The Bolivian Diary
of
Ernesto Che Guevara

The Bolivian Diary *of* Ernesto Che Guevara

PATHFINDER

NEW YORK   LONDON   MONTREAL   SYDNEY

Edited by Mary-Alice Waters

ISBN 0-87348-766-4 paper; ISBN 0-87348-767-2 cloth
Library of Congress Catalog Card Number 93-85736

Manufactured in the United States of America

First edition, 1994

My Campaign with Che is reprinted by permission of Matilde Lara.
COVER AND BOOK DESIGN: Eric Simpson

Pathfinder
410 West Street, New York, NY 10014, U.S.A.
Fax: (212) 727-0150
CompuServe: 73321,414 ● Internet: pathfinder@igc.apc.org

PATHFINDER DISTRIBUTORS AROUND THE WORLD:
Australia (and Asia and the Pacific):
    Pathfinder, 19 Terry St., Surry Hills, Sydney, N.S.W. 2010
    Postal address: P.O. Box K879, Haymarket, N.S.W. 2000
Britain (and Europe, Africa except South Africa, and Middle East):
    Pathfinder, 47 The Cut, London, SE1 8LL
Canada:
    Pathfinder, 4581 rue St-Denis, Montreal, Quebec, H2J 2L4
Iceland:
    Pathfinder, Klapparstíg 26, 2d floor, 101 Reykjavík
    Postal address: P. Box 233, 121 Reykjavík
New Zealand:
    Pathfinder, La Gonda Arcade, 203 Karangahape Road, Auckland
    Postal address: P.O. Box 8730, Auckland
Sweden:
    Pathfinder, Vikingagatan 10, S-113 42, Stockholm
United States (and Caribbean, Latin America, and South Africa):
    Pathfinder, 410 West Street, New York, NY 10014

Contents

Documents and letters by Che Guevara

Accounts by other combatants

TALKS BY CHE GUEVARA TO THE GUERRILLA UNIT

ACCOUNTS BY CUBAN VETERANS

Maps

Bolivia, *8*; the Bolivian campaign, *45*; November 1966, *76*;
December 1966, *88*; January 1967, *104*; February 1967, *122*;
March 1967, *138*; March-April 1967, *157*; April 1967, *162*;
May 1967, *188*; June 1967, *206*; July 1967, *224*; August 1967,
246; September 1967, *264*; October 1967, *290*.

Photographs

Photographs can be found on pages *83, 114, 176, 231, 271,
296, 307, 415*; sixteen pages of photographs follow page *238*.

N

PERU

BRAZIL

Pando

La Paz

B

O

Beni

L

Lake
Titicaca

Las

CARANAVI ○

Yungas

CHAPARE ○

I

Santa Cruz

GUAQUI ○

★ LA PAZ

Cochabamba

V

COCHABAMBA ◉

● SANTA CRUZ

I

ORURO ○

CATAVI ○

A

← AREA OF
GUERRILLA
CAMPAIGN

Oruro

SUCRE ○

POTOSÍ ○

CAMIRI ○

Pacific Ocean

Potosí

Chuquisaca

A

N

TARIJA ○

Tarija

D

VILLAZÓN ○

E

YACUIBA ○

PARAGUAY

S

CHILE

SALTA ○

ARGENTINA

BOLIVIA

SOUTH
AMERICA

350 KILOMETERS

220 MILES

Bolivia

Ernesto Che Guevara

Ernesto "Che" Guevara was born in Argentina on June 14, 1928. After graduating from medical school in 1953, he set off to travel the Americas. While living in Guatemala in 1954, he became involved in political struggle, supporting the elected government of Jacobo Arbenz against the CIA's eventually successful attempts to overthrow it. He then escaped to Mexico, where he soon joined Fidel Castro and other Cuban revolutionaries of the July 26 Movement seeking to overthrow dictator Fulgencio Batista.

In December 1956 Guevara was part of the expedition that landed in Cuba aboard the yacht *Granma* to begin the guerrilla struggle. Originally the troop doctor, Guevara became a commander of the Rebel Army.

Following Batista's fall on January 1, 1959, Guevara became one of the central leaders of the new workers and farmers government. He held a number of posts, including president of the National Bank and minister of industry, and frequently represented Cuba internationally, including at the United Nations and in other world forums. As a leader of the July 26 Movement, he helped bring about the political regroupment that led to the founding of the Communist Party of Cuba in October 1965.

Guevara resigned his government posts and responsibilities in early 1965 and left Cuba in order to return to South America to help advance the anti-imperialist and anticapitalist struggles that were sharpening in several countries. Along with a number of volunteers who would later join him in Bolivia, Guevara went first to the Congo (later Zaire) where he aided the anti-imperialist movement founded by Patrice Lumumba. From November 1966 to October 1967 he led a guerrilla movement in Bolivia against that country's military dictatorship. Wounded and captured by the Bolivian army in a CIA-organized operation on October 8, 1967, he was murdered the following day.

Introduction

Havana, Cuba. New Year's Eve, 1958.

Confronted by rapidly expanding popular support for the July 26 Movement and its advancing Rebel Army guerrilla columns, the military command directed by Washington-backed Cuban dictator Fulgencio Batista collapsed. The hated Batista, together with his government ministers and henchmen hauling the last of their booty, scrambled aboard hastily prepared flights into exile. A general strike swept the island. As the new year broke, the first free territory of the Americas was born.

Among the central leaders of the new revolutionary government soon to be headed by Fidel Castro was Ernesto Guevara—a young Argentine doctor whose leadership capacities, initiative and courage in combat, objectivity in dealing with fellow fighters, and depth of political understanding had won him the rank of commander in the rebel forces. Che, as he was called by his Cuban comrades, soon became one of the best known, most respected, and most popular leaders of the Cuban revolution. He was hated and feared by the fleeing landlords, industrialists, and their Washington and Wall Street overlords. He was loved and emulated by the workers and peasants, who looked to him for leadership and in whose capacities to remake the world and transform themselves in the process he had unshakable confidence.

From the day in 1955 when he joined the July 26 Movement led by Fidel Castro until his death in Bolivia twelve years later,

Guevara's life centered around one single aim: to advance the fight of working people throughout the world to throw off the chains of imperialist oppression and colonial bondage, wrest political power from the propertied classes, and through the struggle to eliminate capitalist exploitation and oppression begin the socialist transformation of society and of humanity itself.

This book, Che's Bolivian diary, records one chapter in that fight.

Long out of print in English, the diary tells the story, in Guevara's own words, of the effort he led to forge a fighting movement of workers and peasants that could win the battle for land and national sovereignty and begin the socialist revolution on the South American continent. Providing a day-by-day chronicle of the eleven-month guerrilla campaign carried out in late 1966 and 1967 by some forty men and one woman in a remote area of Bolivia, the diary is not only a powerful narrative of struggle against great odds. More importantly, it offers an insight into the practical activity, leadership capacities, and strategic thinking of one of the outstanding communist leaders of the twentieth century.

Through the pages of the Bolivian diary we also come to understand more deeply the class character and weight of the Cuban revolution in the world today and the irreconcilable nature of its conflict with Washington and Wall Street.

The overthrow of the Batista dictatorship in 1959 opened the door to the first socialist revolution in the Americas. As the new government took initial steps to implement the revolutionary democratic program to which it was committed—including rolling back rents, electricity and telephone rates; outlawing private beaches and race discrimination in all forms; and organizing the peasants to carry through a land reform—the U.S. government began to retaliate. Acting on behalf of the wealthy U.S. families who owned millions of acres of the best land in Cuba and virtually all major industry, Washington sought to intimidate the new leaders into abandoning their program. When that proved unsuccessful, they tried through accelerating political, economic, and military aggression to overthrow the new regime.

"When the revolution came to power, what did it find?" asked Cuban prime minister Fidel Castro, addressing the General Assembly of the United Nations in New York in September 1960.

> First of all, the revolution found that 600,000 Cubans, able and ready to work, were unemployed—as many, proportionally, as were jobless in the United States during the Great Depression that shook this country, and which almost produced a catastrophe here. This is what we confronted in my country—permanent unemployment. Three million out of a population of a little more than six million had no electricity, possessing none of its advantages and comforts. Three and a half million out of a total population of a little more than six million lived in huts, in shacks, and in slums, without the most minimal sanitary facilities. In the cities, rents took almost one-third of family income. Electricity rates and rents were among the highest in the world.
>
> Some 37.5 percent of our population were illiterate; 70 percent of the rural children lacked teachers; 2 percent of our population suffered from tuberculosis—that is to say, 100,000 persons out of a little more than six million. Ninety-five percent of the children in rural areas suffered from parasites. Infant mortality was astronomical.[1] Life expectancy was very low. On the other hand, 85 percent of the small farmers were paying rent on their land of up to 30 percent of their gross income, while 1.5 percent of the landowners controlled 46 percent of the total area of the country. Of course, the proportion of hospital beds to the number of inhabitants was ridiculously low compared with countries that have even halfway decent medical services.

---

1. In 1958 the infant mortality rate in Cuba was 60 per 1,000 live births. By 1993 it had dropped to 9.4, the lowest in Latin America, and lower than some urban areas of the United States. In the same period average life expectancy in Cuba rose from less than 55 to 74.

Public services, the electricity and telephone companies, all belonged to U.S. monopolies. A major portion of banking, importing, and oil refining; the majority of sugar production; the best land; and the most important industries in all fields in Cuba belonged to U.S. companies.

The balance of payments in the last ten years, from 1950 to 1960, has been favorable to the United States vis-à-vis Cuba to the extent of $1 billion. This is without taking into account the hundreds of millions of dollars extracted from the public treasury by the corrupt officials of the dictatorship and later deposited in U.S. or European banks. One billion dollars in ten years! This poor and underdeveloped Caribbean country with 600,000 unemployed was contributing to the economic development of the most economically developed country in the world!

This was the situation that confronted us. Yet it should not surprise many of the countries represented in this assembly. For what we have said about Cuba is but an X-ray view that could be applied to many of the countries represented here.[2]

The revolutionary government, Castro told the people of the world as he addressed the General Assembly, had one of two choices. It could remain true to the fighting workers and farmers of Cuba and their allies around the globe, thus incurring the enmity of the powerful neighbor to the north. Or it could satisfy Washington, as all previous regimes had done, by protecting the prerogatives of the imperialist-owned monopolies and their allied exploiters in Cuba.

The new workers and farmers government had chosen the only course that could bring dignity and hope to millions of Cubans, begin to improve their conditions of life, and offer a beacon to toiling humanity throughout the world.

---

2. Fidel Castro and Che Guevara, *To Speak the Truth: Why Washington's 'Cold War' against Cuba Doesn't End* (New York: Pathfinder, 1992), pp. 39-40. This book is a collection of speeches by Castro and Guevara given between 1960 and 1979 from the platform of the United Nations and its bodies.

Facing down the Yankee colossus, the workers, peasants, and youth of Cuba mobilized in their millions under the leadership of the revolutionary government to carry out a program, elements of which had been proclaimed many times previously in Latin America, but which had never before been carried through to the end. They implemented land reform and nationalized the banks and basic industry. They organized to eradicate illiteracy; to build homes, clinics, hospitals, schools, and day-care centers throughout the island; to provide education and employment for women; and to root out the institutionalized racism that made prerevolutionary Cuba comparable to the Jim Crow South of the United States. They offered solidarity and support to those fighting for national liberation and socialism around the globe.

Along this line of march, the people of Cuba demonstrated that a profound, popular, socialist revolution could withstand U.S. imperialist pressures. Over more than thirty-five years, Washington has used virtually every weapon in its arsenal—from diplomatic isolation to sabotage, assassination attempts, economic embargo, blockade, nuclear blackmail, and military invasion—to try to destroy the revolutionary power of the workers and peasants ninety miles from its shores. To no avail.

■

Che Guevara was one of the most authoritative representatives of the socialist revolution in Cuba. He was also one of its finest products. His understanding of the world and his capacities as a working-class leader were forged through the experiences of the Cuban revolution. "Wherever I am, I will feel the responsibility of being a Cuban revolutionary, and I shall behave as such," he wrote in 1965 in a letter addressed to Fidel Castro printed in this book.[3]

During the first six years of the Cuban revolution Guevara shouldered a broad range of leadership tasks. "Many were the responsibilities assigned to him," Castro told a solemn meet-

3. See pages 71-73.

ing of hundreds of thousands in Havana in October 1967, one week after Guevara's murder in Bolivia at the hands of a CIA-organized counterinsurgency unit. "His versatile intelligence was able to undertake with maximum assurance any task of any kind. Thus he brilliantly represented our country in numerous international conferences, just as he brilliantly led soldiers in combat, just as he was a model worker in charge of any of the institutions he was assigned to."[4]

Guevara was initially the troop doctor for the revolutionary forces of the July 26 Movement that opened a guerrilla front in Cuba's Sierra Maestra mountains in December 1956. By mid-1957 he was commanding a column of the Rebel Army as well as organizing Marxist education for its cadres. Following the victory in 1959 he served as head of the Department of Industry of the National Institute of Agrarian Reform (INRA); was president of Cuba's National Bank during the crucial year 1960 when domestic- and foreign-owned banks were expropriated, along with most industries; and became head of the Ministry of Industry when it was established in February 1961. Guevara represented Cuba on many trips abroad, in front of the United Nations, and at numerous international conferences. He met often with revolutionists from other countries who were seeking to emulate the Cuban experience, discussing politics and helping them think out the practical tasks of preparing to advance along an anti-imperialist and socialist path.

In the thick of daily central leadership responsibilities in the government, party, and army, Guevara also sought to lay a strategically effective and theoretically consistent programmatic foundation for the transition to socialism in Cuba. He collaborated with groups of Cuban workers and other revolutionary cadres to draw accurate lessons from the proletarian leadership's initial efforts to reorganize industrial production and administration and begin economic planning. He spoke

---

4. Fidel Castro's speech of October 18, 1967, is published as an introduction to *Che Guevara and the Cuban Revolution: Writings and Speeches of Ernesto Che Guevara* (New York: Pathfinder, 1987), pp. 19-29.

and wrote extensively, and debated other currents in the workers movement inside and outside Cuba who did not share his communist views.[5]

The socialist road that Cuban working people set out on at the beginning of the 1960s had been opened some four decades earlier by the October 1917 revolution in Russia. Under the Bolshevik Party leadership headed by V.I. Lenin, for the first time in history, the working class began to use its newly won state power to start building socialism while fighting to advance the world revolution. These efforts—from the overthrow of the tsarist regime in February 1917 and the triumph of the Bolshevik-led workers and peasants government eight months later, through the end of Lenin's active political life in March 1923—left an invaluable legacy to revolutionists such as Guevara and Castro who later shouldered similar responsibilities as they continued and renewed the communist course.

The socialist revolution, as Guevara repeatedly explained, marks the first time in history that expanding revolutionary consciousness and growing political domination by the working class becomes a necessity in order to advance the economic organization of society. The door is opened for working people to cease being the objects of blind economic laws that determine their living and working conditions and social relations, and instead to begin placing the organization of productive forces under their own conscious control.

This is not just one way among others that might be used following a successful popular revolution to advance the transition to socialism. The most committed and self-sacrificing

---

5. The most complete selection of Guevara's writings in English translation are available in books and pamphlets published by Pathfinder Press, including *Che Guevara and the Cuban Revolution: Writings and Speeches of Ernesto Che Guevara; Che Guevara Speaks; Socialism and Man in Cuba;* and *Che Guevara: Economics and Politics in the Transition to Socialism* by Carlos Tablada. Two other articles by Guevara, long out of print in English, are newly translated in issue no. 8 of the Marxist magazine of politics and theory, *New International,* a special issue on "Che Guevara, Cuba, and the Road to Socialism," also available from Pathfinder.

vanguard of the working people, organized in a communist party, *must* lead growing layers of their class in taking more and more control over the political direction and administration of the state and economy. In carrying out whatever leadership task he was assigned, Che organized along a course that made it possible for workers to transform themselves and their social and political consciousness as they collectively transformed the social relations under which they worked, produced, and lived. He explained that this is the only way working people carrying out the revolutionary process can make the new social relations more transparent and direct and, at the same time, base these relations on human solidarity. It is the only way to tear away the veils and fetishes behind which the capitalist system hides the brutal consequences of its exploitation of working people and obscures the unique contribution labor makes to all social and cultural progress.

By the time the Cuban revolution conquered, the balance sheet of twentieth-century experience had demonstrated beyond any doubt that society will not—and cannot—advance toward socialism and communism along any other course. If it is directed down any other road, it will become mired in bureaucratic planning and management, fostering growing demoralization and alienation of working people from their labor. New privileged social layers will be spawned that ape the values and attitudes of the capitalist classes still dominant on a world scale. Willy-nilly, revolutionists will be turned into accomplices of the law of value and its corrosive social consequences. They will begin, at first even unconsciously, to seek support and collaboration from petty-bourgeois layers at home and from bourgeois forces internationally, as they turn their faces away from the toilers of the world, who are humanity's only salvation. Along this road, a workers state will not only regress toward restoration of capitalism but, as Fidel Castro put it in 1986, "to a system worse than capitalism."[6]

6. Fidel Castro, "Important Problems for the Whole of International Revolutionary Thought," speech of December 2, 1986, in *New International* no. 6, p. 217.

Recognizing the fundamentally *political* character of economic questions and decisions during the transition to socialism was central to everything Guevara did as a leader of the Cuban revolution. His experience had given him infinite confidence in the capacities of ordinary working people to understand these questions in the process of taking control over their labor and their lives, and, in fact, to become different human beings.

To this end, Guevara set the example of consistent study and disciplined reading. He did so at the same time that he carried an immense political workload—including international travel, meetings with assemblies of factory workers, and frequent participation on days off in voluntary work mobilizations on priority social projects. He immersed himself in the literature discussing the most technologically advanced industrial processes and automation in use in other countries. He learned the principles of accounting and took classes in higher mathematics so he could help advance the application of computerization to economic planning and financial control in Cuba.

He organized a weekly study group that systematically worked through the pages of *Capital* by Karl Marx. As the references throughout his writings attest, he frequently went back to the works of Lenin, Marx, and Frederick Engels to deepen his knowledge and understanding of the history of the modern working-class movement and draw upon that experience to help chart the way forward for the socialist revolution in Cuba.

The example of Guevara's seemingly inexhaustible work to deepen his understanding of Marxism, and to combine that knowledge with concrete experience to advance the fight for national liberation and socialism worldwide, was one of the attributes Castro pointed to in his 1967 speech commemorating Guevara's life:

> If we looked through the windows of his offices, he had the lights on until all hours of the night, studying, or rather working or studying. For he was a student of all problems; he was a tireless reader. His thirst for learning was practically insa-

tiable, and the hours he stole from sleep he devoted to study.[7]

In the pages of Guevara's Bolivian diary that follow, as well as in the memoirs of his fellow combatants, this Che comes alive—the leader of men and women who challenged all of them to expand their cultural horizons and stretch themselves to take on responsibilities they never dreamed they were capable of. The library of 300-400 books the guerrillas rotated among themselves for reading and discussion; the study classes on political economy, history, mathematics, Quechua, Aymará, and French;[8] Che's study of *The Young Hegel* and *Capital*—all are described in vivid detail here in the accounts by Inti Peredo and by Pombo, both members of the general staff.[9] "The objective Che was pursuing was to raise our cultural level," Pombo notes.

At the same time, he always made us see clearly that even though war presented difficult circumstances, in which one had to live under constant tension, nevertheless we could not let ourselves take an easy-going and conformist attitude that would have us put off study until later. We had to study right there in the guerrilla camp, he said, with an enthusism and determination equal to the way we confronted the vicissitudes and difficulties we faced. And one of the biggest such difficulties to overcome was precisely the one he sought to instill: the habit of study.[10]

The guerrilla unit was a leadership school in another way as

---

7. *Che Guevara and the Cuban Revolution,* p. 26.
8. In the early 1960s some 75 percent of Bolivians were classified as indigenous peoples. Sixty percent spoke only Aymará or Quechua dialects. Study of these languages, with classes taught by Bolivian combatants, was obligatory. French was a voluntary course, taught by Che.
9. Extensive biographical information on all members of the guerrilla column is provided in the glossary on pages 435-54, along with information on other individuals mentioned throughout the book.
10. See page 428.

well. As shown by many examples in his diary, Guevara considered the battle to develop proletarian norms of conduct and leadership relations among the cadres of the unit to be a life-and-death question. The ability to work objectively and impartially with all and encourage the leadership potential of each man and woman; civil discussion among those who held different points of view; intolerance of any abuse of authority; integrity in personal relations—these were indispensable characteristics of revolutionary leadership that Che sought to instill.

Rolando, another member of the general staff, a portion of whose diary is reprinted here, describes a political talk given by Che to the combatants. In it Che rebuked two of the Cuban volunteers for unacceptable behavior but was especially hard on Marcos, who had previously held important leadership responsibilities in Cuba. "Seven years of revolution had left their mark on certain comrades," Rolando quotes Che as saying. "He spoke of how having chauffeurs, secretaries, and others working under them had made them accustomed to giving orders and having things done for them." Che insisted that Marcos change the "insulting manner he employs," which "undermines his authority."

There was no special status in Bolivia for the Cuban volunteers, Che insisted, even though many had proven themselves in combat and in various leadership assignments and had been asked by Che to volunteer for the Bolivian campaign. "What I had in [Cuba] were not friends, but comrades," he said. "Whenever I defended someone in difficulty, I did so because it was correct, and not out of friendship. Whoever is deserving here can have responsibilities and the opportunity to set an example."[11]

■

As Fidel Castro pointed out in his 1960 address to the United Nations General Assembly, the economic, social, and political conditions that made possible the first socialist country in

11. See page 417.

the Americas were not unique to Cuba. The Cuban revolution was only the crest of the rising tide of mass struggles across the continent, which, in turn, registered a new level of energy and explosiveness in the wake of the Cuban victory.

Fear that the example of Cuba would spread and that other proimperialist regimes would be overthrown by mass revolutionary struggle underlay Washington's determination to crush the workers and farmers government in Cuba. At Wall Street's bidding, bourgeois governments throughout the hemisphere rushed to try to isolate the revolutionary regime.

The counterrevolutionary war drive orchestrated by the U.S. government included everything from the CIA-sponsored invasion of Cuba in April 1961 (the "Bay of Pigs" landing, which was wiped out in less than seventy-two hours), to the orchestrated expulsion of Cuba from the Organization of American States in January 1962, to the imposition of a brutal embargo on trade with Cuba by the United States a few days later.

On February 4, 1962, at a mass rally of more than a million in Havana's Plaza of the Revolution, Fidel Castro read the response of the Cuban people, known as the Second Declaration of Havana.

> What is it that is hidden behind the Yankees' hatred of the Cuban revolution? What is it that rationally explains the conspiracy—uniting for the same aggressive purpose the richest and most powerful imperialist power in the contemporary world and the oligarchies of an entire continent, which together are supposed to represent a population of 350 million human beings—against a small country of only seven million inhabitants, economically underdeveloped, without financial or military means to threaten the security or economy of any other country?
>
> What unites them and stirs them up is fear. What explains it is fear. Not fear of the Cuban revolution but fear of the Latin American revolution. . . . Fear that the plundered people of

the continent will seize the arms from their oppressors and, like Cuba, declare themselves free people of the Americas.[12]

Disavowing decades of subordination by the official Communist and Socialist parties of the continent to various bourgeois political parties and currents, the Second Declaration of Havana boldly proclaimed the necessary proletarian leadership and socialist character of the revolution on the agenda throughout the region:

> In the actual historic conditions of Latin America, the national bourgeoisie cannot lead the antifeudal and anti-imperialist struggle. Experience shows that in our nations that class, even when its interests are in contradiction to those of Yankee imperialism, has been incapable of confronting it, for the national bourgeoisie is paralyzed by fear of social revolution and frightened by the cry of the exploited masses.

In ringing terms the fighting people of Cuba explained what was already unfolding across the continent:

> Now history will have to take the poor of the Americas into account, the exploited and spurned of the Americas, who have decided to begin writing their history for themselves for all time. Already they can be seen on the roads, on foot, day after day, in endless march of hundreds of kilometers to the governmental "eminences," there to obtain their rights.
> Already they can be seen armed with stones, sticks, machetes, in one direction and another, each day, occupying lands, sinking hooks into the land which belongs to them and defending it with their lives. They can be seen carrying signs, slogans, flags; letting them flap in the mountain or

---

12. *The Second Declaration of Havana* is available as a pamphlet published by Pathfinder.

prairie winds. And the wave of anger, of demands for justice, of claims for rights trampled underfoot, which is beginning to sweep the lands of Latin America, will not stop. That wave will swell with every passing day. For that wave is composed of the greatest number, the majorities in every respect, those whose labor amasses the wealth and turns the wheels of history. Now they are awakening from the long, brutalizing sleep to which they had been subjected.

For this great mass of humanity has said, "Enough!" and has begun to march.

From the throats of revolutionary-minded youth and class-conscious workers, the cry of *"Cuba sí, yanqui no!"* resounded from Mexico City to Buenos Aires, and into the Yankee metropolis itself.

Within the United States and Canada a new generation of youth, attracted by the power of Cuba's workers and peasants taking their destiny in hand, was won to the communist movement. Responding to the growing mass movement for Black rights and the powerful example of the victorious Cuban revolution, they brought new life to a working-class movement battered by more than a decade of postwar prosperity and anticommunist witch-hunts. A similar admiration and effect spread worldwide, as growing numbers of working people and youth were drawn toward the revolution in Cuba.

Young rebels from across the Americas made their way to Cuba to see the revolution with their own eyes. They hoped to learn from its successes and return home to emulate the "Cuban road." Frequently, in their inexperience and determination, they saw or understood only a one-sided piece of that reality. They saw in bold relief the audacious military victories registered by the guerrillas of the Rebel Army. They often missed the years of party-building work that preceded the landing of the *Granma*; the stature of the July 26 Movement and the mass support it had won even before beginning the struggle in the Sierra Maestra; the caliber of the leadership team carefully put together by Fidel

Castro; the profound roots the movement had among the Cuban toilers and the political astuteness the leadership demonstrated in its feel for the tactical ups and downs of the struggle—in short, the factors that registered almost a decade of work forging and tempering a revolutionary movement that drew on the lessons of a century of struggle, and thus the factors that made possible the victory of the Cuban revolution.

During the first years after the triumph in Cuba, nuclei of guerrilla fighters went into action in the countryside of Venezuela, Colombia, Peru, Guatemala, Nicaragua, Argentina, and elsewhere. Coming from many different political origins, they adopted the banner of the Second Declaration of Havana as their own, challenging the long-established Communist and Socialist parties for leadership of the workers and peasants struggles. Although the majority of these efforts were soon defeated, in a number of countries they had significant and growing political impact.

In hopes of stemming the rising revolutionary tide, the U.S. administration of John Kennedy proclaimed the Alliance for Progress with complicit regimes throughout the hemisphere. Along with plentiful bribes to fill the personal coffers of accommodating bourgeois forces, Washington promised $20 billion in development loans over the span of a decade. As Che Guevara explained with scientific precision to a United Nations–sponsored trade conference in March 1964, the Alliance for Progress was a program that served above all to accelerate, through interest charges and loan repayments, the transfer of billions of dollars of capital to the coffers of the imperialist-owned banks of North America.[13]

More importantly, Kennedy responded to the growing popular struggles throughout Latin America by supporting murderous dictatorships; expanding operations by the Central Intelligence Agency, army special forces units, and others; and employing direct military action. He demonstratively main-

---

13. *To Speak the Truth*, pp. 106-7.

tained U.S. imperialism's insulting and provocative military occupation of the area around Guantánamo Bay in eastern Cuba, a usurpation of Cuba's sovereignty dating back almost sixty years. The administration of Lyndon Johnson continued the same course.

In Brazil the CIA engineered the overthrow of the government of João Goulart in 1964, installing one of the most brutal military dictatorships yet seen in Latin America. The fierce repression unleashed against workers, peasants, and students—much of it carried out by death squads organized by the Brazilian army officer corps and police—became the infamous prototype for fascist-minded military regimes that would follow in other countries.

In the Dominican Republic a mass popular rebellion against a U.S.-backed dictatorship in 1965 was crushed by 20,000 U.S. troops.

Despite such defeats, mass struggles by workers and peasants against their exploitation and oppression deepened in many countries. The specter of revolution hung over the moneyed interests of the Americas.

At the same time, the attention and resources of the U.S. rulers were more and more concentrated on their rapidly escalating war against the people of Vietnam. By late 1963 the Kennedy administration had increased U.S. troop strength in Vietnam to more than 16,000. In August 1964 Washington began bombing North Vietnam, and the war increasingly spread to neighboring Laos and Cambodia. The buildup of U.S. combat forces in Vietnam that eventually exceeded half a million was well under way.

One unintended by-product of Washington's growing difficulties and preoccupation with attempts to crush the tenacious resistance of the Vietnamese people was a relatively larger breathing space for Cuba. Alone among all the governments allied with the Democratic Republic of Vietnam, however, it was the Cuban leadership that fought to close ranks in support of Vietnam. Cuban revolutionists pointed a finger at the criminal refusal of the governments of the Soviet Union and China to provide the level of political, financial, and military aid necessary to win and to lessen the enormous sacrifice of lives and economic devastation being imposed on the people of Vietnam.

Nowhere was this more eloquently stated than in the article by Che Guevara referred to several times in the pages of his diary, his famous message to the Organization of Solidarity with the Peoples of Asia, Africa, and Latin America better known as OSPAAAL, or, at the time, the Tricontinental. Published under the title "Create Two, Three . . . Many Vietnams, That Is the Watchword."[14] Guevara's message was written in 1966 on the eve of his departure for Bolivia, and printed in the magazine *Tricontinental* in April 1967, soon after the launching of the guerrilla front and Guevara's presence in Bolivia had become public knowledge.

In this "Message to the Tricontinental," as it became known, the last major article written by Guevara, Che surveyed the world political situation and explained the decision to open a guerrilla front in Latin America. It was justified not only as a response to the economic and political conditions and deepening social struggles across the continent, he stated. It was also the responsibility of revolutionists everywhere to come to the aid of the embattled Vietnamese people.

> When we analyze the isolation of the Vietnamese we are overcome by anguish at this illogical moment in the history of humanity. U.S. imperialism is guilty of aggression. Its crimes are immense, extending over the whole world. We know this, gentlemen! But also guilty are those who at the decisive moment hesitated to make Vietnam an inviolable part of socialist territory—yes, at the risk of a war of global scale, but also compelling the U.S. imperialists to make a decision. And also guilty are those who persist in a war of insults and tripping each other up, begun quite some time ago by the repre-

---

14. Published in *Che Guevara and the Cuban Revolution,* pp. 347-60.

sentatives of the two biggest powers in the socialist camp.

Defensive weapons, and not in sufficient number, are all these marvelous Vietnamese soldiers have besides love for their country, for their society, and a courage that stands up to all tests. But imperialism is bogged down in Vietnam. It sees no way out and is searching desperately for one that will permit it to emerge with dignity from the dangerous situation in which it finds itself.

Under these conditions, "what is the role that we, the exploited of the world, must play?" Guevara asked. "Since the imperialists are using the threat of war to blackmail humanity, the correct response is not to fear war. Attack hard and without letup at every point of confrontation—that must be the general tactic of the peoples."

Examining the struggles unfolding in Asia, Africa, and the Americas, Guevara concluded that only in Latin America did the conditions prevail to open the kind of anti-imperialist front he envisioned.

In Latin America, the struggle is going on arms in hand in Guatemala, Colombia, Venezuela, and Bolivia, and the first outbreaks are already beginning in Brazil. Other centers of resistance have appeared and been extinguished. But almost all the countries of this continent are ripe for a struggle of the kind that, to be triumphant, cannot settle for anything less than the establishment of a government of a socialist nature.

In Latin America, Guevara pointed out, it was "either a socialist revolution or a caricature of revolution." And the Americas would have the historic responsibility of creating "the world's second or third Vietnam, or second *and* third Vietnam."

How close and bright would the future appear if two, three, many Vietnams flowered on the face of the globe, with their quota of death and their immense tragedies, with their daily heroism, with their repeated blows against imperialism, forcing it to disperse its forces under the lash of the growing hatred of the peoples of the world!

■

"Other nations of the world summon my modest efforts of assistance," Guevara wrote to Fidel Castro before leaving Cuba in 1965. "I can do that which is denied you owing to your responsibility at the head of Cuba."[15]

While preparations for opening the guerrilla front in Bolivia were under way, Guevara spent six months in the Congo (today Zaire) fighting alongside the forces that had been led by murdered independence leader Patrice Lumumba. He then returned secretly to Cuba to continue training the volunteers who would accompany him to Bolivia.

In putting himself on the front lines of a guerrilla struggle in Bolivia, Guevara was carrying out an even broader revolutionary perspective he had long anticipated and prepared for. "This was an old idea of his," Fidel Castro told Italian journalist Gianni Minà in 1987.

> When he joined us in Mexico—and it's not that he made it a condition—he did ask one thing: "The only thing I want after the victory of the revolution is to go fight in Argentina"— his country—"that you don't keep me from doing so, that no reasons of state will stand in the way." And I promised him that. It was a long way off, after all. No one knew, first of all, if we'd win the war or who was going to be alive at the end —and he surely, because of his impetuousness, had little chance of coming out alive—but this is what he asked. Once in a while, in the Sierra and afterward, he would remind me of this idea and promise.[16]

---

15. See page 72.
16. *Un encuentro con Fidel* (Havana: Oficina de Publicaciones del Consejo de Estado, 1987), p. 318.

Che thought and acted as an internationalist. He knew that the future of the Cuban revolution did not ultimately depend on the efforts and capacities of the communist leadership in Cuba of which he was part, however deep-going that revolution might be, however capable the leadership. Only new revolutionary victories elsewhere, especially new socialist advances in the Americas, would change the relationship of class forces internationally and break the isolation that weighed so heavily on Cuba.

As Guevara explained to Bolivian leader Inti Peredo, whose memoirs are printed here in English for the first time, the Bolivian front was chosen because "Bolivia is located in the heart of the southern cone of our continent, bordering five countries,[17] each with a political and economic situation becoming increasingly critical. Bolivia's geographic position thus makes it a strategic region for *extending* the revolutionary struggle to neighboring countries." The struggle would be long and hard, protracted over many years.

"Turn the Andes into the Sierra Maestra of the Americas" became the often-voiced rallying cry of revolutionary forces that sought to emulate the Cuban road toward socialism.

Bolivia had its own recent history of sharp class struggle and growing impoverishment. In 1964 a military dictatorship headed by Gen. René Barrientos had overthrown the presidency of Víctor Paz Estenssoro, ending twelve years of rule by the increasingly corrupt and fractured regime of the Revolutionary Nationalist Movement (MNR).

The MNR, a bourgeois party with strong support from Bolivia's superexploited tin miners, had been thrust into control of the national government in the wake of a revolutionary upsurge in 1952. That powerful upheaval resulted in nationalization of the largest mines, legalization of the trade unions, initiation of land reform, and elimination of the literacy requirement that had effectively disenfranchised the majority of Bolivia's people,

17. Chile, Argentina, Paraguay, Brazil, and Peru.

the Aymará- and Quechua-speaking population. But Bolivia remained one of the poorest countries in the Americas; only Paraguay and Haiti had lower per capita incomes. By the early 1960s average life expectancy was still only forty-three years (compared to sixty-six years in the United States and Canada). With tin prices falling and inflation soaring, the economy was in a shambles. The leadership of the powerful Central Organization of Bolivian Workers (COB), once a supporter of the government, had gone into political opposition.

In 1965 the Barrientos dictatorship provoked a confrontation with the trade union movement by arresting Juan Lechín, the central leader of the COB. When workers responded with a general strike and seizure of the country's tin mines, the regime unleashed a wave of repression, arresting union leaders and sending in troops to occupy the mining camps, killing many. After the strike was defeated, a 40 percent wage cut was imposed on large sections of the working class.

By then, preparations for the guerrilla front were already under way. As Castro recounts here in "A Necessary Introduction," however, these efforts were undermined by the general secretary of the Communist Party of Bolivia, Mario Monje, who "devoted his energies to sabotaging the movement." The accounts by Guevara and Peredo amply detail the extent of this treachery by Monje and those who followed him and its deadly consequences for the guerrilla unit.

■

In the aftermath of Che's death and the defeat of the guerrilla nucleus in Bolivia, a wide-ranging debate inevitably erupted. Was it simply a political adventure doomed from the start?

Not only Guevara's enemies in both Washington and La Paz, but also those political opponents who Castro refers to in his introduction as "the pseudorevolutionaries, opportunists, and charlatans of every stripe"—were quick to proclaim that revolutionary struggle, especially arms in hand, had been

proven to be a romantic death wish at best, a dangerous provocation at worst.

"These people call themselves Marxists, Communists, and
other such titles," Castro continues.

> They have not hesitated, however, to call Che a mistaken
> adventurer or, when they speak more benignly, an idealist
> whose death marked the swan song of revolutionary armed
> struggle in Latin America. "If Che himself," they exclaim, "the
> greatest exponent of these ideas and an experienced guerrilla
> fighter, died in the guerrilla struggle and his movement failed
> to liberate Bolivia, it only shows how mistaken he was!" . . .
>
> That is how they justify themselves. That is how they justify
> their treacherous leaders who, at a given moment, did not hes-
> itate to play at armed struggle, with the true aim—as could be
> seen later—of destroying the guerrilla detachments, putting
> the brakes on revolutionary action, and imposing their own
> shameful and ridiculous political schemes. . . .
>
> That is how they justify those who have made a caricature
> of revolutionary ideas, turning them into an opium-like dog-
> ma with neither content nor message for the masses; those
> who have converted the organizations of popular struggle
> into instruments of conciliation with domestic and foreign
> exploiters; and those who advocate policies that have noth-
> ing to do with the genuine interests of the exploited peoples
> of this continent. . . .
>
> Those who see the outcome of his struggle in Bolivia as
> marking the failure of his ideas can, with the same oversimpli-
> fication, deny the validity of the ideas and struggles of all the
> great revolutionary precursors and thinkers. This includes the
> founders of Marxism, who were themselves unable to com-
> plete the task and to view in life the fruits of their noble efforts.

Noting how many times the small band of Rebel Army
fighters in the Sierra Maestra had been close to annihilation,
Castro emphasized, "In all epochs and under all circum-

stances, there will always be an abundance of pretexts for not fighting; but not fighting is the surest way to never attain freedom."

The plan for the Bolivian campaign, Castro stressed in his 1987 interview with Gianni Minà, was entirely Guevara's. Che selected the territory and supervised the detailed preparations. "The importance of the area he picked seems to have been its proximity to the Argentine border," Castro noted. But "in essence, he made no mistake in his choice."

From his days in the Sierra Maestra on, "because of Che's courage, his qualities, his importance, in our war we gave him the most important missions," Castro remarked. But "this mission we didn't give him. The idea, the plan, everything was his." The political perspective was shared by the entire revolutionary leadership of Cuba, however. "We believed in what [Che] was doing, and we believed he could carry out what he proposed."

> What we did was help him. We helped something we thought was possible. We would not have been able to help something we thought was impossible, something in which we did not believe, because it would have been our duty to tell him: It's not possible, we can't do that, we can't sacrifice comrades on this mission.

As Guevara's diary and the additional accounts make clear, neither Che nor other leaders of the guerrilla unit ever intended for their base of operations to be the area in which they moved and fought for what became eleven months. They had planned, after a preliminary training period, to move to a nearby region with a larger population and conditions more favorable for launching operations. The early detection of the guerrilla unit by the armed forces, however, and the accidental separation of the rear guard from the rest of the unit, kept them from carrying out their plan.

Castro also points out that Cuban leaders strongly disagreed with Guevara's decision to himself join the group in Bolivia at the beginning. The fact that some comrades had already given their lives in an effort to establish a guerrilla front in northern Argentina was "a factor that greatly influenced his impatience to carry out his ideas," Castro told Minà.[18] Nevertheless, Che "should have waited until a stronger movement developed," Castro said. The initial stage "is the most difficult and the most dangerous phase, as the facts showed, and it resulted in his death."

The leadership of the Cuban revolution knew that Guevara's role in the guerrilla struggle in Bolivia would be used by enemies of the revolution to try to escalate attacks on Cuba. But "U.S. imperialism has never needed a pretext to carry out its crimes anywhere in the world," Castro writes in "A Necessary Introduction."

> Its efforts to crush the Cuban revolution began as soon as our country passed its first revolutionary law. This course stems from the obvious and well-known fact that imperialism is the policeman of world reaction, the systematic promoter of counterrevolution, and the protector of the most backward and inhuman social structures that remain in the world.

> Cuba's solidarity with the revolutionary movement may be the pretext, but it will never be the real cause of U.S. aggression. To refuse solidarity in order to avoid providing a pretext is a ridiculous, ostrich-like policy that has nothing to do with the internationalist character of the social revolutions of today.

> "Grave dangers have threatened our country since the tri-

---

18. The guerrilla nucleus in northern Argentina, which began operations in late 1963, was led by Jorge Ricardo Masetti, a journalist from Argentina who had supported the Rebel Army in the Sierra Maestra and was founder of Cuba's Prensa Latina news agency. The Argentine guerrilla unit was wiped out by Argentine government troops in early 1964 and Masetti was killed.

umph of the revolution," Castro noted. "But imperialism will never make us give in for these reasons, because the difficulties that flow from a consistently revolutionary line of action are of no importance to us."[19]

■

Events in the years immediately following the defeat of the guerrilla nucleus in Bolivia amply confirmed what Che had described as the "increasingly critical" economic and political situation throughout Latin America's Southern Cone that had been the objective basis underlying his revolutionary course.

In Bolivia itself a profound working-class upsurge occurred. After several years of deepening instability and a rapid succession of military regimes, in 1970 growing mass mobilizations of workers and students led to an uprising in La Paz. The army split wide open as armed workers took control of the streets, and detachments of peasants and students joined them. The workers established a united "Political Command" to coordinate their struggle. That body soon transformed itself into a People's Assembly, whose delegates set up operations in the chambers previously used by the Bolivian congress.

Neither the workers nor the bourgeoisie were strong enough to decisively gain the upper hand, however. Only after ten months of posturing and wasted opportunities by the officialdom of the workers movement did the counterrevolutionary forces have the strength and cohesion to make their move. They ousted the latest military regime headed by "left-wing" Gen. Juan José Torres, and replaced it with a ferocious dictatorship headed by Gen. Hugo Banzer.

In Argentina a 1966 military coup had installed a regime headed by Gen. Juan Carlos Onganía. By 1969 the class struggle was again on the rise, however, with increasing strike ac-

---

19. See pages 53-54.

tions and student protests. In May of that year, anger over price increases at a university cafeteria triggered a series of events that rapidly led to a general strike in Rosario, Argentina's second-largest city, and a semi-insurrection in Córdoba, the third-largest city and center of Argentina's auto and aviation industry.

The *Cordobazo,* as it became known, ushered in a period of intense class struggle that lasted for more than half a decade, with inevitable ups and downs, and several sharp shifts by the Argentine bourgeoisie as it desperately sought to regain its balance. In 1976 the military installed Gen. Jorge Videla to preside over a dictatorship so bloody that it stood out for its brutality, even in the Latin America of the 1960s and 1970s.

In Chile rising working-class and peasant militancy carried Socialist Party leader Salvador Allende into the presidency in 1970. For the next three years, the increasingly organized popular movement pressed forward the fight for economic and social measures that threatened the prerogatives of capital, both foreign and Chilean. The Communist and Socialist parties that dominated the government, however, refused to prepare to win the approaching showdown, and the U.S.-backed military coup organized by Gen. Augusto Pinochet imposed a crushing defeat on the workers movement in September 1973.

Today, more than a quarter century after the events recounted in these pages, new economic and social crises are looming, and a new generation of young fighters is coming onto the stage of history, not only in the Americas but throughout the world. It is a generation that does not carry the scars of past defeats; nor is it doomed to justify and repeat the same mistakes. As new class battles erupt, Che's socialist perspectives and the lessons for those striving to build a revolutionary party capable of leading the workers and farmers to take political power acquire an ever more immediate weight. The lessons of these turbulent years of struggle are an integral part of the history revolutionists must critically absorb. There could be no better reason to make broadly available once more *The Bolivian Diary of Ernesto Che Guevara.*

■

The history of Che Guevara's Bolivian diary is itself a political saga. At its heart has been the ongoing battle pitting those who have sought to accurately present Che's political legacy against those seeking to discredit him and distort his place, as well as the place of the Cuban revolution, in the history of the twentieth century.

Carried in his knapsack, the diary was among the items that fell into the hands of the Bolivian military when Guevara was wounded and captured on October 8, 1967. The document was immediately relayed to the army high command, with copies to Washington.

The existence of the diary became public knowledge within days of the murder of Guevara. In November 1967 passages were read by the Bolivian military prosecutor in the trial of French journalist Régis Debray. Debray, as Guevara recounts in the diary, had been captured by the Bolivian military following a visit to the guerrilla camp. Sentenced to a thirty-year prison term, he was released in 1970.

The military regime and its backers in Washington used carefully selected quotations—as well as fabrications and rumors about the diary's contents—to justify widespread arrests, incriminate prisoners, and attempt to discredit Guevara and Cuba.

At the same time, Bolivia's dictators instinctively saw the diary as an opportunity for personal financial gain. Although his murderers had no moral or legal basis to exercise literary rights belonging to Guevara's widow, Aleida March, Bolivian government leaders entered into negotiations with major U.S. and French publishers to sell the rights. Figures as high as $400,000 were floated in negotiations.

As condemnation of the Bolivian dictatorship's cold-blooded murder of Che mounted worldwide, however, divisions appeared within the inner circles of the regime. Antonio Arguedas, the country's interior minister and chief of intelligence throughout Che's Bolivian campaign, grew increasingly resentful of CIA pressure on him and growing U.S. dictates. He decided to provide microfilms of the diary to the Cuban government. Supporters of the Cuban revolution organized a clandestine operation that succeeded in delivering the microfilms to Havana in mid-March 1968.

Working with accelerated speed and great secrecy, a team of Cubans including Aleida March verified the authenticity of the diary and arranged for its virtually simultaneous translation and publication inside and outside Cuba in eight different editions.

On July 1, 1968, the Cuban government published the diary, distributing hundreds of thousands of copies free of charge to the Cuban people. News of its publication made front pages around the world.

The Bolivian regime was stunned by this unexpected move. With political machinations and financial hopes shattered, its first response was to claim that the Cuban edition was a fraud. President Barrientos called it "a fictitious diary, falsified and conveniently presented. . . . I am sure that the whole thing is part of a scheme by the Castro hierarchy."

Castro responded to these charges in a televised address on July 3, 1968. "The publication of the diary has upset a few applecarts," Castro explained. "In the first place the imperialists and the Bolivian militarists were most interested in keeping the contents of the document a secret. In the second place, its publication ruined a number of shady and grossly mercenary business deals in connection with the document." He announced that to eliminate any shadow of a doubt, the Cuban government would make photocopies of the diary available to any international journalist accredited in Cuba.

On July 10 the La Paz periodical *Presencia* published the diary. Military chief of staff Alfredo Ovando acknowledged its authenticity and announced the formation of a military tribunal to determine who was responsible for handing it over to the Cuban government. The source of the leak was rapidly traced to Arguedas, since the edition published in Cuba was missing thirteen entries. These were precisely the thirteen entries deleted by Ovando from the version given to the intelligence ministry in order to trace unauthorized duplication. Copies turned over to the CIA had also been marked in an identifiable manner. Arguedas skipped across the border to Chile.

The first English-language edition was published July 2, 1968, in a special issue of *Ramparts* magazine in the United States, under rights granted by the Cuban government on behalf of Aleida March. This version was released a week later as a paperback book by Bantam.

Almost simultaneously a different English version was issued by U.S. publishers Stein and Day, under the title *The Complete Bolivian Diaries of Ché Guevara and Other Captured Documents*. Stein and Day claimed they had been granted "exclusive literary rights" by Bolivia's military dictatorship. The Stein and Day edition contained the thirteen entries missing from the Cuban edition, as well as the captured diaries of three other Cuban combatants. It featured a lengthy introduction attacking Guevara and the Cuban revolution and praising Barrientos and the Bolivian regime. Publisher Sol Stein told the press he had undertaken the project "as an act of conscience," because the Cuban edition was "a clear attempt to build Guevara as the Robin Hood of the 20th century."

Both editions have been out of print for many years.

■

This Pathfinder edition of the Bolivian diary has been newly translated by Michael Taber and Michael Baumann, and contains materials not available in any of the previous editions, in any language. The entries missing from the first Cuban and *Ramparts* editions have been restored. This has been made pos-

sible by the careful work of Editora Política in Cuba, which in
1987 published the complete text of the diary in the Spanish
original. Also included here are other documents written by
Guevara in Bolivia, most of which are referred to in the pages
of the diary, as well as several messages and letters.

Of particular interest are the additional accounts by other
combatants, a number of which are published here for the first
time in English.

My Campaign with Che by Inti Peredo is of special note, offering an extensive account of events paralleling Che's diary. Peredo was a member of the general staff of the guerrilla unit and
one of the five surviving veterans. He had joined the Communist Party of Bolivia in 1951 at the age of fourteen and was secretary of the La Paz region of the party prior to joining Che's
group. In addition to providing a narrative framework for the
events referred to in Guevara's diary, Peredo's memoir adds
substantial information on relations with the Bolivian Communist Party, the guerrillas' political functioning, Che's methods of
leadership, and events following his capture and death.

Excerpts from the diaries and accounts of Rolando, Pombo,
and Benigno record the political talks by Guevara to the guerrilla unit. They expand on Guevara's own one- or two-sen-
tence descriptions of some of these meetings in the camp and
convey the impact these talks had on the combatants.

The accounts of Pombo and Benigno, two of the Cuban veterans of the campaign, shed additional light on Guevara's
thinking, on how and why the fighters got trapped in the unfavorable terrain most were unable to escape from, and on the
political character of the nucleus of combatants. Taken from
interviews that have appeared in the Cuban press over the
years, these eyewitness accounts are part of the living political
continuity of the Cuban revolution. The bulk of the material in
this section appears here in English for the first time.

Numerous explanatory notes, an extensive glossary, chronol-
ogy, list of combatants, and index have been prepared by translator Michael Taber. The aim has been to help readers follow the

story more easily, especially given the passage of time and the nature of the diary itself, which was written under difficult conditions and intended by Guevara as notes for his own use.

Fifteen maps, charting the month-by-month progress of the events recounted, were created for this volume by Eric Simpson, who also designed the book's cover, layout, typography, and photo insert. Virtually every river, mountain range, village, and town mentioned in the diary can be located, along with the route taken by the guerrillas.

This edition of *The Bolivian Diary of Ernesto Che Guevara* would not have been possible without the help and collaboration of numerous individuals in Cuba. Special thanks go to Hugo Chinea, director of Editora Política; Iraida Aguirrechu, who edited *El Diario del Che en Bolivia* for Editora Política in 1987; and Ana Rosa Gort, also of Editora Política.

Gen. Harry Villegas (Pombo) and Col. Leonardo Tamayo (Urbano), Guevara's co-combatants in Bolivia, provided firsthand information and recollections that helped in translating a number of obscure phrases and in preparing the explanatory notes, glossary, maps, and in identifying photos.

Matilde Lara, widow of Inti Peredo, gave permission to publish *My Campaign with Che*. Pedro Álvarez Tabío of the Council of State Office of Publications helped obtain photos. The research conducted over a number of years by Adys Cupull and Froilán González, who annotated and supplied photographs for the 1987 edition of the diary published in Cuba and have authored several other books on the Bolivian campaign, was an irreplaceable aid.

The interest and encouragement of Aleida March was greatly appreciated.

In preparing Pathfinder's new edition of the Bolivian diary, the fundamental aim has been to bring to life for a new generation of revolutionary-minded fighters worldwide this work by one of the great communist leaders of our time. Guevara was not only the revolutionist of action, the great student and practitioner of guerrilla warfare revealed through these pages. He was also the communist leader capable of heading up the reorganization of industry and banking in Cuba; representing the socialist revolution worldwide; promoting the development of volunteer labor as a political necessity for the transition to socialism; and writing some of the most important contributions to Marxism in the twentieth century. All these facets of Che are revealed in other collections of his writings and speeches available in English translation from Pathfinder Press. But without the Che of the Bolivian diary, the rounded communist is missing.

Today, growing numbers of workers and youth throughout the world are seeing with their own eyes what capitalism holds in store for humanity as we enter the twenty-first century. They are repelled by the social consequences of the deepening world capitalist crisis: growing economic conflict and interimperialist competition, trade wars that foretell military confrontations, sharpening inequality and social polarization, unemployment, racism, attacks on women's rights, murders of immigrant workers, growing rightist and fascist movements, famine, disease, devastation, and war.

Through their own observations and experiences, this new generation of rebels will come to the conclusion that the heart of the revolutionary perspective presented by Ernesto Che Guevara some three decades ago remains a burning reality for today—that only working people, through conscious organization and disciplined action, can build a communist organization and lead a fighting humanity out of the abyss and degradation of capitalism toward a socialist future of free men and women.

It is to these fighters above all that this edition is directed, to those who will read the Bolivian diary in the spirit Che wrote it—not as a book about the past, nor as a "manual" of revolution, but as an irreplaceable set of working notes helping us to understand the present and prepare to meet the future.

Mary-Alice Waters
September 1994

Chronology

1965

April 1 – Ernesto Che Guevara delivers letter to Fidel Castro announcing his decision to participate in revolutionary struggles abroad. Shortly afterward he leaves Cuba.

October 3 – Castro reads Guevara's letter during a nationally televised speech.

December – Guevara returns to Cuba from the Congo (today Zaire), where he led a contingent of Cuban volunteers assisting revolutionary forces against that country's proimperialist regime.

1966

January 3-14 – Tricontinental Conference of Solidarity of the Peoples of Asia, Africa, and Latin America is held in Havana, attended by anti-imperialist fighters from around the world.

March – Cuban internationalist Ricardo arrives in Bolivia to organize advance preparations for the guerrilla struggle. He is assisted by Tania, who had been working in Bolivia since 1964 under Guevara's direction, and a number of Bolivian cadres.

June 27 – A 3,000-acre farm in southeastern Bolivia along the Ñacahuazú river is purchased as a possible site for a guerrilla base.

July – Cuban internationalists Pombo and Tuma arrive in Bolivia to help with logistical and political preparations.

July-September – Main body of Cuban volunteers selected by

Guevara for Bolivia mission undergoes training in San Andrés, Pinar del Río province, in eastern Cuba.

September – Exploration conducted of several possible sites in Bolivia for initial guerrilla base.

September 26 – Guevara sends message giving final approval of Ñacahuazú site.

November 3 – Guevara arrives secretly in La Paz.

November 7 – Guevara and several other combatants reach the "zinc house" at the Ñacahuazú site.

November 11 – The guerrillas establish themselves at their first camp, several miles from the zinc house.

November-December – Cuban internationalists and Bolivian fighters arrive at the guerrilla base. Scouting parties explore the area.

December 16 – Guerrilla contingent moves to the site of their main camp (Camp no. 2).

December 31 – Bolivian CP leader Mario Monje comes to the guerrilla camp and meets with Guevara. When his demand for leadership of the column is refused, he breaks off talks and urges Bolivian cadres to desert.

1967

January 8-10 – Bolivian CP Central Committee endorses Monje's stance. Subsequently Bolivian volunteers are dissuaded from joining the guerrillas and several fighters are expelled from the leadership of the CP's youth group.

January 26 – Guevara meets with miners leader Moisés Guevara, who agrees to join the guerrilla movement together with his group.

February 1 – Guerrillas undertake exploratory and training journey. The trip is scheduled to last three weeks, but takes seven. A small group remains at camp.

February-March – New recruits continue to arrive at the Ñacahuazú camp. Régis Debray and Ciro Bustos are brought to the camp for discussions with Guevara on organizing

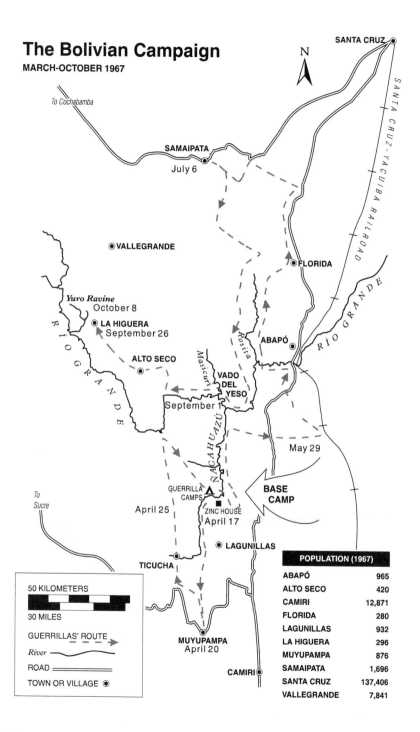

The Bolivian Campaign

MARCH–OCTOBER 1967

N

SANTA CRUZ

To Cochabamba

SANTA CRUZ–YACUIBA RAILROAD

SAMAIPATA
July 6

VALLEGRANDE

FLORIDA

RÍO GRANDE

Yuro Ravine
October 8

Rosita

LA HIGUERA
September 26

ABAPÓ

RÍO GRANDE

ALTO SECO

Masicuri

VADO
DEL
YESO
September 1

RÍO GRANDE

NACAHUAZÚ

May 29

To
Sucre

GUERRILLA
CAMPS

BASE
CAMP

April 25

ZINC HOUSE
April 17

LAGUNILLAS

TICUCHA

50 KILOMETERS	
30 MILES	

GUERRILLAS' ROUTE
River
ROAD
TOWN OR VILLAGE ◉

MUYUPAMPA
April 20

CAMIRI

POPULATION (1967)	
ABAPÓ	965
ALTO SECO	420
CAMIRI	12,871
FLORIDA	280
LAGUNILLAS	932
LA HIGUERA	296
MUYUPAMPA	876
SAMAIPATA	1,696
SANTA CRUZ	137,406
VALLEGRANDE	7,841

international solidarity.

February 26, 1967 – Guerrilla Benjamín drowns in the Río Grande.

February 28 – The guerrilla forward detachment led by Marcos gets separated from the rest of the troops while crossing the Río Grande. Their presence in the village of Tatarenda several days later arouses the army's suspicion.

March 11 – Two new recruits desert from the base camp. They are captured three days later and inform the army of Guevara's presence.

March 12 – The forward detachment led by Marcos arrives back at the Ñacahuazú camp.

March 17 – Carlos drowns while crossing the Río Grande. The Ñacahuazú farm is raided by 60 troops, capturing a guerrilla messenger. One soldier is shot.

March 20 – The main guerrilla force returns to camp. Guevara orders an ambush if the army advances on the camp.

March 23 – Guerrillas ambush an army force along the Ñacahuazú, killing 7. News of the action causes a sensation throughout the country.

March 25 – The guerrillas adopt the name National Liberation Army of Bolivia (ELN). Four Bolivian recruits are expelled from the column.

March 27 – U.S. Lt. Col. Redmond Weber and Maj. Ralph (Pappy) Shelton arrive in Bolivia, followed the next day by 15 U.S. counterinsurgency instructors.

April – U.S. military advisers and CIA personnel continue to arrive in Bolivia. Washington steps up shipment of arms to Bolivian military.

April 10 – An army column is ambushed at the Iripiti river (Monkey Creek), with 10 dead. Rubio is killed.

April 11 – Bolivian government bans Communist Party, Communist Party Marxist-Leninist, and Revolutionary Workers Party (POR).

April 16 – Guevara's "Message to the Tricontinental," written prior to his arrival in Bolivia, is published in Cuba, calling for "two, three, many Vietnams."

April 17, 1967 – Main guerrilla column heads south to escort Debray and Bustos to safety. Rear guard led by Joaquín remains behind. Meant to last three days, the separation of forces becomes permanent.

April 19 – Journalist and likely CIA agent George Andrew Roth reaches the guerrillas. After interrogation he is given an interview prepared by Guevara.

April 19-20 – Debray, Bustos, and Roth are dropped off outside Muyupampa but are arrested hours later. Over the coming months, the imprisonment and trial of Debray and Bustos become a focus of world attention. Roth is released July 8.

April 22 – Guerrillas clash with army troops at Taperillas. Loro becomes separated from the guerrilla column; he is later captured and executed. On the suggestion of Rolando, Guevara's pseudonym is changed from Ramón to Fernando.

April 25 – Army column is ambushed at El Mesón. Rolando is killed in the fighting.

May 1 – Communiqué no. 1 of ELN is published in *Prensa Libre* of Cochabamba.

May 8 – Army column is ambushed at the Ñacahuazú. Three soldiers are killed.

May 23 – Pepe, one of the expelled guerrillas accompanying Joaquín's column, deserts. He is captured by army troops three days later and murdered.

May 30 – Guerrillas ambush government troops at Cuadriculado. Three soldiers are killed.

May 31 – Guerrillas clash with army at at El Espino, killing one.

June 2 – Víctor and Marcos, members of Joaquín's column, are killed in battle.

June 10 – Guerrillas clash with army troops at El Cafetal, killing one.

June 20 – Three army spies are taken prisoner by the guerrillas in Abapó from information provided by Paulino, a village resident who volunteered to join the guerrillas. Several days later Paulino is sent to deliver messages to Cochabamba, in attempt to renew contacts. He is subsequently captured by the army and tortured.

June 23-24 – Troops open fire on miners' settlement at Siglo XX mines while workers and their families sleep; 20 are killed and scores wounded.

June 26 – Guerrillas ambush troops at Florida. Tuma and 3 soldiers are killed.

July 1 – Bolivian dictator Barrientos publicly announces Guevara's presence in the country.

July 6 – A detachment of guerrillas captures Samaipata, capital of Florida province. One soldier is killed and 9 are taken prisoner.

July 9 – Serapio, a member of Joaquín's column, is killed in action.

July 20 – Eusebio and Chingolo, expelled guerrillas accompanying Joaquín's column, desert and are captured. They subsequently lead the army to the guerrillas' strategic supply caves.

July 27 – Guerrillas ambush army troops at La Cruz, killing several.

July 30 – Guerrillas clash with troops at Suspiro river. Ricardo, Raúl, and 4 government troops are killed.

July 31 – August 10 – Organization of Latin American Solidarity (OLAS) conference is held in Havana; conference supports guerrilla movements throughout Latin America; Guevara is elected honorary chair.

August 9 – Joaquín's column clashes with army near Monteagudo. Pedro is killed in the battle.

August 26 – Guerrillas skirmish with troops at the Río Grande.

August 31 – Betrayed by peasant Honorato Rojas, Joaquín's column is annihilated while fording the Río Grande near the Vado del Yeso. Killed in the ambush are Joaquín, Braulio, Alejandro, Tania, Walter, Apolinar, and Moisés Guevara. Ernesto is captured and executed. Negro escapes but is captured and executed four days later.

September 3 – One government soldier is killed in skirmish with guerrillas in the lower Masicuri region.

September 6 – Guerrillas clash with troops.

September 14 – Loyola Guzmán is arrested in La Paz as hundreds of suspected guerrilla collaborators are rounded up and imprisoned.

September 22 – Guerrillas occupy town of Alto Seco. They hold meeting in local schoolhouse addressed by Guevara and Inti.

September 26 – Guerrilla forward detachment falls into army ambush at La Higuera. Coco, Miguel, and Julio are killed. Camba and León desert.

September 27 – Camba and León are captured, and agree to cooperate with the army.

October 8 – The guerrilla column is cornered in the Yuro ravine and a battle ensues. Guerrillas killed in the fighting include Aniceto, Antonio, and Arturo. Four soldiers are killed in the battle. Pacho and Che Guevara, both wounded, are taken prisoner, along with Willy and Chino, and moved to the schoolhouse at La Higuera. Pacho dies of his wounds during the night.

October 9 – After consulting Washington, the Bolivian government orders Guevara's execution. Willy, Chino, and Guevara are shot.

October 12 – Pablito, Eustaquio, Moro, and Chapaco are killed by troops as they try to escape the strategic encirclement. The other group of survivors clash with troops at Naranjal, killing 5, and break out of the encirclement.

November 14-15 – Ñato is killed in combat in Mataral.

November 16 – Debray and Bustos are sentenced to 25 years in prison.

December 16 – After a month in which the 5 surviving guerrillas eluded government troops, Inti and Urbano reach Cochabamba. Arrangements are then made to get the 3 other remaining guerrillas there.

1968

January 6 – Pombo, Benigno, and Darío reach Cochabamba.

January 11-20 – Guerrilla veterans make their way to La Paz.

February 16 – Pombo, Urbano, and Benigno elude a massive army presence at the border and cross into Chilean territory. The two Bolivian veterans, Inti and Darío, stay in Bolivia to attempt to reorganize the ELN.

March 6, 1968 – Pombo, Urbano, and Benigno arrive in Cuba.

Mid-March – microfilms of Guevara's diary are smuggled into
     Cuba.

July 1 – Guevara's diary is published in Cuba.

A Necessary Introduction
by Fidel Castro

It was Che's custom during his days as a guerrilla to carefully record his daily observations in a personal diary. During long marches over rugged and difficult terrain, in the midst of damp woods, when the lines of men, always hunched over from the weight of their packs, ammunition, and weapons, would stop for a moment to rest, or when the column would receive orders to halt and make camp at the end of an exhausting day's march, one would see Che—as he was from the beginning affectionately nicknamed by the Cubans—take out a small notebook and, with his tiny and nearly illegible doctor's handwriting, write his notes.

What he was able to save from these notes he later used in writing his magnificent historical narratives of the revolutionary war in Cuba—accounts full of revolutionary, educational, and human content.[1]

This time, thanks to his invariable habit of jotting down the

---

1. These have been published in English as *Reminiscences of the Cuban Revolutionary War* (New York: Monthly Review Press/Merit Publishers, 1968). Substantial excerpts can be found in *Che Guevara and the Cuban Revolution: Writings and Speeches of Ernesto Che Guevara.*

main events of each day, we have at our disposal detailed, rigorously exact, and priceless information on the heroic final months of his life in Bolivia.

These notes, not written for publication, served as a tool in the constant evaluation of events, situations, and men. They also served as an outlet for the expression of his keenly observant and analytic spirit, often laced with a sharp sense of humor. They are soberly written and form a coherent whole from beginning to end.

It should be kept in mind that they were written during rare moments of rest in the midst of a heroic and superhuman physical effort. Also to be remembered are his exhausting obligations as leader of a guerrilla detachment in the difficult first stages of a struggle of this nature, which unfolded under incredibly harsh material conditions. This reveals once more his habits of work and his will of steel.

While analyzing in detail the incidents of each day, the diary takes note of the shortcomings, critical assessments, and recriminations that are an inevitable part of the development of a revolutionary guerrilla struggle.

Inside a guerrilla detachment such assessments must take place continually. This is especially true during the stage in which the detachment consists of a small nucleus facing extremely adverse material conditions and an enemy infinitely superior in number, when the slightest negligence or the most insignificant mistake can be fatal. The leader must be extremely demanding. At the same time, he must use each event or episode, no matter how insignificant it may seem, to educate the combatants and future cadres of new guerrilla detachments.

The process of training a guerrilla force is a constant appeal to each man's consciousness and honor. Che knew how to touch the most sensitive fibers in revolutionaries. When Marcos, after being repeatedly admonished by Che, was warned that he could be dishonorably discharged from the guerrilla unit, he replied, "I would rather be shot!" Later he gave his life heroically. Similar conduct could be noted among all the men Che placed confidence in and whom he had to admonish for one reason or another in the course of the struggle. He was a fraternal and humane leader, but he also knew how to be demanding and, at times, severe. But above all, and even more so than with the others, Che was demanding and severe with himself. He based discipline on the guerrilla fighter's moral consciousness and on the tremendous force of his own example.

The diary also contains numerous references to Debray, and reflects the enormous concern Che felt over the arrest and imprisonment of the revolutionary writer. Although at heart Che would have preferred to have him stay with the guerrilla unit, Debray had been given a mission to carry out in Europe. That is why Che shows a certain uneasiness and, on occasion, some doubts about his behavior.

Che had no way of knowing the odyssey Debray lived through in the hands of the repressive forces, or the firm and courageous attitude he maintained in face of his captors and torturers.

He noted, however, the enormous political significance of the trial, and on October 3—six days before his death—in the middle of bitter and tense events, he wrote: "An interview with Debray was heard; he was very courageous when faced with a student provocateur." That was his last reference to the writer.

The Cuban revolution and its relation to the guerrilla movement are repeatedly referred to in the diary. Some may interpret our decision to publish it as an act of provocation that will give the enemies of the revolution—the U.S. imperialists and their allies, the Latin American oligarchs—ammunition for redoubling their efforts to blockade, isolate, and attack Cuba.

Those who judge the facts this way should remember that U.S. imperialism has never needed a pretext to carry out its crimes anywhere in the world, and that its efforts to crush the Cuban revolution began as soon as our country passed its first revolutionary law. This course stems from the obvious and well-known fact that imperialism is the policeman of world reaction, the systematic promoter of counterrevolution, and the protector of the most backward and inhuman social structures that remain in the world.

Cuba's solidarity with the revolutionary movement may be the pretext, but it will never be the real cause of U.S. aggression. To refuse solidarity in order to avoid providing a pretext is a ridiculous, ostrich-like policy that has nothing to do with the internationalist character of the social revolutions of today. To refuse solidarity to the revolutionary movement not only does not avoid providing a pretext; it is in effect a show of solidarity with U.S. imperialism and its policy of dominating and enslaving the world.

Cuba is a small country, economically underdeveloped as are all the countries dominated and exploited for centuries by colonialism and imperialism. It is located only ninety miles from the coast of the United States, has a U.S. naval base on its territory,[2] and faces numerous obstacles in attaining socioeconomic development. Grave dangers have threatened our country since the triumph of the revolution. But imperialism will never make us give in for these reasons, because the difficulties that flow from a consistently revolutionary line of action are of no importance to us.

From the revolutionary point of view, there is no alternative but to publish Che's Bolivian diary. It fell into the hands of Barrientos, who immediately sent copies to the CIA, the Pentagon, and the U.S. government. Journalists connected with the CIA had access to the document inside Bolivia. They made photocopies of it with the promise that they would refrain, for the moment, from publishing it.

The Barrientos government and the top-ranking military officers have more than enough reasons not to publish the diary. It reveals the immense incompetence of their army and the countless defeats they were dealt by a handful of determined guerrillas who, in a matter of weeks, seized nearly 200

---

2. A reference to the U.S. naval base at Guantánamo, on the southeastern part of the island.

weapons from them in combat.

Furthermore, Che describes Barrientos and his regime in terms they deserve, with words that cannot be erased from history.

Imperialism also had its own reasons. Che and the extraordinary example he set are becoming more and more powerful in the world. His ideas, image, and name are banners of struggle against the injustices suffered by the oppressed and exploited. They evoke impassioned interest among students and intellectuals the world over.

In the United States itself, the Black movement and progressive students—both of which continue to grow in numbers—have made Che's figure their own. In the most militant demonstrations for civil rights and against the aggression in Vietnam, his image is brandished as an emblem of struggle. Few times in history—perhaps never before—has a figure, a name, an example become a universal symbol so quickly and with such impassioned force. This is because Che embodies, in its purest and most selfless form, the internationalist spirit that characterizes the world of today, and will do so even more in the world of tomorrow.

Out of a continent yesterday oppressed by colonial powers, today exploited and held in backwardness and the most iniquitous underdevelopment by U.S. imperialism, there has emerged this singular figure who has become the universal inspiration of revolutionary struggle, even inside the imperialist and colonialist powers themselves.

The U.S. imperialists fear the power of this example and everything that may help to spread it. The diary is the living expression of an extraordinary personality; a lesson in guerrilla warfare written in the heat and tension of daily events, as flammable as gunpowder; a demonstration in life that Latin Americans are not powerless in face of the enslavers of entire peoples and of their mercenary armies. That is the diary's intrinsic value, and that is what has kept them from publishing it up until now.

Also among those who may be interested in keeping the diary unpublished are the pseudorevolutionaries, opportunists, and charlatans of every stripe. These people call themselves Marxists, Communists, and other such titles. They have not hesitated, however, to call Che a mistaken adventurer or, when they speak more benignly, an idealist whose death marked the swan song of revolutionary armed struggle in Latin America. "If Che himself," they exclaim, "the greatest exponent of these ideas and an experienced guerrilla fighter, died in the guerrilla struggle and his movement failed to liberate Bolivia, it only shows how mistaken he was!" How many of these miserable creatures were happy at Che's death, not even blushing at the thought that their positions and line of reasoning coincide completely with those of imperialism and the most reactionary oligarchs!

That is how they justify themselves. That is how they justify their treacherous leaders who, at a given moment, did not hesitate to play at armed struggle, with the true aim—as could be seen later—of destroying the guerrilla detachments, putting the brakes on revolutionary action, and imposing their own shameful and ridiculous political schemes, because they were absolutely incapable of carrying out any other line. That is how they justify those who do not want to fight, who will never fight for the people and their liberation. That is how they justify those who have made a caricature of revolutionary ideas, turning them into an opium-like dogma with neither content nor message for the masses; those who have converted the organizations of popular struggle into instruments of conciliation with domestic and foreign exploiters; and those who advocate policies that have nothing to do with the genuine interests of the exploited peoples of this continent.

Che envisioned his death as something natural and probable in the process. He made an effort to stress, especially in his last writings, that this eventuality would not hold back the inevitable march of the revolution in Latin America. In his Message to the Tricontinental, he reiterated this thought: "Our every action is a battle cry against imperialism. . . . Wherever death may surprise us, let it be welcome if our battle cry has reached even one receptive ear, if another hand reaches out to take up our arms."[3]

Che considered himself a soldier in this revolution, with absolutely no concern as to whether he would survive it. Those who see the outcome of his struggle in Bolivia as marking the failure of his ideas can, with the same oversimplification, deny the validity of the ideas and struggles of all the great revolutionary precursors and thinkers. This includes the founders of Marxism, who were themselves unable to complete the task and to view in life the fruits of their noble efforts.

In Cuba, Martí and Maceo were killed in combat, followed by Yankee intervention as the war of independence came to an end, frustrating the immediate objectives of their struggle. Brilliant advocates of socialist revolution such as Julio Antonio Mella were killed, murdered by agents in the service of imperialism. But these deaths could not, in the long run, block the triumph of a process that began a hundred years ago. And absolutely no one can call into question the profound justice of the cause and line of struggle of those eminent fighters of the past, nor the timeliness of their basic ideas, which have always inspired Cuban revolutionaries.

From the notations in Che's diary, one can see how real were the possibilities of success, as well as what extraordinary catalyzing power resides in guerrilla struggle. On one occasion, in face of evident signs of the Bolivian regime's weakness and rapid deterioration, he wrote: "The government is disintegrating rapidly. It is a pity we do not have 100 more men at this moment."

Che knew from his experience in Cuba how often our small guerrilla detachment had been on the verge of being wiped out. Whether such things happen depends almost entirely on

---

3. In *Che Guevara and the Cuban Revolution: Writings and Speeches of Ernesto Che Guevara*, pp. 359-60.

chance and the imponderables of war. But would such an eventuality have given anyone the right to consider our line erroneous, and in addition to use it as an example to discourage revolution and inculcate a sense of powerlessness among the peoples? Many times in history revolutionary processes have been preceded by adverse episodes! We ourselves in Cuba—did we not have the experience of Moncada, just six years before the definitive triumph of the people's armed struggle?

From July 26, 1953—the attack on the Moncada garrison in Santiago de Cuba—to December 2, 1956—the landing of the *Granma*—revolutionary struggle in Cuba against a modern, well-equipped army seemed to many people to lack any prospect for success. The action of a handful of fighters was seen as a chimera of idealists and dreamers who were "deeply mistaken." The crushing defeat and total dispersal of the inexperienced guerrilla detachment on December 5, 1956, seemed to confirm entirely these pessimistic forebodings. But only twenty-five months later the remnants of that guerrilla unit had already developed the strength and experience necessary to annihilate that same army.

In all epochs and under all circumstances, there will always be an abundance of pretexts for not fighting; but not fighting is the surest way to never attain freedom. Che did not outlive his ideas; rather, he fertilized them with his blood. On the other hand, his pseudorevolutionary critics, with all their political cowardice and eternal lack of action, will outlive by far the evidence of their own stupidity.

Noteworthy in this respect, as can be seen in the diary, are the actions of one of these revolutionary specimens that are becoming increasingly typical in Latin America—Mario Monje. Brandishing the title of secretary of the Communist Party of Bolivia, Monje sought to dispute with Che the political and military leadership of the movement. Since Monje had stated his intention of resigning his party post to take on this responsibility, he obviously felt that it was enough to have once held that title to claim such a prerogative.

Mario Monje, of course, had no experience in guerrilla warfare and had never been in combat. In addition, the fact that he considered himself a communist should have obliged him, at the very least, to dispense with the gross and mundane chauvinism that had already been overcome by the precursors who fought for Bolivia's first independence.

With such a conception of what an anti-imperialist struggle on this continent should be, "communist leaders" of this type have not gone beyond even the level of internationalism of the aboriginal tribes subjugated by the European colonizers at the time of the conquest.

Bolivia and its historical capital, Sucre, were named after the country's first liberators, both of whom were Venezuelan.[4] And in this country, in a struggle for the definitive liberation of his people, the head of the Communist Party had the possibility of enlisting the cooperation of the political, organizational, and military talent of a genuine revolutionary titan, of a man whose cause was not limited by the narrow and artificial—not to mention unjust—borders of Bolivia. Instead, this person did nothing but engage in disgraceful, ridiculous, and unmerited claims to command.

Bolivia does not have an outlet to the sea. Thus, for its own liberation, to avoid exposure to a cruel blockade, Bolivia more than any other country needs revolutionary victories by its neighbors. Che, because of his enormous authority, ability, and experience, was the man who could have accelerated this process.

Che had established relations with leaders and members of the Bolivian Communist Party, dating back prior to the split that occurred in its ranks.[5] He did so to solicit their help for the

---

4. A reference to Simón Bolívar and Antonio José de Sucre, leaders of the Latin American independence struggle from Spain in the early years of the 19th century.

5. A split occurred in the Bolivian Communist Party in early 1965, leading to the formation of a rival party sympathetic to Maoism led by Oscar Zamora.

revolutionary movement in South America. Under authorization from the party, some of its members worked with Che for years on various assignments. When the split occurred, it created a special situation, given that a number of the people with whom he had been working ended up in one group or the other. However, Che conceived of the struggle in Bolivia not as an isolated occurrence, but as part of a revolutionary liberation movement that would rapidly extend to other countries in South America. His aim was to organize a movement free of sectarianism, one that could be joined by anyone who wanted to fight for the liberation of Bolivia and of all the other peoples of Latin America subjugated by imperialism.

In the initial phase of preparing a base for the guerrilla unit, however, Che depended for the most part on the help of a group of courageous and discreet collaborators who, at the time of the split, remained in the party headed by Monje. Although he certainly felt no sympathy toward Monje, in deference to them he invited Monje to visit his camp first. He then invited Moisés Guevara, a leader of the miners and a political leader who had left the party to join in the formation of another organization, the one led by Oscar Zamora. Because of differences with Zamora, Moisés Guevara later left that group as well. Zamora was another Monje who had once promised Che to help in organizing armed guerrilla struggle in Bolivia. He later backed away from that commitment and cowardly folded his arms at the hour of action. After Che's death, Zamora became one of his most venomous "Marxist-Leninist" critics. Moisés Guevara joined Che without hesitation, as he had sought to do long before Che arrived in Bolivia. He offered his support and gave his life heroically for the revolutionary cause.

The group of Bolivian guerrillas who until then had remained in Monje's organization also joined Che. Led by Inti and Coco Peredo, who later proved to be courageous and outstanding fighters, they left Monje and decisively backed Che. But Monje, seeking revenge, devoted his energies to sabotaging the movement. In La Paz he intercepted well-trained Communist militants who were on their way to join the guerrillas and blocked them from doing so. These facts demonstrate that within the revolutionary ranks are men who possess every quality necessary for struggle, but are criminally frustrated in their development by incapable, maneuvering, and charlatan-like leaders.

Che was a man never personally interested in posts, leadership, or honors. But he was firmly convinced that revolutionary guerrilla struggle was the fundamental form of action for winning the liberation of the peoples of Latin America, basing this conclusion on the economic, political, and social situation of nearly all Latin American countries. And he strongly believed that the military and political leadership of the guerrilla struggle had to be unified, and that the struggle could be led only from the guerrilla unit itself, not from the comfortable offices of bureaucrats in the cities. So he was not prepared to give up leadership of a guerrilla nucleus that, at a later stage of its development, was intended to develop into a struggle of broad dimensions in South America. And he certainly was not prepared to turn over such leadership to an inexperienced emptyhead with narrow chauvinist views. Che believed that such chauvinism, which often infects even revolutionary elements of various countries in Latin America, must be fought, because it represents reactionary, ridiculous, and sterile thinking.

"And let us develop genuine proletarian internationalism," he said in his Message to the Tricontinental. "Let the flag under which we fight be the sacred cause of the liberation of humanity, so that to die under the colors of Vietnam, Venezuela, Guatemala, Laos, Guinea, Colombia, Bolivia . . . to mention only the current scenes of armed struggle—will be equally glorious and desirable for a Latin American, an Asian, an African, and even a European.

"Every drop of blood spilled in a land under whose flag one was not born is experience gathered by the survivor to be applied later in the struggle for liberation of one's own country. And every people that liberates itself is a step in the battle for the liberation of one's own people."[6]

Along these lines, Che believed that fighters from various Latin American countries would participate in the guerrilla detachment, that the guerrilla struggle in Bolivia would be a school in which revolutionaries would serve their apprenticeship in combat. To help him in this task, he wanted to have, together with the Bolivians, a small nucleus of experienced guerrilla fighters, nearly all of whom had been comrades of his in the Sierra Maestra during the revolutionary struggle in Cuba. These were men whose abilities, courage, and spirit of self-sacrifice were known to Che. None of them hesitated to respond to his call, none of them abandoned him, and none of them surrendered.

In the Bolivian campaign Che acted with his proverbial tenacity, skill, stoicism, and exemplary attitude. It can be said that, consumed with the importance of the mission he had assigned himself, Che at all times proceeded with a spirit of irreproachable responsibility. When the guerrilla unit committed an error of carelessness, he quickly called attention to it, corrected it, and noted it in his diary.

Adverse factors built up against him unbelievably. One example was the separation—supposed to last for just a few days—of part of the guerrilla detachment. That unit included a courageous group of men, some of them sick or convalescent. Once contact between the two groups was lost in very rough terrain, this separation continued, and for endless months Che was occupied with the effort to find them. In this period his asthma—an ailment easily treated with simple medication, but one that, lacking the medication, became a terrible enemy—attacked him relentlessly. It became a serious problem since the medical supplies that had been accumulated by the guerrillas beforehand had been discovered and captured by the enemy. This fact, along with the annihilation at the end of August of the part of the guerrilla detachment he

6. *Che Guevara and the Cuban Revolution*, p. 358.

had lost contact with, were factors that weighed heavily in the development of events. But Che, with his iron will, overcame his physical difficulties and never for an instant cut back his activity or let his spirits sag.

Che had many contacts with the Bolivian peasants. Their character—highly suspicious and cautious—would have come as no surprise to Che, who knew their mentality perfectly well because he had dealt with them on other occasions. He knew that winning them over to his cause required long, arduous, and patient work. He had no doubt, however, that in the long run they would obtain the support of the peasants.

If we follow the thread of events carefully, it becomes clear that even in the month of September, a few weeks before his death, when the number of men on whom Che could count was quite small, the guerrilla unit still retained its capacity to develop. It also still had a few Bolivian cadres, such as the brothers Inti and Coco Peredo, who were already beginning to show magnificent leadership potential.

It was the ambush in La Higuera—the sole successful action by the army against the detachment led by Che—that created a situation they could not overcome. In that action, the forward detachment was killed and several more men were wounded as they headed, in broad daylight, toward a peasant area with a higher level of political development—an objective not noted down in the diary, but known through the survivors.[7] It was without doubt dangerous to advance by daylight along the same route they had been following for several days, with unavoidable contact with a large number of residents of an area they were passing through for the first time. It was obvious that the army would certainly intercept them at some point. But Che, fully conscious of this, decided to run the risk in order to help El Médico, who was in very poor physical condition.[8]

---

7. See pages 421-26.
8. A reference to Octavio de la Concepción (Moro), a combatant and the unit's doctor, who suffered near-crippling bouts of lumbago.

The day before the ambush, he wrote: "We reached Pujio early in the day, but there we found people who had seen us down below the day before. In other words, our movements are being announced ahead of time by Radio Bemba [word of mouth]. . . . It is becoming dangerous to travel with mules, but I am trying to make it as easy as possible for El Médico, since he is very weak."

The following day he wrote: "At 1:00 p.m., the forward detachment set out on the road to Jagüey, where a decision was to be made about the mules and El Médico." That is, he was seeking a solution for the sick man, with the aim of getting off the road and taking the necessary precautions. But that same afternoon, before the forward detachment reached Jagüey, the fatal ambush occurred, leaving the detachment in an untenable situation.

A few days later, encircled in the Yuro ravine, Che fought his final battle.

Recalling the feat carried out by this handful of revolutionaries touches one deeply. In and of itself, the struggle against the hostile natural environment in which they operated constitutes an insurmountable page of heroism. Never in history has so small a number of men set out on such a gigantic task. Their faith and absolute conviction that the immense revolutionary capacity of the peoples of Latin America could be awakened, their confidence in themselves, and the determination with which they took on this objective—all these give us a just measure of this group of men.

One day Che said to the guerrilla fighters in Bolivia: "This type of struggle provides us the opportunity to become revolutionaries, the highest level of the human species. At the same time, it enables us to emerge fully as men. Those who are unable to achieve either of these two states should say so and abandon the struggle."

Those who fought at his side until the end became worthy of such honored terms. They symbolize the type of revolutionary and the type of men history is now calling on for a truly difficult task—the revolutionary transformation of Latin America.

The enemy our forefathers faced in the first struggle for independence was a colonial power in decline. Revolutionaries of today have as their enemy the most powerful bulwark of the imperialist camp, equipped with the most modern technology and industry. This enemy not only organized and equipped a new army in Bolivia—where the people had destroyed the previous repressive military apparatus[9]—and immediately sent weapons and advisers to help in the struggle against the guerrillas. It has also provided military and technical support on the same scale to every repressive force on the continent. And when these methods are not enough, it has intervened directly with its troops, as in the Dominican Republic.

Fighting this enemy requires the type of revolutionaries and men Che spoke of. Without this type of revolutionaries and men, ready to do what they did; without the spirit to confront the enormous obstacles they faced; without the readiness to die that accompanied them at every moment; without their deeply held conviction of the justice of their cause and their unyielding faith in the invincible force of the peoples, against a power like U.S. imperialism, whose military, technical, and economic resources are felt throughout the entire world—without these the liberation of the peoples of this continent will not be attained.

The people of the United States themselves are beginning to become aware that the monstrous political superstructure that reigns in their country has for some time no longer been the idyllic bourgeois republic established nearly 200 years ago by the country's founders. They are increasingly subjected to the moral barbarism of an irrational, alienating, de-

---

9. This is a reference to the Bolivian revolution of 1952 that overthrew a military dictatorship. As part of a deep-going mobilization of workers and peasants, popular militias were formed, Bolivia's tin-mining industry was nationalized, and a land reform was decreed.

humanized, and brutal system that takes from the people of the United States a growing number of victims in its wars of aggression, its political crimes, its racial aberrations, its miserable hierarchy of human beings, its repugnant waste of economic, scientific, and human resources on its enormous, reactionary, and repressive military apparatus in the midst of a world where three-quarters of humanity lives in underdevelopment and hunger.

Only the revolutionary transformation of Latin America will enable the people of the United States to settle their own accounts with this very imperialism. At the same time, and in the same way, the growing struggle of the people of the United States against imperialist policy can become a decisive ally of the revolutionary movement in Latin America.

An enormous differentiation and imbalance occurred in the Americas at the beginning of this century. On one side a powerful and rapidly industrializing nation, in accordance with the very law of its social and economic development, was marching toward imperial heights. On the other side, the weak and stagnant countries in the balkanized remainder of the Americas were kept under the boot of feudal oligarchies and their reactionary armies. If this part of the hemisphere does not undergo a profound revolutionary transformation, that earlier gap will seem but a pale reflection of the enormous present unevenness in economics, science, and technology. And even more, it will foretell the horrible imbalance that, at an increasingly accelerated rate, the imperialist superstructure will impose on the peoples of Latin America in the next twenty years.

Along this road, we are condemned to be increasingly poor, weak, dependent, and enslaved to imperialism. This gloomy perspective also confronts, to an equal degree, all the underdeveloped nations of Africa and Asia.

If the industrialized and educated nations of Europe, with their Common Market and supranational scientific institutions, are worried about the possibility of being left behind and contemplate with fear the prospects of being converted into economic colonies of U.S. imperialism—what then does the future have in store for the peoples of Latin America?

This is unquestionably the real situation that decisively affects the destiny of our peoples. What is urgently needed is a deep-going revolutionary transformation that can gather together all the moral, material, and human forces in this part of the world and launch them forward so as to overcome the centuries-old and constantly increasing economic, scientific, and technological backwardness relative to the industrialized world to which we are tributaries and will continue to be to an even greater degree, especially to the United States. Is there some liberal or bourgeois reformist, or some pseudorevolutionary charlatan incapable of action, who has a different answer—and with a magic wand for carrying it out? Does he possess a formula different from Che's conception—one that can sweep away the oligarchs, despots, and petty politicians (the servants) and the Yankee monopolists (the masters) and do so with all the urgency the circumstances require? Only such a person can stand up to berate Che.

But not one of them really has an honest answer or a consistent policy that will bring genuine hope to the nearly 300 million human beings who make up the population of Latin America. Devastatingly poor in their overwhelming majority and increasing in number to 600 million within twenty-five years, they have the right to the material things of life, to culture, and to civilization. So the most dignified thing would be to remain silent about the actions of Che and those who fell with him, courageously defending their ideas. Because the feat carried out by this handful of men, guided by the noble idea of redeeming a continent, will remain the strongest proof of what determination, heroism, and human greatness can accomplish. It is an example that will illuminate the consciousness and preside over the struggle of the peoples of Latin America. Che's heroic cry will reach the receptive ear of the poor and exploited for whom he gave his life, and many

hands will come forward to take up arms to win their definitive liberation.

On October 7, Che wrote his last lines. The following day,
at 1:00 p.m., in a narrow ravine where he proposed waiting
until nightfall in order to break out of the encirclement, a
large enemy force made contact with them. The small group
of men who now made up the detachment fought heroically
until dusk. From individual positions located on the bottom
of the ravine, and on the top edges, they faced a mass of soldiers who surrounded and attacked them. There were no survivors among those who fought in the positions closest to
Che. Since at his side were El Médico in the grave state of
health mentioned before, and a Peruvian guerrilla who was
also in very poor physical condition, everything seems to indicate that until he fell wounded, Che did his utmost to safe-
guard the withdrawal of these comrades to a safer place. El
Médico was not killed in this battle, but rather several days
later at a place not far from the Yuro ravine. The ruggedness
of the rocky, irregular terrain made it difficult—at times impossible—for the guerrillas to maintain visual contact with
each other. Those defending positions at the other entrance to
the ravine, several hundred meters from Che—among them
Inti Peredo—resisted the attack until dark, when they man-
aged to lose the enemy and head toward the previously
agreed point of regroupment.

It has been possible to establish that Che continued fighting
despite being wounded, until a shot destroyed the barrel of his
M-2 rifle, making it totally useless. The pistol he carried had
no magazine. These incredible circumstances explain how he
could have been captured alive. The wounds in his legs kept
him from walking without help, but they were not fatal.

Moved to the town of La Higuera, he remained alive some
24 hours. He refused to exchange a single word with his captors, and a drunken officer who tried to annoy him received a
slap across the face.

At a meeting in La Paz, Barrientos, Ovando, and other high

military leaders made the cold-blooded decision to murder Che. Details are known of the way in which the treacherous agreement was carried out in the schoolhouse at La Higuera. Major Miguel Ayoroa and Colonel Andrés Selnich, rangers trained by the Yankees, ordered warrant officer Mario Terán to proceed with the murder. Terán, completely drunk, entered the school yard. When Che, who heard the shots that had just killed a Bolivian and a Peruvian guerrilla fighter,[10] saw the executioner hesitate, he said firmly, "Shoot! Don't be afraid!" Terán left, and again it was necessary for his superiors, Ayoroa and Selnich, to repeat the order. He then proceeded to carry it out, firing a machine-gun burst from the belt down. A version had already been given out that Che died a few hours after combat; therefore, the executioners had orders not to shoot him in the chest or head, so as not to induce immediately fatal wounds. This cruelly prolonged Che's agony until a sergeant, also drunk, killed him with a pistol shot to the left side. Such a procedure contrasts brutally with the respect shown by Che, without a single exception, toward the lives of the many officers and soldiers of the Bolivian army he took prisoner.

The final hours of his existence in the hands of his contemptible enemies must have been very bitter for him. But no man was better prepared than Che to be put to such a test.

The way in which the diary came into our hands cannot be told at this time; suffice it to say there was no monetary payment involved. It contains all the notes he wrote from November 7, 1966, the day Che arrived in Ñancahuazú, until October 7, 1967, the evening before the battle in the Yuro ravine. There are a few pages missing, pages that have not yet arrived in our hands; but they correspond to dates on which nothing of any importance happened, and therefore do not alter the content of the diary in any way.[11]

---

10. The two fighters murdered together with Guevara were the Bolivian Willy (Simón Cuba) and the Peruvian fighter Chino (Juan Pablo Chang).
11. The present work includes the entries missing from the original 1968 edition.

Although the document in itself offers not the slightest doubt as to its authenticity, all the photocopies have been subjected to a rigorous examination to establish not only their authenticity, but also to check on any possible alteration, no matter how slight. The dates were compared with the diary of one of the surviving guerrilla fighters; the two documents coincide in every aspect. Detailed testimony of the other surviving guerrilla fighters, who were witnesses to each one of the events, also contributed to corroborating the document's authenticity. In short, it has been established with absolute certainty that all the photostats were faithful copies of Che's diary.

Deciphering the tiny letters and the difficult handwriting was a laborious job, a task that was carried out with the tireless assistance of his wife and comrade, Aleida March de Guevara.

The diary will be published almost simultaneously in France by the publishing house of François Maspero; in Italy by Feltrinelli publishers; in the Federal Republic of Germany by Trikont Verlag; in the United States by *Ramparts* magazine; in France, in a Spanish edition, by Ediciones Ruedo Ibérico; in Chile by the magazine *Punto Final*; in Mexico by Editorial Siglo XXI; and in other countries.

Hasta la victoria siempre! [Ever onward to victory!]

June 1968

'Other nations of the world summon my assistance'

Letter to Fidel Castro by Ernesto Che Guevara

This letter announcing Guevara's decision to pursue internationalist missions was delivered April 1, 1965, prior to his departure for the Congo (today Zaire) to aid revolutionary forces fighting the imperialist-installed regime. The letter was read aloud by Castro on October 3, 1965, during a televised speech at the close of the founding meeting of the Communist Party of Cuba.

Havana
Year of Agriculture

Fidel:

At this moment I remember many things—when I met you in María Antonia's house, when you proposed I come along, all the tensions involved in the preparations.[1] One day they came by and asked who should be notified in case of death, and the real possibility of it struck us all. Later we knew it was true, that in a revolution one wins or dies (if it is a real one). Many comrades fell along the way to victory.

Today everything has a less dramatic tone, because we are more mature, but the event repeats itself. I feel that I have

---

1. Guevara and Castro met in Mexico in July-August 1955, at the home of Cuban revolutionary María Antonia González. Guevara became one of the first recruits to the guerrilla expedition Castro was planning, which sailed for Cuba in November 1956 aboard the *Granma*.

fulfilled the part of my duty that tied me to the Cuban revolution in its territory, and I say farewell to you, to the comrades, to your people, who now are mine.

I formally resign my positions in the leadership of the party, my post as minister, my rank of commander, and my Cuban citizenship. Nothing legal binds me to Cuba. The only ties are of another nature—those that cannot be broken as can appointments to posts.

Reviewing my past life, I believe I have worked with sufficient integrity and dedication to consolidate the revolutionary triumph. My only serious failing was not having had more confidence in you from the first moments in the Sierra Maestra, and not having understood quickly enough your qualities as a leader and a revolutionary.

I have lived magnificent days, and at your side I felt the pride of belonging to our people in the brilliant yet sad days of the Caribbean crisis.[2] Seldom has a statesman been more brilliant than you were in those days. I am also proud of having followed you without hesitation, of having identified with your way of thinking and of seeing and appraising dangers and principles.

Other nations of the world summon my modest efforts of assistance. I can do that which is denied you owing to your responsibility at the head of Cuba, and the time has come for us to part.

You should know that I do so with a mixture of joy and sorrow. I leave here the purest of my hopes as a builder and the dearest of those I hold dear. And I leave a people who received

---

2. A reference to the October 1962 crisis when President John F. Kennedy demanded removal of Soviet nuclear missiles installed in Cuba following the signing of a mutual defense agreement between the Soviet and Cuban governments. Washington ordered a total naval blockade of Cuba, stepped up its prior course toward an invasion of the island, and placed U.S. armed forces on nuclear alert. Cuban workers and farmers responded by mobilizing massively in defense of the revolution. Following an exchange of communications between Moscow and Washington, Soviet premier Nikita Khrushchev decided to remove the missiles, without consulting the Cuban government.

me as a son. That wounds a part of my spirit. I carry to new battlefronts the faith that you taught me, the revolutionary spirit of my people, the feeling of fulfilling the most sacred of duties: to fight against imperialism wherever one may be. This is a source of strength, and more than heals the deepest of wounds.

I state once more that I free Cuba from all responsibility, except that which stems from its example. If my final hour finds me under other skies, my last thought will be of this people and especially of you. I am grateful for your teaching and your example, to which I shall try to be faithful up to the final consequences of my acts.

I have always been identified with the foreign policy of our revolution, and I continue to be. Wherever I am, I will feel the responsibility of being a Cuban revolutionary, and I shall behave as such. I am not sorry that I leave nothing material to my wife and children; I am happy it is that way. I ask nothing for them, as the state will provide them with enough to live on and receive an education.

I would have many things to say to you and to our people, but I feel they are unnecessary. Words cannot express what I would like them to, and there is no point in scribbling pages.

Hasta la victoria siempre! [Ever onward to victory!]

Patria o muerte! [Homeland or death!]

I embrace you with all my revolutionary fervor.

Che

The Bolivian Diary *of* Ernesto Che Guevara

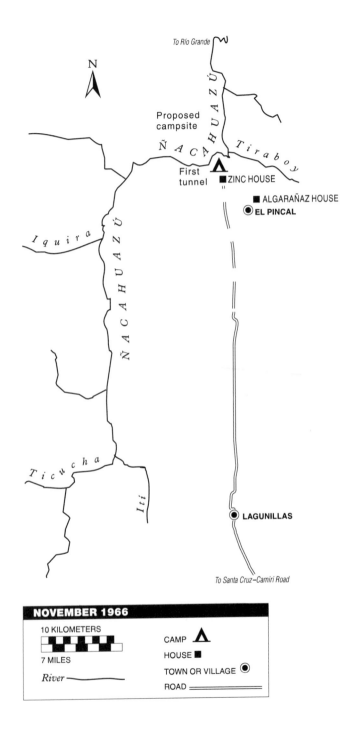

NOVEMBER 1966

November 7

Today a new stage begins. We arrived at the farm at night. The trip went fairly well. After arriving in Cochabamba, suitably disguised, Pachungo and I made the contacts. We then traveled by jeep for two days, in two vehicles.[1]

Approaching the farm, we stopped the vehicles and continued on in one jeep to avoid arousing the suspicion of the landowner nearby,[2] who is muttering about our being involved in cocaine manufacturing. Curiously enough, the ineffable Tumaini is indicated as the chemist of the group. Continuing on toward the farm during the second trip, Bigotes, who had just been informed of my identity, almost drove into

---

1. Arriving in La Paz on November 3, Guevara had traveled to the guerrilla base with Cubans Pacho (Pachungo), Tuma (Tumaini), and Pombo, and the Bolivian Bigotes (who was also known as Loro and Jorge). [See the glossary on pp. 435-54 for the identities of the guerrillas and biographical information.] The guerrilla base, a farm along the Ñacahuazú river, had a house with a corrugated zinc roof that came to be known as the "zinc house."
2. Ciro Algarañaz (also referred to by Guevara as Argañaraz).

a ditch, leaving the jeep stuck out over the edge. After walking about 20 kilometers, we arrived at the farm past midnight. There are three workers from the [Bolivian Communist] party there.[3]

Bigotes states he is prepared to collaborate with us whatever the party might do, but he is loyal to Monje, whom he respects and seems to like. According to him, Rodolfo feels the same way, as does Coco,[4] but it is necessary to try to get the party to join the struggle. I asked him to help us, and requested he not inform the party until Monje—who is on his way to Bulgaria—arrives. He agreed to both things.

November 8

We spent the day in the brush, barely 100 meters from the house, and next to the creek. We were attacked by a type of *yaguasa*,[5] very annoying although they do not bite. The insects we have seen, up to now, are yaguasas, gnats, *mariguís*,[6] mosquitoes, and ticks.

Bigotes got his jeep out with the help of Argañaraz and stayed to buy a few things, such as pigs and chickens.

I intended to write a message about the latest developments, but will leave that for next week, when we expect the second group to arrive.

November 9

An uneventful day. Tumaini and I scouted the area along the Ñacahuasi river[7] (actually a creek), but did not reach its source.

---

3. Apolinar, Serapio (Serafín), and León (Antonio), had been assigned as workers at the farm.
4. Rodolfo Saldaña was a leader of the urban support network. Coco Peredo, formal "proprietor" of the farm, was centrally involved in the guerrilla preparations, together with Jorge Vázquez (Bigotes or Loro). All were members of the Bolivian Communist Party.
5. A gnat-type insect common to the region.
6. A yellow-winged, biting insect.
7. Different spellings for the Ñacahuazú are used by Guevara throughout the diary. The river's flow is south to north.

The river runs through a steep gully, and the region appears to be seldom visited. With proper discipline, one could stay here a long time.

During the afternoon a heavy rain drove us into the house. I removed six ticks from my body.

November 10

Pachungo and Pombo went scouting with one of the Bolivian comrades, Serafín. They got farther than we had and found where the creek branches out, turning into a stream that appears good. After returning they stayed at the house, loafing, and were seen by Algarañaz's driver, who had come to drop off the men and some items they had purchased. I exploded, and we decided that tomorrow we would move out into the brush, where we will set up a permanent camp. Tumaini will let himself be seen, since he is already known as one of the employees at the farm. The situation is deteriorating rapidly; we shall see whether it will at least be possible to bring our men in. Once they are here I will rest easier.

November 11

An uneventful day spent at the new camp, on the other side of the house, where we slept.

The insects are a torment; the only protection is in one's hammock under mosquito netting (which only I have).

Tumaini went to visit Argañaraz and bought some chickens and turkeys from him. It appears he does not yet harbor any great suspicions about us.

November 12

An entirely uneventful day. We conducted a brief scouting trip to prepare the camp area for the arrival of the six men from the second group. The area selected is on a little rise, about 100 meters from the clearing. Nearby is a hollow in which caves can be made to store food and other objects. By then the first of three groups of two, into which the men are di-

vided, should start to arrive. They should reach the farm by
the end of this coming week. My hair is growing, although
very sparsely, and the gray hair is turning blond and beginning to disappear.[8] In addition, my beard is coming back. In a
couple of months I'll be myself again.

November 13

Sunday. Some hunters passed by our house—farmhands employed by Argañaraz. They are men of the outdoors, young and
single, ideal for recruitment, with an intense hatred for their
boss. They said that eight leagues[9] along the river are houses,
and some ravines with water. There is nothing else of note.

November 14

One week at the camp. Pachungo appears to be having
some difficulty adapting and is unhappy, but he should recover. Today we begin digging to construct a tunnel in which to
put everything that could be compromising. We will camou-
flage it with a grating of branches and sticks, and will protect
it from the humidity as much as possible. A shaft one and a
half meters deep has already been dug, and work on the tunnel has begun.

November 15

Work on the tunnel continued—Pombo and Pachungo in
the morning, Tumaini and I in the afternoon. At six o'clock we
stopped work; by then the tunnel had reached a depth of two
meters. Tomorrow we intend to finish it and place all compromising items inside. During the night rain forced me from my
hammock, which got wet because the nylon cover is too small.
There was nothing else of any note.

---

8. To make the trip to Bolivia, Guevara had posed as a middle-aged official of the
   Organization of American States, trimming his hair and dying it gray. The
   newly grown blond hair, which later disappeared, was caused by the bleach-
   ing.
9. One league is roughly 3.5 miles (5.5 kilometers).

November 16

The tunnel was finished and camouflaged; the only task remaining is to disguise the path. Tomorrow we will move the things to our little house and secure them, covering up the opening with a grating of sticks and clay. The diagram of this tunnel, known as number 1, is contained in document 1. Everything else was uneventful. Starting tomorrow we can reasonably expect news from La Paz.

November 17

The tunnel has been filled with items that could be compromising for those remaining at the house, as well as some canned food. It has been well camouflaged.

There was no news from La Paz. The fellows in the house spoke with Argañaraz, and purchased a few things from him. He again raised with them his desire to participate in the manufacture of cocaine.

November 18

No news from La Paz. Pachungo and Pombo went out again to explore the creek, but are not particularly convinced it is a suitable site for the camp. Tumaini and I will scout it out on Monday. Argañaraz came to repair the road and take rocks from the river, spending a considerable amount of time in this effort. It seems he does not suspect our presence here. Everything goes on monotonously; the bites from the mosquitoes and ticks are beginning to get infected and create painful sores. It is starting to get a bit chilly in the mornings.

November 19

No news from La Paz. No news here. We spent the day confined since it is Saturday, when the hunters are out.

November 20

Marcos and Rolando arrived at noon. There are now six of us. They immediately proceeded to tell us the details of the trip.[10] The reason for the considerable delay was that they did not receive the notice until a week ago. The two of them made the trip via São Paulo, faster than any of the others. We cannot expect the other four to arrive before next week.

With them came Rodolfo, who made a very good impression on me. He seems more determined than Bigote to break with everything. Papi[11] informed him of my presence; he also told Coco. This was a violation of instructions, apparently a case of jealousy of authority. I wrote to Manila with some recommendations[12] (documents 1 and 2), and to Papi, answering his questions. Rodolfo left at dawn.

November 21

The first day of the expanded group. It rained quite hard, and the move to our new location cost us a good drenching. We are now settled in. The tent turned out to be a canvas tarp meant for a truck; it leaks but offers some protection. We have our hammocks with nylon coverings. Some additional weapons have arrived: Marcos has a Garand and Rolando will be issued an M-1 from the cache. Jorge[13] has remained with us, but will be in the house; there he will direct efforts to improve the farm. I asked Rodolfo to send us an agronomist who can be trusted. We will try to maintain this facade as long as possible.

November 22

Tuma, Jorge, and I made a tour along the river (Ñacahuzu) to inspect the newly discovered creek. Owing to the previous

10. Marcos and Rolando were the first of the group of six Cubans Guevara was expecting. Both were former members of the Central Committee of the Cuban Communist Party, who had resigned their posts and responsibilities before leaving Cuba.
11. Papi, known also as Ricardo, was one of the Cuban coordinators of guerrilla preparations, functioning out of La Paz.
12. "Manila" refers to Cuba. For the text of the message, see page 315.
13. Beginning with this date Bigotes is referred to as Jorge. After December 5 he is also known as Loro.

The Ñacahuazú river.

day's rain, the river was unrecognizable and it took a considerable effort to find the desired spot: a tiny stream well concealed at the point where it joins the river. With suitable preparation it could serve as the site of a permanent camp. We returned a little after 9:00 p.m. There is nothing new here.

November 23

We set up an observation post overlooking the little house at the farm, to provide warning against any surveillance or unwanted visits. With two people out scouting, the others are called on to do three hours of guard duty each. Pombo and Marcos explored the area around the camp as far as the creek, which is still swollen.

November 24

Pacho and Rolando left on a scouting mission along the creek; they should return tomorrow.

At night two of Argarañaz's farmhands came by "taking a stroll," a rather unusual visit. Nothing strange was going on here, but Antonio[14] was absent (he was with the scouts), as was Tuma, who officially lives at the house. Their pretext: hunting.

Aliucha's birthday.[15]

November 25

From the observation post we learned that a jeep with two or three passengers was approaching. It turned out they were from an antimalaria agency, and they left immediately after collecting blood samples. Pacho and Rolando arrived very late at night. They found the creek that was on the map and explored it; they also followed along the river's main course until coming to some abandoned fields.

---

14. Until mid-December "Antonio" refers to León. After that, the name refers to a Cuban combatant who arrived on December 11.

15. Aleida Guevara March, his second-eldest daughter.

November 26

Since it was Saturday, all of us remained at quarters. I asked Jorge to scout out along the river bed on horseback, to see where it led. The horse was not here so he left on foot to ask Don Remberto[16] for one (20-25 kilometers away). He had not returned by nightfall. No news from La Paz.

November 27

Jorge has still not appeared. I ordered an all-night watch, but at nine o'clock the first jeep arrived from La Paz. Coco had brought Joaquín and Urbano and a Bolivian who will be staying: Ernesto, a medical student. Coco went out again and brought back Ricardo with Braulio and Miguel and another Bolivian, Inti, who will also be staying.[17] We are now twelve insurgents, plus Jorge, who acts as owner. Coco and Rodolfo will be in charge of contacts.

Ricardo brought some uncomfortable news: Chino[18] is in Bolivia and wants to send 20 men and to see me. This causes some difficulties since we would be internationalizing the struggle before having worked things out with Estanislao.[19] We agreed that Chino would go to Santa Cruz, and that Coco would pick him up there and bring him here. Coco left at dawn with Ricardo, who will take the other jeep and continue on to La Paz. Coco will stop by Remberto's house to check on Jorge. In a preliminary discussion, Inti expressed the view that Estanislao will not take up arms. However, he seems determined to cut his ties.

---

16. Remberto Villa was the former owner of the Ñacahuazú property who had sold it to Coco Peredo.
17. Joaquín, Urbano, Braulio, and Miguel were the Cuban fighters Guevara had been expecting. Joaquín had been a member of the Communist Party of Cuba's Central Committee prior to resigning his posts and responsibilites in preparation for leaving Cuba. The two Bolivians were Inti Peredo and Freddy Maymura (Ernesto).
18. Chino was the Peruvian revolutionary Juan Pablo Chang.
19. A reference to Bolivian Communist Party leader Mario Monje.

November 28

Jorge had not appeared by morning, and Coco had not returned. They arrived later on; what happened was simply that he had stayed at Remberto's.

Somewhat irresponsible. In the afternoon I called a meeting of the Bolivian group to raise with them the Peruvian offer to send 20 men. Everyone agreed, but only after action has begun.

November 29

We went out to examine the river and explore the creek, which will be the site of our next camp. The group consisted of Tumaini, Urbano, Inti, and myself. The creek is quite safe but very murky. We will try to look at another one an hour away. Tumaini fell down and apparently suffered a broken ankle. We arrived at camp at night, after measuring the depth of the river. Nothing new here. Coco left for Santa Cruz to wait for Chino.

November 30

Marcos, Pacho, Miguel, and Pombo left with instructions to scout out a creek farther away; they should be gone two days. It rained hard. Nothing new at the house.

ANALYSIS OF THE MONTH

Everything has gone quite well. My arrival went without incident. Half the people have arrived, also without incident, although with some delay. Ricardo's main collaborators have joined the struggle, come hell or high water. The general picture appears good in this remote region; everything indicates we shall be able to stay here practically as long as we wish.

The plans are to wait for the rest of the people, increase the number of Bolivians to at least 20, and begin operations. We still need to ascertain Monje's reaction and how Guevara's people will conduct themselves.[20]

---

20. "Guevara" here and elsewhere in the diary refers to Moisés Guevara, the Bolivian miners leader who subsequently joined the guerrillas.

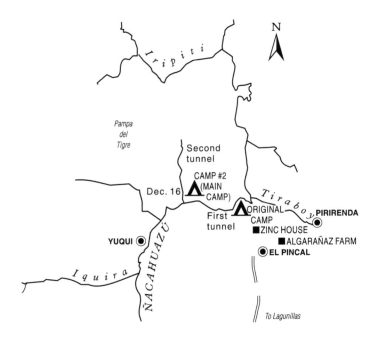

N

Iripiti

Pampa
del
Tigre

Second
tunnel

CAMP #2
(MAIN
Dec. 16 CAMP)

Tiraboy **PIRIRENDA**

ORIGINAL
CAMP

First
tunnel

■ ZINC HOUSE

■ ALGARAÑAZ FARM

◉ **EL PINCAL**

YUQUI ◉

Ñacahuazu

Iquira

To Lagunillas

DECEMBER 1966

10 KILOMETERS

7 MILES

ROAD ========

TOWN OR VILLAGE ◉

River ～

DECEMBER 1966

December 1

The day passed uneventfully. At night Marcos and his comrades returned. Their trip took longer than it was supposed to; they had wasted time roaming around in the hills. At 2:00 a.m. I was told that Coco had arrived with a comrade; I will leave it for tomorrow.

December 2

Chino arrived early, very effusive. We spent the day talking. The essence of it is this: He will go to Cuba to report on the situation in person. Within two months five Peruvians will be able to join us, that is, when action has begun. For now, two will come: a radio technician and a doctor, both of whom will stay with us a while. He requested weapons and I agreed to give him a BZ, some Mausers and grenades, and to purchase an M-1 for them. I also decided to provide them assistance to enable them to send five Peruvians to establish a conduit for relaying arms to a region close to Puno, on the other side of Titicaca. He told me about his troubles in Peru, including an audacious plan to free Calixto,[1] which strikes me as a bit unreal. He believes that some survivors of the guerrilla movement are functioning in that region. They cannot be certain, however, since they have not been able to reach the area.

The rest of the conversation dealt with incidentals. He bid us farewell with the same enthusiasm, heading for La Paz, taking our photos with him. Coco has instructions to work with Sánchez[2] (whom I will see subsequently) on preparing contacts, and to get in touch with the head of the president's information office, who has offered to provide us information since he is Inti's brother-in-law.[3] The network is still in its infancy.

December 3
Uneventful. There are no scouting parties as it is Saturday. The three permanent workers at the farm left for Lagunillas to run errands.

December 4
Nothing new. Everything is still, since it is Sunday. I gave a talk on our approach toward the Bolivians who will be coming and toward the war.[4]

December 5
Uneventful. We intended to leave but it rained all day long. There was a small alarm when a few shots were fired by Loro without warning.

December 6
We left to begin work on the second cave at the first creek.

---

1. A reference to Héctor Béjar, the Peruvian guerrilla leader captured in 1966.
2. Julio Dagnino Pacheco, a Peruvian revolutionary working in the guerrillas' underground network in La Paz.
3. Gonzalo López, head of information at the Presidential Palace, was married to a cousin of Inti Peredo's wife.
4. For an account of this talk, see pages 410-11.

The group was made up of Apolinar, Inti, Urbano, Miguel, and myself. Miguel is replacing Tuma, who has not recovered from his fall. Apolinar has requested to join the guerrilla unit, but wants to take care of some matters in La Paz. I told him yes, but that he should wait a bit. We reached the creek close to 11:00 a.m. We made a camouflaged path and went looking for a suitable place for the cave. The ground is all rock, however, and the creek, after drying up, continues through steep banks of solid rock. We will continue scouting tomorrow. Inti and Urbano left to hunt deer, since our supply of food is very skimpy and must last us until Friday.

December 7
Miguel and Apolinar found a suitable location and began work on the tunnel. The tools are inadequate. Inti and Urbano returned empty-handed, but at nightfall Urbano killed a turkey with an M-1. Since we had already eaten, we left it for tomorrow's breakfast. Today, in point of fact, marks one month of our stay here, but for convenience I will write the summaries on the last day of each month.

December 8
We went with Inti to a ridge overlooking the creek. Miguel and Urbano continued digging the shaft. In the afternoon Apolinar relieved Miguel. Marcos, Pombo, and Pacho arrived at nightfall; the latter was very tired and lagged far behind. Marcos asked that I remove Pacho from the forward detachment if he does not improve. I marked down the path to the cave in diagram 2. I went over the most important tasks for them to do during their stay. Miguel will remain with them, and we will return tomorrow.

December 9
We made the return trip slowly during the morning, arriving close to noon. Pacho was ordered to remain behind when the group returns. We tried to make contact with camp no. 2,

but were unable to. There is no other news to report.

December 10

The day went by uneventfully, except that the first batch of bread was baked at the house. I spoke with Jorge and Inti about some urgent tasks. There is no news from La Paz.

December 11

The day went by uneventfully, but during the night Coco showed up with Papi. He brought Alejandro and Arturo and a Bolivian, Carlos. The other jeep was left on the road, as is customary. Later he brought Moro the doctor, Benigno, and two Bolivians, both of them *cambas* from the Caranavi farm.[5] The night was spent listening to the usual talk about the trip and discussing the absence of Antonio and Félix, both of whom should have been here by now.[6]

I spoke with Papi and we decided that two trips will still be needed to bring Renán and Tania.[7] The safe houses will be closed down and the caches will be emptied; from this, $1,000 will be given to Sánchez as aid. He will keep the van; we will sell one jeep to Tania and hold onto the other. One trip will be needed to transport weapons here. I ordered the shipment brought in one jeep to avoid having to switch it from one vehicle to another, which could be more easily spotted. Chino left for Cuba, apparently very enthusiastic, and he intends to return here on his way back. Coco remained here in order to obtain food supplies in Camiri, and Papi left for La Paz.

---

5. *Camba* refers to natives of the Santa Cruz region of Bolivia. Guevara is referring here to combatants Julio Méndez (Ñato) and Orlando Jiménez, known subsequently as Camba. The two had previously been assigned to the guerrilla-owned farm in Caranavi, northeast of La Paz, which had been considered as an alternate site for the guerrilla base.

6. Antonio and Félix (Rubio) were Cuban combatants. The Bolivian Antonio becomes "León" following the two Cubans' arrival on December 19.

7. Renán was a leader of the urban support network. Tania was Tamara Bunke; on Guevara's instructions, she had been living in Bolivia under a false identity since 1964, and was involved in various guerrilla support tasks.

A dangerous incident occurred: the Vallegrandino,[8] a hunter, discovered a set of footprints left by us. He saw the tracks, apparently spotted one of us, and found a glove lost by Pombo. This changes our plans and we must be very careful. The Vallegrandino will go with Antonio tomorrow to show him where he set his traps for catching tapir.

Inti expressed to me his reservations about the student Carlos, who, as soon as he arrived, began a discussion on the Cuban participation; previously he had stated that he would not take up arms if the party did not participate. Inti said that Carlos had been sent by Rodolfo as a result of a misunderstanding.

December 12

I spoke before the entire group, lecturing them about the realities of war. I stressed the need for unity of command and for discipline, and warned the Bolivians of the responsibility they were assuming in violating their party's discipline by adopting a different line. I assigned the following responsibilities: Joaquín, second in command militarily; Rolando and Inti, commissars; Alejandro, head of operations; Pombo, in charge of services; Inti, finances; Ñato, provisions and armaments; Moro, for the time being, will be in charge of medical services.[9]

Rolando and Braulio left to warn the group there to keep quiet, waiting for the Vallegrandino to set his traps or go exploring with Antonio. They returned in the evening; the traps are not very far away. They got the Vallegrandino drunk, and when they left he was quite content, with a bottle of singani inside of him. Coco returned from Caranavi, where he bought some essential food items. However, he was seen by some people in Lagunillas, who were astounded by the quantity he had.

---

8. Tomás Rosales, from Vallegrande, was a farmhand of Ciro Algarañaz.

9. For an additional account of this talk, see pages 412-13.

Later on, Marcos arrived with Pombo. Marcos had slashed his eyebrow while cutting a stick; he was given two stitches.

December 13

Joaquín, Carlos, and El Médico [Ernesto][10] left to join Rolando and Braulio. Pombo accompanied them, with instructions to return the same day. I ordered them to cover up the path and make another one, starting where the first one had begun and leading to the river. They did this so successfully that Pombo, Miguel, and Pacho got lost on their return and followed the river back.

I spoke with Apolinar, who will be leaving to spend a few days at his house in Viacha. He was given money for his family and urged to observe absolute secrecy. Coco left last night, but at 3:00 a.m. the alarm was sounded when we heard whistling sounds and noises, and the dog barked. It turned out to be Coco, lost in the woods.

December 14

An uneventful day. The Vallegrandino passed by the house to check his traps, since he had set them yesterday, contrary to what he said previously. Antonio was shown the path we had created in the woods, through which he was to take the Vallegrandino, to avoid suspicion.

December 15

Nothing new. Preparations were made for departure (eight men), to establish ourselves permanently in camp no. 2.

December 16

In the morning, Pombo, Urbano, Tuma, Alejandro, Moro, Arturo, Inti, and I left for good, heavily loaded down. The

---

10. "El Médico" (the doctor) is used in the diary to refer both to Moro and Ernesto. Brackets have been inserted, where possible, to indicate which one is being referred to. The guerrillas Julio, Negro, and Che himself were also trained as doctors.

trip took three hours.[11]

Rolando remained with us, while Joaquín, Braulio, Carlos, and El Médico [Ernesto] returned. Carlos has proven himself a good hiker and a good worker. Moro and Tuma discovered a cave by the river with very large fish in it and caught 17, making a good meal; a catfish cut Moro on his hand. A search was made for a spot to build the secondary cave, since the first one had been finished. We then stopped work until morning. Moro and Inti tried to hunt tapir and left to spend the night on lookout.

December 17

Moro and Inti were only able to bring back a turkey. Tuma, Rolando, and I concentrated on building the secondary cave, which can be ready tomorrow. Arturo and Pombo scouted out an area where we can set up the radio; later they worked on fixing up the entrance path, which is in pretty bad condition. It began raining during the night, and it went on nonstop until morning.

December 18

The rain kept up throughout the day, but we continued working on the cave, and are close to reaching the requisite 2.5 meters. We inspected a hilltop for setting up the radio system. It seems quite good, but the tests will tell.

December 19

Another rainy day, and a hike was not very appealing. But close to 11:00 a.m., Braulio and Ñato arrived with news that the river was deep but passable. As we were leaving, we ran into Marcos and his forward detachment, who were arriving to establish themselves at the camp. He will remain in charge,

---

11. On this day the guerrillas moved to their main camp (camp no. 2). In addition to the original camp near the Ñacahuazú farmhouse (no. 1), the guerrillas also established two others in the vicinity, known subsequently as Bear Camp and Monkey Camp.

and was ordered to send three to five men, depending on the possibilities. We made the trip in a little more than three hours.

At midnight, Ricardo and Coco arrived, bringing Antonio and Rubio (they were unable to obtain passage last Thursday) and Apolinar, who has come to join up for good. Iván arrived as well, to discuss a whole series of matters.[12]

It was a virtually sleepless night.

December 20

We were discussing various points and everything was being put in order, when a group arrived from Camp no. 2, led by Alejandro. They brought word that the body of a deer killed by gunshot had been found on the path close to the camp, with a ribbon tied around its leg. Joaquín had passed by the spot an hour before and reported nothing. It was assumed that the Vallegrandino had dragged it there, and that for some unknown reason he had dropped it and fled. A guard was posted at the rear and two men were sent to apprehend the hunter if he appeared. Later came word that the deer had been dead for some time and was decomposing; Joaquín on his return confirmed that this was what he had seen. Coco and Loro brought the Vallegrandino to see the animal, and he reported having wounded it several days ago. That closed the incident.

It was resolved to speed up contacts with the man in the information office, whom Coco has neglected. Megía[13] will be asked to serve as contact between Iván and the man in the information office. Iván will maintain ties with Megía, Sánchez, Tania, and a representative of the party who has not been named. It is possible that the person designated may be from Villamontes, but this has not been concretized. A telegram was received from Manila indicating that Monje will be coming from the south.

A system of contacts has been devised, but I am not satisfied

---

12. Iván was a member of the underground support network in La Paz.
13. A member of the urban support network.

with it since it demonstrates a clear distrust of Monje on the part of his own comrades.

At 1:00 a.m. a message will be radioed from La Paz about whether they have gone to get Monje.

Iván has the potential for some business dealings, but his sloppily made passport does not permit it. The next step is to improve the document; he should write to Manila to ask our friends to speed it up.

Tania will come shortly to receive instructions. I will probably send her to Buenos Aires.

It was finally resolved that Ricardo, Iván, and Coco will leave Camiri by plane, and that the jeep will remain here. When they return, they will telephone Lagunillas to say they have arrived; Jorge will go at night to see if there is news, and will look for them if the answer is affirmative.[14] At 1:00 a.m. we were unable to receive any signals from La Paz. At dawn they left for Camiri.

December 21

Loro did not leave me the maps made by the scout,[15] so I remained in the dark as to the type of road to Yaqui[16] that exists. We left during the morning and made our way without difficulty. We will try to have everyone here by the 24th, when we plan to hold a celebration.

We crossed paths with Pacho, Miguel, Benigno, and Camba, who were supposed to carry the radio equipment. At 5:00 p.m., Pacho and Camba returned without the equipment, which had been left hidden in the brush because of its weight. Tomorrow five men from here will go and bring it back. The cave for supplies was completed; tomorrow we will begin building the one for the radio.

---

14. The contact person in Lagunillas to be telephoned with news of Mario Monje's arrival was the wife of the local police chief.
15. A reference to Mario Chávez, a guerrilla collaborator assigned to live in Lagunillas; also referred to as the Lagunillero.
16. A reference to the Iquira river.

December 22

We began work on the radio operator's cave. It went well at first, when the ground was soft, but we soon ran into very hard rock that obstructed our progress.

They brought the generator, which is quite heavy, but has not been tested due to a lack of gasoline. Loro relayed word that maps had not been sent because the [scout's] report was verbal, and that he would come tomorrow to present it.

December 23

I went out with Pombo and Alejandro to explore the ridge on the left. We will have to clear a path, but my impression is one can walk along it comfortably. Joaquín arrived with two comrades, bringing word that Loro would not be coming because a pig had escaped and he had gone to look for it.

There is no news about the trip made by the Lagunillero.

In the afternoon the pig arrived, quite large in size, but the drinks are not here yet. Loro is incapable of obtaining even these things; he appears very disorganized.

December 24

A day devoted to Christmas Eve. Some people had made two trips and arrived late, but in the end we were all together and things went well, with some of the people getting a bit drunk.

Loro explained that the Lagunillero's trip was not very fruitful; the only small result was a sketch he drew, which was very imprecise.

December 25

Back to work. There were no trips to the original camp. This has been named C-26 at the suggestion of El Médico (Bolivian) [Ernesto]. Marcos, Benigno, and Camba left to make a path along the ridge on our right. They returned in the afternoon, reporting they had spotted a barren plain two hours from here. Tomorrow they will reach it. Camba returned with a fever. Miguel and Pacho created some diversionary paths along the left bank, as well as a path providing access to the radio cave. Inti, Antonio, Tuma, and I continued working on the radio cave. The job is very difficult, because it is solid rock. The rear guard was instructed to make their camp and find an observation spot overlooking access to both sides of the river; the place is very good.

December 26
Inti and Carlos left to scout as far as the point on the map called Yaki; the trip is estimated to last two days. Rolando, Alejandro, and Pombo continued work on the cave, which is extremely difficult. Pacho and I went out to inspect the paths made by Miguel; it is not worthwhile to continue the one along the ridge. The access path to the cave is quite good and difficult to spot. Two snakes were killed in addition to one yesterday; it appears there are many of them. Tuma, Arturo, Rubio, and Antonio went out to hunt, while Braulio and Ñato remained on guard at the other camp. They came back with news that Loro had overturned the jeep, together with an explanatory note announcing Monje's arrival. Marcos, Miguel, and Benigno left to work on the path along the ridge, but did not return the entire night.

December 27
Tuma and I went out to try to find Marcos; we walked two and a half hours until reaching the beginning of a ravine, which descended on the left side, to the west. We followed the tracks, climbing down very steep embankments. I thought we could make it back to camp along this route, but as the hours passed, the camp did not appear. At 5:00 p.m. we arrived at the Ñacahuasu, some five kilometers below camp no. 1, and at 7:00 we reached camp. We then learned that Marcos had spent the previous night there. I did not send anyone to report our whereabouts, since I assumed that Marcos would have told them of my possible route.

We saw the jeep; it is quite banged up. Loro had gone to Camiri to look for some spare parts; according to Ñato, he fell asleep at the wheel.

December 28

As we were heading off for the camp, Urbano and Antonio arrived looking for me. Marcos had continued on with Miguel to make a pathway to the camp along the ridges and had not arrived. Benigno and Pombo went to look for me along the same path we were taking. When I arrived at camp, I found Marcos and Miguel, who had slept on a ridge, as they were unable to reach the camp. Marcos complained to me of the way I had been treated. The complaint was apparently directed at Joaquín, Alejandro, and El Médico [Moro]. Inti and Carlos returned having found no inhabited houses, only an abandoned one that presumably is not the place marked as Yaki on the map.

December 29

Together with Marcos, Miguel, and Alejandro, I climbed the barren hill to gain a better grasp of the area. It appears to be the beginning of the Pampa del Tigre, a mountain range of uniform elevation and barren hills, situated at an altitude of 1,500 meters. The ridge on the left should be rejected because it forms a semicircle around the Ñacahuasu. We climbed down and arrived at camp in an hour and 20 minutes. Eight men were sent to bring back supplies, but did not get the entire load. Rubio and El Médico [Ernesto] relieved Braulio and Ñato. Braulio made a new path before coming back; it begins at some rocks along the river and leads into the woods on the other side along some more rocks, so that no tracks are left. There was no work done on the cave. Loro left for Camiri.

December 30

Despite the rain, which has caused the river to rise, four men were sent to clear out the remaining items at camp no. 1;

it is now empty. There is no news from the outside. Six men went to the cave, and in two trips they stored everything that was to be put there.

The oven could not be finished because the clay was soft.

December 31

At 7:30 a.m. El Médico [Ernesto] arrived with news that Monje was over there. I went with Inti, Tuma, Urbano, and Arturo. The reception was cordial but tense. The question "What are you here for?" pervaded everything. Monje was accompanied by "Pan Divino," the new recruit;[17] Tania, who has come to receive instructions; and Ricardo, who will now remain with us.

The discussion with Monje began with generalities, but soon came down to his fundamental views. These were summarized in three basic conditions he laid down:

1. He would resign from the party leadership, but would obtain at least its neutrality, as well as procuring cadres for the struggle.

2. The political-military leadership of the struggle would rest with him as long as the revolution was taking place on Bolivian soil.

3. He would handle relations with other South American parties, trying to get them to support liberation movements (he gave Douglas Bravo[18] as an example).

I answered him that the first point was up to him as party secretary, although I considered his position to be a serious error. It was a vacillating and adaptationist stance that served to shield those who should be historically condemned for their unwillingness to struggle. Time will show I am right.

As to the third point, I told him I had no objections to his trying to do this, although he was destined to fail. Asking

---

17. A leader of the Bolivian Communist youth organization, known subsequently as Pedro.
18. Douglas Bravo was a leader of the guerrilla movement in Venezuela; he was expelled from the Communist Party in 1967.

Codovilla[19] to support Douglas Bravo would be like asking him to condone an uprising within his own party. Time will also be the judge.

As to the second point, I told him I could not accept this under any circumstance. I would be the military leader and would accept no ambiguities on this score. Here the discussion bogged down and went around and around in a vicious circle.

We left it that he would think it over and speak with the Bolivian comrades. We went to the new camp and there he spoke with all of them, laying out the choice of either staying here or supporting the party. Everyone decided to stay, which he seemed to take as a blow.

At midnight we drank a toast, where he pointed to the historic importance of the date.[20] I answered, taking advantage of his words and marking this moment as a new Grito de Murillo of the continent-wide revolution.[21] I said that our lives meant nothing faced with the fact of the revolution.

Fidel sent me the attached messages.

ANALYSIS OF THE MONTH

Assembling the team of Cubans has been successfully completed. Morale is good and there are only a few small problems. The Bolivians are doing well, although there are few of them. Monje's stance may retard things on the one hand, but on the other it will help free me from political commitments. The next steps, in addition to waiting for more Bolivians, will

---

19. Victorio Codovilla was president of the Communist Party of Argentina.
20. January 1, 1959, marked the victory of the Cuban revolution.
21. The Grito de Murillo (cry of Murillo) refers to the onset of Bolivia's uprising against Spanish colonial rule in 1809; the revolt was led by Pedro Domingo Murillo.

consist of speaking with Guevara and with the Argentines Mauricio and Jozami (Massetti and the dissident party).[22]

---

22. Mauricio (Ciro Roberto Bustos) was an Argentine painter who had supported the failed 1963-64 guerrilla nucleus in the Salta mountains of Argentina,
led by Jorge Ricardo Masetti, who had supported the Rebel Army in the Sierra Maestra and was the founder of Cuba's Prensa Latina. Eduardo Jozami
belonged to a split-off from the Communist Party of Argentina.

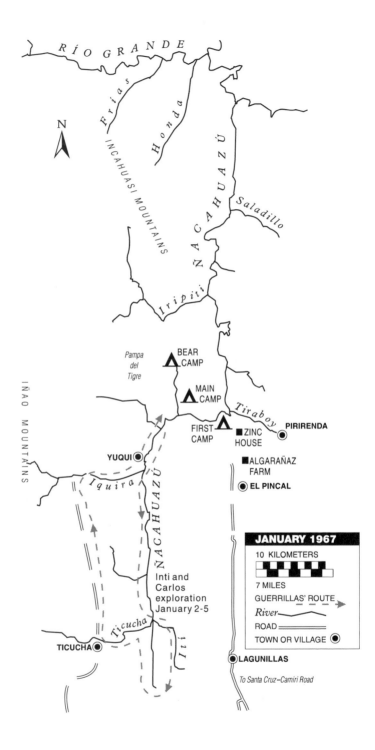

RÍO GRANDE

Frias

Honda

ÑACAHUAZÚ

Saladillo

INCAHUASI MOUNTAINS

Iripiti

N

Pampa
del
Tigre

INAO MOUNTAINS

▲ BEAR
CAMP

▲ MAIN
CAMP

Tirabov

FIRST ▲
CAMP   ■ ZINC
       HOUSE

PIRIRENDA ◉

YUQUI ◉

Iquira

ÑACAHUAZÚ

■ ALGARAÑAZ
  FARM

‖ ◉ EL PINCAL

Inti and
Carlos
exploration
January 2–5

JANUARY 1967

10 KILOMETERS

7 MILES

GUERRILLAS' ROUTE ▸▸▸

River

ROAD ══════

TOWN OR VILLAGE ◉

Ticucha

Iti

TICUCHA ◉

◉ LAGUNILLAS

To Santa Cruz–Camiri Road

JANUARY 1967

January 1

In the morning, without discussing it with me, Monje announced he was leaving and would submit his resignation to the party leadership on January 8. According to him, his mission had finished. He left looking like a man being led to the gallows. My impression is that when Coco informed him of my decision not to yield on strategic matters, he dug in his heels on this question to force the break, since his arguments lack consistency.

In the afternoon I met with the whole group and explained Monje's position. I announced that we would unite with all those who wanted to make the revolution, and I predicted difficult moments ahead and days of moral anguish for the Bolivians. I said we would try to solve any problems through collective discussion or through the commissars.

I laid out plans for Tania's trip to Argentina to speak with Mauricio and Jozami and bring them here. We went over Sánchez's tasks, and resolved to leave Rodolfo, Loyola, and

Humberto in La Paz for the time being.[1] Loyola's sister will remain in Camiri, and Calvimonte will stay in Santa Cruz. Mito will travel through the Sucre region to see where he should set himself up. Loyola will be in charge of finances, and has been sent 80,000 pesos; of this, 20,000 is for a truck that Calvimonte is to buy. Sánchez will contact Guevara to set up a meeting. Coco will go to Santa Cruz to meet with Carlos's brother and put him in charge of receiving three people who are coming from Havana. I wrote Fidel the message that appears in document CZO #2.

January 2

The morning was spent encoding the letter. Sánchez, Coco, and Tania left in the afternoon, after Fidel had completed his speech. He referred to us in terms that obligate us to give an even greater effort, if that is possible.[2]

At the camp, the only work done was on the cave; the others went out to get things from the first camp. Marcos, Miguel, and Benigno left to scout the area up north; Inti and Carlos left to explore the Ñacahuazu up to where they encounter people, presumably at Yaki. Joaquín and El Médico [Moro] were assigned to scout the Yaki river up to its source or until they run into people. They have all been given five days maximum.

The men came back from the camp and reported that Loro had not returned from dropping off Monje.

January 3

We worked on the roof of the cave, but did not finish it; we must do so tomorrow. Only two men were sent to bring sup-

---

1. Loyola Guzmán and Humberto Rhea were, with Rodolfo Saldaña, leaders of the urban support network.
2. In his speech of January 2, 1967, Castro stated, "The imperialists have killed Che many times in many places, but we anticipate that any day now, where imperialism least expects it, Commander Ernesto Guevara will rise from the ashes like a Phoenix, seasoned by war, a guerrilla fighter, healthy; and that some day we will again have very concrete news of Che."

plies over, and they reported that everyone had left last night. The rest of the comrades worked on building a roof for the kitchen; it is now ready.

January 4
Nothing much to report. People went out to bring back supplies. We have finished the roof of the radio operator's cave. Target practice was suspended owing to rain.

January 5
We continue transporting supplies. A few more trips are still needed. The cave was finished, together with its accessories (a smaller cave for the generator). We tested the rear guard's rifles, as well as some of the center group's. They are all in good shape, except for Apolinario's rifle. The scouting parties have all returned. Inti and Carlos hiked along the Ñacahuasu until running into people. They encountered several houses, among them those of two middle-sized landowners, one of whom has 150 head of cattle and lives in Lagunillas. There is a little settlement called Iti, which has a cattle trail leading to Lagunillas. From there they went to Ticucha, which is linked by a truck route to Vaca Guzmán. They returned by a path along the Iquiri river, which we have been calling the Yaki. The place called Yuki is a pasture close to our camp; it was abandoned by its inhabitants due to a cattle disease. Joaquín and El Médico [Moro] continued along the Iquiri until coming to some impassable rocks; they did not run into people but did see signs of their presence. Marcos, Miguel, and Benigno traveled along the ridges until reaching an inaccessible point, blocked off by a cliff.

We have a new recruit: a little turkey hen caught by Inti.

January 6
In the morning, Marcos, Joaquín, Alejandro, Inti, and I went up to the barren plateau. There I made the following decisions: Marcos, with Camba and Pacho, will try to reach the Ñacahuasu along the right, avoiding any people; Miguel, with

Braulio and Aniceto, will look for a passageway along the ridge to try to create the main trail; Joaquín, with Benigno and Inti, will look for a path to the Frías river, which according to the map runs parallel to the Ñacahuasu, on the other side of the plateau that would appear to be the Pampa del Tigre.

In the afternoon Loro arrived with two mules he had bought for 2,000 pesos, a good buy; the animals are strong and tame. I sent someone to go and get Braulio and Pacho, so that they can set out tomorrow; Carlos and El Médico [Ernesto] will relieve them.

After class I spoke to the group, launching forth a little "salvo" on the necessary characteristics of a guerrilla unit and the need for greater discipline. I explained that our mission, above all, was to form a steeled nucleus that could serve as an example. In this context I explained the importance of study, which is indispensable for the future.[3]

I then met with those holding responsibilities: Joaquín, Marcos, Alejandro, Inti, Rolando, Pombo, El Médico [Moro], Ñato, and Ricardo. I explained that Joaquín had been selected as second in command, owing to repeated errors committed by Marcos. I criticized Joaquín's attitude in the incident with Miguel on New Year's Day, and then explained some of the tasks that had to be carried out to improve the organization of our work. At the end, Ricardo told me of an incident between him and Iván, in Tania's presence, where they had insulted each other and Ricardo had ordered Iván to get out of the jeep. These unpleasant incidents among comrades are damaging our work.

January 7

The scouting parties set out. The "gondola"[4] consisted solely of Alejandro and Ñato. The others worked on tasks around the camp: the generator was installed along with all of Arturo's

---

3. For an additional account of this talk, see page 416.
4. The guerrillas' expression for their regular trips back and forth to haul supplies to the camp, coined from a Bolivian term for bus.

things; an additional little roof for the cave was made; and a source for water was fixed up by building a little bridge on the creek bed.

January 8
Sunday. The gondola was expanded to eight, and almost everything was brought over. Loro announced he is going to Santa Cruz on an unscheduled trip, apparently to find harnesses for the mules. There were no classes or any other activities. It was my turn for guard duty, in very inclement weather.

January 9
It rained, and everything is wet. The river has risen and is unpassable, so we were unable to relieve those on guard duty at the old camp.

Otherwise the day was uneventful.

January 10
The guard was changed at the observation post at the old camp, with Rubio and Apolinar relieving Carlos and El Médico [Ernesto]. The river is still swollen, although the water level continues to drop. Loro went to Santa Cruz and has not returned.

Together with El Médico (Moro), Tuma, and Antonio, who is to remain in charge of the camp, we climbed up to the Pampa del Tigre. I then explained to Antonio his task for tomorrow in scouting what looks like a creek west of our camp. From there we looked for a junction with Marcos's old path, which we found with relative ease. As it got dark six of the scouts returned: Miguel, with Braulio and Aniceto; Joaquín, with Benigno and Inti. Miguel and Braulio found a tributary to the river that cuts across the ridge, and stumbled across another one, which appears to be the Ñacahuasu. Joaquín was able to go downriver along what is apparently the Frías, and continued for a short distance. This appears, however, to be the same river followed by the other group. That indicates that our maps are very bad, since they show two rivers, separated by a large plateau and emptying separately into the Río Grande. Marcos has still not returned.

A message was received from Havana, announcing that Chino is leaving January 12, with the doctor and the radio technician, and Rea is leaving on the 14th. There was no word on our two remaining comrades.

January 11

Antonio left to scout the nearby creek with Carlos and Arturo; he returned during the night. The only concrete news he brought back was that the creek ends at the Ñacahuasu, across from the pastureland where we hunt. Alejandro and Pombo worked on making maps in Arturo's cave. On returning they brought word that my books had gotten wet, and some of them were ruined. In addition, the radio equipment was wet and had rusted. Coming on top of the two radios being broken, this reflects sadly on Arturo's abilities.

Marcos arrived during the night. He had come upon the Ñacahuasu far downstream, but had still not reached the point where it joins what is presumed to be the Frías river. I am not at all sure of the maps, nor of the identity of this watercourse.

We began the study of Quechua, taught by Aniceto and Pedro.

Boro[5] day. Fly larvae were removed from Marcos, Carlos, Pombo, Antonio, Moro, and Joaquín.

January 12

The gondola was sent to bring back the final items. Loro has still not returned. We did some practice climbs of the banks of our creek. Along the sides of the creek it took over two hours; at the center, only seven minutes. That is where we should set up our defense.

---

5. A type of fly of the region, which deposits larvae upon biting.

Joaquín told me that Marcos feels hurt by my reference to his errors at the meeting the other day. I must speak with him.

January 13

I spoke with Marcos. His complaint is that I had criticized him in front of the Bolivians. His argument is groundless. Apart from his emotional state, which is worthy of attention, everything else was unimportant.

He referred to some harsh words Alejandro had addressed to him. I took this up with Alejandro, and it appears there were none, only some idle chatter. Marcos calmed down somewhat.

Inti and Moro went to hunt, but did not get anything. Several teams left to construct a cave in the place accessible by mule. Nothing could be done in this regard, however, and it was decided to build a small, sunken shed. Alejandro and Pombo made a study of the defense of the entranceway and marked out trenches. Tomorrow they will continue.

Rubio and Apolinar returned, and Braulio and Pedro went to the old camp. There is no word on Loro.

January 14

Marcos, with the forward detachment minus Benigno, headed downriver to build the shed. They were supposed to return at night, but came back at midday owing to rain, without having finished the shed.

Joaquín led a group that began digging the trenches. Moro, Inti, Urbano, and I left to create a path bordering our position along the ridge at the right of the creek. But we went off course and had to go around somewhat dangerous cliffs. At noon it began to rain and activities were suspended.

No word on Loro.

January 15

I remained at the camp, drafting some instructions for cadres in the cities. It being Sunday, we worked only half a day.

Marcos, with the forward detachment, worked on the shed. The rear guard and the center group worked on the trenches. Ricardo, Urbano, and Antonio spent their time improving the path we made yesterday; this was unsuccessful, however, as a big rock juts out between the ridge and the hillside leading down to the river.

No trips were made to the old camp.

January 16
Work continued on the trenches, which are still not completed. Marcos almost finished his task, building a nice little hut. El Médico [Ernesto] and Carlos relieved Braulio and Pedro, who returned with word that Loro had arrived along with the mules. He did not appear, however, even though Aniceto went to meet him.

Alejandro is showing symptoms of malaria.

January 17
A day of little activity. The frontline trenches and the shed were finished.

Loro came to tell me about his trip. When I asked him why he had gone, he answered that he thought the purpose of his trip was understood, and confessed that he had gone to visit a girlfriend of his there. He brought the harness for the mule, but could not get it to walk through the river.

There is no news of Coco. This is now somewhat alarming.

January 18
It was cloudy at daybreak, so I did not inspect the trenches. Urbano, Ñato, El Médico (Moro), Inti, Aniceto, and Braulio left on the gondola. Alejandro did not work due to feeling ill.

Shortly afterward, it began to pour. Loro arrived in the rain to say that Argañaraz had spoken with Antonio, indicating that he knows about many things and offering to collaborate with us on cocaine or whatever, thereby showing that he suspects there is something more. I instructed Loro to make an agreement with him without offering much—only payment for what he brings in his jeep, and threatening him with death if he betrays. Owing to the heavy downpour, Loro left immediately to avoid being cut off by the river.

The "gondola" had not arrived by 8:00, so I gave the green light to eat the food set aside for them, and it was devoured. A few minutes later, Braulio and Ñato arrived, saying that the rising water had surprised them along the way. They had all tried to continue but Inti had fallen into the water, losing his rifle and suffering bruises. The others decided to spend the night there, and the two of them made it back with considerable difficulty.

January 19

The day began routinely, working on the defenses and improving the camp. Miguel came down with a high fever and shows all the symptoms of malaria. All day I felt like I was coming down with something, but the illness did not break out.

At 8:00 a.m., the four stragglers showed up, bringing a good supply of *choclos*.[6] They spent the night huddled around a fire. As soon the river goes down, an attempt will be made to recover the rifle.

Around 4:00 p.m., after Rubio and Pedro had gone to relieve the pair on guard duty at the other camp, El Médico [Ernesto] came to announce that the police had arrived at the other camp. Lieutenant Fernández and four police officers, in civilian clothes, arrived in a rented jeep looking for the cocaine factory. The only place they searched was the house, where they took note of a few strange things, such as the carbide for our lamps, which had not been moved to the cave. They took away Loro's pistol but left him his Mauser and the .22. They made a big deal about having taken a .22 from Argañaraz, which they showed Loro. They left with the warning that they

---

6. Baby corn.

The guerrillas' main camp. *Top,* the "amphitheater," where classes were held on political economy, languages, history, and other topics. *Bottom,* Bolivian combatant Raúl at work.

knew everything, and that he had better take them into account. Loro could reclaim the pistol in Camiri, Lieutenant Fernández said, "No fuss, just come and talk to me." He asked about the "Brazilian."

Loro was instructed not to talk with the Vallegrandino and Argañaraz, who must be the ones responsible for spying and informing on us. He was also told to go to Camiri, under the pretext of getting the pistol, to make contact with Coco (I am doubtful that he is still at liberty). As much as possible they should live in the woods, away from the house.

January 20

I inspected the positions and issued orders to implement the plan of defense that was explained at night. It is based on the rapid defense of an area adjacent to the river. This site will become the base for a counterattack by some members of the forward detachment along paths running parallel to the river, leading into positions manned by the rear guard.

We intended to stage some trial runs, but the situation in the old camp continues to be insecure. A gringo showed up firing an M-2; he is a "friend" of Argañaraz and will be spending ten days' vacation at his house.[7] Scouting parties will be sent out and we will move the camp to a spot closer to Argañaraz's house. If this blows up into something, we will make our influence felt on this individual before leaving the area.

Miguel continues to have a high fever.

January 21

We staged the exercise drill, which went well in general although there were problems in some areas. It will be necessary to work on the withdrawal, which was the weakest part of the exercise. Afterward, the teams were sent out: Braulio's group went to create a path parallel to the river toward the west; another group, led by Rolando, went off to do the same toward

---

7. The "gringo" was Cristian Reese, a Bolivian of German descent.

the east. Pacho went to the barren hill to test a walkie-talkie, and Marcos set out with Aniceto to look for a path from which we can to keep a careful watch on Argañaraz. Everyone was supposed to return before two o'clock, except for Marcos. Creating the paths and testing the radio equipment went successfully. Marcos returned early because rain made visibility impossible.

Pedro arrived in the midst of the rain, bringing Coco and three new recruits: Benjamín, Eusebio, and Walter.[8] The first of these has just come from Cuba and will be assigned to the forward detachment, since he has knowledge of weapons; the other two will be assigned to the rear guard. Mario Monje spoke with three others who were returning from Cuba and dissuaded them from joining the guerrillas. Not only did he not resign from the leadership of the party, but he sent a letter to Fidel (attachment D-4). I received a note from Tania informing us of her departure[9] and of Iván's illness, plus another one from Iván, which is attachment D-5.

At night I met with the entire group and read them Monje's document, pointing out the distortions contained in his points (a) and (b), and making a few additional points.[10] They appeared to respond well. Of the three new recruits, two seem firm and conscious. The youngest is an Aymará peasant, who looks very healthy.

---

8. The three recruits were Bolivians; Benjamín had been studying in Cuba.

9. For Argentina.

10. In his January 11 letter to Castro, Monje wrote: "The discussions [with Guevara] centered on the following premises raised by us: (a) Broad political front for the armed struggle and the party's contribution with the incorportion of cadres and organizers. (b) International solidarity necessary for the success of the Bolivian people's struggle. In this sense we believe the meeting of the Communist and Workers Parties of the continent to be crucial. (c) The Bolivian revolution and the armed struggle must be planned and led by Bolivians. Our leadership does not evade its responsibility in this sphere and takes it seriously. Such a need does not downplay or reject the voluntary assistance that can be provided by experienced revolutionary and military cadres from other countries."

January 22

A "gondola" of 13 persons plus Braulio and Walter was sent to relieve Pedro and Rubio. They returned in the afternoon, without having brought all the cargo. Everything is calm over there. On the return trip Rubio suffered a spectacular fall but was not seriously hurt.

I have written to Fidel (document no. 3) to explain the situation and test the mail drop. I plan to send it to La Paz with Guevara, if he appears in Camiri on the 25th as scheduled.

I wrote some instructions for urban cadres (D-3).[11] Owing to the gondola there was no activity at the camp. Miguel felt better, but now Carlos has fallen ill with a high fever.

The tuberculosis test was given today. Two turkeys were caught; a small animal stepped into the trap, but its foot was severed and it was able to escape.

January 23

Tasks at camp were divided up and scouting parties were sent out. Inti, Rolando, and Arturo went to look for a possible hiding place for El Médico [Moro] and any wounded. Marcos, Urbano, and I went to explore the hill in front of us, to find a suitable place for viewing Argañaraz's house. This was accomplished, and the house can be seen clearly.

Carlos still has a fever; typical of malaria.

January 24

The "gondola" left with seven men, returning early with the entire load and some corn. This time it was Joaquín who wound up taking a swim, losing his Garand but then recovering it. Loro is on his way back and is now in hiding. Coco and Antonio are still out; they should be arriving tomorrow or the day after with Guevara.

We improved one of the paths, so that in the event of having to defend these positions, we can surround the soldiers. We

---

11. "Instructions for Cadres Assigned to Urban Areas." See pages 299-304.

held a meeting at night where I reviewed the other day's exercise, pointing to a few shortcomings.

January 25

Marcos and I went out to scout the path that will be used to lead the attackers toward our rear guard. It took us almost an hour to get there, but the place is very good.

Aniceto and Benjamín went to test the transmitter from a hill overlooking Argañaraz's house, but they got lost and nothing could be heard. The exercise will have to be repeated. Work began on another cave for personal effects. Loro arrived and was assigned to the forward detachment. He spoke with Argañaraz along the lines I had instructed. The latter admitted sending the Vallegrandino to spy, but denied being the one who informed the police. Coco scared the Vallegrandino away from the house, since he had been sent by Argañaraz to spy. A message was received from Manila acknowledging the smooth receipt of everything and informing us that Kolle is on his way there; Simón Reyes is already there waiting for him.[12] Fidel states he will listen to what they have to say, but will be hard on them.

January 26

We had hardly begun work on the new cave when we received word that Guevara had arrived with Loyola. We left for the little house at the intermediate camp and they arrived there at noon.

I laid out my conditions to Guevara: dissolution of his group, no ranks for any of them, no political organization as of yet, and all polemics concerning international or national points of disagreement are to be avoided. He accepted everything with great modesty and sincerity. After an initial coolness, his relations with the Bolivians became cordial.

Loyola made a very good impression on me. She is very

---

12. Jorge Kolle and Simón Reyes were leaders of the Communist Party of Bolivia.

young and mild-mannered, but one can detect a strong sense of determination. She is on the verge of being expelled from the [Communist Party] youth organization, although they are trying to get her to resign. I gave her the instructions for urban cadres and another document. In addition, I repaid her the money that has been spent, which comes to 70,000 pesos. We are becoming short of money.

Dr. Pareja was named head of the urban network and Rodolfo will come and join our ranks within two weeks.

I sent a letter to Iván (D-6) with instructions.[13]

I instructed Coco to sell the jeep but to ensure communication with the farm.

At about 7:00 p.m., with night falling, we said goodbye. They will leave tomorrow night and Guevara will arrive with the first group between February 4 and 14. He said he could not come any sooner owing to problems of communication, and that his men are scattered for the moment owing to the carnivals.

More powerful radio transmitters will be coming.

January 27

A strong "gondola" was sent, which brought almost everything, although there are still some items remaining. Coco and the visitors left at night; they will stay in Camiri while Coco goes on to Santa Cruz to arrange the sale of the jeep, to take place after February 15.

Work on the cave continued. A *tatú*[14] was caught in the traps. The job of preparing provisions for the journey is being finished. The plan is to leave when Coco returns.

January 28

The gondola cleaned out the old camp. They reported having come across the Vallegrandino by surprise circling the

---

13. For the text, see pages 316-17.
14. A type of armadillo common to the area.

cornfield, but he escaped. All indications are that the hour of decision concerning the farm is approaching.

Provisioning has been completed for a ten-day march. The date has been set: a day or two after Coco's return on February 2.

January 29

A day of absolute idleness, except for those doing the cooking, hunting, and guard duty.

Coco arrived during the afternoon; he had not gone to Santa Cruz but to Camiri. He dropped off Loyola and Moisés. She will continue on to La Paz by plane, while he will go by bus to Sucre. They set next Sunday as the day for making contact.

February 1 was set as the day of departure.

January 30

The gondola consisted of 12 men, and they transferred most of the food supplies; five men will be needed to bring the rest. The hunters came back empty-handed.

The cave for storing personal objects was finished; it did not turn out well.

January 31

Last day at camp. The gondola cleared out the old camp, and the sentries were withdrawn. Antonio, Ñato, Camba, and Arturo remained behind. Their instructions are the following: They will make contact with us at least every three days. As long as there are four of them, two will be armed. Sentries will be posted at all times. New recruits will receive instruction in general norms, but must not know any more than absolutely necessary. The camp will be emptied of all personal effects, and weapons will be hidden in the woods, covered by a tarp. The money reserves will remain at the camp on someone's person at all times. The paths already made will be patrolled, along with the nearby creeks. In the event of a hasty retreat, two men—Antonio and Arturo—will go to Arturo's cave, and

Ñato and Camba will withdraw along the creek; one of them will run ahead to leave word for us, at a site we will select tomorrow. If more than four men are present, one group will be assigned to guard the supply cave.

I spoke to the troops, giving them final instructions about the march. I also gave final instructions to Coco. (D-7)

ANALYSIS OF THE MONTH

As expected, Monje's stance was first evasive and then treacherous.

The party has now taken up arms against us, and I do not know how far they will go. This will not stop us, however, and over the long run will perhaps be beneficial (of that I am almost certain). The most honest and militant people will be with us, although they will go through a crisis of conscience to a greater or lesser degree.

Guevara has responded well up to now. We will see how he and his people conduct themselves in the future.

Tania departed, but the Argentines have shown no signs of life, nor has she. Now begins the guerrilla stage, properly speaking, and we will test the troops. Time will tell what they are capable of, and what the prospects of the Bolivian revolution are.

Of all the elements foreseen, what is going most slowly is the incorporation of Bolivian combatants.

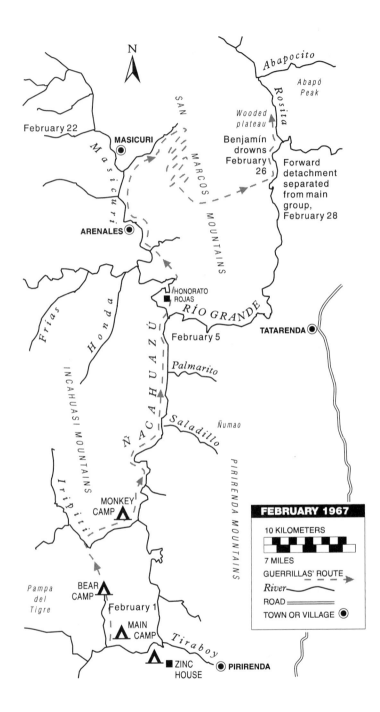

N

Abapocito

Abapó
Peak

February 22

Rosita

SAN

Wooded
plateau

MASICURI

Benjamín
drowns
February
26

Masicuri

MARCOS

Forward
detachment
separated
from main
group,
February 28

ARENALES

MOUNTAINS

Honda

Frías

HONORATO
ROJAS

RÍO GRANDE

TATARENDA

INCAHUASI MOUNTAINS

ÑACAHUAZÚ

February 5

Palmarito

Saladillo

Ñumao

Iripiti

PIRIRENDA MOUNTAINS

MONKEY
CAMP

Pampa
del
Tigre

BEAR
CAMP

February 1

MAIN
CAMP

Tiraboy

ZINC
HOUSE

PIRIRENDA

FEBRUARY 1967

10 KILOMETERS

7 MILES

GUERRILLAS' ROUTE

River

ROAD

TOWN OR VILLAGE

FEBRUARY 1967

February 1
The first stage was carried out.[1] The group arrived somewhat tired, but in general they conducted themselves well. Antonio and Ñato came up to work out the message system with us, and they brought my knapsack and that of Moro, who is recovering from malaria.

A warning system was established. Messages will be put inside a bottle under a bush close to the path.

In the rear guard, Joaquín is having trouble carrying his load. This is holding up the entire group.

February 2
A slow and arduous day. El Médico [Moro] slowed the march down somewhat, although the general pace is already sluggish. At 4:00 p.m. we reached the last site with water and made camp. The forward detachment was ordered to reach

---

1. A reference to the beginning of the exploratory training march, which extended into the middle of March.

the river (presumably the Frías), but they too were unable to set a good pace. It rained during the night.

February 3
The morning started out rainy, so we delayed our departure until 8:00 a.m. As we began to move out, Aniceto arrived with the rope to help us through difficult footing. Shortly afterward the rain began again. We reached the creek at 10:00 a.m., completely soaked, and decided to halt for the day. The creek cannot be the Frías river; it simply does not appear on the map.

Tomorrow the forward detachment will head out, with Pacho leading the way. We will communicate with each other every hour.

February 4
We hiked from daybreak until 4:00 p.m., with a two-hour stop at noon for some soup. The path follows along the Ñacahuasu; it is relatively good, but fatal on shoes. Several comrades are already almost barefoot.

The troops are fatigued but have responded very well. I have been relieved of almost 15 pounds and can now walk with agility, although the pain in my shoulders is unbearable at times.

We have encountered no traces of people having been along the river recently. However, sooner or later we will come across inhabited areas, according to the map.

February 5
Unexpectedly, after walking five hours during the morning (12-14 kilometers), the forward detachment sent word that they had come across animals (it turned out to be a mare and a colt). We halted and I sent out a scouting party, to avoid our walking into a populated area. We debated whether we were at the Iripiti river or at the spot on the map where the Saladillo branches off. Pacho came back with news of a large river several times bigger than the Ñacahuasu, and that it was impass-

able. We went there and found ourselves at the genuine Río Grande, swollen moreover. There were signs of people, but these were not very recent. The footprints come to an end at a thick undergrowth, where there are no signs of passage.

We camped at a bad spot; it is close to the Ñacahuasu so that we can make use of the water. Tomorrow we will scout both sides of the river (east and west) to get to know the area. The other group will try to cross it.

February 6

A day of calm and of replenishing our strength. Joaquín left with Walter and El Médico [Moro] to explore the Río Grande following its flow. They hiked eight kilometers without finding any fording areas; all they found was a creek with salt water. Marcos, accompanied by Aniceto and Loro, walked a short distance against the current, but did not reach the Frías. Alejandro, Inti, and Pacho tried unsuccessfully to swim across the river. We moved our camp site back almost a kilometer, looking for a better spot. Pombo is somewhat ill.

Tomorrow we will begin work on a raft to try to make the crossing.

February 7

The raft was built under Marcos's direction. It turned out very big and difficult to maneuver. At 1:30 p.m. we begin moving toward the site of the crossing, which began at 2:30. The forward detachment made it in two trips; the third trip brought over half the center group plus my clothes, although not my knapsack. During the next trip, which was to bring over the rest of the center group, Rubio miscalculated and the raft was carried downstream and could not be recovered, coming apart. Joaquín began work on another one, which was ready at 9:00 p.m. However, it was not necessary to make the crossing at night since it was not raining and the water level was continuing to drop. Of the center group, Tuma, Urbano, Inti, Alejandro, and I remain behind. Tuma and I slept on the ground.

February 8

At 6:30 a.m. the rest of the center group began making the crossing. The first part of the forward detachment had set out at 6:00, and after the center group crossed over, the rest of the forward detachment left. At 8:30, after the entire rear guard had crossed over to this side, the center group departed. The rear guard was instructed to hide the raft and to follow behind us. The path became irregular, and it was necessary to clear the way with machetes. At 6:00 p.m., hungry and thirsty, we arrived at a creek with a small pond, where we decided to camp. There are many signs that pigs have been here.

Braulio, Aniceto, and Benigno went down to the river three kilometers away. Upon returning, they reported having spotted footprints made by a pair of sandals, plus tracks of three animals, one of them wearing horseshoes. All the tracks are recent.

February 9

After we had been walking for a little more than half an hour, I decided we should abandon the trail, which was ascending, and follow along the creek. Shortly thereafter a cornfield appeared. I sent Inti and Ricardo to scout and then pandemonium broke out. Those behind us did not see the marker we had left for them, and thought I was lost. Teams were coming and going all over the place.

The forward detachment spotted a house and awaited my arrival. Inti and Ricardo encountered some little children and went to the house of a young peasant with six children; he was very friendly and gave them a multitude of information. In a second conversation with the peasant, Inti said he was the head of the guerrillas and bought two pigs, out of which we made *humita*.[2]

We remain at the same spot eating corn and pork. A punch made of milk and sugar was prepared early in the morning, but we left it for the following day.

---

2. A Bolivian dish made from crushed baby corn and meat.

February 10

Posing as Inti's assistant, I went to speak with the peasants. I do not think the act was very convincing, however, owing to Inti's shyness.

The man is a typical peasant. He is unable to help us, but also unable to foresee the dangers he can cause, and thus potentially dangerous. He told us a few things about the peasants, but was unable to be very specific due to uncertainty.

El Médico [Moro] treated the children; they are full of parasites, and one of them was kicked by a mare. Then we departed.

The afternoon and evening were spent preparing humita (it is not very good). At night we had a meeting of all the comrades and I made a few observations about the next ten days. My plan is to continue the march for ten more days in the direction of Masicuri, and have all the comrades get a firsthand view of the soldiers. We will then try to return along the Frías in order to explore another path.

(The peasant's name is Rojas.)[3]

February 11

The old man's birthday: 67.[4]

We followed a clearly marked trail along the river bank until it became difficult to pass through. At times it disappeared altogether, showing that no one had been through for a long time. At noon we reached a spot where it simply ended, alongside a large river. We were suddenly seized by doubt as to whether or not this was the Masicuri. We halted at a creek while Marcos and Miguel went off to explore upriver and Inti, with Carlos and Pedro, went downriver, trying to find the mouth. They reached it and confirmed that this is the Masicuri. The first shallow crossing appears to be farther down, where some peasants were seen in the distance load-

---

3. Honorato Rojas. Months later he was to lead a section of the guerrillas into an army ambush.
4. Ernesto Guevara Lynch, his father.

ing some horses. They have probably seen our tracks, so from now on we must take greater precautions. We are one or two leagues from Arenales, according to the peasant's information.

Altitude = 760 meters.

February 12

We walked rapidly through the two kilometers cleared yesterday by the forward detachment. After that, clearing a trail went very slowly. At 4:00 p.m. we fell upon a main road, which looks like the one we have been looking for. Across from it on the other side of the river was a house, which we decided to ignore. Instead we looked for another one on this side of the river, that of Montaño, whom Rojas had recommended to us. Inti and Loro went there, but did not find anyone at home, although there were indications this was the house.

At 7:30 we set out on a night march, which served to demonstrate how much we still have to learn. At about ten o'clock, Inti and Loro went back to the house. The news they brought back was not very good: the man was drunk and not very cordial; all he had was some corn. He had gotten drunk at Caballero's house, on the other side of the river, at the site of a shallow crossing. We decided to stay and get some sleep in a nearby wooded area. I was dreadfully tired, since the humitas had not agreed with me and I had gone a day without eating.

February 13

A heavy rain began at dawn, lasting all morning and causing the river to rise. The news improved. Montaño is the owner's son; he is about 16 years old. The father is away and will not be back for a week. He gave us quite a bit of detailed information, going as far as the low-lying area a league away. A stretch of road runs along the left side of the river, but it is very small. Along this bank the only house is that of a brother of Pérez, a middle peasant whose daughter is the girlfriend of a member of the army.

We moved to a new campsite, alongside the creek and next to a cornfield. Marcos and Miguel cut a path to the main road.

Altitude = 650 meters (stormy weather).

February 14

A peaceful day, spent at the same campsite. The boy from the house came three times. One of these trips was to warn us that some people had crossed over from the other side of the river looking for some pigs, although they did not go any farther. He was paid additional money for the damage to the cornfield.

The path clearers spent the entire day using their machetes, without coming to any houses. They estimate having prepared about six kilometers, which is half our goal for tomorrow.

A long message from Havana was deciphered, the heart of which is news of the meeting with Kolle. There in Havana Kolle claimed he had not been informed of the continent-wide scope of the undertaking. This being the case, he would be prepared to collaborate with us on a plan of action, and he asked to discuss the details of it with me. Kolle, Simón Rodríguez,[5] and Ramírez would be coming here. I am also told that Simón has expressed his willingness to help us, independently of what the party decides.

In addition, the message states that the Frenchman,[6] traveling on his passport, will be arriving in La Paz on February 23, and will stay at the house of either Pareja or Rhea. Part of the message has not yet been deciphered.

We shall see how this new conciliatory offensive should be confronted. Other news: Merci[7] appeared without the money, alleging robbery; misappropriation is suspected although the possibility of something more serious has not been discounted.

---

5. Kolle, Simón Reyes (not Rodríguez), and Humberto Ramírez were leaders of the Communist Party of Bolivia.
6. Régis Debray.
7. The pseudonym of an individual sent from Cuba to collaborate with the underground network in Bolivia.

Lechín is going to ask for money and training.[8]

February 15
Hildita's birthday (11).[9]

A calm day on the march. At 10 a.m. we caught up with the path clearers. After that, progress went slowly. At 5:00 p.m. we were told that a cultivated field had been encountered; this was confirmed at 6:00. Inti, Loro, and Aniceto were sent to speak with the peasant, who turned out to be Miguel Pérez, the brother of Nicolás, who is a rich peasant. Miguel, however, is poor and is exploited by his brother; for this reason he seemed willing to collaborate. We did not eat owing to the lateness of the hour.

February 16
We moved our position a few meters to shield us from the brother's curiosity, setting up camp on high ground overlooking the river 50 meters below. The position is good in that it shields us from surprises, but is a bit uncomfortable. We began the task of preparing a large amount of food for the journey across the mountain range toward the Rosita.[10]

In the afternoon a driving and persistent rain began, continuing all night without letup. This delayed our plans and made the river rise, cutting us off once again. We will loan the peasant 1,000 pesos to purchase some pigs and fatten them up; he has capitalistic ambitions.

February 17
The rain continued all morning—eighteen hours of rain. Everything is wet and the river is very high. I sent Marcos, with Miguel and Braulio, to find a path leading to the Rosita. They returned in the afternoon having created a trail four kilo-

---

8. Juan Lechín was head of the Central Organization of Bolivian Workers, the main trade union body.
9. Hilda Guevara Gadea, his eldest daughter.
10. For an account of Guevara's reasons for this journey, see page 413.

meters long. They brought word that a barren plateau rises up ahead, similar to the one we call the Pampa del Tigre. Inti is not feeling well, the result of overeating.

Altitude = 720 meters (atmospheric conditions abnormal).

February 18

Josefina's birthday (33).[11]

A partial failure. We walked slowly, following behind the path clearers. By 2:00 p.m., however, they had ascended to the plateau, where machetes were no longer needed. We slowed down a little more, and at 3:00 p.m. we reached a water hole where we camped, intending to cross the plateau in the morning. Marcos and Tuma went on a scouting party but returned with very bad news: the hill has sharp cliffs on all sides, making it impossible to climb down. There is no alternative but to turn back.

Altitude = 980 meters.

February 19

A wasted day. We descended the hill until we got to the creek. We then attempted to climb along its banks, but this was impossible. I sent Miguel and Aniceto to climb up the new outcropping of rock and try to cross over to the other side, without success. We spent the day waiting for them. They returned with news that the cliffs were like the others: unpassable. Tomorrow we will attempt to climb along the last of the ridges past the creek, which descends toward the west (the others lead toward the south, where the hill ends).

Altitude = 760 meters.

February 20

A day of slow and uneven progress. Miguel and Braulio headed out along the old path to the small creek by the cornfield. After that they lost the trail, and returned to the creek at sunset. When we reached the next creek, I sent Rolando and

---

11. Aleida March, his wife.

Pombo to scout it out as far as the cliff. They had not returned
by 3:00 p.m., however, so we followed the path that Marcos had
been making, leaving Pedro and Rubio behind to wait for them.
At 4:30 we arrived at the creek by the cornfield, where we made
camp. The scouts did not return.

Altitude = 720 meters.

February 21

A slow hike along the creek, heading upstream. Pombo and
Rolando returned with news that the other creek could be
crossed. Marcos had scouted it out and reported the same thing.
We set off at 11:00 a.m., but at 1:30 we came to some deep pools
of very cold water, which could not be waded through. Loro
was sent out to explore; he was gone a long time, so I sent for
Braulio and Joaquín in the rear guard. Loro returned with news
that the creek got wider upstream, and could be crossed more
easily there. We therefore resolved to continue on, without waiting for word from Joaquín. At 6:00 p.m., as we were setting up
camp, Joaquín brought news that it was possible to climb the
ridge and that there were a number of suitable paths. Inti does
not feel well; he has gas pains for the second time in a week.

Altitude = 860 meters.

February 22

The entire day was spent climbing along difficult ridges,
through thick undergrowth. After an exhausting day, it was
time to set up camp. We had still not reached the top, however,
so I sent Joaquín and Pedro to try to do it alone. When they returned at 7:00 p.m., they brought word that at least three
hours of path clearing would be needed.

Altitude = 1,180 meters. We are at the source of the creek
that empties into the Masicuri, but headed toward the south.

February 23

A bad day for me. I was exhausted and made it through on
will-power alone. Marcos, Braulio, and Tuma set off in the

morning to clear the path, while we waited for them at camp. There we deciphered a new message, acknowledging receipt of the one I had sent via the French mail drop. We left at noon, under a sun so strong it split open rocks. Shortly thereafter, we reached the top of the highest hill and I began to feel faint. From that moment on, I walked under the power of sheer determination.

The highest altitude in the area is 1,420 meters, overlooking a vast region that includes the Río Grande, the mouth of the Ñacahuasu, and part of the Rosita. The topography is different from what appears on the map. After a clear divide, it drops abruptly into a tree-lined plateau eight to ten kilometers wide, at the end of which flows the Rosita. Behind that there is another range, with altitudes equal to those in this chain. A plain is visible in the distance.

We decided to descend through an area that was suitable although very steep, in order to follow along a creek bed that leads to the Río Grande, and from there to the Rosita. It looks like there are no houses along the banks, contrary to the map. After a hellish trek, without water, and already past dark, we set up camp at an altitude of 900 meters.

Yesterday morning I overheard Marcos telling a comrade to go to hell; today I heard him say the same thing to another comrade. I must speak with him.

February 24

Ernestico's birthday (2).[12]

An arduous and unproductive day. We made very little progress and were without water, because the creek bed we are following is dry. At noon the path clearers were replaced because of exhaustion. At 2:00 p.m. it rained a little and we filled up the canteens. A little later we came across a small pool of water, and at 5:00 we made camp on level ground alongside the water. Marcos and Urbano continued scouting. Marcos re-

---

12. Ernesto Guevara March, his youngest child.

turned with news that the river was a couple of kilometers away, but that the path along the creek was very poor, because it turned into a marsh.

Altitude = 680 meters.

February 25

A bad day. Very little progress was made; and to top it off, Marcos, who was with Miguel and Loro, took the wrong path and the whole morning was lost. At noon he reported this and asked for relief and radio communication. Braulio, Tuma, and Pacho were sent. At 2:00 p.m. Pacho returned saying that Marcos had sent him back because reception was poor. At 4:30 I sent Benigno to tell Marcos that if he did not find the river by 6:00 he should return.

After Benigno had left, Pacho called me over to tell me that he and Marcos had had an argument and that Marcos had ordered him around in an arrogant way, threatening him with a machete and hitting him in the face with the handle. When Pacho returned and told him he could go no further, Marcos again threatened him with a machete, giving him a shove and tearing his clothes.

Due to the seriousness of the incident, I summoned Inti and Rolando. They confirmed the bad atmosphere inside the forward detachment as a result of Marcos's personality, but also mentioned acts of insolent behavior by Pacho.

February 26

In the morning I spoke with Marcos and Pacho. Through this I became convinced that Marcos is guilty of insulting behavior and mistreatment, and possibly of threatening with a machete, but not of striking him. Pacho, for his part, is guilty of insulting replies and has an innate tendency toward bravado, of which there have been some previous incidents.

I waited until everyone was together, and then spoke of the significance of our effort to reach the Rosita. I explained how the type of privations we were experiencing were an introduction to what we would suffer in the future. And I explained that as a result of difficulty in adapting, shameful incidents had occurred, such as this one between two Cubans. I criticized Marcos for his attitude, and I warned Pacho that another incident of this type would lead to his dishonorable discharge from the guerrilla force. In addition to refusing to continue with the radio equipment, Pacho returned without informing me of the incident; and later, according to all indications, he lied to me about Marcos having struck him.

I told the Bolivians that anyone who felt weak and discouraged should not resort to deceitful methods but should speak to me, and we would discharge him from the group peacefully.[13]

We continued our march, attempting to reach the Río Grande and then to continue along it. We did so, and were able to follow it for a little more than a kilometer. But then it was necessary to climb the bank once again because jutting rock made it impossible to continue along the river.

Benjamín had fallen behind because of difficulties with his knapsack and physical exhaustion. When he reached our position, I ordered him to continue, which he did. He walked about fifty meters but then lost the ascending trail; in attempting to find it he stepped out onto a ledge. Just as I was instructing Urbano to help him regain the trail, Benjamín made a sudden movement and fell into the water. He did not know how to swim. The current was swift and dragged him along. We ran to try to save him, but while we were undressing he disappeared in a pool of water. Rolando swam toward him and tried to dive under, but the current dragged him far off. After five minutes we gave up all hope. He was a weak young man and absolutely unfit, but his determination to prevail over all obstacles was great. He was not up to the test; his physical abilities did not match his will. We have now had our baptism of death on the banks of the Río Grande, in an absurd way.

---

13. For additional accounts of this talk, see pages 413-14 and 416-17.

We set up camp at 5:00 p.m., before reaching the Rosita. We ate our last ration of beans.

February 27

After another exhausting day hiking along the river bank and climbing jutting rocks, we reached the Rosita river. It is bigger than the Ñacahuasu but smaller than the Masicuri, with reddish water.

We ate our last reserve rations. We did not come across any signs of people nearby, despite our proximity to populated areas and roads.

Altitude = 600 meters.

February 28

A partial rest day. After breakfast (tea), I gave a short talk analyzing the death of Benjamín and relating some experiences from the Sierra Maestra.

Scouting teams were then sent out. Miguel, Inti, and Loro were ordered to hike three and a half hours upstream along the Rosita. I thought this was the time it would take to reach the Abaposito river, but it turned out not to be so, owing to the lack of a trail. They encountered no recent signs of life. Joaquín and Pedro climbed the bluffs facing us. However, they did not see anything, nor did they find a trail or any traces of one. Alejandro and Rubio crossed the river and did not find a trail, although their search was superficial.

Marcos directed the construction of a raft. As soon as it was completed, the crossing was begun at a bend in the river into which the Rosita flows. The knapsacks of five men went across. But while Benigno went across and Miguel stayed behind, the pattern was reversed with their knapsacks. And to top it off, Benigno left his shoes behind.

The raft could not be recovered. Since the second one was not finished, we suspended the crossing until tomorrow.

ANALYSIS OF THE MONTH

Although I have not received news from the camp, everything is going more or less satisfactorily, with some exceptions—fatal in one case.

There is no news from the outside concerning the two men who are due to arrive to complete the group. The Frenchman should be in La Paz by now, and will be arriving at the camp any day. I have received no word on the Argentines or Chino. Radio messages are being received satisfactorily in both directions. The party's stance continues to be vacillating and two-faced, at best. However, when I speak with the new delegation we will receive an explanation, which could be definitive.

The march has gone fairly well, but was tarnished by the accident that cost the life of Benjamín. The men are still weak, and not all the Bolivians will withstand it. The recent days of hunger have revealed a slackening of enthusiasm. This became more obvious when the group got split up.[14]

As far as the Cubans are concerned, two of the relatively inexperienced ones, Pacho and Rubio, have yet to respond; Alejandro has done so fully. Among the old-timers, Marcos is a constant headache and Ricardo is not up to standard. The others are doing well.

The next stage will be one of combat and decision.

---

14. On February 28, the forward detachment was separated from the rest of the unit during the crossing of the Río Grande, when the raft drifted away. The two groups remained separated for the remaining weeks of the expedition.

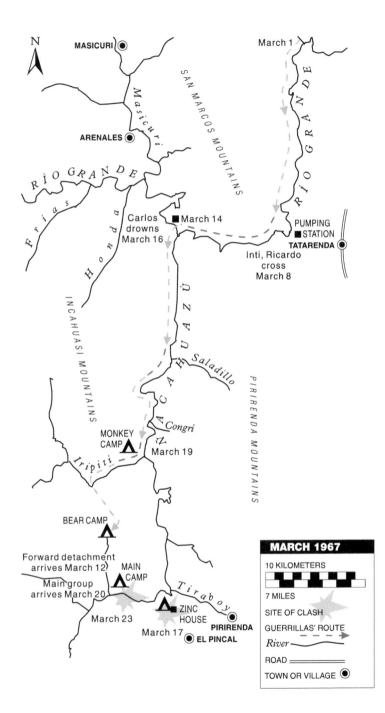

N

MASICURI

Masicuri

SAN MARCOS MOUNTAINS

March 1

RÍO GRANDE

ARENALES

RÍO GRANDE

Frias

Honda

Carlos
drowns
March 16

■ March 14

PUMPING
■ STATION
TATARENDA

Inti, Ricardo
cross
March 8

INCAHUASI MOUNTAINS

ACAHUAZÚ

Saladillo

PIRIRENDA MOUNTAINS

Congrí

MONKEY
CAMP
March 19

Iripiti

BEAR CAMP

Forward detachment
arrives March 12

MAIN
CAMP

Main group
arrives March 20

Tiraboy

ZINC
HOUSE
PIRIRENDA

March 23

March 17 ● **EL PINCAL**

MARCH 1967

10 KILOMETERS

7 MILES

SITE OF CLASH

GUERRILLAS' ROUTE

River

ROAD

TOWN OR VILLAGE ●

MARCH 1967

March 1

At 6:00 a.m. it began to rain. We postponed the crossing until it stopped, but the rain only got heavier, and it continued until 3:00 p.m. By that time the water level had risen and we decided it would not be wise to try the crossing. The river is now very high, and there is no indication that the water level will drop anytime soon. I moved into an abandoned hut to get out of the rain, and set up the new camp there. Joaquín stayed where he was. At night I was informed that Polo had consumed his can of milk, and Eusebio his can of milk and his sardines. As punishment, they will not eat when the others have their rations of these items. A bad sign.

March 2

The day started out rainy and people were restless—especially me. The river rose even higher. We decided to leave camp as soon the rain stopped and continue parallel to the river along the path we had been following. We left at noon with a good stock of hearts of palm. We stopped at 4:30, having deviated from our path in an attempt to utilize an old trail, which we were unable to find. There is no news of the forward detachment.

March 3

We began with enthusiasm, walking well. As the hours wore on, however, the pace slackened. It was necessary to move up to higher ground, since I was afraid of another accident in the area where Benjamín fell. It took us four hours to hike a distance that took less than half an hour down below. At 6:00 p.m. we reached the bank of a creek, where we made camp. Since only two hearts of palm remained, Miguel and Urbano, followed later by Braulio, went out to find some farther away. They returned at 9:00, and we ate close to midnight. Hearts of palm (called *totai* in Bolivia) are saving the day.

Altitude = 600 meters.

March 4

Miguel and Urbano left during the morning and spent the entire day cutting a trail with machetes. They returned at 6:00 p.m., having advanced some five kilometers. They spotted a plain through which we should be able to advance. Since there is no place there to set up camp, however, we decided to stay where we are until the trail is lengthened. The hunters caught two small monkeys, a parrot, and a dove, which was our dinner, together with hearts of palm, which are abundant around this creek.

People's spirits are low, and physical deterioration is setting in more and more each day. My legs are beginning to swell.

March 5

Joaquín and Braulio went out in the rain to clear the path. They are both weak, however, and did not make much progress. Twelve hearts of palm were collected and a few small birds were caught. This enables us to save the canned food for one more day, and to build up a two-day reserve of hearts of palm.

March 6

A day of intermittent hiking, lasting until 5:00 p.m. Miguel, Urbano, and Tuma were path clearers. They made some progress, and in the distance they saw some hilltops that appear to be the ones overlooking the Ñacahuaso. The only thing bagged was a small parrot, which was given to the rear guard. Today we ate hearts of palm with meat. We have three very skimpy meals left.

Altitude = 600 meters.

March 7

Four months. The men are becoming more and more discouraged, seeing the end of the provisions but not of the journey. Today we advanced four to five kilometers along the river bank and finally came across a promising trail. Food for the day: three and a half small birds and the remaining hearts of palm. Starting tomorrow, and for the next two days we will have canned food by itself, with one-third of a can per person. Then, the condensed milk, which is the end of it.

The Ñacahuasu must be two or three days away.

Altitude = 610 meters.

March 8

A day of little hiking, full of surprise and tension. At 10:00 a.m., we broke camp without waiting for Rolando, who was hunting. After only an hour and a half we caught up with the path clearers (Urbano, Miguel, and Tuma) and the hunters (El Médico [Moro] and Chinchu[1]). The latter group had caught a bundle of parrots, but then came to a spot where they could see a water tank [on the other side of the river] and halted. After ordering the troop to make camp, I went to see the place, and it turned out to be an oil-pumping station.

Instructed to cross over and pose as hunters, Inti and Ricardo dived into the river. They jumped in with their clothes

---

1. Ricardo.

on, trying to make it in two stages, but Inti ran into difficulty and almost drowned. Ricardo came to his aid and they finally made it to the other side, drawing the attention of everybody. They did not give the signal indicating danger, and disappeared.

They began the crossing at noon, but when I left at 3:15 we had received no sign from them. They did not show up all afternoon and evening. The last crew on watch left at 11:00 p.m., having seen no new signs from them.

I was very concerned, having two valuable comrades exposed in this way and not knowing what had happened to them. We resolved that Alejandro and Rolando, our best swimmers, would cross over tomorrow to find out.

We ate better than on other days, despite the lack of hearts of palm, because of the abundance of parrots and two small monkeys that Rolando killed.

March 9

We began the crossing early in the day. However, it was necessary to build a raft, which delayed things considerably. At 8:30 a.m., the lookouts reported seeing some semi-clad people on the other side, and the crossing was suspended. A little path had been made leading to the other side, but it ended up in a clearing where we could be seen. This will make it necessary to effect the departure in the early morning, taking advantage of the mist from the river.

Close to 4:00 p.m., after an exasperating watch that for me had gone on since 10:30 a.m., the providers (Inti and Chinchu) jumped into the river, reaching our shore far downstream. They brought with them pork, bread, rice, sugar, coffee, canned goods, ripe corn, etc. We treated ourselves to a small feast of coffee and bread, and authorized the use of a can of condensed sweetened milk that we had been keeping in reserve. They explained that they had gone out every hour so we would see them, but to no avail.

Marcos and his people passed through here three days ago,

and it seems that in typical fashion, Marcos paraded his weapons.[2] The operators at the plant do not know for sure how far the Ñacahuasu is from here, but estimate it to be a five-day hike. If that is true, our provisions should last. The pump is part of a pumping plant under construction.

March 10
We departed at 6:30 a.m., and after walking 45 minutes we caught up to the path clearers. At 8:00 it began to rain, lasting until 11:00. We put in about three hours of hiking, all told, and made camp at 5:00. Some hills are visible in the distance, which could be the Ñacahuasu. Braulio left to scout the area. On his return, he reported there is a trail, and that the river leads due west.

Altitude = 600 meters.

March 11
The day began auspiciously. We walked for over an hour along a perfect trail, but then it suddenly ended. Braulio took his machete and worked hard with it until he reached a sandy area. We allowed time for Urbano and him to clear a path, but when we set out to follow them, rising water barred our way. It happened quite suddenly, as the river's level rose by several meters.

We remained cut off from the path clearers, and were forced to make our way through thick undergrowth. We stopped at 1:30 p.m. and I sent Miguel and Tuma to catch up with the forward detachment and instruct them to return, providing they have not been able to reach the Ñacahuaso or some other suitable place. The two of them returned at 6:00 p.m. After walking about three kilometers, they had run into a steep cliff.

We appear to be close, but the final days will be very difficult

---

2. The forward detachment had been through the village of Tatarenda, the site of the oil-pumping station belonging to the state oil enterprise, on March 4. The appearance of strangers there became known to the army.

if the river does not go down, which looks unlikely. We covered four to five kilometers today.

An unpleasant incident has arisen. The rear guard's supply of sugar is low; suspicions are that either each person was issued less, or that Braulio has taken certain liberties. I must speak with him.

Altitude = 610 meters.

March 12

We covered the stretch of ground that was cleared yesterday in an hour and ten minutes. When we arrived, Miguel and Tuma, who had set out before we did, were already exploring a passageway around the steep cliff. The entire day was spent in this way. Our only activity was to catch four small birds, which we ate as a side dish to rice and mussels. We have two meals left. Miguel remained on the other side; it appears he has been able to find a path to the Ñacahuaso.

We covered about three to four kilometers.

March 13

From 6:30 to noon we climbed through hellish cliffs, in a gigantic effort, following the trail created by Miguel. We thought we had almost reached the Ñacahuaso when we ran into some bad stretches, and in five hours we made very little progress. We set up camp at 5:00 p.m. under a moderate shower. The men are very tired and a little demoralized again. Only one meal remains. We covered about six kilometers, but of little benefit.

March 14

Almost without realizing it, we arrived at the Ñacahuazu. (I was—I am—dead tired, and feel as if a boulder had fallen on top of me.) The river is rough, and we were not eager to cross. But Rolando stepped forward to volunteer, and went across easily, beginning his trip to the base camp at precisely 3:20 p.m. I expect him to arrive in two days.

We ate our last meal: *mote*[3] with meat, and are now dependent on what we hunt. As of when I am writing this, we have caught one small bird and three shots have been heard. El Médico [Moro] and Inti are the hunters.

Altitude = 600 meters.

We heard parts of Fidel's speech. In blunt language, he castigates the stance of the Venezuelan Communists and harshly criticizes the position of the USSR toward the Latin American puppet regimes.[4]

March 15

We crossed the river; but only the center group went, with Rubio and El Médico [Ernesto] to assist us. We intended to reach the mouth of the Ñacahuaso, but we were bringing over three men who did not know how to swim and a great deal of weight. The current dragged us almost a kilometer, and the raft was no longer usable for further crossings, which had been our intention. Eleven of us will stay on this side. Tomorrow El Médico [Ernesto] and Rubio will go back across.

We shot four sparrow hawks for our meal, which was not as bad as might have been expected. Everything is wet, and the weather continues full of rain. The morale of the men is low. Miguel's feet are swollen, and there are several others in a similar condition.

Altitude = 580 meters.

March 16

We decided to eat the horse, since by now people's swellings have reached alarming proportions. Miguel, Inti, Urbano, and Alejandro all showed various symptoms, and I was extremely weak. We made an error in calculation, thinking that Joaquín would be crossing over, but this was not the case. El

---

3. A dish made of boiled kernels of corn.
4. Castro's speech of March 13, 1967, can be found in *Selected Speeches of Fidel Castro* (New York: Pathfinder, 1992).

Médico [Ernesto] and Rubio tried to cross over to assist them, but they were thrown downstream and lost from view. Joaquín requested authorization [for the rear guard] to cross over and I gave it to him. They too were lost downstream. I sent Pombo and Tuma to catch up with them, but they could not find them, and the two returned at night. At 5:00 p.m., we began to gorge ourselves on horsemeat, for which we will probably suffer the consequences tomorrow. I calculate that Rolando should be arriving today at the camp.

Message no. 32 was completely deciphered, announcing the arrival of a Bolivian who will be joining up with us, together with another shipment of Glucantine, an antiparasitic drug (leismania). Up to now we have had no cases of this illness.

March 17

Tragedy struck again prior to the first taste of combat. Joaquín's group appeared mid-morning. Miguel and Tuma had gone to reach them, bringing large pieces of meat. Their odyssey had been a great one. They had been unable to control the raft and it was carried downstream along the Ñacahuaso. The raft eventually got caught up in a whirlpool and overturned, several times according to them. The end result was the loss of a number of knapsacks, almost all the ammunition, six rifles, and one man: Carlos. He had been thrown into the whirlpool together with Braulio, but their fates were different: Braulio reached the bank and could see Carlos being helplessly dragged off. Joaquín and the rest of his men had already reached shore farther down, and they did not see him go by. Up until that point, Carlos was considered to be the best among the Bolivians in the rear guard, owing to his seriousness, discipline, and enthusiasm.

The weapons lost are one Brno (Braulio), two M-1s (Carlos and Pedro), and three Mausers (Abel, Eusebio, and Polo). Joaquín reported having seen Rubio and El Médico [Ernesto] on the other side, and had already ordered them to build a small raft and come across. At 2:00 p.m. they appeared, recounting their trials and tribulations; they were naked and Rubio was barefoot. Their raft was destroyed at the first whirlpool. They made it ashore almost at the spot we did.

Our departure is set for early tomorrow morning, and Joaquín will leave at noon. I anticipate receiving news tomorrow during the course of the day. The morale of Joaquín's men appears good.

March 18

We set out early, leaving Joaquín behind to eat and finish cooking his half of the horsemeat. His instructions were to head out as soon as they felt strong.

I fought to maintain a reserve supply of meat, against the view of those who wanted to devour it all. By mid-morning, Ricardo, Inti, and Urbano had fallen behind, and we had to wait for them. This went contrary to my wishes of not resting until we reach the camp from which we started the journey. We are progressing poorly in any case.

At 2:30 p.m. Urbano showed up with a *urina*[5] shot by Ricardo, which allowed us to eat our fill and maintain a reserve supply of horse ribs. At 4:30 we reached what should have been the halfway point, but there we stopped for the night. Several of the men have become lazy and are in foul spirits, including Chinchu, Urbano, and Alejandro.

March 19

Those of us in front made good progress in the morning, stopping at 11:00, as had been agreed. Again, however, Ricardo and Urbano fell behind, joined this time by Alejandro. They arrived at 1:00 p.m., but with another urina; this one too was killed by Ricardo. Along with them came Joaquín. There was an incident between Joaquín and Rubio, where the two exchanged words. I had to be harsh with Rubio, although I was not convinced he was the guilty party.

---

5. A deerlike animal common to the region.

I decided to continue on to the creek at all costs, but a small plane was circling overhead, which did not bode well. In addition, I was concerned about the lack of news from the base camp. I thought the distance would be longer, but even with the men's half-heartedness, we arrived at 5:30 p.m.

There we were met by the Peruvian doctor, Negro, who had come with Chino and the telegraph operator. They brought word that Benigno was awaiting us with food, that two of Guevara's men had deserted, and that the police had raided the farm.[6] Benigno explained that he had left to meet us with food and had crossed paths with Rolando three days ago. Benigno had spent two days at this spot, but was not eager to continue on because the army might be advancing along the river, since the plane had been circling overhead for three days. Negro had witnessed the attack on the farm by six men. Neither Antonio nor Coco were present. Coco had gone to Camiri to meet another group of Guevara's men, while Antonio had left immediately after to warn him of the desertion.

I received a long report from Marcos (D-8), where he explains his typical doings—he had gone to the farm, against my specific orders.[7] There were also two reports from Antonio explaining the situation (D-9 and D-10).

At the base camp now are the Frenchman, Chino and his comrades, Pelado, Tania, and Guevara with the first part of his group.[8] After eating a lavish meal of rice and beans with urina, Miguel left to look for Joaquín, who had not arrived, and to find Chinchu, who had fallen behind yet again. Miguel re-

---

6. On March 11 Orlando and Daniel, two new recruits who had arrived as part of Moisés Guevara's group, deserted. Three days later they were captured and provided detailed information to the army on the Ñacahuazú camp and Che Guevara's presence. This led to a raid on the farm March 17 and to continual air surveillance.

7. The forward detachment arrived back at camp on March 12.

8. During the exploratory march, Tania had brought the Argentine Ciro Bustos (Pelado or Pelao) and the Frenchman Régis Debray to the camp; Chino and two other Peruvian fighters were there; and Moisés Guevara and eleven of his men arrived. Several other Bolivian recruits also came.

turned with Ricardo, and Joaquín showed up at dawn. We are now all together here.

March 20

We set out at 10:00 a.m., walking at a good pace. Benigno and Negro left ahead of us with a message for Marcos, ordering him to take charge of the defense and to leave the administrative tasks to Antonio. Joaquín's group left after erasing the tracks leading to the creek, but they did so quite slowly. Three of his men are barefoot. At 1:00 p.m., while we were taking a long break, Pacho arrived with a message from Marcos. It explained in more detail what Benigno had reported earlier, although things are now more complicated. Soldiers, 60 of them, had entered the area through the Vallegrandino's trail, and had captured a messenger of ours named Salustio, one of Guevara's people. They seized a mule from us and the jeep is lost. There was no word from Loro, who had been keeping watch at the little house.

We decided at any rate to reach Bear Camp, as it is now called, since a bear was killed there. We sent Miguel and Urbano to prepare food for hungry men, and we arrived there at dusk. At the camp were Danton,[9] Pelao, and Chino, in addition to Tania and a group of Bolivians who in gondola fashion were bringing food and leaving. Rolando had been sent to organize the withdrawal of everything. A mood of defeat was in the air.

Shortly afterward, there arrived a Bolivian doctor who has recently joined us,[10] with a message for Rolando, telling him that Marcos and Antonio were by the pond, and that he should go meet them there. I ordered the same messenger to go back and tell them that wars are won with bullets, and that they should immediately return to the camp and wait for me there. Everything gives the impression of total chaos; no one knows what to do.

---

9. Régis Debray.
10. A reference to Julio.

I had a preliminary discussion with Chino. He is asking for $5,000 a month for ten months; when he was in Havana they told him to discuss it with me. He also brought a message that Arturo was unable to decipher because of its length. I told him that I was in agreement in principle, provided they took up arms within six months. He intends to do so in the Ayacucho region, with 15 men under his command. We also agreed that he would send us 5 men now and 15 more after a period of time, and that they would be sent back with their weapons after receiving training in combat. He is to send me a pair of medium-range (40 mile) transmitters, and we will work out a code for our own use and for keeping in permanent contact with each other. He seems very enthusiastic.

He also brought several reports by Rodolfo that are very old by now. We learned that Loro has appeared, announcing he had killed a soldier.

March 21

I spent the day going over several points with Chino and holding discussions with the Frenchman, Pelao, and Tania. The Frenchman brought news we had already heard concerning Monje, Kolle, Simón Reyes, etc. He has come to stay, but I asked him to go back and organize a support network in France, stopping off in Cuba along the way. This would coincide with his desire to get married and have a child with his companion. I am to write letters to Sartre and B. Russell, asking them to organize an international aid fund for the Bolivian liberation movement.[11] In addition, he is to speak with a friend who will organize the channels for sending aid. It will consist primarily of money, medicine, and electronics, the latter in the form of an electrical engineer and equipment.

Pelao, of course, is ready to put himself under my command. I proposed that he act as a type of coordinator, dealing for the

---

11. French writer Jean-Paul Sartre and British liberal philosopher Bertrand Russell were prominent opponents of the U.S. war in Vietnam.

time being solely with the groups led by Jozamy, Gelman, and Stamponi, and that he send me five men to begin training.[12] He is to convey greetings to María Rosa Oliver and to the old man.[13] He will be given 500 pesos to send out and a thousand to get around with. If they agree, they are to begin exploratory activity in northern Argentina and send me a report.

Tania made the contacts and the people came. According to her, however, it became necessary that she herself bring them here in her jeep. She had intended to stay one day, but things got complicated. Jozamy was unable to stay the first time; the second time, it was not even possible to make contact with him since Tania was here. She referred to Iván with considerable derision; I do not know what is behind this. We received Loyola's financial balance sheet through February 9 ($1,500). (She also reports that she has been removed from the leadership of the youth organization.)

Two reports by Iván were received. One of them, with photos, concerns a military school and is of no interest. The other has information on a few points, but is also not very important.

The main thing is that we have been unable to decipher the written message (D-13). Antonio sent a report in which he tries to justify his behavior (D-12). We heard over the radio a report announcing one death, which was later retracted; this would seem to confirm Loro's account.

March 22

We left at [illegible], leaving the [illegible] camp abandoned, with a little food, lightly guarded [illegible]. We reached the area downstream at 12:00 noon. There are 47 of us, counting visitors and all.

When we arrived, Inti raised with me a series of acts of dis-

---

12. Juan Gelman was a member of the Communist Party of Argentina; Luis Faustino Stamponi, of the Argentine Socialist Party.
13. María Rosa Oliver was an Argentine writer. The "old man" refers to Guevara's father.

respect committed by Marcos. I exploded and told Marcos that if this were true, he would be expelled from the guerrilla unit. He answered that he would rather be shot.

Orders were given to set an ambush of five men ahead, along the river, and to send out a scouting party of three men headed by Antonio, with Miguel and Loro. Pacho was sent to the barren hill overlooking Argañaraz's house to keep watch, but he saw nothing. At night the scouts returned, and I gave them a real tongue-lashing. Olo[14] reacted very emotionally and denied the charges. The meeting was extremely heated, and did not end well. It is not clear what Marcos said. I sent for Rolando to straighten out once and for all the problem of the recruits, the numbers and the distribution of supplies, since more than 30 of us in the center group went hungry.

March 23

A day of military events. Pombo wanted to organize a gondola upriver to recover supplies, but I was opposed to it until the question of Marcos's replacement was clarified. Shortly after 8:00 a.m., Coco came running to report that a section of the army had fallen into the ambush. The final tally, as of now, is 3 60-mm. mortars, 16 Mausers, 2 BZs, 3 Uzis, 1 .30-caliber machine gun, 2 radios, boots, etc., 7 killed, 14 uninjured prisoners, and 4 wounded. We were unable to seize any food supplies, however. We captured their plan of operations, which was to advance along both sides of the Ñacahuasu, meeting up midway.

We rapidly moved people to the other side, and I positioned Marcos with almost the entire forward detachment at the end of the path of operations, while the center group and part of the rear guard remained behind in defensive positions, and Braulio set up an ambush at the end of the other path of operations.[15] We will spend the night in these positions, to see if the

---

14. Antonio.
15. For a description of the paths of operations, see the entries for January 20 and January 24.

famous Rangers arrive tomorrow. A major and a captain taken prisoner sang like canaries.

The message sent via Chino was deciphered. It speaks of Debray's trip, the sending of $60,000, Chino's requests, and an explanation of why they have not written to Iván. I have also received a communication from Sánchez reporting on the possibilities of getting Mito set up in several places.

March 24

The final tally is 16 Mausers; 3 mortars, with 64 shells; 2 BZs; 2,000 Mauser rounds; 3 Uzis, with 2 clips each; 1 .30-caliber machine gun, with 2 cartridge belts. There are 7 dead and 14 prisoners, including 4 wounded. Marcos was sent to scout and did not see anything, but the planes bombed close to our house.

I sent Inti to speak with the prisoners for the last time and to set them free, stripping them of every article of clothing we could use. The two officers were spoken to separately and kept their clothing. We told the major that we were giving him until noon on the 27th to remove the bodies, and offered him a truce covering the entire Lagunillas region if he stayed here. However, he replied that he was resigning from the army. The captain reported that he had reentered the army a year ago at the request of people from the party, and that he had a brother studying in Cuba. He also gave us the names of two other officers willing to collaborate. When the planes began bombing, it gave them a terrible fright, but it had the same effect on two of our men, Raúl and Walter. The latter was also weak during the ambush.

Marcos conducted a scouting mission and did not find anything in the area. Ñato and Coco went with the rejects up the river to carry supplies, but they had to be brought back because they did not want to walk. They must be discharged from our ranks.

March 25

There were no new developments during the day. León,

Urbano, and Arturo were sent to an observation spot overlooking the access ways at both sides of the river. At noon,
Marcos withdrew from his ambush position, and all the people were concentrated at the principal ambush site.

At 6:30 p.m., with almost everyone present, I made an analysis
of the journey and its significance. I reviewed Marcos's errors and
announced his demotion, naming Miguel to replace him as head
of the forward detachment. At the same time I announced the
discharge of Paco, Pepe, Chingolo, and Eusebio, informing them
that they will not eat if they do not work.[16] In addition, their cig-
arette ration was suspended and their personal belongings will
be redistributed to the comrades who need them most. I referred
to Kolle's plan of coming to hold discussions with us, while at the
very same time they expel members of the youth organization
who are here.[17] What interests us are deeds; words at variance
with deeds have no importance. I announced we would try to
find a cow and that study classes will be resumed.[18]

I spoke to Pedro and El Médico [Ernesto], announcing they
had almost completely graduated as guerrilla fighters; I also
spoke to Apolinar, encouraging him along these lines. I criticized
Walter for becoming soft during the journey, for his attitude in
combat, and for the fear he displayed toward the planes; he did
not react well. We went over details with Chino and Pelado, and
I gave the Frenchman a long oral report about the situation.

In the course of the meeting, this group was named the National Liberation Army of Bolivia.[19] Coming out of the meeting
a public statement will be issued.

---

16. These four expelled Bolivian recruits are referred to subsequently in the diary as the "rejects."

17. On February 5, Antonio Jiménez (Pedro, Pan Divino), Aniceto Reinaga (Aniceto), and Loyola Guzmán were removed from the Executive Committee
and Political Bureau of the Bolivian Communist Youth (JCB) for "indiscipline, abandonment of the organization's work, and disagreement with the
line of the JCB."

18. For an additional account of this talk, see pages 417-19.

19. Ejército de Liberación Nacional de Bolivia (ELN).

March 26

Early in the day Inti left with Antonio, Raúl, and Pedro to look for a cow in the area around Ticucha. Three hours after leaving, however, they ran into troops and turned back; apparently they were not seen. They reported that the soldiers had a lookout post in a clearing along with a house with a shiny roof, from which about eight men were seen leaving. They are near the river that we used to call Yaki. I spoke with Marcos and sent him to the rear guard. I do not believe his conduct will improve very much.

We organized a small gondola and the usual sentries. From the observation post overlooking the Argarañaz house, 30-40 soldiers were spotted, and a helicopter was seen landing.

March 27

Today the news exploded onto the scene, monopolizing the air waves and producing mountains of public statements, including a press conference by Barrientos.[20] The official report lists as dead one more than we do, and gives them as wounded and later shot. It also gives our losses as 15 dead and 4 captured, 2 of them foreigners. In addition, they speak about a foreigner who killed himself and about the composition of the guerrilla unit. It is evident that either the deserters or the prisoner talked; what is not known is how much information they gave and in what form. Everything seems to indicate that Tania has been identified; with that we have lost two years of good and patient work. The departure of the people will now become very difficult. When I told this to Danton, I got the impression he was not very pleased. We shall see later on.

Benigno, Loro, and Julio set out to find the route to Pirirenda, and should be gone two or three days. Their instructions are to reach Pirirenda without being seen and then travel on to Gutiérrez. The reconnaissance plane dropped some para-

---

20. Gen. René Barrientos had become Bolivia's president following a military coup in 1964.

troops, and the lookouts reported they landed in the hunting ground. Antonio and two others were sent to investigate and try to take prisoners, but there was nothing.

At night we held a meeting of the general staff, where we agreed on plans for the days ahead. Tomorrow we will send a gondola to our little house to gather corn; later another crew will be sent to Gutiérrez to purchase supplies. Finally, we will stage a small diversionary attack; this could be conducted in the forest between Pincal and Lagunilla, against passing vehicles.

Communiqué no. 1 was produced (D-17). We will try to get it to the newspaper reporters in Camiri.[21]

March 28

The air waves continue to be saturated with news about the guerrillas. According to the reports, we are surrounded by 2,000 men within a 120-kilometer radius, and the circle is tightening, complemented by napalm bombing, and we have suffered 10-15 casualties.

I sent Braulio, with nine men under him, to try to gather corn. They returned at night with a string of crazy items to report:

1. Coco, who had left earlier to warn us, has disappeared.

2. They reached the farm at 4:00 p.m. They found that the cave had been rummaged through, but they began gathering things. While they were doing this, there appeared seven men from the Red Cross, two doctors, and several unarmed military personnel. They were taken prisoner and told that the truce had expired, but were given permission to continue their work.

3. A truckload of soldiers appeared, and instead of firing at them, our people made them promise to withdraw.

4. The soldiers withdrew in disciplined fashion, and our

---

21. The ELN's Communiqué no. 1 was eventually printed in Cochabamba's *Prensa Libre* on May 1; it was the only guerrilla communiqué published during the war For the text, see pages 305-6.

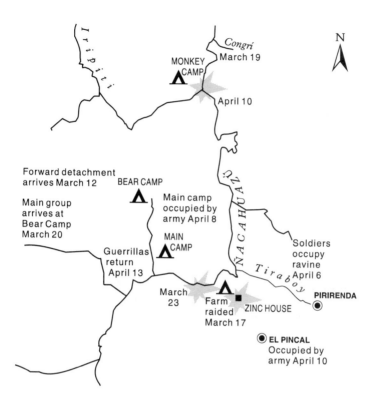

Iripiti

Congrí
March 19

MONKEY
CAMP

April 10

N

Forward detachment
arrives March 12

BEAR CAMP

Main group
arrives at
Bear Camp
March 20

Main camp
occupied by
army April 8

NACAHUAZÚ

Soldiers
occupy
ravine
April 6

Guerrillas
return
April 13

MAIN
CAMP

Tiraboy

PIRIRENDA

March
23

Farm
raided
March 17

ZINC HOUSE

EL PINCAL
Occupied by
army April 10

MARCH-APRIL 1967

10 KILOMETERS

7 MILES

SITE OF CLASH

River

ROAD

TOWN OR VILLAGE ⦿

men accompanied the health workers to the rotting corpses. But they were unable to carry the bodies and said they would return tomorrow to burn them.

Our men confiscated two horses from Argarañaz and returned, leaving Antonio, Rubio, and Aniceto at the spot where the animals were unable to continue. As we were about to go look for Coco, he showed up; it seems he had fallen asleep. There is still no word of Benigno.

The Frenchman raised, with excessive vehemence, how useful he could be abroad.

March 29

A day of little action but of a flurry of news. The army is giving out many details which, if true, could be of much value to us. Radio Havana has now reported the news, and the Bolivian government has announced its support for the action by Venezuela in presenting the case of Cuba before the OAS [Organization of American States]. Among the news items is one that has me concerned: it mentions an encounter at the Tiraboy[22] ravine in which two guerrillas were killed. This spot is on the way to Pirienda, where Benigno was to explore. Moreover, he should have returned today but did not. Their orders were not to go through the ravine, but in recent days they have repeatedly disobeyed orders I have given.

Guevara is making very slow progress in his work. He was given dynamite but they were unable all day to set it off. One of the horses was killed and generous portions of meat were eaten, even though it must last four days. We will try to bring the other one here, although it looks like it will be difficult. To judge by the birds of prey, the bodies have still not been burned. As soon as the cave is finished we can move from this camp, which is now uncomfortable, plus its location is known quite well. I informed Alejandro that he would remain here together with El Médico [Moro] and Joaquín (probably at Bear

---

22. Also known as Piraboy.

Camp). Rolando is also quite exhausted.

I spoke with Urbano and Tuma. I could not even get the latter to understand the source of my criticisms.

March 30

Things returned to calm. In the middle of the morning Benigno and his comrades appeared. They had in fact passed through the Piraboy ravine, but all they encountered were two sets of footprints. They reached their destination, although they were seen by peasants, and headed back. They report that it takes four hours to reach Pirirenda, and that there is apparently no danger. The little house was strafed continuously from the air.

I sent Antonio and two others to scout up the river. They reported that the soldiers remain stationary, although there are signs of a scouting patrol along the river. They have dug trenches.

The remaining mare arrived at camp, so that in the worst of cases we have a four-day supply of meat. Tomorrow we will rest and the following day the forward detachment will set out on the next two operations: the seizure of Gutiérrez and an ambush along the road leading from the Argarañaz farm to Lagunillas.

March 31

A relatively uneventful day. Guevara announced that the cave will be finished tomorrow. Inti and Ricardo reported that the soldiers had reoccupied our little farm, following an attack with artillery (mortars), aircraft, etc. This will obstruct our plans to go to Pirirenda for supplies. Nevertheless, I instructed Manuel[23] to advance with his people toward the little house. If it is vacant, he is to seize it and send two men to inform me, so we can move out the day after tomorrow. If it is occupied by soldiers and a surprise attack is not possible, they should return and scout out the possibilities for bypassing the Argara-

---

23. Miguel.

ñaz farm to mount an ambush between El Pincal and Lagunillas.

The radio continues to clamor away, with statements coming on top of official combat communiqués. They have fixed
our position with absolute precision between the Yaki and
the Ñacahuasu, and I fear they may make an effort to surround us. I spoke with Benigno about his mistake in not going to find us, and I explained the situation of Marcos. He reacted well.

At night I spoke with Loro and Aniceto. The discussion
went very badly. Loro went so far as to say we were falling
apart, and when I pressed him he referred me to Marcos and
Benigno. Aniceto expressed partial agreement with Loro. Later, however, he confessed to Coco that he was complicit in the
theft of some cans of food. He also told Inti that he did not
agree with Loro's statements about Benigno, about Pombo,
and about the "general disintegration of the guerrilla unit,"
more or less.

ANALYSIS OF THE MONTH

The month has been packed with events, but the general
picture has the following characteristics:

The stage of consolidating and purifying the guerrilla unit—
fully accomplished;

The slow stage of development, with the incorporation of
some elements that have come from Cuba, who do not seem
bad, plus Guevara's people, whose general level is quite poor
(two deserters, one "talking" prisoner, three cowards, two
fainthearts);

The stage of the beginning of the struggle, characterized by
a well-aimed and spectacular blow, but marked by gross in-

decision before and after the event (withdrawal of Marcos, Braulio's action[24]);

The stage of the beginning of the enemy counteroffensive, characterized up to now by: (a) a tendency to establish measures of control to isolate us; (b) creating a clamor on the national and international levels; (c) total ineffectiveness up to now; (d) mobilization of peasants.

We will evidently have to take to the road earlier than I anticipated, dropping off one group of people and with the dead weight of four potential informers. The situation is not good, but now begins another stage that will test the guerrilla force, and it will be of great benefit after it has been surpassed.

The composition:

Forward detachment—Miguel (head), Benigno, Pacho, Loro, Aniceto, Camba, Coco, Darío, Julio, Pablo, Raúl.

Rear guard—Joaquín (head), Braulio (second in command), Rubio, Marcos, Pedro, El Médico [Ernesto], Polo, Walter, Víctor (Pepe, Paco, Eusebio, Chingolo).

Center group—myself, Alejandro, Rolando, Inti, Pombo, Ñato, Tuma, Urbano, Moro, Negro, Ricardo, Arturo, Eustaquio, Guevara, Willy, Luis, Antonio, León, (Tania, Pelado, Danton, Chino—visitors), (Serapio—from the refuge[25]).

---

24. For Marcos's withdrawal from camp, see March 20 entry; for Braulio's action at the farm, see March 28.
25. A reference to the house at the Ñacahuazú farm.

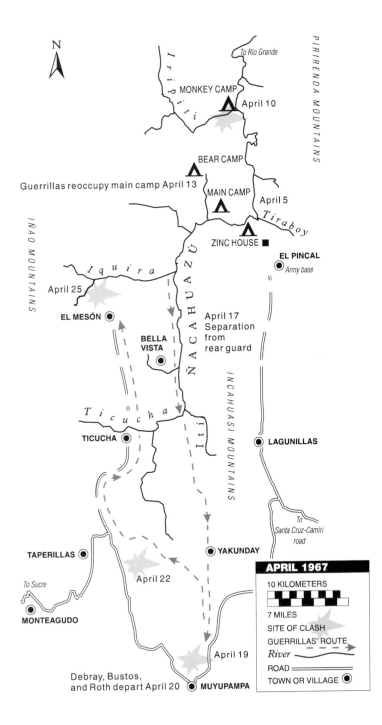

N

To Río Grande

PIRIRENDA MOUNTAINS

MONKEY CAMP
April 10

Iripiti

BEAR CAMP

Guerrillas reoccupy main camp April 13

MAIN CAMP

April 5

Tiraboy

ZINC HOUSE

EL PINCAL
Army base

IÑAO MOUNTAINS

Iquira

ÑACAHUAZÚ

April 25

EL MESÓN

BELLA VISTA

April 17
Separation
from
rear guard

Ticucha

Itití

INCAHUASI MOUNTAINS

TICUCHA

LAGUNILLAS

To
Santa Cruz-Camiri
road

TAPERILLAS

YAKUNDAY

April 22

To Sucre

MONTEAGUDO

April 19

Debray, Bustos,
and Roth depart April 20   MUYUPAMPA

APRIL 1967

10 KILOMETERS

7 MILES

SITE OF CLASH

GUERRILLAS' ROUTE

River

ROAD

TOWN OR VILLAGE

APRIL 1967

April 1

The forward detachment left at 7:00 a.m., after a considerable delay. It did not include Camba, who had not returned from his expedition with Ñato to hide the weapons at the cave at Bear Camp.

At 10:00 Tuma arrived from the observation post to tell us he had seen three or four soldiers in the little plain where we hunt. We took positions. Walter, on lookout, reported seeing three soldiers and a mule or burro, and they were setting up something. He pointed it out to me, but I did not see anything. At 4:00 p.m. I withdrew, judging that in any case it was no longer necessary to stay since they would not be attacking. It seems to me, however, that it was an optical illusion on Walter's part.

I decided we would evacuate everything tomorrow and that Rolando would be in charge of the rear guard in Joaquín's absence. Ñato and Camba arrived at 9:00 p.m., having stored everything except food for the six who remained behind. These are Joaquín, Alejandro, Moro, Serapio, Eustaquio, and Polo—the three Cubans under protest. The other mare was killed, in order to leave *charqui*[1] for the six. At 11:00 p.m. Antonio arrived with a sack of corn, bringing word that everything had gone without incident.

At 4:00 a.m., Rolando headed off, encumbered by the four fainthearts (Chingolo, Eusebio, Paco, Pepe). Pepe wanted them to give him a weapon, and let him stay behind. Camba went with him.

Coco arrived at 5:00 with another message saying they had slaughtered a cow and were waiting for us.

I set the meeting place as the creek downhill from the farm, the day after tomorrow at 12:00 noon.

April 2

The incredible quantity of items we have accumulated made it necessary to spend the entire day storing them in their respective caves. We finished the transfer at 5:00 p.m. Four men were kept on guard duty, but the day was absolutely calm; there were not even any planes flying overhead. The radio reports speak of a "tightening of the encirclement," and say that the guerrillas are digging in at the canyon of the Ñacahuasu. They report that Don Remberto has been taken prisoner, and tell how he sold the farm to Coco.

Due to the lateness of the hour, we decided not to depart today. Instead, we will leave at 3:00 a.m. and gain time going directly along the Ñacahuasu, despite the fact that the meeting place is in the other direction. I spoke with Moro, explaining why I had not included his name as one of the best. He has certain weaknesses regarding food, and a tendency to exasperate comrades with his joking. We discussed these topics for a while.

April 3

The plans went without a hitch. We left at 3:30 a.m. and hiked slowly until we passed the bend in the shortcut at 6:30, reaching the edge of the farm at 8:30. When we passed by the

1. Meat that is salted and sun-dried.

ambush site, we saw the seven bodies, which are now bare skeletons. It appears the birds of prey went about their responsibilities with the utmost seriousness. I sent two men (Urbano and Ñato) to make contact with Rolando. In the afternoon we set up camp at the Piraboy ravine, where we went to sleep after having stuffed ourselves on beef and corn.

I spoke with Danton and Carlos[2] and laid out three alternatives for them: continue on with us; leave on their own; or we could occupy Gutiérrez and from there they could try their luck as best they can. They chose the third option. We will give it a try tomorrow.

April 4

An almost total failure. At 2:30 p.m., we came across the tracks of soldiers, including a paratrooper's beret and remnants of U.S.-made individual food rations. I decided to take by assault the first house belonging to [*illegible*], which we did at 6:30 p.m. Guaraní Indian farmhands came out and told us that approximately 150 army soldiers had been withdrawn from the area yesterday, and that the owner of the house had left to move his cattle far away. A meal of pork and yucca was prepared. Meanwhile, Loro, Coco, Aniceto, and later Inti went to occupy the second house belonging to [*illegible*], accompanied by one of the other peasants.

The couple was not at home, but when they arrived, the young farmhand escaped in the confusion. We were finally able to establish that approximately one company belonging to the Second Regiment, the Bolívar, had been there and had left that morning. Their orders had been to climb down the Piraboy ravine, but they chose instead to set out along a different ridge, which is why we did not clash with them. There are no soldiers in Gutiérrez, but they will return tomorrow, so it is not advisable to stay.

At the first house we found items left by the army, including

---

2. Debray and Bustos.

plates, canteens, even ammunition and equipment, and we confiscated everything. After a good but not excessive meal, the rear guard left at 3:00 a.m. and we set out at 3:30. The forward detachment was to have left as soon as they ate their last portion. We got lost and left farther down from the ambush site, causing confusion that lasted until morning.

April 5

A day lacking in events, but somewhat tense. At 10:00 a.m. we were all together. A little later Miguel's group departed, carrying their knapsacks, to occupy the approach to the ravine. They were ordered to tell the three men from the rear guard on sentry duty there to come back and get their knapsacks. To speed up the journey, I instructed Urbano, Ñato, and León to take the place of the three men from the rear guard. At 3:30 I halted the center group to set up an ambush for any troops coming down the sides of the ravine. The forward detachment and rear guard will defend both entrances into the little creek at its mouth.

At 2:00 p.m. I sent Tuma to see what was happening with the three men, and he returned at 5:00 without any information. We moved to the previous campsite and I repeated the order. At 6:15 Rolando arrived; they had brought the three knapsacks since the men had not met up with them. Braulio made some comments that raise very serious doubts about Marcos's combat capability at present.

I had intended for us to leave in the early morning heading downstream, but soldiers were seen bathing some 300 meters from our position. We then resolved to cross the river without leaving tracks and walk along the other trail toward our creek.

April 6

A very tense day. We crossed the Ñacahuasu river at 4:00 a.m. and decided to wait for daybreak before continuing on. Later Miguel began to scout out the area, but had to return twice because of mistakes that brought us very close to the soldiers. At 8:00 Rolando reported that approximately 10 soldiers were at the approach to the ravine we had just abandoned. We departed, walking slowly, and by 11:00 a.m. we were out of danger, on a ridge. Rolando brought word that more than 100 soldiers were stationed in the ravine.

At night, before we had reached the creek, we heard the voices of cattle herders in the river. We went there and detained four peasants who were watching over cattle owned by Argarañaz. They had a safe-conduct pass from the army to look for 12 head of cattle; some of the animals had been through much earlier and could not be found. We took two cows for ourselves and brought them along the river to our creek. The four civilians turned out to be the contractor and his son, a peasant from Chuquisaca, and another from Camiri who appeared very receptive. We gave him the document and he promised to disseminate it.

We held them a little while and then let them go, requesting they not say anything, which they promised.

We spent the night eating.

April 7

We moved into the creek, bringing the surviving cow, which was slaughtered to make charqui. Rolando remained on ambush along the river, with orders to fire on anything that appeared. There was nothing all day. Benigno and Camba followed the path that should take us to Pirirenda. They reported hearing what sounded like the motor of a sawmill in a canyon close to our creek.

I sent Urbano and Julio with a message for Joaquín. They did not return all day.

April 8

A relatively uneventful day. Benigno went out and returned to his work, but did not finish; he stated he will not finish it tomorrow either. Miguel left to look for a canyon that Benigno saw from a hilltop, but he did not return. Urbano and Julio came back with Polo. The soldiers have captured the camp and are sending reconnaissance patrols through the hills. They passed by the "elevator"[3] on their way down. Joaquín reports on these and other questions in the attached document (D-19).

We ran into three cows with their calves, although one escaped; this leaves us with four animals. One or two of these will be used to make charqui, with our remaining salt.

April 9

Polo, Luis, and Wyly left on a mission to deliver a note to Joaquín, and to help them return and position themselves in a hidden area upstream, which Ñato and Guevara will select. According to Ñato there are good locations a little over an hour from our present spot, although they are close to the creek. Miguel arrived; according to his reconnaissance, the gorge leads to Pirirenda, and the trip takes a day with knapsack. For this reason I ordered Benigno to suspend what he was doing, which will take him at least another day.

April 10

The day began uneventfully and continued that way throughout the morning. We were preparing to leave the creek, after clearing away all traces of our presence, and to cross through Miguel's ravine toward Pirirenda-Gutiérrez. At mid-morning, Negro arrived, very excited, to warn us that 15 soldiers were coming down the river. Inti went to warn Rolando, at the ambush site. There was nothing else to do but wait, which we did. I sent Tuma out, so that he would be ready to bring me any news. Soon the first reports arrived, on an unpleasant note: Rubio—Jesús Suárez Gayol—had been fatally wounded. His body was brought back to our camp, with a bullet in the head.

What happened was this: The ambush was composed of eight men from the rear guard reinforced by three from the for-

---

3. A guerrilla-built pathway up a dry waterfall, leading to one of the supply caves.

ward detachment, distributed along both sides of the river. When Inti had gone to warn them of the approach of the 15 soldiers, he passed by Rubio's position and noticed he was in a very bad spot, clearly visible from the river. The soldiers advanced with few precautions, searching the banks of the river for trails. Along one of these they clashed with Braulio or Pedro before entering the ambush. The shooting lasted a few seconds. Left on the battlefield were 1 dead and 3 wounded, plus 6 prisoners. Later a low-ranking officer also fell, and four escaped. Lying next to one of the wounded was Rubio, who was dying. His Garand was jammed, and at his side was an unexploded grenade with the pin loosened. It was not possible to interrogate the captured officer because of the seriousness of his wounds, and he soon died, as did the commanding lieutenant.

From interrogating the prisoners, the following picture emerges: These 15 men belong to the company that was up the Ñacahuaso, where they had passed through the canyon, gathered the skeletons, and later captured the camp. According to the soldiers, they did not find anything there, although the radio speaks of photos and documents found there. The company consists of 100 men, 15 of whom were sent to accompany a group of journalists to our camp. These 15 then set out on reconnaissance, with orders to return at 5:00 p.m. The main force is at El Pincal, and there are about 30 soldiers in Lagunillas. It is assumed that the group that passed through Piraboy has been withdrawn to Gutiérrez. The prisoners recounted their group's odyssey, lost in the woods and without water, making it necessary for a rescue mission to be sent for them.

Estimating that the rescuers would be arriving later in the day, I decided to leave in place the ambush, which Rolando had moved up by some 500 meters, but to reinforce it now with the entire forward detachment. At first I ordered the rear guard to move back, but it then seemed logical to me to leave it in place. About 5:00 p.m., word arrived that a large number of troops were advancing toward us. There was nothing to do but wait. I sent Pombo to bring me a clear picture of the situation. Scattered shots were heard lasting a few minutes, and then Pombo returned with news that the soldiers had again fallen into the ambush. He reported that a number of them were killed and that a major had been taken prisoner.

What had happened this time was that the soldiers were advancing along the river spread out, but without taking any great precautions. The surprise was total. This time there were 7 dead, 5 wounded, and a total of 22 prisoners. The balance sheet is the following: (It is not possible to total it up due to lack of data).

April 11

In the morning we began transferring all the goods, and we buried Rubio in a small, shallow grave, given the lack of materials. Inti stayed with the rear guard to accompany the prisoners and set them free, in addition to searching for more weapons scattered around. The only result of the search was two new prisoners with their Garands. Two copies of Communiqué no. 1 were given to the major, who promised to deliver them to the newspapers.

The total number of casualties is 10 dead, among them 2 lieutenants; 30 prisoners, including a major and some noncommissioned officers, with the rest being soldiers; there were 6 wounded, one in the first battle and the remainder in the second.

They are under the command of the Fourth Division, although elements from other regiments are mixed in. These include Rangers, paratroopers, and soldiers from the area who are not much older than children.

It took us until the afternoon to finish hauling all the matériel. We located the cave to store the remnants, although we have still not been able to prepare it properly. During the last stretch the cows became frightened and ran off, leaving us with only a single calf.

Right when we were arriving at the new camp, we ran into Joaquín and Alejandro, who were coming down with all of their people. From their report, it is apparent that the soldiers seen were only a fantasy of Eustaquio's imagination, and that shifting our location here was a useless effort.[4]

The radio issued a report of "a new and bloody clash" and speaks of 9 dead from the army and 4 "confirmed" dead on our side.

A Chilean journalist gave a detailed account of our camp and reported the discovery of a photo of me, without a beard and smoking a pipe. It is necessary to investigate further how this was obtained. There is no evidence that the upper cave has been discovered, although certain indications point to this.

April 12

At 6:30 a.m. I gathered all the combatants together, minus the four rejects, and gave a short eulogy of Rubio, stressing that the first blood to be shed was Cuban. I sought to put a halt to a tendency observed in the forward detachment of finding fault with the Cubans. This came to the surface yesterday when Camba stated, following an incident with Ricardo, that he had less and less confidence in the Cubans. I issued another call for unity as the only possibility for our army to grow. Although our firepower and combat experience have increased, our army has not grown in size; on the contrary, it has decreased in recent days.

After storing all the captured goods in a cave that was well prepared by Ñato, we left at 2:00 p.m., walking slowly—so slowly that we made virtually no progress. We had barely started the march when we had to stop for the night at a small water hole.

The army now concedes 11 dead. It seems they found another body, or else one of the wounded died. I began a short study course on Debray's book.[5]

---

4. A reference to the events of April 1.
5. *Revolution in the Revolution? Armed Struggle and Political Struggle in Latin America*. An English-language edition was published in 1967 by Monthly Review Press.

We have deciphered part of a message. It does not appear very important.

April 13

We divided the group in half to be able to walk more rapidly. But in spite of everything, the march went slowly and we reached the camp at 4:00 p.m., with the last ones arriving at 6:30. Miguel had arrived during the morning. The caves have not been discovered and nothing has been touched. The benches, the kitchens, the oven, and the seed beds remain intact.

Aniceto and Raúl went on a scouting patrol, but did not do a very good job. We must keep at it tomorrow, and scout as far as the Ikira river.

The North Americans are announcing that sending advisers to Bolivia corresponds to a plan long in place, and has nothing to do with the guerrillas.[6] We are perhaps witnessing the first episode of a new Vietnam.

April 14

A monotonous day. Several items were brought from the infirmary area, giving us a five-day supply of food. We went to the upper cave to look for cans of milk, but found that 23 are missing. This seems inexplicable since Moro left 48 cans, and there does not appear to have been time for anyone to take them. Milk is one of our elements of corruption. A mortar and a machine gun were taken out of the special cave to fortify our position until Joaquín comes.

It is not clear how we should conduct the operation. It seems to me, however, that the best course of action would be for the entire group to set out and operate for a short time in the Muyupampa region, later withdrawing toward the north. If possible, Danton and Carlos will be dropped off on the Sucre-to-Cochabamba road, depending on circumstances.

---

6. It was reported on April 12 that U.S. military experts were arriving to organize counterinsurgency training and coordination of operations.

Communiqué no. 2 was written, addressed to the Bolivian people (D-21).[7] I am also writing report no. 4 for Manila, which the Frenchman will deliver.

April 15
Joaquín and the entire rear guard arrived, and it was decided we will leave tomorrow. He reported that planes were flying over the area, and that artillery was being fired at the hills. The day went by without incident. The task of arming the group was completed. The .30-caliber machine gun was assigned to the rear guard (Marcos), which will have the rejects as their assistants.

At night I announced the journey and issued a severe warning about the missing cans of milk.[8]

A long message from Cuba was partially deciphered. In essence, it states that Lechín knows about me and is going to issue a declaration of support. He will reenter the country clandestinely in three weeks.

I have written a note to Fidel (no. 4), informing him of the most recent events. It is being coded and written in invisible ink.

April 16
The forward detachment left at 6:15 a.m., and we followed at 7:15. We made good progress up to the Ikira river, although Tania and Alejandro fell behind. When we took their temperatures, Tania's was over 39 degrees [102° F] and Alejandro was at 38 [100.4° F]. Moreover, their lagging was delaying the schedule of our march. We left the two of them plus Negro and Serapio one kilometer up the Ikira river, and continued on to a hamlet that we occupied, called Bella Vista. More precisely, this is a settlement of four peasants, who sold us potatoes, a pig, and some corn. They are poor peasants and are very frightened by our presence here. We spent the night cooking

---

7. For the text, see pages 308-9.
8. For accounts of this talk, see pages 414 and 419-20.

and eating, and did not move from the spot. We will wait until early morning to head out to Tikucha without our presence being observed.

April 17

The news kept changing, and with it the decisions. Going to Tikucha is a waste of time, according to the peasants, since there is a direct road to Muyupampa (Vaca Guzmán) that is shorter and whose last stretch is wide enough for vehicles to pass. After much vacillation on my part, we decided to continue on directly to Muyupampa.

I sent for the four stragglers, who will remain behind with Joaquín. I instructed Joaquín to make a show of presence through the area to forestall any excessive troop movement, and to wait for us three days. After this they are to remain in the area, but without engaging in frontal combat, awaiting our return.[9]

At night it was learned that one of the peasant's sons had disappeared and might have gone to inform on us. Despite this, we still decided to depart, so we can get the Frenchman and Carlos out once and for all. Moisés was added to the group of stragglers; he has to stay behind due to an acute gall bladder attack.

Here is a drawing of our situation:

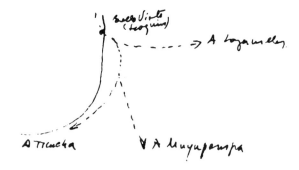

---

9. The April 17 separation with the rear guard led by Joaquín, meant to last three days, turned out to be permanent.

In returning along the same road we risk clashing with army units alerted in Lagunillas or with a column coming from Tikucha. However, it is necessary to run this risk to avoid becoming separated from the rear guard.

We left at 10:00 p.m., walking with rest breaks until 4:30 a.m. We then stopped to sleep a little, having advanced about ten kilometers. Of all the peasants we have seen, there is one, Simón, who displays a willingness to cooperate, although he is afraid. There is another one, Vides, who could be dangerous; he appears to be the "rich man" of the area. It is also necessary to remember the disappearance of Carlos Rodas's son, who may be an informer (although under the influence of Vides, the economic kingpin of the region).

April 18

We walked until dawn, catching a nap the last hour of the night under a considerable chill. In the morning the forward detachment went out to explore and found a house inhabited by Guaraní Indians, who gave very little information. Our sentries stopped a person on horseback, who turned out to be a son of Carlos Rodas (another one) on his way to Yakunday, and we took him prisoner.

We walked slowly, and at 3:00 we reached Matagal, at the house of A. Padilla, a poor peasant whose brother has a house a league away, which we passed. The man was frightened and tried every way possible to get us to leave. Then, on top of everything, it began to rain and we had to seek shelter in his house.

April 19

We remained in the area the entire day, detaining peasants coming from both directions, so that we obtained a wide assortment of prisoners.

At 1:00 p.m. the sentries brought us a strange gift: an English journalist named Roth, who had been guided to us by some children from Lagunilla who had followed our tracks.

Che with Peruvian volunteer Chino.

His documents were in order, but there were some suspicious things. In his passport the occupation of student was crossed out and changed to that of journalist (in fact he claims to be a photographer). He has a Puerto Rico visa, and when asked about an organizer's card from Buenos Aires, he confessed to having taught Spanish to students from the [Peace] Corps. He stated that he had been at the camp and had been shown a diary of Braulio's, where the latter relates his experiences and journeys. It is the same old story; indiscipline and irresponsibility are everywhere.[10]

Through reports by the young boys who guided the journalist, it was learned that the very night of our arrival here, this information was known in Lagunillas thanks to an informant. We pressed Rodas's son and he confessed that his brother and a farmhand of Vides's had gone to collect the reward of 500 to 1,000 pesos. We confiscated a horse from him as a reprisal, and made this known to the peasants being held.

The Frenchman asked us to raise with the Englishman, as a test of his good faith, that he help get them out. Carlos agreed reluctantly, and I washed my hands of it. At 9:00 p.m. we reached [*illegible*], and continued on toward Muyupampa, where, according to the peasants' reports, all is quiet. The Englishman accepted the conditions Inti put to him, and was handed a short account that I drafted. At 11:45 p.m., after shaking hands with those leaving us, we began our march to take the town. I stayed behind with Pombo, Tuma, and Urbano. There was an intense chill in the air, and we built a small fire.

At 1:00 a.m. Ñato arrived to report that the town was in a state of alert, with 20 army troops stationed there, in addition to self-defense patrols. One of these patrols, with two M-3s and two revolvers, surprised our forward detachment, but surrendered to us without a fight.

---

10. George Andrew Roth's story about a diary by Braulio found at the camp was untrue; Braulio's real diary was captured after his death on August 31.

They asked me for instructions and I told them to withdraw due to the lateness of the hour, and to release the English journalist. I said that the Frenchman and Carlos should make whatever decision they deemed best. At 4:00 a.m. we began the return trip, without having achieved our objective. Nevertheless, Carlos decided to remain behind and the Frenchman followed him—this time it was the latter who did so reluctantly.

April 20

Shortly before 7:00 a.m. we reached the house of Nemesio Caraballo; we had met him during the night and he had offered us coffee. He was gone, having left the house locked, with only some frightened servants remaining. We prepared a meal right there, purchasing corn and *jocos* (pumpkin) from the hired hands.

Around 1:00 p.m. a van arrived bearing a white flag. In it were the subprefect, the doctor, and the priest from Muyupampa, the latter of whom was German. Inti spoke with them. They came on a mission of peace, but the peace was to be on a national level, for which they offered themselves as intermediaries. Inti offered peace for Muyupampa, provided they brought us a list of supplies prior to 6:30 p.m. They did not agree to this because, according to them, the army is in charge of the town. They asked us to extend the deadline until 6:00 a.m., which was not accepted.

As a gesture of good will, they brought two cartons of cigarettes along with news that the three who left us have been taken prisoner in Muyupampa, and that two of them were implicated by having false documents on them. Things look bad for Carlos; Danton should come out all right.

At 5:30 p.m., three AT-6 aircraft came and dropped a few bombs on the very house where we were cooking. One of them fell 15 meters away, wounding Ricardo slightly with a piece of shrapnel. This was the army's response. We must make known our proclamations in order to achieve the total demoralization of the army's troops. Judging by their emissaries, the soldiers are scared stiff.

We left at 10:30 p.m. with two horses: the one we had confiscated and the one belonging to the journalist. We walked in the direction of Ticucha until 1:30 a.m., when we stopped to sleep.

April 21

We walked a short distance until we reached the house of Roso Carrasco. He treated us very well, selling us what we needed. At night we walked as far as the crossing of the Muyupampa-to-Monteagudo road, at a place called Taperillas. The idea was to remain by a pond and send out reconnaissance to find a place for an ambush. There was an additional reason: the radio is reporting the death of three mercenaries—a Frenchman, an Englishman, and an Argentine. This uncertainty must be cleared up so we can inflict a special punishment in response.[11]

Before dinner we passed by the house of the older Rodas, the stepfather of Vargas, the one killed at Ñacahuasu.[12] We explained to him what had happened, and he seemed satisfied. The forward detachment did not understand instructions and continued along the road, waking up a few dogs that barked loudly.

April 22

The mistakes began in the morning. After we had withdrawn into the woods, Rolando, Miguel, and Antonio went to scout out a place for an ambush. However, they surprised a small truck belonging to the YPFB,[13] which was examining

---

11. The announcement of the death of Debray, Bustos, and Roth in combat was designed to give the military a free hand to murder them if they refused to cooperate. Photographs of the prisoners were obtained within a few days by journalist Hugo Delgadillo and published in the La Paz daily *Presencia,* refuting the military's lie.

12. Epifanio Vargas, a peasant, was killed in the ambush of March 23 while being forced to act as army guide.

13. Yacimientos Petrolíferos Fiscales Bolivianos (Bolivian State Petroleum Reserves).

our tracks while a peasant informed them of our presence the previous night. At this point our people decided to take everyone prisoner.

This altered our plans. We decided to set up an ambush during the day and capture any passing trucks containing merchandise, and to ambush the army if it came. A truck was captured, containing some supplies, a large stock of bananas, and a considerable number of peasants. However, they let another one by that was seen observing our tracks; above all, other YPFB small trucks were let through. We were delayed by waiting for the meal, with the temptation of bread that was offered but never came.

My aim was to load the YPFB truck with all the foodstuffs, and advance with the forward detachment until we reached the road leading to Ticucha, four kilometers away. At nightfall, a plane began to circle our position and the barking of dogs from neighboring houses become more persistent. At 8:00 p.m. we were ready to set out despite evidence that our presence had been detected.

Right at that time, a short battle began, followed by voices calling on us to surrender. We were all caught off guard, and I had no idea what was happening. Fortunately, our belongings and the merchandise were already loaded in the truck. Things soon got organized. Loro was the only one missing, but up to now there is no indication that anything has happened to him, since Ricardo was the one involved in the fighting. Ricardo had surprised the soldiers' guide as they were walking along the ridge above to surround us. It is possible that the guide was hit.

We left with the truck and all the available horses, six in all, alternating the men on foot and on horseback. In the end, everyone got into the truck except for six from the forward detachment, who rode the horses. We reached Tikucha at 3:30 a.m., and after getting stuck in a hole, we arrived at El Mesón at 6:30. The area is owned by the priest.

The balance sheet of the action is negative: first of all, lack of discipline and foresight. Secondly, the loss of a man (temporary I hope)[14] and of supplies that we paid for but did not take with us. Finally, there is the loss of a packet of dollars that fell out of Pombo's bag. These are the results of the action. In addition, there is the fact that we were taken by surprise and forced to retreat by a group that must have been small. Much is needed to turn this group into a fighting force, although morale is very high.

April 23

Today was declared a rest day, and it passed uneventfully. At midday, the AT-6 aircraft flew over the area. The sentries were reinforced, but nothing happened. At night instructions were given for tomorrow. Benigno and Aniceto will go look for Joaquín—four days. Coco and Camba will explore the trail to the Río Grande and make it passable—four days. As for us, we will remain close to the cornfield, awaiting Joaquín's reincorporation while watching to see if the army comes. Joaquín's instructions are to bring everyone here, except for any of the rejects who may be ill.

The fate of Danton, Pelado, and the English journalist remains unknown. There is press censorship, and they are now announcing another clash, in which three to five prisoners were taken.

April 24

The reconnaissance team departed. We positioned ourselves one kilometer upstream, on a small ridge. From the lookout, one can see as far as the house of the last peasant, which is about 500 meters before one gets to the farm owned by the priest. (We found marijuana in the fields.)

The peasant arrived again and was snooping around. In the

---

14. Separated from the unit, Loro was wounded and captured two weeks later. Kept incommunicado, he was subjected to severe torture before being murdered. His body was tossed from a helicopter into the jungle.

afternoon an AT-6 plane fired two machine-gun bursts at the little house. Pacho has mysteriously disappeared; he was ill and remained behind. Antonio showed him the path and he set out in our direction. It should have taken him five hours, but he did not arrive. We will look for him tomorrow.

April 25

A black day. At around 10:00 a.m., Pombo returned from the lookout, warning that 30 soldiers were advancing on the little house. Antonio remained at the observation post. As we were making preparations, Antonio brought word that there were 60 men, and that they were preparing to continue their advance. The lookout proved ineffective in giving us prior warning.

We decided to improvise an ambush along the path leading to the camp. We hurriedly selected a small stretch bordering the creek, with a visibility of 50 meters. There I positioned myself with Urbano and Miguel, who had the automatic rifle. El Médico,[15] Arturo, and Raúl occupied the position on the right, to cut off any attempt to advance or retreat along that side. Rolando, Pombo, Antonio, Ricardo, Julio, Pablito, Darío, Willi, Luis, and León occupied the lateral position on the other side of the creek, to completely cover the flank. Inti remained at the river bed, to attack anyone seeking refuge there. Ñato and Eustaquio went to the lookout point, with orders to withdraw toward the rear when the shooting began. Chino remained behind, guarding the camp. My meager forces were reduced by three: Pacho is lost and Tuma and Luis are out looking for him.

Soon the army's advance unit appeared. To our surprise, it included three German shepherds and their guide.[16] The animals were restless, but I did not think they would give us away. However, they continued advancing and I shot at the first dog, but missed. When I went after the guide, my M-2

---

15. From here through the end of the diary, "El Médico" refers to Moro.
16. The dogs were being used to follow the guerrillas' scent.

jammed. Miguel shot the other dog, according to what I could see, although it could not be confirmed. No one else entered the ambush.

Intermittent firing began along the army's flank. When it stopped I sent Urbano to order the withdrawal, but he came back with news that Rolando was wounded. They brought his lifeless body back a short time later, and he died as they began to give him plasma. A bullet had split open his thighbone and the entire nerve and vascular bundle; he bled to death before we could act.

We have lost the best man in the guerrilla unit, one of its pillars. He was a comrade of mine from the time when, barely a child, he served as messenger for Column no. 4, through the invasion, to this new revolutionary venture.[17] Concerning his obscure and unheralded death, all that can be said, with eyes toward a hypothetical future that may come about, is: "From the ashes of your mortal remains, valiant captain, a lustrous image extends over the horizon."

The rest of the day was spent in the slow operation of the withdrawal, gathering all the things and the body of Rolando (San Luis). Pacho joined us later. He had taken the wrong trail and caught up with Coco, returning during the night. At three o'clock we buried the body under a thin layer of dirt. At 4:00 p.m., Benigno and Aniceto arrived, announcing they had fallen into an army ambush (more precisely, a little skirmish). They lost their knapsacks but returned unharmed. This occurred, according to Benigno's calculations, right before they reached the Ñacahuasu.

The two natural outlets are now blocked off, and we will have to "head toward the mountains." The exitway along the Río Grande is not propitious, both because it is predictable and because it would move us away from Joaquín, whom we

---

17. Rolando served in Column 4 of the Cuban Rebel Army, commanded by Guevara, which participated in the 1958 invasion westward from the Sierra Maestra to central Cuba.

have not heard from. At night we reached the crossing of the two roads, one leading to the Ñacahuasú and one to the Río Grande, and there we slept. We will wait here for Coco and Camba in order to gather together all our small forces.

The balance sheet of the operation is extremely negative. first of all, there is Rolando's death. But not only that: the army's losses were two at most, plus the dog, since our positions were neither adequately planned nor prepared, and those doing the shooting could not see the enemy. Finally, our lookout system was very bad, which prevented us from making preparations with adequate time.

A helicopter landed twice at the priest's house; possibly to withdraw some wounded. Planes bombed our previous positions, which indicates they have not advanced at all.

April 26

We walked a few meters and I ordered Miguel to look for a place to camp while we sent someone to search for Coco and Camba. However, he appeared at noon with the two of them. They report having cleared a path for a four-hour hike with supplies, and say that climbing the ridge is a possibility. Nevertheless, I sent Benigno and Urbano to explore a possible ascent near the canyon of the creek emptying into the Ñacahuasu. They returned at sundown, with word that the route was very bad. We decided to continue along the trail opened by Coco, with the aim of trying to find another one that leads to the Iquiri.

We have a mascot: Lolo, a little baby urina. We shall see if it survives.

April 27

Coco's four hours turned out to be two and a half. We came to a place with many orange trees, which we believed to be the spot on the map known as Masico. Urbano and Benigno continued creating the path and prepared an additional hour's journey. There is an intense chill at night.

Bolivian radio is broadcasting official statements from the army reporting the death of a civilian guide, a dog trainer, and a dog named Rayo. Our losses are given as two dead: one person presumed to be Cuban nicknamed Rubio, and a Bolivian. It has been confirmed that Danton is being held prisoner near Camiri. Clearly the others are also alive with him.

Altitude = 950 meters.

April 28

We walked slowly until 3:00 p.m. At that time we reached a point where the creek, which had run dry, began heading in a different direction, so we stopped. It was too late to explore the area, so we went back toward the water and set up camp. All we have left is a four-day supply of food at short rations. Tomorrow we will try to reach the Ñacahuasu by way of the Ikiri. We will have to cut through the mountains.

April 29

We did further exploring along some clearings that could be seen. The result was negative. At this point, at least, the canyon appears unbroken. Coco thinks he has seen a canyon that intersects this one but was never explored; tomorrow we will go there with the entire troop.

With considerable delay, message no. 35 has been completely deciphered. It contains a paragraph requesting authorization to add my signature to an appeal in support of Vietnam headed up by Bertrand Russell.

April 30

We began the assault on the hill. The supposed canyon ends up at steep cliffs, but we found a ridge we could climb. Night came upon us close to the top, and we slept there. It was not very cold.

Lolo died, victim of Urbano's impulsiveness. He shot it in the head.

Radio Havana is broadcasting a report by Chilean journalists stating that the guerrillas are now strong enough to threaten the cities, and that they have recently captured two military trucks full of supplies. The magazine *Siempre* interviewed Barrientos. Among other things, he acknowledges the presence of U.S. military advisers and concedes that the guerrillas arise out of Bolivia's social conditions.

SUMMARY OF THE MONTH

Things are proceeding within normal limits, although we must acknowledge two grievous losses: Rubio and Rolando. The death of the latter is a severe blow, since I had intended to put him in charge of the eventual second front. We had four more battles, all of which were positive in general, and one of them—the ambush in which Rubio died—was very good.

On other aspects, we continue to be totally cut off from the outside. Illness has undermined the health of some comrades, compelling us to divide our forces, which has greatly reduced our effectiveness. We have still not been able to make contact with Joaquín. Our peasant base still needs to be developed, although it appears that through planned terror we can obtain the neutrality of most; support will come later. We have not had a single recruit; and in addition to the deaths there is the loss of Loro, who disappeared following the action at Taperillas.

Regarding the points previously noted concerning military strategy, the following should be stressed:

(a) The measures to keep track of and control our movements have not been effective up to now. They have been an annoyance, but have not stopped our movements, due to the army's poor mobility and its weakness. Moreover, after the most recent ambush against the dogs and the trainer, we can presume they will be extremely careful in entering heavily wooded areas.

(b) The clamor continues, but now it is on both the national and international levels. And after the publication of my article in Havana, there can be no doubt about my presence here.[18] It appears certain that the North Americans will intervene here in force. They are already sending helicopters, and apparently Green Berets as well, although these have not been seen here.

(c) The army (one or two companies at least) has improved its technique. They surprised us at Taperillas and did not become demoralized at El Mesón.

(d) The mobilization of peasants against us is nonexistent, except as informants, which has bothered us somewhat. However, they are not very rapid or efficient, and we should be able to nullify them.

The status of Chino has changed, and he will be a combatant until a second or third front is formed. Danton and Carlos fell victim to their haste—desperation almost—to leave, and to my lack of energy in preventing them from doing so. As a result, communication with Cuba was cut (Danton) and the plan of action in Argentina has been lost (Carlos).

To summarize: This has been a month in which everything has gone within normal limits, keeping in mind the exigencies of guerrilla warfare. Morale is good on the part of all the combatants, who have passed their preliminary examinations as guerrilla fighters.

---

18. Guevara's "Message to the Tricontinental," written before he left Cuba in 1966, was published by the Cuban government on April 16, 1967. It can be found in *Che Guevara and the Cuban Revolution*, pp. 347-60.

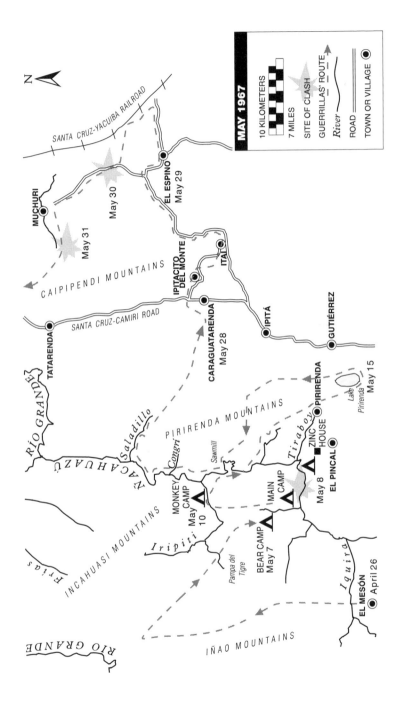

MAY 1967

10 KILOMETERS
7 MILES

SITE OF CLASH
GUERRILLAS' ROUTE
River
ROAD
TOWN OR VILLAGE

N

SANTA CRUZ-YACUIBA RAILROAD

MUCHURI

May 31

May 30

EL ESPINO
May 29

CAIPIPENDI MOUNTAINS

IPITACITO
DEL MONTE

ITAI

IPITÁ

GUTIÉRREZ

TATARENDA

SANTA CRUZ-CAMIRI ROAD

CARAGUATARENDA
May 28

RÍO GRANDE

Saladillo

NACAHUAZÚ

PIRIRENDA MOUNTAINS

Congri

Sawmill

Tirabo

PIRIRENDA

Lake
Pirirenda

May 15

ZINC
HOUSE

EL PINCAL

MONKEY CAMP
May 10

MAIN
CAMP

May 8

INCAHUASI MOUNTAINS

Iripiti

BEAR CAMP
May 7

*Pampa del
Tigre*

Frías

Iquira

EL MESÓN
April 26

RÍO GRANDE

IÑAO MOUNTAINS

MAY 1967

May 1

We celebrated the date by clearing undergrowth from the path, but we walked very little. We have still not reached the watershed.

Almeida[1] spoke in Havana, referring to me and the famous Bolivian guerrillas. The speech was a bit long, but good. We have sufficient food for three days. Today Ñato killed a small bird with a slingshot. We are now entering the era of the bird.

May 2

A day of slow progress and confusion about our geographic position. We walked two hours all told due to the difficulty of the path clearing. From an elevation I could make out a point close to the Ñacahuaso, which indicates we are very far north, although there are no signs of the Iquiri. I ordered Miguel and Benigno to spend the entire day clearing the trail, trying to reach the Iquiri, or at the very least, to reach water, since we are without it. We have food for five days, but very meager rations.

---

1. Juan Almeida, a central leader of the Cuban revolution.

Radio Havana continues its news offensive about Bolivia, with exaggerated reports.

Altitude = 1,760 meters (highest point); we slept at 1,730.

May 3

After a day of continuous path clearing, which made it possible to walk productively for a little more than two hours, we reached a creek with a sizable amount of water that appears to lead north. Tomorrow we will scout the creek to see whether it changes direction; at the same time we will continue the path clearing. We have only a two-day supply of very short rations remaining. Our altitude is 1,080 meters, 200 above the level of the Ñacahuasu. The noise of a motor can be heard in the distance, although we cannot tell from which direction.

May 4

We continued the march in the morning, while Coco and Aniceto explored the creek. They returned close to 1:00 p.m., stating that the creek turned toward the east and south, which would seem to make it the Iquiri. I ordered the machete team to be found, and to continue walking downstream. We set out at 1:30, and stopped at 5:00. By this time we were sure that the creek's direction was east-northeast, so that it could not be the Iquiri, unless it changed course. The path clearers reported they had not found water and continued seeing hilltops. We decided to continue forward, under the impression that we are heading toward the Río Grande. The hunting netted only a *cacaré*,[2] which, because of its small size, was given to the path clearers. We have a two-day supply of light rations.

The radio is reporting the arrest of Loro, wounded in the leg. His statements have been good up to now. Everything seems to indicate that he was not wounded at the house but somewhere else, possibly trying to escape.

Altitude = 980 meters.

---

2. A small bird of the area.

May 5

We walked for five hours all told, and progressed 12-14 kilometers, reaching a campsite made by Inti and Benigno. It seems we are at the Congrí Creek,[3] which is not on the map, and that we are much farther north than we thought. This raises a series of questions: Where is the Iquiri? Could this be the place where Benigno and Aniceto were attacked by surprise? And could their attackers have been Joaquín's people?

Our aim now is to head toward Bear Camp, where there should be breakfast left for two days, and from there go to the old camp. Today two big birds and a cacaré were killed, enabling us to save food, and we continue to have a two-day reserve, consisting of powdered soup packets and canned meat. Inti, Coco, and El Médico are hunting from a hidden position.

It was reported that Debray will be tried by a military court in Camiri as the alleged head or organizer of the guerrillas. His mother is arriving tomorrow and there is plenty of noise about the whole affair. Nothing about Loro.

Altitude = 840 meters.

May 6

The calculations about the arrival at Bear Camp were wrong, since the distance to the little house by the creek turned out to be greater than foreseen. In addition, the path was blocked off and it was necessary to clear it. We arrived at the little house at 4:30 p.m., having reached altitudes of 1,400 meters with the men walking half-heartedly. We ate our next-to-last meal, a very skimpy one. The only thing hunted was a partridge, which was given to the machete user (Benigno), and to the two people right behind him on the march.

The news reports center around the Debray case.

Altitude = 1,100 meters.

---

3. Named as such by the guerrillas for the amount of *congrí* (a Cuban dish of rice and beans) served there in March, as they returned from the exploratory journey.

May 7

We arrived at Bear Camp early in the day. Waiting for us there were eight cans of milk, from which we made a satisfying breakfast. We took a few things out of the nearby cave. Among these was a Mauser for Ñato, who will be our bazooka man, with five antitank shells. He is feeling poorly, after an attack of vomiting.

Right after arriving at the camp, Benigno, Urbano, León, Aniceto, and Pablo went to scout the little farm. We ate the last of the soup and meat, but we have a supply of lard that had been in the cave. Footprints were visible and there is some debris indicating that soldiers were here. At dawn the scouting party arrived empty-handed: the farm is occupied by soldiers and they have cut down the corn.

(Today marks six months since the official start of the guerrilla movement, from the time of my arrival.)

Altitude = 880 meters.

May 8

Early in the morning I insisted that the caves be put in order and that we bring down the other can of lard to refill the bottles, since it is all we have to eat.

At about 10:30 scattered shots were heard coming from the ambush site. Two unarmed soldiers had come up the Ñacahuasu. Pacho, thinking they were an advance column, wounded them both, one in the leg and the other in the stomach. He said he fired because they did not halt when instructed. They of course heard nothing. The ambush was poorly coordinated and Pacho's conduct was not good; he was very nervous. We strengthened the forces there by sending Antonio and a few others to the right side. The soldiers said their unit is stationed close to the Iquiri, but in fact they were lying.

At 12:00 noon, two other soldiers were captured running at full speed down the Ñacahuasu. The reason they were moving so rapidly, they stated, was because they had gone out to hunt, and when they returned along the Iquiri, they found that their company had disappeared, and they set out to find them. They too were lying. In fact, they were camped at the hunting plain, and snuck out to look for food at our farm, because the helicopter bringing their supplies had not arrived.

From the first two prisoners we captured sacks of roasted and raw corn, four cans of onions, plus sugar and coffee. This solved our food problems for the day, with the help of the lard, which we ate in large amounts. Some of the men got sick from this.

Later on, the sentry post reported that army reconnaissance patrols were repeatedly going back and forth up to the edge of the river. Everyone waited tensely until the soldiers arrived, 27 of them it appears. The soldiers had seen something strange, and advanced. They were commanded by Second Lieutenant Laredo. He himself was the one to open fire and was killed on the spot, along with two other recruits. Night had already fallen and our forces advanced, capturing 6 soldiers. The rest of them retreated.

The totals are 3 dead and 10 prisoners, 2 of them wounded. We captured 7 M-1s and 4 Mausers, personal gear, ammunition, and a little food, which we ate with the lard to mitigate our hunger. We slept there.

May 9

We arose at 4:00 a.m. (I did not sleep) and released the soldiers after giving them a speech. We took their shoes and exchanged clothing with them. The liars were sent back in their underwear. They headed toward the little farm, taking their wounded.

At 6:30 we completed our withdrawal toward the creek at Monkey Camp[4] along the path by the cave, where we stored the items we had captured. Our only remaining food is the lard. I felt faint and had to sleep for two hours to be able to

---

4. The site of the April 10 ambush; named for the number of monkeys in the area.

continue at a slow and halting pace. This was how the march went in general. At the first water hole we ate lard soup. The men are weak and there are a number of cases of swollen extremities.

At night the army issued a statement on the action. They named their dead and wounded but not their prisoners, and announced great battles with heavy losses on our side.

May 10

We continued our slow advance. When we arrived at the camp where Rubio's grave is located, we found charqui that had been left there, in bad condition, along with tallow. We gathered it all up. There were no signs that soldiers had been there. We crossed the Ñacahuazú, taking precautions, and began the journey toward Pirirenda. We walked through a ravine previously explored by Miguel, although the path has not been completed. We stopped at 5:00 p.m. and ate the piece of charqui and the tallow.

May 11

The forward detachment left first. I remained behind, listening to the news reports. In a little while Urbano came with word that Benigno had killed a peccary and was asking permission to build a fire and skin it. We decided to stay put and eat the animal while Benigno, Urbano, and Miguel continued clearing the trail to the lake. At 2:00 p.m. we started up the march again, camping for the night at 6:00 p.m. Miguel and the others went on ahead.

I must have a serious talk with Benigno and Urbano. The former ate a can of food the day of the battle and denied it, while the latter ate a piece of charqui at the camp where Rubio is buried.

The radio is announcing that Colonel Rocha, head of the Fourth Division, which operates in the region, is being replaced.

Altitude = 1,050 meters.

May 12

We walked slowly. Urbano and Benigno opened up the trail. At 3:00 p.m. we saw the lake about five kilometers away, and a little later we found an old trail. An hour later we came to a huge cornfield with calabash trees, but without water. We prepared roasted and salted jocos with lard and corn kernels; we also made toasted corn.

The scouting party brought back news that they had come across the house of Chicho, the same one as before, who is named as a good friend by Lt. Henry Laredo in his diary.[5] He was not at home, but his four farmhands were, along with a servant, whose husband came to look for her and was detained. We cooked a large pig with rice and fritters, plus calabash fruit. Pombo, Arturo, Willi, and Darío remained to guard the knapsacks. Unfortunately, we have not located the water outside the house.

We withdrew at 5:30, walking slowly. Almost everyone was sick. The owner of the house had not arrived and we left a note for him listing the damages and expenses. The farmhands and the servant were paid 10 pesos apiece for their work.

Altitude = 950 meters.

May 13

A day of belching, farting, vomiting, and diarrhea—a veritable organ concert. We remained absolutely immobilized, trying to digest the pig. We have two cans of water. I was quite sick until I vomited, and then felt better. At night we ate fried corn and roasted calabash, plus the remnants of yesterday's feast—those who were able to.

All the radio stations are emphatically reporting the news of a Cuban landing in Venezuela that was crushed. The Leoni government presented two of the captured men, with their

---

5. Lieutenant Laredo, the army commander killed in the battle of May 8, had left a diary. For an account of its contents, see page 373.

name and rank. I do not know them, but everything indicates something went wrong.[6]

May 14
We set out early, half-heartedly, for the Pirirenda lake. We followed a path that Benigno and Camba had found while scouting.

Before leaving I held a meeting with everyone, letting forth a "salvo" on the problems we have faced, primarily that of food. I criticized Benigno, for having eaten a can of food and denied it; Urbano, for having surreptitiously eaten a piece of charqui; and Aniceto, for his willingness to do anything related to food while being reluctant when it comes to doing anything else. In the midst of the meeting we heard the sound of approaching trucks. In a nearby hiding place, we stored about 50 jocos and two *quintales* [200 pounds] of kerneled corn for future use.

While we were away from the road picking beans, explosions could be heard nearby. Shortly afterward, we saw planes "ferociously bombing us"—two or three kilometers away from our positions. As the army continued making noise, we climbed a little hill and spotted the lake. At nightfall we approached a house recently abandoned by its occupants. It was well stocked and had water. We ate a delicious fricassee of chicken with rice, and remained there until 4:00 a.m.

May 15
An uneventful day.

May 16
As we began the hike I was overcome with intense abdominal pain, with vomiting and diarrhea. I was given demerol, which stopped it, but I lost consciousness and had to be car-

---

6. A landing by Venezuelan guerrillas assisted by several Cubans was crushed by government troops May 8. Raúl Leoni was president of Venezuela.

ried in my hammock. When I awoke I felt much relieved, but was covered in my own filth like a newborn infant. They loaned me a pair of pants, but without water my stench could be smelled a league away.

We spent the entire day there, while I nodded off. Coco and Ñato went scouting to find a path that leads due north. At night we followed it under moonlight and then rested. Message no. 36 was received, through which we can see our complete isolation.

May 17

We continued the march until 1:00 p.m., when we reached a sawmill bearing signs of having been abandoned about three days ago. In it were sugar, corn, lard, flour, and bottled water that appears to have been transported from far away. We remained camped here, while scouting parties were sent out along the paths leading from the camp to the woods. Raúl has an abscess on his knee that is intensely painful and prevents him from walking. He was administered a powerful antibiotic and will have to lance it tomorrow. We walked about 15 kilometers.

Altitude = 920 meters.

May 18

Roberto and Juan Martín.[7]

We spent the day in ambush, in case either the workers or the army came, but nothing happened. Miguel left with Pablito and found water two hours from the camp, along an intersecting road. Raúl's abscess was lanced, and 50 cc of pus was drained. He is being treated with a general antiseptic, and can barely walk a step. I did my first tooth extraction of this guerrilla war. The lucky victim: Camba; it went well. We ate bread baked in a small oven, and at night filled up on a delicious stew that left me bursting at the seams.

---

7. This refers to the birthday of two of his brothers.

May 19

The forward detachment left early, taking positions at the ambush site at the crossroads. We left afterward, replacing part of the forward detachment while they went back and brought Raúl to the crossing. The other part of the center group continued on to the pond to drop off their knapsacks, and then returned to get Raúl, who is slowly improving. Antonio scouted a short distance downstream and found an abandoned army camp, where there are remnants of dried rations. The Ñacahuasu must not be far, and I calculate that we should come out below the Congrí Creek. It rained all night, surprising the experts.

We have food for ten days, and there is calabash and corn in the immediate vicinity.

Altitude = 780 meters.

May 20

Camilo.[8]

A day without movement. In the morning the center group was placed on ambush, followed by the forward detachment in the afternoon. The whole time it was under the command of Pombo, who expressed the view that the position chosen by Miguel was very poor. Miguel scouted the creek downstream, reaching the Ñacahuasu after a two-hour hike without a knapsack. A gunshot was clearly heard, although it was not known who fired it. There are signs of another military camp along the banks of the Ñacahuasu, composed of a couple of squads. There was an incident with Luis. As a result of his grumbling he was punished by not being sent on the ambush. He appears to have reacted well.

At a press conference Barrientos rejected Debray's claim to journalist status, and announced he will request that congress reinstate the death penalty. Almost all the journalists, including all the foreigners, asked him about Debray. He defended

---

8. A reference to the birthday of his son, Camilo Guevara March.

himself with an incredible lack of intelligence. He is the most incompetent person one could ask for.

May 21

Sunday. A day without movement. The ambush remained in place, as the 10 men were rotated with another 10 at noon. Raúl is slowly getting better. A second lancing drained another 40 cc of pus. He no longer has a fever, but is in pain and can barely walk. He is my main concern at the moment. At night we ate extravagantly: stew, corn flour, shredded charqui, and calabash topped with mote.

May 22

As was to be expected, the attendant at the sawmill showed up, arriving in a broken-down jeep. His name is Guzmán Robles, and he was accompanied by one of his sons and the driver. At first they appeared to be an advance patrol of the army to investigate the scene, but he gradually opened up to us and eventually agreed to go to Gutiérrez at night, leaving his son as hostage. He should be returning tomorrow. The forward detachment remained on ambush all night. Tomorrow we will wait until 3:00 p.m. After that it will be necessary to withdraw since the situation will become increasingly dangerous.

The man gives the impression that he will not betray, but we do not know how capable he is of making the purchases without arousing suspicion. We paid him for all the items consumed at the mill. He reported on the situation in Tatarenda, Limón, and Ipitá. There are no soldiers in any of these places except for a lieutenant in Ipitá. What he told us about Tatarenda is secondhand, since he has not been there.

May 23

A day of tension. The attendant did not appear all day. Although nothing much was going on, we decided to pull out at night, taking the hostage, a big 17-year-old boy. We walked for an hour along the trail under the moonlight, and slept on the road. We left with a 10-day supply of food.

May 24
We reached the Ñacahuasu in two hours, and it was free of soldiers. After about four hours of hiking downstream, we came to the Congrí Creek. We are walking slowly, held back by the slow and half-hearted pace of Ricardo, who was joined in this today by Moro. We arrived at the camp that we used the first day of our first journey. We did not leave any tracks, and there were no signs of any recent ones. The radio is reporting that Debray's petition for a writ of habeas corpus has been denied. I estimate we are one or two hours away from the Saladillo. When we reach the top we will decide what to do.

May 25
We reached the Saladillo in an hour and a half, without leaving tracks. We then walked two hours upstream to the water's source, where we ate. At 3:30 p.m., we continued on, walking another couple of hours, and made camp at 6:00. We are at an altitude of 1,100 meters, and have still not reached the ridge at the top. According to the boy, this leaves us a couple of leagues from his grandfather's farm plot. Benigno says we are also a full day's hike from Varga's house overlooking the Río Grande. We will decide tomorrow where to go.

May 26
After a two-hour march, in which we passed the summit at an elevation of 1,200 meters, we reached the farm plot belonging to the boy's great uncle.[9] Two farmhands were working and had to be apprehended, since they were walking in our direction. They turned out to be brothers-in-law of the old man, who is married to a sister of theirs. Their ages are 16 and 20.

---

9. The man was incorrectly identified in the previous day's entry as his grandfather.

They reported that the father of the boy made the purchases but was arrested and confessed to everything. There are 30 soldiers in Ipitá patrolling the village. We ate fried pork with a stew made of calabash and lard, since there is no water in the area and it has to be brought in bottles from Ipitá. At night we headed out toward the boys' farm plot. It is eight kilometers away—four toward Ipitá and four toward the west. We arrived at dawn.

Altitude = 1,100 meters.

May 27

A day of idleness, along with a bit of despair. Of all the marvels promised, the farm plot contained only a little bit of old sugarcane, and the mill was useless. As was to be expected, the old man who owned it came at noon with a cart full of water for the pigs. On his way back, he saw something strange as he passed by the spot where the rear guard was hiding in ambush; they apprehended him together with a farmhand. They were held prisoner until 6:00 p.m., when we let them go, together with the younger of the brothers. We instructed them to remain there until Monday [May 29], and to say nothing.

We walked for two hours and slept in a cornfield. We are now headed along the road that will take us to Caraguatarenda.

May 28

Sunday. We rose early and began the march. In an hour and a half we reached the edge of the farms at Caraguatarenda. Benigno and Coco were sent to explore, but were seen by a peasant and apprehended him. In a little while we had a whole colony of prisoners. They did not show signs of any great fear until an old woman, when told to halt, began to scream, together with her children. Neither Pacho nor Pablo were especially eager to stop her, and she fled back to the village.

We occupied the village at 2:00 p.m., posting sentries on both sides. A little later a jeep owned by the YPFB fell into our hands. A total of two jeeps and two trucks were captured—half of them owned by individuals, half belonging to the oil company. We had something to eat, drank some coffee, and after four dozen arguments, we departed at 7:30 en route to Ipitacito. There we broke into a store and took 500 pesos' worth of merchandise. We left the money in the custody of two peasants, drawing up a very elaborate receipt.

We continued our pilgrimage, reaching Itay. There we were well received at a house that turned out to belong to the woman who owned the store at Ipitacito, and we went over the prices with her. I joined in and it appeared they knew who I was. They had some cheese and a little bread, and they gave these to us along with some coffee. There appeared to be a false note in their reception, however.

We continued on toward Espino, following the railroad tracks leading to Santa Cruz. However, the truck—a Ford with the front-wheel drive removed—stalled out, and it took us all morning to travel the three leagues to Espino. The vehicle finally broke down for good two leagues from the place. The forward detachment occupied the little settlement and the jeep made four trips to transport us all.

Altitude = 880 meters.

May 29

The settlement of El Espino is relatively new, since the old one was demolished by the flood of 1958. It is a Guaraní community whose members are very timid and who speak—or pretend to speak—very little Spanish. The oil company has people working nearby, so we inherited another truck, in which we were able to load everything. But the opportunity was wasted when Ricardo got it stuck and we were unable to pull it out. The place was utterly peaceful, as if it were in a separate world.

Coco was put in charge of finding out information about the roads. The information he brought back was inadequate and contradictory. As a result, we were about to embark on a somewhat dangerous journey that would have taken us close to the

Río Grande. At the last moment, however, there was a change of plans and we decided to go instead to Muchiri, a place where there is water. With all the organizational problems, we left at 3:30. The forward detachment (six—seven including Coco) went in the jeep while the rest went on foot.

The radio brought us news of Loro's escape, which occurred in Camiri.[10]

May 30
During the day we reached the railroad tracks and discovered that the road that was to have taken us to Muchiri does not exist. Searching around, we found a straight road 500 meters from the crossing, used by the oil company, and the forward detachment followed it in the jeep. As Antonio was leaving, a little boy with a shotgun and a dog came toward us along the tracks. When ordered to halt, he fled. In view of this, I left Antonio hidden in ambush at the entrance of the road, and we moved 500 meters back. At 11:45 a.m. Miguel appeared with the news that he had walked 12 kilometers east without finding any houses or water; only a road that headed north. I gave the order for him to take three men in the jeep to explore this road, going 10 kilometers north and returning before sunset.

At 3:00 p.m., while sleeping peacefully, I was woken up by gunfire coming from the ambush site. The news arrived quickly: the army had advanced and fallen into the trap. The toll appears to be three dead and one wounded. Those involved were Antonio, Arturo, Ñato, Luis, Willy, and Raúl—the latter of whom was weak.

We withdrew on foot and walked the 12 kilometers to the crossing, without running into Miguel. We learned that the jeep was sputtering because the radiator was dry. We found it three kilometers farther up the road. After we all urinated into

---

10. The news of Loro's escape was false; in fact he had been murdered by the army.

it and added a canteen of water, we were able to make it to the farthest point reached, where Julio and Pablo were waiting. At 2:00 a.m., with everyone gathered around a fire, we roasted three turkeys and fried the pork meat. We are keeping one animal so it can drink from the water holes, just in case.

We are descending: from 750 meters, we have now reached 650 meters.

May 31
The jeep continued along bravely with its urine and some canteen water. Two events occurred that changed the pace of things. First, the road heading north suddenly ended, causing Miguel to suspend the march. Second, one of the groups on security detained a peasant named Gregorio Vargas, who was riding his bicycle along a side road to set his traps, which is his trade. The man's attitude was not totally clear, but he gave us valuable information about water holes. One of them was behind us, and I sent a group to find water and to cook, taking him as guide.

As they approached the location, they spotted two army trucks and hastily set up an ambush. Two soldiers were apparently hit by our fire. After missing with a blank from his grenade launcher, Ñato fired a real one that blew up in his face. He was unhurt, but the barrel was destroyed.

We continued our withdrawal, without harassment from the air, and walked about 15 kilometers before finding the second water hole after dark. The jeep finally sounded its death rattle, due to a lack of gasoline and overheating. We spent the night eating.

The army issued a statement acknowledging their dead yesterday: one second lieutenant and one soldier, and attributing to us several deaths "that were seen." My aim for tomorrow is to cross the railway tracks and head toward the mountains.

Altitude = 620 meters.

SUMMARY OF THE MONTH

The negative point is the impossibility of making contact with Joaquín, despite our pilgrimage through the mountains. There are indications that he has moved north.

From the military point of view, there were three new battles, inflicting losses on the army without suffering any of our own. In addition, our forays into Pirirenda and Caragatarenda are indications of success. The dogs have been declared incompetent and have been withdrawn from circulation.

The most important characteristics are:

1. A total lack of contact with Manila, La Paz, and Joaquín, which reduces us to the 25 men who presently comprise the group.

2. A total lack of peasant recruitment, although they are gradually losing their fear of us and we are winning their admiration. This is a slow and patient task.

3. The party, through Kolle, offers its collaboration, apparently without reservations.

4. The clamor around the Debray case has given our movement more aggressiveness than ten victorious battles.

5. The morale and confidence of the guerrilla force, already powerful, continues to grow. Properly handled, this is a guarantee of success.

6. The army remains disorganized, and its technique has not improved substantially.

News of the month: the capture and escape of Loro, who should now be rejoining us or heading to La Paz to make contact.

The army issued a statement reporting the arrest of all the peasants who collaborated with us in the Masicuri region. Now comes a stage in which the peasants will feel terror from both sides, although of a different nature. Our triumph will serve as the qualitative change necessary for their leap in development.

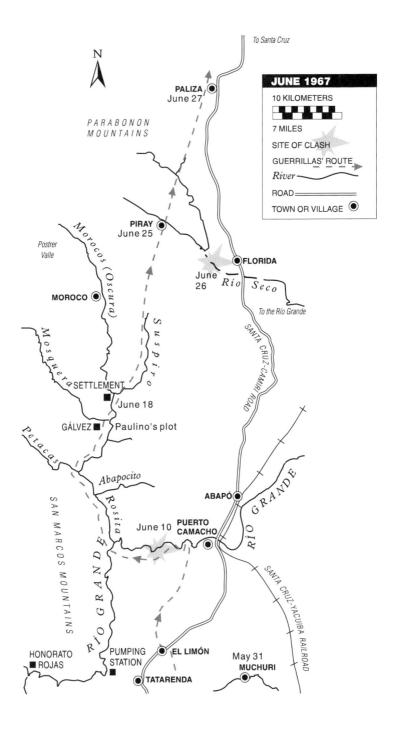

N

PARABONON MOUNTAINS

PALIZA
June 27

To Santa Cruz

JUNE 1967

10 KILOMETERS

7 MILES

SITE OF CLASH

GUERRILLAS' ROUTE

River

ROAD

TOWN OR VILLAGE

PIRAY
June 25

Postrer Valle

Morocos (Oscura)

MOROCO

Mosquera

Suspiro

FLORIDA

June 26

Río Seco

To the Río Grande

SANTA CRUZ–CAMIRI ROAD

SETTLEMENT
June 18

GÁLVEZ ■   Paulino's plot

Petacas

Abapocito

Rosita

ABAPÓ

June 10   **PUERTO CAMACHO**

RÍO GRANDE

SAN MARCOS MOUNTAINS

RÍO GRANDE

SANTA CRUZ–YACUIBA RAILROAD

HONORATO
ROJAS ■

PUMPING
STATION ■

EL LIMÓN

May 31
MUCHURI

TATARENDA

JUNE 1967

June 1

I sent the forward detachment to set up a lookout along the road and to scout the area up to the intersection of the road used by the oil company, about three kilometers away. Planes began to fly over the area. According to radio reports, the bad weather of previous days made it difficult for them to operate, and now the flights are to resume. A strange statement was issued concerning two dead and three wounded; it is unclear whether these are the old casualties or the new ones.

After eating at 5:00 p.m., we set out toward the railroad tracks. We traveled seven to eight kilometers without incident. After walking along the tracks for a kilometer and a half, we headed down an abandoned lane that should take us to a farm seven kilometers away. However, since everyone was tired, we slept halfway there. The only thing heard during the entire journey was a single shot far away.

Altitude = 800 meters.

June 2

Altitude = 800 meters.

We walked the seven kilometers foreseen by Gregorio and

reached the farm. There we caught and killed a healthy-looking pig. Just then a cattle herder named Braulio Robles appeared, together with his son and two farmhands, one of whom turned out to be a stepson of the owner, Symuní. We used his horses to transport the quartered pig three kilometers away, and we held the four men there. Meanwhile we kept Gregorio hidden from view, since his disappearance was known.

Just as the center group was arriving, an army truck passed by with two very young soldiers in it and some large bottles. It would have been an easy catch, but this was a day of gaiety and pork. We spent the night cooking, and at 3:30 a.m. we released the four peasants, paying them 10 pesos apiece for the day. Gregorio left at 4:30, after waiting for the food and his re-enlistment bonus, and receiving 100 pesos. The water in the creek is bitter.

June 3

We left at 6:30 along the left side of the creek, walking until noon. Then Benigno and Ricardo were sent to scout the road, finding a good place for an ambush. At 1:00 p.m. we took positions. Ricardo and I each headed a group positioned at the center; Pombo was placed on the far side; and Miguel, with the entire forward detachment, was stationed at the best spot. At 2:30 a truck drove by with pigs in it, and we let it pass. We did the same with a small truck carrying empty bottles that drove by at 4:20.

At 5:00 p.m. an army truck came by—the same one as yesterday—with two very young soldiers lying down in back wrapped in blankets. I did not have the heart to shoot them and did not think fast enough to apprehend them, and we let them pass. At 6:00 we lifted the ambush and continued down the road until we ran into the creek once again. Just as we were arriving, four trucks passed by in a row, followed by three more later on. There did not appear to be soldiers in them.

June 4

We continued walking along the side of the creek, with the aim of setting up another ambush if conditions were right. However, we came across a path leading west and followed it. Later it continued along a dry gully and turned south. At 2:45 p.m. we stopped at a little puddle of muddy water, to make coffee and oatmeal. It took so long, however, that we set up camp right there. At night a cold front from the south passed over the area, accompanied by a fine drizzle that lasted all night.

June 5

We abandoned the trail and continued cutting our way through underbrush, under the constant drizzle of the cold front. We walked until 5:00 p.m., spending two and a quarter hours, all told, chopping through the fierce tangle of undergrowth along the hill slopes. Fire became the great god of the journey. The day was a blank as far as food was concerned. We saved the brackish water in our canteens for tomorrow's breakfast.

Altitude = 250 meters.

June 6

After a meager breakfast, Miguel, Benigno, and Pablito left to clear a path and to scout. At about 2:00 p.m., Pablo returned with news that they had reached an abandoned farm with cattle in it. We all began the march, following the course of the creek. We crossed the farm and continued on until reaching the Río Grande. From there a scouting party was sent out, with instructions to capture a house if one was nearby and was set out of the way. This was done and the first reports indicated we were three kilometers from Puerto Camacho, where about 50 soldiers are stationed, and that it is connected by a road. We spent the entire night cooking pork and *locro*.[1] The day's journey did not yield the anticipated results, and we left past dawn, tired.

---

1. A dish made of meat, potatoes, rice, and root vegetables.

June 7

We walked at a leisurely pace, passing by old pastureland. Then the guide, one of the owner's sons, announced we had reached the last one. We followed along the sand embankment until encountering another farm, which the guide had not mentioned, with jocos, sugarcane, bananas, and a few beans, and we made camp there. The boy who is guiding us began to complain of sharp stomach pains; we do not know if they are genuine.

Altitude = 560 meters.

June 8

We moved the camp some 300 meters to free ourselves of the double responsibility of having to watch both the sand embankment and the farm. Later, however, we learned that the owner had not gone on foot, but instead always arrived by barge. Benigno, Pacho, Urbano, and León left to try to create a path that would cut across the cliffs, but they returned in the afternoon saying this was impossible. I had to issue another warning to Urbano on account of his insolence. We decided that tomorrow we will build a raft, close to the cliff.

News of the state of siege and the threat from the miners was broadcast, but it all comes to nothing.

June 9

We walked two hours until we reached the cliff. There Ñato began working on the raft with vigor. But it took too long and did not turn out well. It has still not been tested. I sent Miguel to find another way out, but he had no success. Benigno caught a large *dorado*.[2]

Altitude = 590 meters.

June 10

As was to be expected, the raft could not carry more than

---

2. A river fish in eastern Bolivia, similar to a porgy.

three knapsacks. The swimmers dived into the water but could not do anything because of the cold. I decided to send a team to the prisoner's house to look for a barge. Coco, Pacho, Aniceto, and Ñato accompanied him.

Shortly after this, mortar fire was heard. Ñato returned to report that they had clashed with the army, which was on the other side of the river. By all indications, our people did not take precautions as they walked, and were spotted. The soldiers began their usual noisemaking, and Pombo and Coco fired back without rhyme or reason, alerting them.

We decided to remain where we are, and to begin clearing a trail tomorrow to make our exit. If they decide to attack us in force, however, the situation will be a bit uncomfortable, since under the best of circumstances, we would have to make our way through arid and rocky terrain.

June 11
A day of utter calm. We remained in ambush, but the army did not advance. All they sent was a small plane that flew over the area for a couple of minutes. It is possible they are waiting for us at the Rosita. Work on the trail along the ridge is progressing, and it now almost reaches the top of the hill. We will leave tomorrow in any case. We have an ample supply of food for five to six days.

June 12
When we began the march it was felt we would be able to reach the Rosita, or at least the Río Grande once again. Upon arriving at a small water hole, however, we saw how difficult this would be, so we remained there awaiting news. At 3:00 p.m. word came of a larger water hole, but it was still not possible for us to descend, and we decided to remain here. The day began to come apart. On top of everything, a southern cold front blessed us with a wet and chilly night.

The radio is reporting some interesting information: the newspaper *Presencia* is announcing army casualties of one dead and one wounded from Saturday's clash. This is almost certainly true, and is very good since it continues the pattern of clashes with enemy dead. Another communiqué speaks of three dead on our side, among them Inti, one of the guerrilla leaders. It also announces the foreign composition of the guerrilla unit: 17 Cubans, 14 Brazilians, 4 Argentines, and 3 Peruvians. The number of Cubans and Peruvians corresponds to reality. It would be good to find out where they got the information.

Altitude = 900 meters.

June 13

We walked only an hour, making it to the next water hole, since the trail clearers did not reach either the Rosita or Río [Grande]. It is very cold. Possibly they will reach their destination tomorrow. We have five days of light rations remaining.

Of considerable interest is the political upheaval shaking the country, the fabulous quantity of pacts and counterpacts all over the place. Rarely has a guerrilla movement's catalyzing potential been seen so clearly.

Altitude = 840 meters.

June 14

Celita (4?)[3]

We spent the day at the icy water hole, around a fire, awaiting news from Miguel and Urbano, who were clearing the trail. The time set for moving out was 3:00 p.m., but Urbano arrived after that time with news that they had reached a creek where some fences could be seen. This led them to believe the creek might lead to the Río Grande. We remained where we were, eating up the last of the stew. All that is left is a single ration of peanuts, and three rations of mote.

I've reached my 39th birthday, and am inevitably approaching the age when my future as a guerrilla must be considered. For now, I'm still in one piece.

---

3. A reference to the birthday of his youngest daughter, Celia Guevara March.

Altitude = 840 meters.

June 15

It took us a little less than three hours to reach the banks of the Río Grande. We recognized the spot, which I estimate to be two hours from the Rosita. Nicolás, the peasant, says it is three kilometers away. He was given 150 pesos and the opportunity to leave, and he took off like a rocket. We are remaining where we are. Aniceto explored the area and believes the river can be crossed. We ate peanut soup and a few hearts of palm from the totaí tree, boiled and cooked in lard. All that is remaining is a three-day supply of mote.

Altitude = 610 meters.

June 16

One kilometer into the hike we spotted people from the forward detachment along the opposite side of the river. Pacho had crossed over to scout and found the ford. The icy water was waist-deep and had a fairly strong current, but we crossed without incident. An hour later we reached the Rosita, where there are a few old footprints, apparently made by the army. We found that the Rosita has more water in it than what we had foreseen, and there are no traces of the trail that is indicated on the map.

We walked for an hour in the icy water and decided to make camp, in order to take advantage of the totaí palm hearts and to try and find a beehive that Miguel had encountered on a previous scouting expedition. The beehive was not found, and all we ate was mote and hearts of palm with lard. There is food left for tomorrow and the day after (mote). We walked about three kilometers along the Rosita and another three along the Río Grande.

Altitude = 610 meters.

June 17

We walked about 15 kilometers along the Rosita in five and

a half hours. In the course of the trip we crossed four creeks, even though the map indicates only one, the Abapocito. There are abundant signs of recent passage through the area. Ricardo killed a *hochi*,[4] which, together with the mote, was our food for the day. We have mote for tomorrow, but we assume we will come across a house.

June 18

Many of us burned our bridges, eating up all the mote at breakfast. At 11:00 a.m., after walking two and a half hours, we ran into a farm plot with corn, yucca, sugarcane and a mill to grind it, jocos, and rice. We prepared a meal without protein, and sent Benigno and Pablito to scout. At 2:00 p.m. Pablo returned with news that they had run into a peasant whose plot of land is 500 meters from this one. Behind him came other peasants, who were apprehended when they arrived.

At night we changed our campsite, sleeping in the boys' farm plot, located right at the start of the road leading to Abapó seven leagues away. Their houses are 10 to 15 kilometers above the junction of the Mosquera and Oscura rivers, located on the latter.

Altitude = 680 meters.

June 19

We walked slowly for about 12 kilometers, until we reached the settlement. It is composed of three houses, with one family each. Two kilometers farther down, right at the junction of the Mosquera and Oscura rivers, lives a family named Gálvez. To speak with the inhabitants, you have to hunt them down, as they are like little animals. We were well received in general, although Calixto—who was appointed mayor by a military commission that passed through here a month ago—appeared reserved and was reluctant to sell us a few small things.

After it was dark, three pig merchants came by, carrying a

---

4. A rodent common to eastern Bolivia.

revolver and a Mauser. The sentry from the forward detachment let them pass. Then Inti interrogated them but did not take their weapons. Finally Antonio, who was keeping watch on them, did so very carelessly. Calixto assures us they are merchants from Postrer Valle and that he knows them.

Altitude = 680 meters.

There is another river called the Suspiro, which runs into the left side of the Rosita; no one lives along it.

June 20

During the morning, Paulino,[5] one of the boys from the farm plot downstream, informed us that the three individuals were not merchants. One of them was a lieutenant, and the other two were not in this line of work either. This information was obtained by Calixto's daughter, who is Paulino's girlfriend.

Inti went with a number of men and gave them until 9:00 a.m. for the officer to come out; otherwise they would all be shot. The officer came out immediately, in tears. He is a second lieutenant in the police, and was sent with a carabinero and the teacher at Postrer Valle, who came as a volunteer. They were sent by a colonel stationed in that village, with 60 men under him. Their mission included making a long trip, for which they were given four days; their journey was to include visiting other points along the Oscura. We considered killing them, but I later decided to send them back with a severe warning about the norms of warfare.

After an investigation of how they could have been let through, it was established that Aniceto abandoned his sentry post to call Julio, and it was during this time gap that they passed through. In addition, Aniceto and Luis were found asleep at their post. As punishment they were given seven days' kitchen duty, and one day without eating the roasted and fried pork and the stew that was served to excess.

---

5. Paulino Baigorria, who accompanied the guerrillas and volunteered to be their messenger.

The prisoners will be stripped of all their belongings.

June 21

The old lady.[6]

After two days of profuse dental extractions, in which I gained fame as Fernando the Toothpuller,[7] I closed my consulting office and we left in the afternoon, walking a little more than an hour. For the first time in this war, I left riding a mule. The three prisoners were taken an hour down the road by the Mosquera and stripped of all their belongings, including watches and sandals. We intended to take Calixto the mayor as a guide along with Paulino, but he was sick, or pretended to be, and we left him with a serious warning that will probably be of no avail.

Paulino has agreed to go to Cochabamba with my message. He will be given a letter for Inti's wife, a coded message for Manila, and the four communiqués. The fourth one explains the composition of our guerrilla force and clears up the lie about Inti's death.[8] It is document no. [*blank in original*]. We shall see if we can now establish contact with the city. Paulino pretended to come along as our prisoner.

Altitude = 750 meters.

June 22

We walked about three hours, all told, leaving behind the Oscura or Morocos river and reaching a water hole in the area called Pasiones. We consulted the map and everything indicates we are no more than six leagues from Florida, or from Piray, the nearest place where there are houses. Although his brother-in-law lives there, Paulino does not know the way. We considered continuing ahead by moonlight, but it was not

6. A reference to the birthday of his mother, Celia de la Serna.
7. Known previously as Ramón, Guevara had changed his pseudonym to Fernando on April 22. The change, suggested by Rolando, was made after it was learned that the army knew the guerrillas were led by "Ramón."
8. For the text, see page 311.

worth the effort given the distance.

Altitude = 950 meters.

June 23

We made only an hour's worth of progress, since we lost the trail and wasted all morning and part of the afternoon looking for it, and later spent the rest of the time clearing it for tomorrow. San Juan Eve was not as chilly as legend would have one believe.[9]

Altitude = 1,050 meters.

My asthma threatens to become much worse, and there is very little medication in reserve.

June 24

We walked about 12 kilometers, four hours' worth of progress. There were stretches where the trail was good and was visible; at others, one could only guess at it. We climbed down an unbelievable cliff, following the tracks of some cattlemen driving their herd. We made camp by a trickle of water on the slopes of Durán hill. The radio is reporting news of the battle in the mines.[10]

Altitude = 1,200 meters.

June 25

We followed the trail created by the cattlemen without catching up to them. At midmorning we came to a burning pasture and a plane flew over the area. We remained unclear about the relationship between these two events, but continued ahead. At 4:00 p.m. we reached the Piray, where Paulino's sister lives. There are three houses here. One of them was

---

9. San Juan Eve, a holiday celebrated in the region, is traditionally considered the coldest night of the year.

10. On the night of June 23-24, in the midst of an upsurge of struggle by Bolivia's tin miners, the army opened fire on miners' housing at the Siglo XX mines. The initial reports were 16 dead and 71 wounded, with the number of dead rising to 20.

abandoned; at the second, no one was home; at the third, there was the sister with four children. The husband was not there; he had gone to Florida together with Paniagua, who lives in the other house. Everything seemed normal. One kilometer away was the house of a daughter of Paniagua, which was the place chosen for our campsite. A calf was purchased and immediately slaughtered. Coco was sent to Florida to make some purchases, together with Julio, Camba, and León. However, they found that the army is there: about 50 men, with more expected, which will raise the total to 120-130. The owner of the house is an old man named Fenelón Coca.

Argentine radio is reporting 87 victims at the Siglo XX mines. The Bolivian stations are silent about the number. My asthma continues to get worse, and will now not let me sleep well.

Altitude = 780 meters.

June 26

A black day for me. Everything seemed to be going peacefully as I sent five men to relieve those stationed on ambush at the Florida road. Suddenly shots were heard. We left rapidly on horseback and came across a strange spectacle: amid total silence, the bodies of four little soldiers were lying in the sun, on the sand by the river. We were unable to take their weapons since we did not know the enemy's position.

It was 5:00 p.m., and we were waiting for nightfall to recover the weapons. Miguel then sent word that the sound of cracking branches could be heard to his left. Antonio and Pacho went there, but I gave the order not to fire unless they could see something. Almost immediately gunfire broke out, which became generalized on both sides. I gave the order to withdraw, since we were at a disadvantage under these circumstances. The withdrawal was delayed and we received word of two wounded: Pombo in the leg and Tuma in the stomach.

We brought them rapidly to the house so we could operate

on them with what we had. Pombo's wound is superficial, and will merely result in headaches for us due to his lack of mobility. Tuma's wound had destroyed his liver and he had suffered intestinal perforations. He died during the operation. With his death I have lost an inseparable comrade and companion over all the recent years. His loyalty was unwavering, and I feel his absence almost as if he were my own son. After he fell he asked that I be given his watch, and since they did not do so while he was being treated, he took it off and gave it to Arturo. Behind this gesture was the desire that it be given to the son whom he did not know, as I had done with the watches of many comrades who had died in the past. I shall carry it throughout the entire war. We loaded the body onto an animal and will bury it far from here.

Two new spies were taken prisoner: a lieutenant in the carabineros and a carabinero. They were given a lecture and set free in their underwear, due to a misinterpretation of my order that they be stripped of anything of value. We left with nine horses.

June 27

After carrying out the painful task of burying Tuma in a poorly made grave, we continued our trip, arriving during the day at Tejería, properly speaking. At 2:00 p.m. the forward detachment set out on a 15-kilometer trip, and we followed at 2:30. The trip took a long time for those at the back, since nightfall fell upon them and they had to wait for the moonlight. They arrived at 2:30 a.m. at the house in Paliza where the guides were from.

Altitude = 850 meters.

We returned two animals to the owner of the house in Tejería, who is the nephew of the old lady Paniagua, so that they could be returned to her.

June 28

We obtained a guide who for 40 pesos offered to take us as

far as the road leading to Don Lucas's house. However, we stayed at a house that came before it, which had a water hole. We left late, but the last ones, Moro and Ricardo, dallied forever, and I heard no word from them. We averaged a kilometer an hour.

According to broadcasts, the army, or a radio station on its own, is speaking about three dead and two wounded in an encounter with guerrillas in the Mosquera region. This has to be a reference to our battle. But we saw, with virtual certainty, four bodies—unless one of them was able to perfectly simulate being dead.

There is no one home at the house of someone named Zea, although there are a number of cows whose calves are fenced in.

Altitude = 1,150 meters.

June 29

I had harsh words with Moro and Ricardo because of the delay, especially with Ricardo. Coco and Darío from the forward detachment, plus Moro, left with the horses, loaded with knapsacks. Ñato took his own, since he is in charge of all the animals. In addition, Pombo's and mine were put on a mule. Pombo was able to make the trip with relative ease, riding on a mare. We put him up at the house of Don Lucas, who lives on the summit at an altitude of 1,800 meters. He has two daughters with him, one of whom has a goiter. There are two other houses: one belongs to a seasonal worker and has almost nothing inside, while the other is well stocked.

The night was cold and rainy. According to reports, Barchelón is a half-day walk, although peasants who traveled the path say it is very bad. The owner of the house disagrees, assuring us it can be easily cleared. Some peasants came to see the person from the other house, and were detained as being suspicious.

Along the way I had a discussion with the troops, now consisting of 24 men. I added Chino to the list of the exemplary. I explained the significance of our losses, and spoke of the personal loss that Tuma's death meant for me, as I considered him almost like a son. I criticized the lack of self-discipline and the slowness of the march. In addition, I promised to present some additional thoughts so that future ambushes do not see a repeat of what happened here: a needless loss of life due to failure to abide by norms.

June 30

The old man Lucas gave us some information about his neighbors, from which we gather that the army has already begun its preparations for this area. One of them, Andulfo Díaz, is the general secretary of the peasants union of the area—a "union" that supports Barrientos. Another is an old chatterbox who was let go because he is paralytic. Another one is a coward who might talk, according to his colleagues, to avoid complications. The old man promised to accompany us and to help us clear the path to Barchelón; the two peasants will follow. We spent the day resting, since the weather was rainy and inclement.

On the political level, the most important development is Ovando's official declaration that I am here. In addition, he stated that the army is confronting perfectly trained guerrillas, including Viet Cong commanders who have defeated the best U.S. regiments. Ovando's declaration is based on the statements made by Debray. It appears the latter said more than was necessary, although we cannot know the implications this may have, nor the circumstances in which he said what he did. It is also rumored that Loro was murdered. They have charged that I am the mastermind of the planned insurrection in the mines, coordinating it with the uprising at Ñacahuasú. Things are starting to look pretty. Soon I will cease being Fernando the Toothpuller.

A message from Cuba was received explaining the low level of development in organizing the guerrilla movement in Peru. There are hardly any weapons or men, but a ton of money has been spent. The message also speaks of the organization of a supposed guerrilla front involving Paz Estenssoro, a Colonel Seoane, and a certain Rubén Julio, a wealthy fat cat belonging to the [Revolutionary National] Movement from the Pando region. The front would be in Guayamerín.[11] The document is number [*Illegible in original*].

ANALYSIS OF THE MONTH

The negative points are the impossibility of making contact with Joaquín and the gradual loss of men, with each loss constituting a serious defeat, although the army does not know it. We had two small battles during the month, causing the army four dead and three wounded, according to their own information.

The most important characteristics are:

1. The total lack of contact continues. This reduces us now to the 24 men on hand, with Pombo wounded and mobility reduced.

2. The lack of peasant recruitment continues to be felt. It is a vicious circle: to achieve this recruitment we need to carry out ongoing action in populated territory, and for this we need more men.

3. The legend of the guerrilla grows like wildfire. We are now invincible supermen.

4. The lack of contact extends to the party, although we have made an attempt through Paulino that might bear fruit.

5. Debray continues to be in the news, although it is now

---

11. Víctor Paz Estenssoro was former president of Bolivia, ousted by Barrientos in a 1964 military coup. The Revolutionary National Movement (MNR), the major political party following the 1952 revolution, had split into several wings in the early 1960s. Rubén Julio Castro was the major landowner in the Pando region and most of Beni.

linked with my presence as leader of this movement. We shall see what this step by the government will result in, and whether it will be positive or negative for us.

6. The guerrillas' morale continues to be firm, and their resolve to fight is growing. All the Cubans are exemplary in battle, and only two or three Bolivians are weak.

7. The army's military tactics are nil, although they are undertaking work among the peasants that we must not ignore, since it is transforming all the members of the community into informers, either through fear or deception about our aims.

8. The massacre in the mines greatly clarifies the general picture for us. If our proclamation can be disseminated, it will play a great part in clarifying things.[12]

Our most urgent task is to reestablish contact with La Paz, resupply ourselves with military and medical supplies, and incorporate 50-100 men from the city—although the actual number of combatants from this group would be reduced in practice to 10-25.

---

12. The text of Communiqué no. 5, "To the Miners of Bolivia," can be found on pages 312-14.

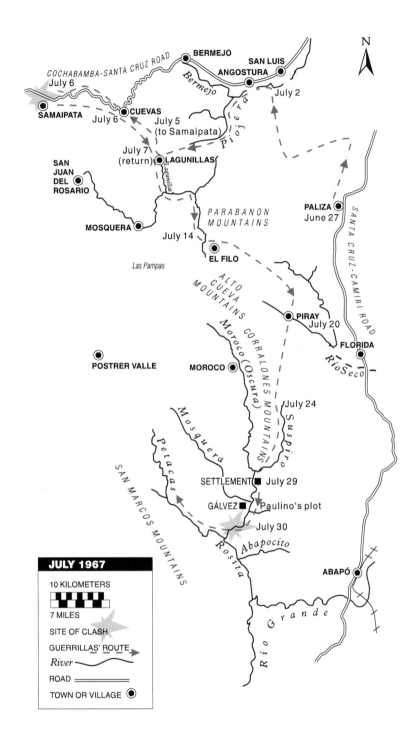

JULY 1967

July 1

Although the weather had not completely cleared up, we set out in the direction of Barchelón—Barcelona on the map. The old man Lucas gave us a hand in fixing up the path, but despite everything it remained quite jagged and slippery. The forward detachment left in the morning and we followed at noon, spending all afternoon climbing up and down the ravine. We had to stop for the night at the first farm plot we came to, separated from the forward detachment, which continued on ahead. There were three extremely timid children there with the last name Yépez.

Barrientos held a press conference where he acknowledged my presence but predicted I would be wiped out in a few days. He spoke his usual string of nonsense, calling us rats and snakes, and repeated his intention of passing sentence on Debray.

Altitude = 1,550 meters.

We detained a peasant named Andrés Coca, whom we ran into along the trail. We also took the other two with us, Roque and his son Pedro.

July 2

In the morning we met up with the forward detachment, which had camped at the crest of the hill, at the house of Don Nicomedes Arteaga. An orange grove is there, and they sold us cigarettes. The main house is down below, by the Piojera river. We went there and ate lavishly.

The Piojera river runs entirely through steep canyon, and it is only through the river that one can follow its course on foot toward Angostura. The way out is toward the Junction, another point along the same river; however one must cross over a rather steep hill to get there. The Junction is important because it is the point where two paths cross.

The spot we are at is only 950 meters in altitude, and the weather is much milder. Here the ticks are replaced by gnats. The settlement is composed of Arteaga's house and the houses of a number of his children. They have a little coffee plantation, where people from various areas nearby come to sharecrop. It now has about six farmhands from the San Juan region.

Pombo's leg is not progressing with sufficient speed, probably due to the endless trips on horseback. There are no complications, however, and at this point none are feared.

July 3

We remained here all day, trying to give Pombo's leg more time to rest. Our purchases are being made at high prices, and thus the peasants' fear is mixed with self-interest, so they are obtaining things for us. I took some photographs, which earned me the attention of all. The three problems now are developing the pictures, enlarging them, and getting them here.

A plane passed overhead during the afternoon. In the evening someone mentioned the danger of nighttime bombings, which sent everyone scattering into the night. After stopping them, we explained there was no danger.

My asthma continues to act up.

July 4

Moving slowly, we walked two leagues to the Junction, arriving at 3:30 p.m. A peasant named Manuel Carrillo lives there, and our presence left him terrified and panic-stricken. We ate extravagantly, as has become our custom in recent days, and we slept in an abandoned shack. My asthma is punishing me with a fury, and for the first time it is preventing me from sleeping.

Altitude = 1,000 meters.

Two days ago, seven soldiers passed through, coming from El Filo and en route to Bermejo.

July 5

The entire region—families with their belongings—is fleeing to escape the army's reprisals. Along the route we mingled with oxen, pigs, chickens, and people until we reached Lagunillas.[1] There we paid leave to the Piojera river and took its tributary, the Lagunillas, for one kilometer. Our guide was a very unhappy peasant named Ramón, whose family has the proverbial fear that is common to this region. We slept on the side of the road. Along the way we passed an uncle of Sandoval Morón; the uncle lives in San Luis and seems to be much more alert.

Altitude = 1,160 meters.

July 6

We set out early in the direction of Peña Colorada, crossing an inhabited area that greeted us with terror. At dusk we reached the Alto de Palermo, a peak 1,600 meters high. We began our descent toward a spot where there is a small grocery, at which we purchased some things we might need. It was past dark when we came to the highway, where there was only one little house

---

1. A reference to the area by the Lagunillas river in Florida province; not to be confused with the town of Lagunillas to the south, close to the guerrillas' base camp.

belonging to an old widow. The forward detachment did not do very well in capturing it, owing to indecision.

The plan was to capture a vehicle coming from Samaipata, investigate the situation prevailing in town, and head there with the driver of the vehicle. Then we would capture the DIC[2] office, purchase items in the pharmacy, raid the hospital, buy some canned food and sweets, and return. The plan was changed because no vehicles were coming from Samaipata, and it was learned that vehicles heading there were not being stopped; in other words, the barrier had been raised.

Those assigned to the action were Ricardo, Coco, Pacho, Aniceto, Julio, and Chino. They stopped a truck coming from Santa Cruz without any trouble, but behind it was another one, which stopped to offer assistance and had to be detained as well. Then a give-and-take began with a woman traveling in the truck who did not want her daughter to get out. A third truck stopped to see what was going on, and with the road now blocked off, a fourth one had to stop, owing to the men's indecision. Things were straightened out and the four vehicles remained parked on one side. One of the drivers, when asked, spoke of taking a rest stop.

Our people set out in a truck and arrived in Samaipata. There they captured two carabineros, followed by Lieutenant Vacaflor, the head of the post. Then they made him give the password to the sergeant, and in a lightning action they captured the post, with 10 soldiers in it. There was a brief exchange of fire with one soldier who resisted. They were able to capture five Mausers and one BZ-30. The 10 prisoners were put in the truck and driven one kilometer outside of Samaipata, where they were left, stripped of their clothes.

In terms of supplies, the action was a failure. Chino let himself be influenced by Pacho and Julio, and did not purchase anything of value. With regard to medicine, he bought none of the things I need, although he did get the most indispensable

---

2. Department of Criminal Investigations—the police force.

things for the guerrilla unit.

The action was carried out in front of the entire population and a multitude of travelers, so word of it will spread like wildfire.[3] By 2:00 a.m. we were already on our way back with the captured goods.

July 7

We walked without a rest until reaching a canefield, where there was a man who had received us well the previous time; it is one league from Ramón's house. The people continue to be gripped by fear. The man sold us a pig and was amiable, but warned us there were 200 men in Los Ajos and that his brother had just come from San Juan, where there were 100 soldiers. I wanted to pull some teeth, but he preferred not to have it done. My asthma is getting worse.

July 8

We walked with caution from the house by the canefield to the Piojera river. The coast was clear, however, and there were not even rumors of soldiers. The people coming from San Juan deny that soldiers have been there. It seems this was a trick by the man to get us to leave. We walked along the river for about two leagues until coming to the Piray, and from there we traveled one league to the cave, arriving at dusk. We are close to El Filo.

I gave myself several injections so I could continue, finally using an adrenaline solution, at 1:900, prepared as an eyewash. If Paulino's mission is not successful, we will have to return to the Ñacahuaso to look for medicine for my asthma.

The army released a statement on the action, acknowledging one dead, which must have occurred in the exchange of fire. Ricardo, Coco, and Pacho were the ones who captured the little garrison.

---

3. The guerrillas' brief occupation of Samaipata (pop. 1,700), the capital of Florida province, caused a sensation internationally.

July 9

In setting out, we lost the trail and spent the morning looking for it. At midday we followed a path that was not very
clear, which took us to the highest altitude we have yet
reached—1,840 meters. Shortly afterward we reached a shack,
where we spent the night. We are uncertain about the path to
El Filo.

The radio is announcing a 14-point agreement between the
workers at the Catavi and Siglo XX mines and the Comibol Enterprise, amounting to a total defeat of the workers.

July 10

We left late because a horse was missing, which turned up
later. We passed our highest altitude, 1,900 meters, along a sel-
dom-used path. At 3:30 p.m. we reached a shack, where we
decided to spend the night. However, the unpleasant surprise
was that the paths ended. Men were sent out to explore some
old, long-unused trails, but these led nowhere. Ahead of us
some farms are visible, which might be El Filo.

The radio reported a clash with guerrillas in the El Dorado
region, which does not figure on the map and is between
Samaipata and the Río Grande. It admits to one wounded
while claiming two dead on our part.

On another matter, the statements by Debray and Pelado are
not good. Above all they have made a confession concerning
the continental aims of the guerrilla struggle, something they
did not have to do.

July 11

The day was rainy, with an intense fog. As we were making
our way back, we lost all the trails. In so doing we became
completely separated from the forward detachment, which
descended the hill after reopening an old trail. We slaughtered
a calf.

The guerrillas on the march.

July 12

We spent the entire day awaiting news from Miguel. However, it was not until dusk that Julio arrived with word that they had gone down into a creek running south. We remain at the same spot. I have been having regular asthma attacks.

The radio is now reporting other news that appears to be true in its most important part. It speaks of a battle at the Iquira, with one dead on our part, and says that the corpse was brought to Lagunillas. The euphoria about the corpse indicates there is an element of truth in the report.[4]

July 13

In the morning we climbed down a steep hill that was slippery due to the poor weather, and met up with Miguel at 11:30. He had sent Camba and Pacho to explore a trail that branched off from the one along the creek. They returned an hour later, reporting they had spotted farms and houses, and had been inside an abandoned one. We headed there and later, following the course of a stream, arrived at the first house, where we stopped for the night. The owner of the house arrived later and told us that a woman, the mother of the mayor, had seen us and must have already informed the soldiers at the settlement of El Filo a league away. A watch was kept all night.

July 14

There was a steady drizzle all night, which continued throughout the entire day. Nevertheless, we left at 12:00 noon, bringing along two people as guides. These were Pablo, the brother-in-law of the mayor, and Aurelio Mancilla, the man from the first house. The women remained behind crying.

We reached a fork in the road, with one path leading to Florida and Moroco and the other to Pampa. The guides proposed following the one to Pampa, where it is possible to take

---

4. Serapio, a member of Joaquín's column, was killed in combat July 9.

a newly created trail to the Mosquera. This was agreed to, but after walking about 500 meters, a young soldier and a peasant appeared carrying a load of corn flour on a horse. They also brought a message for the second lieutenant in El Filo from his colleague in Pampa, where there are 30 soldiers. We decided to change course, and set out on the path to Florida, making camp shortly afterward.

The PRA and the PSB have withdrawn from the Revolutionary Front, and the peasants are warning Barrientos about an alliance with the Falange.[5] The government is disintegrating rapidly. It is a pity we do not have 100 more men at this moment.

July 15
We walked very little owing to the poor condition of the path, which has been abandoned for many years. On the advice of Aurelio, we killed a cow belonging to the mayor and ate a lavish meal. My asthma has abated somewhat.

Barrientos has announced Operation Cynthia, to wipe us out in a few hours.

July 16
We began the march very slowly due to the strenuous job of clearing the trail. The animals suffered greatly due to the path's poor condition. However, we reached the end of the day's march without serious incident, at a deep canyon, where it is impossible to continue with the horses loaded down. Miguel and four men from the forward detachment continued ahead and slept apart from us.

There was no news of any importance on the radio. We passed an altitude of 1,600 meters close to Durán hill, which we passed by on our left.

---

5. A reference to the Authentic Revolutionary Party (PRA) and the Bolivian Socialist Falange (FSB). The Revolutionary Front was the progovernment coalition.

July 17

We continued walking slowly, owing to stretches of the trail that had disappeared. We had hoped to reach an orange grove that the guide had mentioned, but on getting there we found that the trees were bare. There is a pond that we used for setting up camp. We did not make more than three hours' progress, all told, during the march. My asthma is much better. It appears we will wind up on the path we used before to reach Piray. We are beside Durán hill.

Altitude = 1,560 meters.

July 18

Shortly after we set out, the guide lost the trail and claimed he was unfamiliar with the rest of it. Finally, an old path was found. While it was being cleared, Miguel followed it ahead, cutting through underbrush, and arrived at the intersection of the road to the Piray.

Upon reaching a little creek where we made camp, the three peasants and the young soldier were released after being given a lecture. Coco left with Pablito and Pacho to investigate whether Paulino left anything in the hollow. If all calculations are correct, they should return tomorrow night. The soldier says he is going to desert.

Altitude = 1,300 meters.

July 19

We made the short trip to the old camp and remained there, under reinforced guard, waiting for Coco. He arrived after 6:00 p.m., announcing that things remain as they were: the rifle is in its place and there are no signs of Paulino. On the other hand, there are many signs that soldiers have passed through, and they have also left tracks on the part of the road we are on.

The political news is of a tremendous crisis whose outcome cannot be foreseen. For the moment, the agricultural unions of Cochabamba have formed a political party "under Christian inspiration," which supports Barrientos. The latter asks "to be allowed to govern for four years." He is almost pleading. Siles Salinas threatens the opposition that our rise to power would cost everyone their heads. He is calling for national unity, declaring the country to be in a state of war. He seems to be pleading on the one hand, while appearing as a demagogue on the other. Perhaps a replacement of leaders is being prepared.

July 20

We walked with caution until we reached the first two little houses, where we found one of Paniagua's sons and the son-in-law of Paulino.[6] Of the latter's fate they knew nothing, except that the army was looking for him for having been our guide. The tracks belong to a group of 100 men that passed through here a week after we did and then continued on to Florida. It seems the army suffered three dead and two wounded in the ambush.[7] Coco was sent to scout Florida, along with Camba, León, and Julio, and to purchase whatever could be found there. They returned at 4:00 with some provisions and a person named Melgar, the owner of two of our horses, who offered to help us any way he could. He gave us some detailed—although somewhat exaggerated—information, from which the following can be extracted:

Four days after our departure, Tuma's body was discovered, eaten by animals. The army did not advance until the day after the battle, when the lieutenant without clothes turned up. The action at Samaipata was known about in minute detail, with a few things added, and is the subject of jokes and ridicule among the peasants. Tuma's pipe and some scattered belongings were found. A major named Soperna appears to be halfway sympathetic or an admirer of ours. The army arrived at Coca's house, where Tuma died, and from there went to Teje-

6. Actually his brother-in-law.
7. A reference to the battle on June 26.

ría before returning to Florida.

Coco considered using the man to carry a letter, but I thought it more prudent to first test him by sending him to purchase some medicines. Melgar told us about a group [of guerrillas] that was heading in this direction, with a woman among them. He learned this through a letter written by the mayor of Río Grande to the one here. Since the latter lives on the road to Florida, we sent Inti, Coco, and Julio to speak with him. He denied having any news of the other group, but confirmed in general the statements made by Melgar.

We spent a miserable night because of the rain. The radio is identifying the dead guerrilla as Moisés Guevara. At a press conference, however, Ovando was very cautious about this, putting the responsibility for the identification on the Ministry of the Interior. It is still possible that the supposed identification is a total farce or an invention.[8]

Altitude = 680 meters.

July 21

We spent a calm day. The old man Coca was spoken to about the cow he sold us that did not belong to him. He later said that he had not been paid, and emphatically denied the fact. We insisted that he pay for it.

At night we went to Tejería, where we purchased a large pig and *chankaka*.[9] Inti, Benigno, and Aniceto were the ones who went; they were received very well by the people there.

July 22

We left early, carrying a heavy load on our shoulders and atop the animals. Our aim was to throw everyone off our scent. We left the path leading to Moroco and took the one by the lagoon, one or two kilometers to the south. Unfortunately, we did not know the rest of the way and had to send out

---

8. The guerrilla killed was Serapio, not Moisés Guevara.
9. Brown sugar and water cooked in a pan.

scouts. In the meantime, Mancilla and the Paniagua boy appeared along the lagoon, herding cattle. They were warned not to say anything, but now things have changed. We walked a couple of hours and slept at the edge of a creek that has a trail leading southeast along its course. There are also other trails, less marked, heading south.

The radio is reporting that the wife of Bustos (Pelao) is confirming that he saw me here. However, she says he came with other aims.

Altitude = 640 meters.

July 23

We remained at the campsite while scouting was done along the two possible routes. One of these leads to the Río Seco, at a point beyond where it receives water from the Piray and before it is absorbed by the sand. In other words, this is between the site of the ambush we set and Florida. The other path leads to a shack, about two or three hours away. According to Miguel, who did the scouting, from there it is possible to reach the Rosita. Tomorrow we will take this path, which could be the one mentioned by Melgar in one of the stories he told Coco and Julio.

July 24

We walked about three hours along the explored trail, which took us over heights of 1,000 meters. We camped at 940 meters, at the bank of a creek. Here the paths end, and the entire day tomorrow will have to be spent searching for the best way out. There are a number of farm plots under cultivation here, indicating its relationship to Florida; it might be the place called Canalones.

We are trying to decipher a long message from Manila. Raúl [Castro] spoke at a graduation ceremony for officers from the Máximo Gómez School. Among other things, he refuted the attacks by the Czechs on my article about the many Vietnams. The friends are calling me a new Bakunin, and are lamenting the blood that has been shed and that would be shed in the event of three or four Vietnams.[10]

July 25

We spent the day resting, sending three pairs of scouts to explore different areas. Coco, Benigno, and Miguel were the ones in charge. Coco and Benigno both came out at the same place, and from there one can take the path to Moroco. Miguel reported that the creek definitely leads into the Rosita and that it is possible to follow it along, although a path will have to be cleared with machetes.

Two actions have been reported, one in Taperas and the other in San Juan del Potrero. These could not have been conducted by the same group, which raises a question as to the actual existence of the events or the truthfulness of the reports.[11]

July 26

Benigno, Camba, and Urbano were assigned to create a path along the creek, avoiding Moroco. The rest of the personnel stayed in camp, and the center group set up an ambush in the rear. Nothing happened.

Accounts of the action in San Juan del Potrero were reported over foreign radio in minute detail: 15 soldiers and a colonel were captured, stripped of belongings, and freed—our technique. This place is on the other side of the Cochabamba-to-

---

10. In Guevara's "Message to the Tricontinental," written in Cuba before leaving for Bolivia at the end of 1966, he had called for coming to the aid of the Vietnamese people by creating "two, three, many Vietnams," and extending the number of fronts in the worldwide struggle against imperialism. Mikhail Bakunin was a 19th-century anarchist who opposed the course charted by Karl Marx and Frederick Engels, founders of the modern communist movement. Bakunin fought bitterly against those who advocated that a conscious international working class should aim to take political power and establish revolutionary workers and farmers governments to help lead the transformation of economic and social relations.

11. The army had clashed with Joaquín's column at Taperas on July 21; the other report was false.

In the years prior to and following the guerrilla struggle led by Guevara in 1966-67, Bolivia was the scene of mounting political battles by workers, peasants, and youth demanding better wages and working conditions, land, and an end to U.S. imperialist domination.

Above, March 1959 demonstration in front of Bolivia's presidential palace in La Paz, two months after the triumph of the Cuban revolution. The action was part of a wave of protests against U.S. imperialist domination, including a strike by 24,000 tin miners. It was touched off by an article in the Latin American edition of *Time* magazine that quoted a United States embassy official in La Paz saying, "We're wasting money [here]. The only solution to Bolivia's problems is to abolish Bolivia. Let her neighbors divide up the country and its problems." (AP/Wide World)

Oruro, Bolivia, October 28, 1964.

Top, miners carrying dynamite protest killings of student demonstrators by police the day before. *Bottom,* secondary school students assemble at barricades. Similar protests took place in Cochabamba and La Paz. One week later, Gen. René Barrientos seized power from President Víctor Paz Estenssoro in a military coup. (Photos: AP/Wide World)

Top, tin miners demonstrate in La Paz, December 1963, demanding release of two arrested union leaders at the Siglo XX mines. The portrait is of Juan Lechín, leader of the Central Organization of Bolivian Workers (COB).

Bottom, armed miner and family, May 1965, near Milluni mine north of La Paz. Hundreds were killed when Barrientos ordered troops to occupy the mines in an effort to break the miners union. Workers militias resisted government troops. (Photos: AP/Wide World)

Above, Guevara's Uruguayan passport photo used to enter Bolivia, identifying him as an official of the Organization of American States.

Top, with Tuma (at left) on November 7, 1966, during final stage of trip from La Paz to the Ñacahuazú.

Top, Cuban volunteers during training in San Andrés, Pinar del Río, Cuba, fall 1966, prior to departure for Bolivia. Left to right: Joaquín, Braulio, Rolando, Urbano, Alejandro, Marcos, Benigno, Antonio, Che (Ramón), Miguel, Rubio.

Bottom, Che addressing guerrillas late December–early January. Left to right: Rubio (seated on ground), Sánchez, Braulio, and Tania.

At the guerrilla camp.

This page, top, left to right: Urbano, Miguel, Marcos, Che, Chino, Pacho, Inti, Coco. *Bottom,* left to right: Alejandro, Pombo, Urbano, Rolando, Che, Tuma, Arturo, and Moro (El Médico).

Facing page, top: Che with urban underground leader Rodolfo Saldaña, November 20, 1966. *Bottom photos:* Che reading and demonstrating ambush position.

Top, left to right, Coco, Ricardo, Loyola Guzmán, and Inti on January 26, 1967. *Above,* Benjamín and Eustaquio, late January 1967. *Right,* Joaquín.

Above, Tania. *Right,*
Moisés Guevara.
Below, Bolivian
Communist Party
leader Mario Monje.

Above, Guevara talking to villagers in Picacho, September 26, 1967.

Facing page: Top, left to right, Pombo, Antonio, Rolando. *Middle,* fording the Río Grande. *Bottom,* Pombo, Braulio (with machete), and Moro (El Médico).

Top, Che with Honorato Rojas and his children,
February 10, 1967. *Bottom,* as "Fernando the
Toothpuller" in Moroco, June 20-21, 1967.

Top, the Peruvian doctor Negro treats residents of a peasant village.
Bottom, Urbano (left) with Paulino Baigorría, a peasant who volunteered
to accompany the guerrillas and serve as their messenger, June 1967.

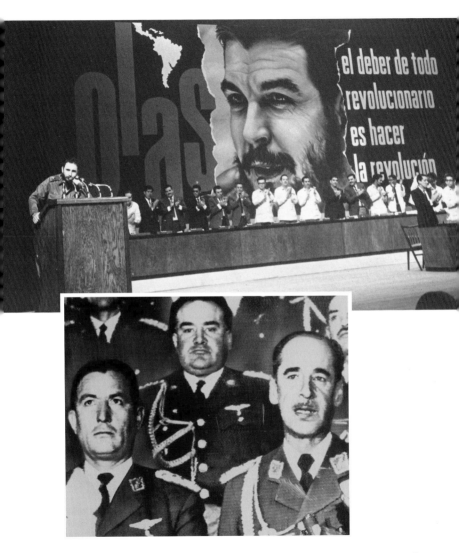

Top, delegates from revolutionary organizations throughout the Americas hear Fidel Castro address the Organization of Latin American Solidarity (OLAS) conference in Havana, August 1967. The slogan, taken from the Second Declaration of Havana, reads, "The duty of every revolutionary is to make the revolution." (Joseph Hansen/*Militant*)

Above, village of Pucará, where the guerrillas were headed in September 1967. *Right,* Yuro ravine.

Facing page, bottom, Generals René Barrientos, left, and Alfredo Ovando, right, leaders of Bolivia's military dictatorship. Behind them is Col. Carlos Alcoreza, minister of finance. (AP/Wide World)

In a July 3, 1968, televised broadcast, Fidel Castro answered charges that the Cuban edition of Che Guevara's Bolivian diary was a fabrication. *Above,* Castro displays photograph of Bolivian generals celebrating Guevara's murder.

Events in the years immediately following the defeat of the guerrillas in Bolivia confirmed what Guevara described as the "increasingly critical" economic and political situation throughout Latin America's Southern Cone, and the revolutionary upsurge that was coming. The class struggle in Bolivia reached a peak in 1970-71. *Top of page,* armed miners arrive in La Paz August 1971 in an unsuccessful attempt to block a military coup led by Gen. Hugo Banzer. (AP/Wide World)

Santa Cruz highway.

At night I gave a short talk on the significance of July 26, a rebellion against oligarchies and against revolutionary dogmas. Fidel made a small mention of Bolivia.[12]

July 27

We were all set to leave, and the people in ambush had received the order to depart automatically at 11:00 a.m., when Willy arrived a few minutes before the designated time to report the presence of the army. Willi, Ricardo, Inti, Chino, León, and Eustaquio were sent, joining Antonio, Arturo, and Chapaco in conducting the action.

It happened as follows: Eight soldiers appeared on the crest of the hill, walking south along an old path. Then they returned, firing some mortar rounds and making signals with a rag. At one point a soldier called out the name of a Melgar, possibly the one from Florida.[13] After a short rest, 8 soldiers began walking toward the ambush. Only 4 of them fell into it, however, as the rest were lagging behind. There are 3 confirmed and 1 probable dead; the latter was wounded in any case. We withdrew without taking any weapons or equipment because of the difficulty of recovering them, and we headed downstream. After passing the mouth of another little canyon, we set up a new ambush. The horses advanced as far as the end of the path.

My asthma gave me a hard time, and the tiny supply of sedatives is being used up.

Altitude = 800 meters.

---

12. July 26 was the anniversary of the 1953 attack on the Moncada garrison in Santiago de Cuba that launched the modern Cuban revolutionary struggle. In his speech Castro spoke of "the continued victories of the Bolivian Army of Liberation. Their actions began barely four months ago, and the military thugs are already confessing they are powerless in their attempts to defeat the guerrillas."

13. Antonio Melgar, the army courier killed in this battle, was not the same person as Pedro Melgar, the peasant whom the guerrillas had met in Florida on July 20.

July 28

Coco was sent, accompanied by Pacho, Raúl, and Aniceto, to cover the mouth of the river, which we believe is the Suspiro. We did very little walking, clearing a path through a very steep canyon. We camped apart from the forward detachment, since Miguel had advanced farther than was possible for the horses, which sank into the sand and suffered because of the rocks.

Altitude = 760 meters.

July 29

We continued walking through a canyon that descends toward the south, with good cover along both sides and plenty of water. At about 4:00 p.m. we met up with Pablito, who informed us that we had reached the mouth of the Suspiro without any problems. For a moment I thought the canyon was not the Suspiro because it was heading due south, but at the last stretch it turned west and emptied into the Rosita.

At approximately 4:30 p.m. the rear guard arrived and I decided to continue the journey, to put some distance between us and the mouth of the river. However, I did not feel like demanding the effort necessary to go any farther than Paulino's plot of land. We therefore made camp along the side of the road, one hour's march from the mouth of the Suspiro. At night I had Chino give a talk on the anniversary of his country's independence, July 28.[14] Afterward I explained why this camp was poorly situated and gave the order to pull out at 5:00 a.m., and head toward Paulino's farm.

Radio Havana announced that a number of army troops fell into an ambush and were rescued by helicopter, but it was not very audible.

July 30

My asthma bothered me greatly and I was up all night. At

---

14. Peru proclaimed its independence on July 28, 1821.

4:30 a.m., while Moro was making coffee, he reported seeing a lantern coming across the river. Miguel, who was awake because of the guard change, was sent together with Moro to stop those approaching. From the kitchen area I heard the following dialogue:

"Who goes there?"

"Trinidad Detachment."

Shooting broke out right then and there. Immediately Miguel brought back an M-1 and a cartridge belt taken from a wounded soldier, along with news that the group consisted of 21 men en route to Abapó, and that there were 150 more in Moroco. Other casualties were inflicted on the enemy, although the exact number could not be determined in the confusion.

Loading up the horses took a long time, and the black one got lost with the axe and a mortar that had been taken from the enemy. It was already close to 6:00 a.m., and we lost even more time because several loads fell off. The end result was that by the time the last ones were crossing, we were under fire from the soldiers, who were growing bolder. Paulino's sister was at her house, and received us, very calm, saying that all the men from Moroco had been taken prisoner and were in La Paz.

I hurried the men and, again under fire, Pombo and I passed the river canyon where the path ended. There it was finally possible to organize the resistance. I sent Miguel, with Coco and Julio, to take up the forward position while I helped with the horses. Covering the retreat were seven men from the forward detachment, four from the rear guard, and Ricardo, who fell behind to reinforce the defense. Benigno was on the right side, with Darío, Pablo, and Camba; the rest came along the left.

I had just given the order to rest, at the first suitable location, when Camba arrived with news that Ricardo and Aniceto had been hit crossing the river. I sent Urbano, with Ñato and León and two horses, and sent for Miguel and Julio, leaving Coco on forward lookout. They passed by without receiving my instructions, and shortly afterward, Camba came once again. He reported that together with Miguel and Julio, they had been taken by surprise, that the soldiers had advanced far, and that Miguel had withdrawn and was awaiting instructions. I sent Camba back, along with Eustaquio, so that only Inti, Pombo, Chino, and I remained.

At 1:00 p.m. I sent for Miguel, leaving Julio on forward lookout, and withdrew together with the men and the horses. When we reached the high ground where Coco was keeping watch, we were informed that all the survivors had appeared, that Raúl was dead, and that Ricardo and Pacho had been wounded.

What happened was this: Ricardo and Aniceto were imprudently crossing the clearing when Ricardo was wounded. Antonio organized a line of fire and Arturo, Aniceto, and Pacho were able to rescue him. However, Pacho was wounded and Raúl was killed by a bullet through the mouth. The withdrawal was difficult, carrying the two wounded men, with little help from Willi and Chapaco—the latter in particular. Later they were joined by Urbano's group and the horses, plus Benigno and his men. This left the other side unguarded, through which the soldiers advanced, taking Miguel by surprise. After an arduous trip through dense underbrush, they reached the river and met up with us. Pacho came on horseback, but Ricardo could not mount a horse and had to be carried in a hammock.

I sent Miguel, with Pablito, Darío, Coco, and Aniceto, to occupy the mouth of the first creek, on the right side, while we tended the wounded. Pacho has a superficial wound through the buttocks and the skin of his testicles. Ricardo, however, was in grave condition, and the last of the plasma was lost in Willi's knapsack. At 10:00 p.m. Ricardo died, and we buried him close to the river in a well-hidden spot, so that the soldiers will not find him.

July 31

At 4:00 a.m. we set out along the river. After taking a shortcut, we headed downstream without leaving tracks. In the morning we reached the creek where Miguel had set up ambush. He had not understood the order and had left tracks. We walked upstream about four kilometers and entered the woods, erasing our tracks and setting up camp near a tributary of the creek.

At night I explained the mistakes made during the action: (1) poor location of the campsite; (2) poor use of time, enabling the soldiers to fire at us; (3) overconfidence, leading to the loss of Ricardo, and of Raúl during the rescue; (4) lack of resolve in saving all the goods and matériel. Eleven knapsacks were lost, containing medicine, binoculars, and some useful items such as the tape recorder used for copying messages from Manila, the book by Debray with my notations in it, and a book by Trotsky. This is apart from the political value the government will derive from this capture, and the confidence it will give to the soldiers.

We calculate enemy losses at about 2 dead and up to 5 wounded. However, there are two contradictory reports: one, from the army, acknowledges 4 dead and 4 wounded on July 28; the other, from Chile, speaks of 6 wounded and 3 dead on the 30th. Later the army released another statement announcing the recovery of a body, and stating that an officer, a second lieutenant, was out of danger.

Regarding our dead, it is hard to categorize Raúl, owing to his introspection. He was not much of a combatant or worker, but he was always interested in political matters, even though he never asked questions. Ricardo was the most undisciplined of the Cuban group, and the least resolute in face of daily sacrifice. But he was an extraordinary combatant and an old comrade-in-adventure going back to the defeat of Segundo,[15] the Congo, and now here. His death is another tangible loss,

---

15. A reference to the guerrilla nucleus in the Salta mountains of northern Argentina from late 1963 to early 1964, led by Jorge Ricardo Masetti (Segundo). In July 1963 Ricardo had gone to southern Bolivia, where he helped coordinate logistical support, recruitment, and other forms of assistance to the guerrillas. In these tasks he was aided by Inti and Coco Peredo, Rodolfo Saldaña, Jorge Vázquez (Loro), and other Bolivian revolutionaries. In early 1964 the Argentine guerrillas were wiped out by government troops.

owing to his attributes. There are now 22 of us, including two wounded (Pacho and Pombo) and myself, with my asthma at full throttle.

ANALYSIS OF THE MONTH

The negative points of the previous month remain. These are: the impossibility of making contact with Joaquín and the outside, and the loss of men. We are now 22, with 3 disabled (myself among them), which diminishes our mobility. We had three encounters, including the taking of Samaipata, and inflicted casualties of 7 dead and 10 wounded. The figures are approximate because of confused dispatches. Our losses were 2 dead and 1 wounded.

The most important characteristics are:

1. The total lack of contact continues.

2. The lack of peasant recruitment continues to be felt, although there are several encouraging signs, based on the reception given us by peasants whom we have known for a long time.

3. The guerrilla legend is acquiring continental dimensions. Onganía is closing the borders[16] and Peru is taking precautions.

4. The effort to establish contact through Paulino was a failure.[17]

5. The morale and combat experience of the guerrillas grows with each battle. Camba and Chapaco remain weak.

6. The army still cannot do anything right, but several units

---

16. Juan Carlos Onganía was military dictator of Argentina.

17. Paulino, who had volunteered to join the guerrillas, had been arrested before he could deliver the messages to Matilde Lara, Inti Peredo's wife, in Cochabamba. He was subjected to severe torture, but refused to betray the guerrillas.

appear to be more combative.

7. The political crisis of the government is growing. However, the United States is granting small loans, which on the Bolivian level are a big help in stemming discontent.

The most pressing tasks are reestablishing contacts, incorporating new combatants, and obtaining medical supplies.

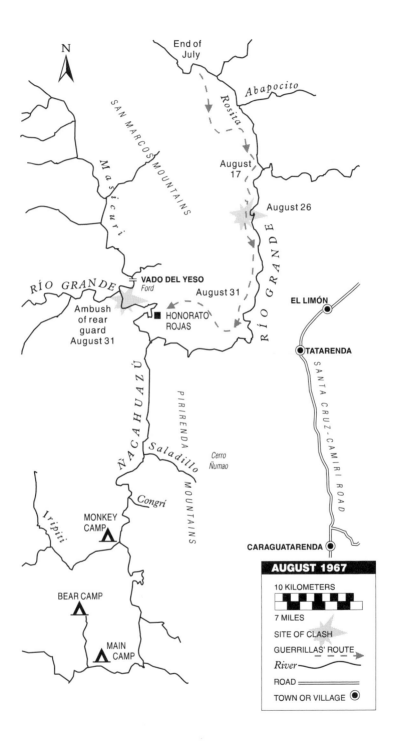

AUGUST 1967

August 1

A quiet day. Miguel and Camba began work on the trail, but progressed little more than a kilometer due to the difficult terrain and the vegetation. We killed a wild colt, which should give us meat for five to six days. Small trenches were dug to set an ambush for the army should they come through here. If they come tomorrow or the day after and do not discover the camp, the idea is to let them pass and then open fire.

Altitude = 650 meters.

August 2

The path seems to be progressing well thanks to Benigno and Pablo, who are working on it. It took them almost two hours to return to camp from the farthest point of the trail. There is no news about us on the radio, except for the announcement that the body of an "antisocial" had been moved. My asthma is hitting me hard, and I have already used up the last anti-asthma injection. All that is left is about a 10-day supply of tablets.

August 3

The path turned out to be a fiasco. It took Miguel and Urbano 57 minutes to return today; progress is very slow. There is no news.

Pacho is recuperating well, but I am doing poorly. I had a difficult day and night, and no short-term solution is in sight. I tried an intravenous novocaine injection, but it did not help.

August 4

The men reached a canyon that turns in a southwest direction and may lead to the creeks flowing toward the Río Grande. Tomorrow two pairs of men will work on clearing the path and Miguel will ascend the trail we are currently on to scout out what appears to be abandoned farmland. My asthma improved somewhat.

August 5

Benigno, Camba, Urbano, and León were divided into pairs to make better progress, but they ended up at a creek that flows into the Rosita and had to continue cross-country. Miguel went to scout the farm plot but did not find it. We finished the horsemeat; tomorrow we will try to catch some fish, and the following day we will slaughter another animal. Tomorrow we will advance to the next water hole. My asthma was implacable. Despite my aversion for splitting up, I will have to send a group on ahead. Benigno and Julio volunteered; I will need to see if Ñato is willing.

August 6

The campsite was moved. Unfortunately, the path cleared was sufficient for only a one-hour trip, not three, which means we are still a long way off. Benigno, Urbano, Camba, and León continued clearing the trail with machetes, while Miguel and Aniceto went to scout the new creek up to its confluence with the Rosita. They had not returned by nightfall, so precautions were taken, especially because I heard something sounding like a mortar shell in the distance. Inti, Chapaco, and I said a few words about today's date, the anniversary of Bolivia's independence.[1]

Altitude = 720 meters.

August 7

At 11:00 a.m. I concluded that Miguel and Aniceto were lost, and ordered Benigno to advance very cautiously up to the creek's outlet into the Rosita, and to investigate the direction the others had taken, if they had made it that far. However, at 1:00 p.m. the lost ones turned up; they had simply run into difficulties along the way and stopped for the night before reaching the Rosita. Miguel made me go through some difficult moments.

We remained at the same location but the path clearers found another creek, and we will head there tomorrow. The old horse Anselmo died today, and we now have only one beast of burden left. My asthma remains unchanged but the medicine is being used up. Tomorrow I will make a decision about sending a group to the Ñacahuazú.

Today marks exactly nine months since the founding of the guerrilla movement, beginning with our arrival. Of the initial six, two are dead, one is missing, and two are wounded; then there is me with asthma, which I don't know how to stop.

August 8

We walked for about an hour, all told, although it took me two owing to the exhaustion of the little mare. At one point I slashed its neck, opening up quite a wound. The new camp is probably the last one with water until we reach the Rosita or the Río Grande. The path clearers are 40 minutes away (2-3 kilometers).

I selected a group of eight men for the following mission: Tomorrow they will leave from here and travel all day. The following day Camba will return to report how things are going.

---

1. Bolivia won its independence in 1825.

The day after, Pablito and Darío will return with the day's news. The remaining five will continue on to Vargas's house, at which time Coco and Aniceto will return to report on things. Benigno, Julio, and Ñato will continue on to the Ñacahuazu to get my medication. They must proceed with great care to avoid ambushes. We will follow behind them, with the following meeting points: Vargas's house or beyond, depending on our speed; the creek facing the cave on the Río Grande; the Masicuru (Honorato); or the Ñacahuazu. The army is reporting they have discovered an arms cache at one of our camps.

At night I gathered everyone together and spoke along the following lines: We are in a difficult situation. Pacho is recuperating, but I am a real mess, and the episode with the mare proves that at times I have lost control. The situation will improve, but each and every one of us will bear the burden. Whoever feels unable to withstand it should say so. We have reached a moment when great decisions are called for. This type of struggle provides us the opportunity to become revolutionaries, the highest level of the human species. At the same time, it enables us to emerge fully as men. Those who are unable to achieve either of these two states should say so and abandon the struggle.

All the Cubans and some of the Bolivians stated they would continue on to the end. Eustaquio did the same, but he also criticized Muganga[2] for having loaded up the mule with his knapsack and for not carrying firewood. This provoked an angry retort by the latter. Julio sharply criticized Moro and Pacho for similar things, which was met by another sharp response, this time by Pacho. I ended the discussion by saying that two separate things were being raised, of a very different nature. One was whether or not each person was willing to continue on; the other involved petty squabbles or internal problems among the guerrillas, which detract from the more important

---

2. Moro.

decision. I did not like the statements made by Eustaquio and Julio, but neither did I like the responses by Moro and Pacho. In short, we must be more revolutionary and more exemplary in our conduct.

August 9

Altitude = 780 meters.

The eight explorers left in the morning. Miguel, Urbano, and León cleared 50 minutes' additional trail from the camp, using machetes. An abscess on my heel was lanced, enabling me to put weight on my foot, although I am still in great pain and feverish. Pacho is doing very well.

August 10

Antonio and Chapaco went out hunting in the area behind us, and shot a urina—or *guaso*—and a turkey. They scouted the first campsite, where there is nothing unusual, and brought back a load of oranges. I ate two, and immediately had an asthma attack, although it was mild.

At 1:30 p.m. Camba arrived, one of the eight, with the following news: Yesterday they went to sleep without water, and continued on today until 9:00 a.m. without finding any. Benigno recognizes the area and will head off to the Rosita to obtain water. If the water arrives, Pablo and Darío will be sent back.

Fidel gave a long speech in which he attacks the traditional [Communist] parties, above all the Venezuelan. It appears there was a great struggle behind the scenes.[3] My foot was treated again. I am getting better, but am still not well. Nonetheless, tomorrow we must move our base closer to the path clearers, who lengthened the trail by only 35 minutes during the day.

---

3. A reference to the conference of the Organization of Latin American Solidarity (OLAS), which met in Havana July 31 to August 10, attended by leaders of revolutionary and national liberation movements from throughout the Americas. Castro gave the closing speech.

August 11

The path clearers progressed very slowly. At 4:00 p.m. Pablo and Darío arrived with a note from Benigno announcing they are close to the Rosita, and estimating it will take three more days to reach Vargas's house. Pablito had left the water hole where they spent the night at 8:15 a.m., and at approximately 3:00 p.m. he ran into Miguel. This means that the path clearers have far to go. It appears that turkey meat upsets my asthma, so I gave my little bit to Pacho. We shifted campsites to another creek that disappears at noon and reappears at midnight. It rained but was not cold. There are many mariguí.

Altitude = 740 meters.

August 12

A dreary day. The path clearers made little progress. There was nothing new here, nor was there very much food. Tomorrow we will slaughter another horse, which should last six days. My asthma has leveled off to a tolerable level. Barrientos has announced the decline of the guerrillas and is again threatening an attack on Cuba. He is as stupid as ever.

The radio reported a battle near Monteagudo, with one dead on our part: Antonio Fernández from Tarata. This is very similar to the real name of Pedro, who is from Tarata.[4]

August 13

Miguel, Urbano, León, and Camba left to set up camp by the water hole discovered by Benigno, and to continue on from there. They brought a three-day supply of food consisting of meat from Pacho's horse, which was slaughtered today. There are four animals left, and everything seems to indicate we will have to slaughter another one before we reach the food. If all goes well, Coco and Aniceto should arrive here tomorrow. Arturo shot two turkeys, which they awarded to me since

---

4. Antonio Jiménez (Pedro, Pan Divino), a member of Joaquín's column, was killed August 9 in the mountains of Iñao.

there is almost no corn left. Chapaco is showing increasing signs of becoming unbalanced. Pacho's recovery is proceeding well. Since yesterday my asthma has been getting worse; I now take three tablets a day. My foot is almost all better.

August 14
A black day. The day's activities went by drearily and things were uneventful, but at night the news reported the capture of the cave where our travelers are heading. The details being given are so precise that the report is impossible to doubt. Now I am condemned to suffer from asthma indefinitely. They also captured documents of every type, and photographs. This is the hardest blow they have yet dealt us. Someone talked. The question is who.

August 15
Early in the day I sent Pablito with a message to Miguel, ordering him to send two men to find Benigno, provided that Coco and Aniceto had not arrived. But Pablito ran into them along the way and the three of them returned. Miguel sent word that he was remaining at the spot where night overtook them, and asked for some water to be sent. Darío was sent to notify him that we would be leaving tomorrow in any event. However, he met León along the way, who was coming to inform us that the trail was completed.

A radio station in Santa Cruz announced, in passing, that two prisoners had been taken by the army unit stationed in Muyupampa. There is no longer any doubt that this refers to Joaquín, who must be under hot pursuit, not to mention the two prisoners who talked.[5]

It was cold, but I did not have a bad night. Another abscess on my foot will have to be lanced. Pacho is on his feet.

---

5. Eusebio and Chingolo, two of the discharged guerrillas accompanying Joaquín's column, deserted in late July. Taken prisoner several days later they led the army to the supply caves at the Ñacahuazú, mentioned in the previous day's entry.

Another clash in Chuyuyako was announced, with no army casualties.[6]

August 16

We marched along a relatively good path for a total of 3 hours and 40 minutes, in addition to an hour's rest. The mule threw me clear out of the saddle after it stepped on a sharp stick, but I was all right. My foot is getting better. Miguel, Urbano, and Camba continued clearing the trail and reached the Rosita.

Today was the day when Benigno and his comrades were supposed to reach the cave. Planes flew over the area several times. This could be due to some tracks they might have left near Vargas's house, or it could be related to some troops going down along the Rosita or advancing along the Río Grande. At night I warned the men about the dangers of the crossing tomorrow, and precautions were taken.

Altitude = 600 meters.

August 17

We set out early, and reached the Rosita at 9:00 a.m. There Coco thought he heard two shots, and an ambush was set; but nothing happened. The rest of the journey went slowly owing to continually losing the trail and to miscommunication. We reached the Río Grande at 4:30 p.m. and camped there. I considered continuing under moonlight, but the men were very tired. We have a two-day supply of rationed-out horsemeat remaining; for me, there is mote for one day. By all indications, we will have to slaughter another animal.

The radio announced that documents and evidence will be presented from the four caves at the Ñacahuazu. This means they have also located the one at Monkey Camp. My asthma is not treating me too badly, under the circumstances.

---

6. On August 9 the army clashed with Joaquín's column at this settlement in the Iñao hills, resulting in the death of the guerrilla Pedro.

Altitude = 640 meters (which is illogical considering that yesterday we were at 600).

August 18

We set out even earlier than usual, but we had to ford four crossings—one of them a bit deep—and create trails in several places. After all this, we reached the creek at 2:00 p.m., with the men dead tired. There was no further activity. Clouds of *niboriguises* are flying around in this area, and it continues to be cold at night.

Inti raised with me that Camba wants to quit. According to Camba, his physical condition prevents him from continuing; moreover, he sees no prospects for the struggle. This is obviously a typical case of cowardice, and letting him go would be a healthy thing for us. But he now knows our future route in trying to reunite with Joaquín, so he cannot leave. Tomorrow I will speak with him and with Chapaco.

Altitude = 680 meters.

August 19

Miguel, Coco, Inti, and Aniceto left to scout the best route to Vargas's house, where it appears there is an army detachment. However, there is nothing new there and it seems we must continue following the old trail. Arturo and Chapaco went hunting and bagged a urina. Then the very same Arturo, while on guard duty with Urbano, killed a tapir, which put the entire camp on alert since it took seven shots. This animal will supply meat for four days, and the urina will supply one. There is also a reserve stock of beans and sardines. Total food: six days. It appears that the white horse, the next one on the list, has a chance to be spared.

I spoke with Camba, explaining to him that it would not be possible for him to leave until we complete our next step, which is reuniting with Joaquín. Chapaco stated he would not leave, since that would be cowardice, but he would like some hope of leaving within six months to a year. I gave it to him.

He made a series of disjointed statements. He is not in good shape.

The radio is full of news about Debray; they do not mention the other defendants. There is no news of Benigno; he should have been here by now.

August 20

Miguel and Urbano, the path clearers, and Willy and Darío, my "public works department," made little progress, so we decided to remain right here for another day. Coco and Inti hunted without success, but Chapaco killed a monkey and a urina. I ate urina and at midnight suffered a severe attack of asthma. El Médico continues to be ill with an apparent attack of lumbago, which is affecting his overall health and is turning him into an invalid. There is no news of Benigno, which has now become cause for concern.

The radio is reporting the presence of guerrillas 85 kilometers from Sucre.[7]

August 21

Another day at the same place, and another day without news of Benigno and his comrades. Five monkeys were shot, four by Eustaquio and one by Moro when it passed near him. The latter continues doing poorly from his lumbago, and was given a dose of meperidine. My asthma does not get along with urina.

August 22

We finally moved out, but not before an alarm was sounded when a man was seen, apparently fleeing along the river bank. It turned out to be Urbano, lost. I gave El Médico a local anesthetic, and with this he was able to ride the mare, although he arrived in pain. He seems to be a little better. Pacho made the trip on foot.

---

7. The report was untrue.

We made camp along the right bank. Only a little bit of machete work is needed to ready the trail leading to Vargas's house. We have tapir meat remaining for tomorrow and the day after, but starting tomorrow we will be unable to hunt. There is no news of Benigno's people, ten days after they separated from Coco.

Altitude = 580 meters.

August 23

The day was very fatiguing, as we had to climb around a very difficult cliff. The white horse refused to go any farther and they left it buried in the mud, without even taking the bones. We reached a small cabin for hunters that showed signs of recent inhabitants. We set up an ambush, and two people soon fell into it. Their story is that they were there to check on ten traps they had set. They report that the army is at Vargas's house, at Tatarenda, Caraguatarenda, Ipitá, and Yumon,[8] and that a couple of days ago there was a clash at Caraguatarenda, with one wounded on the army's side. This could possibly be Benigno, pressed by hunger or encirclement. The men stated that tomorrow the army would come to fish, in groups of 15 to 20.

Tapir meat was distributed, along with some fish that were caught with a cartridge bag. I ate rice, which went down very well. El Médico is doing better. It was announced that Debray's trial has been postponed until September.

Altitude = 580 meters.

August 24

Reveille was sounded at 5:30 a.m., and we headed to the ravine we intended to follow. The forward detachment began the march and had gone a few meters when three peasants appeared along the other side. Miguel and his men were called back, and everyone went into ambush. Eight soldiers appeared. The instructions were to let them cross the river

---

8. A reference to Cerro Ñumao.

through the ford in front of us, and then open fire as they reached the other side. But the soldiers did not cross, limiting themselves to going around a few times and passing in front of our rifles, which we did not fire. Our civilian prisoners claim to be only hunters.

Miguel and Urbano, with Camba, Darío, and Hugo Guz-mán—the hunter—were sent to follow a trail heading west, although we do not know where it ends. We remained on ambush all day. At nightfall the path clearers returned with the traps, containing a condor and a rotting cat. Everything was eaten together with the last of the tapir. All that is remaining are the beans and whatever can be hunted. Camba is reaching the extreme limit of his moral degradation; he now trembles at the very mention of soldiers. El Médico continues in pain and is administering himself talamonal. I am doing pretty well, but am ravenously hungry.

The army issued a dispatch stating they had captured another cave and that two of their men had been slightly wounded, in addition to "guerrilla casualties." Radio Havana reports an unconfirmed battle in Taperillas with one wounded on the army's side.

August 25

The day passed uneventfully. Reveille was at 5:00 a.m. and the path clearers left early. The army, seven men in all, approached and came within a few steps of our position, but they did not try to cross. They appear to be calling the hunters with their gunshots. We will attack them tomorrow if the opportunity should arise. Insufficient progress was made on clearing the trail, as Miguel sent Urbano to us with a message that the latter transmitted poorly, at a time when it was too late to do anything.

The radio reported a battle in Monte Dorado, which seems to be within Joaquín's jurisdiction. It also announces the presence of guerrillas three kilometers from Camiri.

August 26

Everything went badly. The seven soldiers came, but they divided themselves up: five went downstream and two went across. Antonio, who was in charge of the ambush, opened fire prematurely and missed. This enabled the two men to run off for reinforcements. The other five ran off, at full speed. Inti and Coco gave chase, but the soldiers found shelter and held them off. While watching the hunt, I noticed that bullets were landing close by, coming from our side. I ran out of there and found that Eustaquio was doing the shooting, since Antonio had not told him what was going on. I got so furious that I lost control and treated Antonio harshly.

We left at a very slow pace, since El Médico cannot do much. Meanwhile, the army had recovered and was advancing along the island in front of us with 20 to 30 men; there was no point in attacking them. They might have suffered two wounded, maximum. Coco and Inti distinguished themselves with their decisiveness.

Things went all right until El Médico became exhausted and began to hold up the march. At 6:30 p.m. we stopped, without having caught up to Miguel, who nevertheless was only a few meters away and made contact with us. Moro remained in a ravine, without being able to climb the last stretch, and we slept divided in three parts. There are no signs of pursuit.

Altitude = 900 meters.

August 27

The day was spent in a desperate search for a way out, although the results of the search are not yet clear. We are close to the Río Grande and have already passed Yumao, but according to our reports there are no fording places ahead. We could go there by way of Miguel's cliff, but the mules will not be able to make it. There is a possibility of crossing a small mountain chain and then heading toward the Río Grande–Masicuri. However, we will not know until tomorrow whether this is feasible. We passed an altitude of 1,300 meters, which is

more or less the highest altitude of the area, and we slept at
1,240 meters under a considerable chill. I am quite well, but El
Médico is doing very poorly. We are now out of water, but
have kept a little for him.

The good news, or the good development, was the appearance of Benigno, Ñato, and Julio. Their odyssey was a great one,
since there are soldiers at Vargas's house and in Yumao, who almost clashed with them. Later they followed behind troops
heading down the Saladillo and up the Ñacahuasu, and they
discovered that the Congrí Creek has three passageways made
by the soldiers. The cave at Bear Camp, which they arrived at on
the 18th, is now an antiguerrilla camp with about 150 soldiers.
They were almost spotted there, but were able to return without
being seen. They were at the grandfather's farm,[9] where they
obtained jocos, the only thing there, since everything is abandoned. They then passed by the soldiers again and heard our
gunfire. They slept close by, so they could follow our tracks and
catch up with us. According to Benigno, Ñato conducted himself very well, but Julio got lost twice and was a little bit afraid
of the soldiers. Benigno believes that some of Joaquín's people
went through the area a few days ago.

August 28

A dreary and somewhat troubled day. We assuaged our
thirst with *caracoré* leaves, which is more like playing games
with one's throat. Miguel sent Pablito out by himself with one
of the hunters to look for water, and to top it off, with only a
small revolver. He had not returned by 4:30 p.m., and I sent
Coco and Aniceto to look for him; they did not return all night.

The rear guard remained down at the bottom and was unable to hear the radio. It appears there is a new message. We
finally slaughtered the little mare, after she had accompanied
us for two difficult months. I did all I could to save her, but our

---

9. This was the farm visited on May 26 belonging to the great uncle of Moisés
   Robles, the guerrillas' peasant guide.

hunger was getting worse. Now, at least, the only thing we suffer from is thirst. It appears we will not reach water tomorrow either.

The radio reported one soldier wounded in the Tatarenda region. The mystery to me is this: Why, if they are so scrupulous in reporting their losses, do they lie in all their other dispatches? And if they are not lying, who is inflicting casualties in places as far apart as Caraguatarenda and Taperillas? Unless Joaquín's group is divided in two, or unless there are new independent guerrilla groups in existence.

Altitude = 1,200 meters.

August 29

A tough and very difficult day. The path clearers made little progress, and at one point took the wrong route, thinking they were heading toward the Masicuri. We made camp at an altitude of 1,600 meters, in a relatively humid place that has a cane-like plant whose pulp mitigates thirst. Some comrades—Chapaco, Eustaquio, and Chino—are collapsing from lack of water. Tomorrow it will be necessary to decide the closest place where water can be found. The mules are bearing up very well.

There was nothing of note on the radio. The most important item is the trial of Debray, which is being extended another week or two.

August 30

The situation was becoming distressing. The machete users were suffering fainting spells. Miguel and Darío drank their own urine, as did Chino, with the unfortunate result of diarrhea and cramps. Urbano, Benigno, and Julio climbed down into a canyon and found water. They informed me that the mules were unable to make it down, and I decided to remain with Ñato. However, Inti came back up with water, and the three of us stayed there eating horsemeat. The radio remained below, so there was no news.

Altitude = 1,200 meters.

August 31

In the morning Aniceto and León left to scout the area below. They returned at 4:00 p.m. with word that there was a route the mules could take, leading from the camp to the water ahead. The most difficult part came first, but from what I could see, it really is possible for the animals to make it through. Therefore, for tomorrow I ordered Miguel to create a detour around the last cliff and continue clearing the path ahead, along which we will be able to lead the mules down the hill. There is a message from Manila, but it could not be copied.

SUMMARY OF THE MONTH

This was without doubt the worst month we have had in the war. The loss of all the caves, with the documents and medicine in them, was a hard blow—psychologically above all. The loss of two men at the end of last month and the subsequent march on a horsemeat diet demoralized the men. It also led to the first request to abandon our ranks, from Camba; this could only be counted as a net gain, but not under these circumstances. The lack of contact with the outside and with Joaquín, and the fact that prisoners taken from his group have talked, is also somewhat demoralizing to the troop. My illness led to uncertainty among a number of others. All this was reflected in our only engagement, where we should have inflicted a number of casualties on the enemy, but only wounded one of them. Moreover, the difficult march through the hills without water brought to the surface some negative traits among the men.

The most important characteristics are:

1. We continue without contact of any kind, and have no reasonable hope of establishing any in the near future.

2. We continue without any peasant recruitment. This is un-

derstandable given the lack of dealings we have had with them in the recent period.

3. There is a decrease—temporary I hope—in combat morale.

4. The army has not improved either in effectiveness or aggressiveness.

We are at a low point in our morale and in our revolutionary legend. The most urgent tasks are the same as those of last month: reestablishing contacts, incorporating new combatants, and supplying ourselves with medicine and equipment.

It should be noted that Inti and Coco are distinguishing themselves more and more as revolutionary and military cadres.

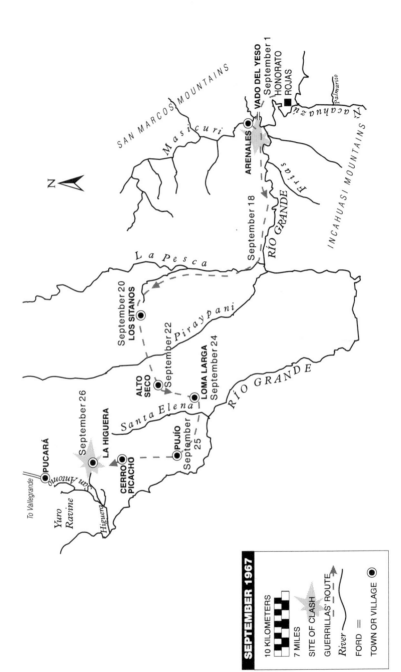

N

SAN MARCOS MOUNTAINS

Masicuri

VADO DEL YESO
September 1
HONORATO
ROJAS

ARENALES

September 18

RÍO GRANDE

Frías

INCAHUASI MOUNTAINS

Palmarito

Ñacahuazú

La Pesca

September 20
LOS SITANOS

Piraypani

September 22

RÍO GRANDE

ALTO
SECO

LOMA LARGA
September 24

Santa Elena

September 26

PUJIO
September 25

LA HIGUERA

PUCARÁ

CERRO
PICACHO

San Antonio

Higuera

To Vallegrande

Yuro
Ravine

SEPTEMBER 1967

10 KILOMETERS

7 MILES

SITE OF CLASH

GUERRILLAS' ROUTE

River

FORD ▥

TOWN OR VILLAGE ◉

SEPTEMBER 1967

September 1

We led the mules down early in the day, with a few incidents, including a spectacular fall by one of them. El Médico has not recovered, but I have, and I walked fine while leading the mule. The trip took longer than we thought, and it was not until 6:15 p.m. that it dawned on us that we were at the creek by Honorato's house.[1]

Miguel continued ahead at full speed, but got only as far as the main road before it got completely dark. Advancing with caution, Benigno and Urbano noticed nothing abnormal, so they entered the house, which was empty. However, several barracks had been added by the army, which were vacant at

---

1. Two days earlier Joaquín's unit had reached the same house belonging to Honorato Rojas, whom the guerrillas had met on February 10. Working with the army, Rojas led the ten remaining members of the column into an ambush on August 31 while wading across the Río Grande at Puerto Mauricio, near the Vado del Yeso. Joaquín, Braulio, Alejandro, Tania, Moisés, Apolinar, and Walter were killed; Ernesto was wounded and later murdered; Paco, one of the discharged guerrillas accompanying them was taken prisoner; Negro escaped but was captured and murdered four days later.

present. We found flour, lard, salt, and goats, killing two of them. This together with the flour made for a feast, although waiting for it to be cooked took all night. We left at dawn, posting a lookout at the little house and at the entrance to the road.

Altitude = 740 meters.

September 2

Early in the morning we withdrew to the farm plots, leaving behind an ambush at the house headed by Miguel, with Coco, Pablo, and Benigno. A guard was kept posted on the other side. At 8:00 a.m. Coco came to report that a herdsman had come by looking for Honorato. There were four of them and I ordered him to let the other three pass. All of this took time, since our position was an hour away from the house.

At 1:30 p.m. several shots were heard. We learned later that a peasant had approached, along with a soldier and a horse. Chino, who was keeping guard together with Pombo and Eustaquio, shouted, "A soldier!" and cocked his rifle. The soldier shot at him and fled, while Pombo opened fire, killing the horse. I threw a tremendous fit, as this was the height of incompetence. Poor Chino feels crushed.

We released the four, who had passed by in the meantime, along with our two prisoners, and sent everyone heading up the Masicuri. We purchased a young bull from the herdsmen for 700 pesos, and Hugo was given 100 pesos for his work and 50 pesos for some items taken from him. The dead horse turned out to be one left at Honorato's house because it was crippled.

The herdsmen told us that Honorato's wife had complained that the army had beaten her husband and eaten everything they had. When the herdsmen passed by a week ago, Honorato was in Valle Grande recovering from a tiger bite. In any event, there was someone in the house, as a fire was burning when we arrived.

Due to Chino's mistake, I decided to leave during the night along the same route the herdsmen were taking, and to try to reach the first house. The assumption was that the soldiers were few in number and would have continued their retreat. However, we left very late and did not cross the ford until 3:45 a.m. We did not find the house and slept on a cowpath, awaiting daylight.

The radio reported an ugly piece of news concerning the annihilation of a group of ten men led by a Cuban named Joaquín, in the Camiri region. However, this item was broadcast on the Voice of America; the local stations have said nothing.

September 3

As one would expect on a Sunday, there was a clash. At dawn we followed the Masicuri downstream to its mouth, and then went up the Río Grande for a stretch. At 1:00 p.m. Inti, Coco, Benigno, Pablito, Julio, and León set out to try to reach the house. If the army was not there, the instructions were to purchase the items most needed to make our lives more bearable. The group first captured two farmhands, who told them the owner was not in, that no soldiers were there, and that a large quantity of food supplies could be obtained. Other news: yesterday five soldiers galloped by without stopping at the house. Honorato passed by two days ago on the way to his house, with two of his children.

Upon reaching the landowner's house, the group found that 40 soldiers had just arrived. A confused skirmish resulted, in which our forces killed at least one soldier, who had a dog with him. The soldiers reacted and surrounded them, but later retreated in the face of our shouts. Our group was unable to gather even a single grain of rice. A plane flew over the area and fired a few small rockets, apparently over the Ñacahuasu.

Another piece of information provided by the peasants was that no guerrillas have been seen in the area. Their first news of us came from the herdsmen who passed through yesterday.

The Voice of America reported again on battles with the army, this time naming José Carrillo as the sole survivor of a group of ten men. Since this Carrillo is Paco, one of the rejects, and the annihilation occurred in Masicuri, everything seems to indicate this is a trick.

Altitude = 650 meters.

September 4

A group of eight men under Miguel's command set up an ambush along the road from Masicuri to Honorato's house. It lasted until 1:00 p.m., without incident. Meanwhile, with great effort, Ñato and León brought back a cow. Later on they were able to obtain two magnificent oxen. Urbano and Camba walked about 10 kilometers up the river. Four crossings must be forded, one of them fairly deep. The young bull was killed. A request was made for volunteers to go search for food and information. Inti, Coco, Julio, Aniceto, Chapaco, and Arturo were selected, under Inti's command. Pacho, Pombo, Antonio, and Eustaquio also volunteered. Inti's instructions are to reach the house during the early morning, watch for any movement, and stock up on supplies if there are no soldiers. If soldiers are there his instructions are to circle around and continue ahead, trying to capture one of them. He was reminded that the main thing is not to suffer any casualties, and to exercise a maximum of caution.

The radio is reporting news of a death at the Vado del Yeso, in a new clash, close to where the group of ten men was annihilated. This would appear to confirm that the report about Joaquín is a trick. On the other hand, they did give a physical description of Negro, the Peruvian doctor, killed in Palmarito, whose body was transported to Camiri. Pelado helped in the identification. This death does indeed appear to be a real one; the others could be fictitious, or might be some of the rejects. In any case, there is a strange tone to the dispatches, which are now being shifted to Masicuri and Camiri.

September 5

The day went by uneventfully as we awaited the results. At 4:30 a.m. the group returned, bringing a mule and some merchandise. There were soldiers at the house of the farmer Morón, and they very nearly discovered us because of the dogs. It appears the army is moving at night. The men circled around the house and cut through the woods to Montaño's house, where no one was home. However, there they found corn, and took a quintal. At about 12:00 noon they crossed the river and came across two houses on the other side. At one of these everyone had escaped and they requisitioned a mule. At the other house they received very little collaboration and had to resort to threats. The information given them was that the inhabitants had never seen guerrillas before, and that the only place visited by guerrillas was Pérez's house before the carnival (us).

They made their way back during the day and waited for nightfall to sneak by Morón's house. Everything was going fine until Arturo got lost and fell asleep on the path, causing them to lose two hours looking for him. They left footprints that could be tracked, provided the cattle do not erase them all. In addition, they dropped a few things along the way. The men's spirit changed at once.

The radio reported that the dead guerrillas have not been identified, but that new developments are possible at any moment. A message [from Cuba] was deciphered completely. It states that OLAS was a triumph, but that the Bolivian delegation was shit. Aldo Flores of the PCB [Bolivian Communist Party] pretended to represent the ELN, and they had to unmask the lie. They have asked for one of Kolle's men to come for discussions. Lozano's house was raided and he has gone underground.[2] They think they can arrange an exchange for Debray. That is all. Evidently they did not receive our last message.

September 6

Benigno.
Benigno's birthday looked promising. In the early morning

---

2. Hugo Lozano was a member of the guerrillas' support network in La Paz.

we cooked some cornmeal we were carrying, and drank some *mate* with sugar. Later Miguel, with eight men under him, set up an ambush, while León caught another young bull to take with us. Shortly past 10:00 a.m., since it was getting a little late and they had not returned, I sent Urbano to notify them to lift the ambush at noon.

A few minutes later a shot was heard, followed by a short burst of fire, and a shot sounded in our direction. As we took positions, Urbano arrived on the run. He had clashed with a patrol that had dogs with them. With nine of our men on the other side, and not knowing their exact location, I was quite desperate. The path was cleared for passage not quite to the river bank, and along it I sent Moro, Pombo, and Camba, with Coco. My aim was to leave with the knapsacks and make contact with the rear guard if possible, reincorporating them into the group. On the other hand, there was also the possibility that they could fall into an ambush. Nevertheless, by cutting through the woods, Miguel and all his people were able to rejoin the group.

The explanation for the events: Miguel had advanced without posting a guard along our little trail while they devoted themselves to looking for cattle. León heard a dog barking, and Miguel, becoming suspicious, decided to retreat. At that moment they heard shots and noticed that a patrol had passed between them and the woods along a trail, and was now in front of them. They then cut through the woods.

We withdrew calmly, with the three mules and three head of cattle. After wading through four crossings, two of them rough, we made camp about seven kilometers from the previous one. There we slaughtered a cow and ate extravagantly. The rear guard reported hearing sustained gunfire from the direction of the camp, with a number of machine guns.

Altitude = 640 meters.

September 7

A short march. We crossed only one ford, and later ran into difficulties due to jutting rock. This led Miguel to decide to

Top, crossing the Río Grande. *Bottom,* Arturo, the guerrillas' radio operator, tuning in Radio Havana, in a photo taken earlier in the campaign.

make camp and wait for us. Tomorrow we will explore the area thoroughly.

The situation is this: there are no aircraft searching for us here, despite the army having reached the camp, and despite the radio reports that even state that I am head of the group. So the question is: Are they afraid? Unlikely. Do they believe it is impossible for us to make it through up above? With the experience of what we have done, of which they are aware, I do not think so. Are they letting us advance to await us at some strategic point? It is possible. Do they think we will stick to the Masicuri region to obtain supplies? That is also possible. El Médico is much better, but I had a relapse and spent a sleepless night.

The radio is reporting on the valuable information supplied by José Carrillo (Paco). It would be worthwhile to make a lesson out of him. Debray responded to the charges Paco made against him, stating that he sometimes went hunting, which is why he might have been seen with a rifle.

Radio Cruz del Sur is announcing the discovery of the body of Tania the guerrilla on the banks of the Río Grande. This piece of news does not have the same ring of truth as the one about Negro. The body was brought to Santa Cruz according to this radio station, and this one alone; it has not been reported on Radio Altiplano.

Altitude = 720 meters.

I spoke with Julio. He is doing well but feels the lack of contact and recruitment.

September 8

A quiet day. Two ambushes, involving eight men, were kept from morning until night under the command of Antonio and Pombo. The animals ate well in a *chuchio*[3] field and the mule is recovering from its blows. Aniceto and Chapaco went scouting upstream and reported that the path is a relatively good

---

3. A type of hollow cane similar to wicker or bamboo.

one for the animals. Coco and Camba crossed the river, with the water up to their chests, and climbed a hill in front of them, although they did not bring back any new information. I sent Miguel, with Aniceto, on a longer scouting mission; the news Miguel brought back was that it will be very difficult for the animals to pass. For tomorrow we will stick to this side, since it is always possible to have the animals walk through the water, without weight on their backs.

The radio reported that Barrientos attended the interment of the remains of the guerrilla Tania, who was given a "Christian burial." Later he was in Puerto Mauricio, where Honorato's house is. He has made an offer to those deceived Bolivians who have not been paid the promised salary, asking them to turn themselves in to army posts with their hands on their head, and nothing will happen to them. A small plane bombed Honorato's house in the area below us, as if to make a demonstration for Barrientos.

A Budapest daily is criticizing Che Guevara, a pathetic and apparently irresponsible figure. It salutes the Marxist stance of the Chilean Communist Party, which takes practical positions in the face of practical events. How I would like to take power, if for no other reason than to unmask cowards and lackeys of every stripe and rub their snouts in their own filth.

September 9

Miguel and Ñato went scouting, bringing news that the river is indeed passable, but that the animals will have to swim across; the men can cross at a ford. There is a fairly big creek along the left side, where we will make camp. The ambushes continued in place with eight men, under the command of Antonio and Pombo, with nothing to report.

I spoke with Aniceto. He appears to be very firm, although he thinks several of the Bolivians are weakening. He complained of the lack of political work by Coco and Inti. We finished off the cow, so that all that is remaining are the four hooves for a soup tomorrow morning.

The only news on the radio is the postponement of Debray's trial to September 17 at the earliest.

September 10

A bad day. It began promisingly, but then, as a result of the poor state of the trail, the animals began to put up a struggle. Finally the mule refused to go any farther and we had to leave it on the other side. The decision was made by Coco due to the rising water and the turbulence of the river. However, four weapons were left on the other side, including Moro's gun and three antitank shells for Benigno's rifle.

I swam across the river with the mule, but lost my shoes in the process. I am now wearing sandals, and do not particularly enjoy it. Ñato made a bundle out of his clothing and wrapped his weapons in a sheet of cloth. He jumped in when the current was strong, losing everything. The other mule got bogged down and jumped into the river by itself. It was necessary to bring her back, however, since there was no way she could make it across. When an attempt was made by León to bring the mule across, they both almost drowned in a torrent of water. Finally we reached the creek that was our objective. El Médico was in a very bad state, and complained all night of acute pain in his extremities.

From here our plan was to make the animals swim to the other side again, but the rising water made us abandon the idea, at least until the water level drops. In addition, planes and helicopters are flying over the area. I do not at all like this development with the helicopters, since they could be placing ambushes along the river. Tomorrow scouting parties will be sent up the river and up the creek to try to determine exactly where we are.

Altitude = 780 meters. Progress: 3-5 kilometers.

I forgot to highlight an event. Today, after more than six months, I bathed. This constitutes a record that several others are already approaching.

September 11

A quiet day. Scouts were sent up the river and up the creek. The ones scouting the river returned late in the afternoon with news that it will very probably be passable when the river goes down some more, and that there are sandy areas along the banks that the animals can walk through. Benigno and Julio scouted the creek, but very superficially and they returned at noon. Ñato and Coco, assisted by the rear guard, went to get the items left behind, passing the mule and leaving behind only one bag of machine-gun bullet casings.

There was an unpleasant incident: Chino came to tell me that Ñato had roasted and eaten an entire piece of meat in front of him. I gave him a real tongue-lashing, since it was his responsibility to prevent it. However, after further investigation the matter became more complicated, since it could not be determined whether Chino had authorized the act or not. He asked to be replaced and I gave the responsibility to Pombo once again. But it was a bitter pill for Chino.

In the morning the radio reported a statement by Barrientos that I have been dead for some time and that everything was propaganda. At night it reported that he was offering 50,000 pesos (US$4,200) for information leading to my capture, dead or alive. It appears the armed forces gave him a [*illegible*]. Leaflets were dropped over a region, probably containing my physical description. Requeterán[4] says that Barrientos's offer should be considered a psychological move, since the guerrillas' tenacity is well known and a prolonged war is being prepared for.

I had a long discussion with Pablito. Like everyone, he is concerned about the lack of contact and believes that our fundamental task is reestablishing contact with the city. But he appears firm and determined, in the spirit of *"patria o muerte,"*[5] wherever it may lead.

---

4. A reference to army colonel Luis A. Reque Terán.
5. "Homeland or death," a slogan of the Cuban revolution.

September 12

The day began with a tragicomic episode. At 6:00 a.m., the time for reveille, Eustaquio came to warn that there were people advancing along the creek. The call to arms was sounded and everyone was mobilized. Antonio saw them, and when I asked how many there were, he signaled with his hand that there were five. When all was said and done, it turned out to be a hallucination. This was a dangerous thing for the troops' morale, since right away there began talk of psychosis. I later spoke with Antonio and he is clearly out of sorts. Tears came to his eyes, but he denied that there was anything on his mind. He asserted that the only thing affecting him was lack of sleep, since for six days he has been on kitchen duty for having fallen asleep on guard duty and then denied it.

Chapaco disobeyed an order and was penalized with three days of kitchen duty. At night he spoke with me, requesting to be assigned to the forward detachment since he says he is not getting along with Antonio. I refused. Inti, León, and Eustaquio left to do a thorough exploration of the creek, to see if it would be possible to follow it to the other side of a large mountain range visible in the distance. Coco, Aniceto, and Julio went upriver to try to locate fording places and to find a way to bring the animals in the event we follow that route.

It seems that Barrientos's offer has caused quite a sensation. In any case, a demented reporter has ventured the opinion that US$4,200 is very little money given how dangerous I am. Radio Havana reports that OLAS received a message of support from the ELN. A miracle of telepathy!

September 13

The scouts returned. Inti and his group spent all day climbing along the creek. They slept at a high altitude, where it was quite cold. The creek apparently originates in a mountain chain ahead of us and runs west. There is no passage for the animals. Coco and his comrades tried unsuccessfully to cross the river. They passed over 11 cliffs before reaching the canyon of what would appear to be the La Pesca river. Signs of life can be seen there: fields that had been cleared by fire, and an ox. The animals would have to cross over to the other side, unless we can bring everything over together on a raft. This is what we will try to do.

I spoke with Darío, raising with him the question of his departure if he so desires. At first he answered that leaving was very dangerous, but I warned him that this is not a refuge, and that if he decides to stay, it is for good. He said he would stay, and that he would correct his shortcomings. We shall see.

The only news on the radio is of the shot fired over the head of Debray's father, and of the seizure of all the papers Debray had gathered in preparation for his defense. The pretext is that they do not want this material turned into a political pamphlet.

September 14

An exhausting day. At 7:00 a.m. Miguel departed with the entire forward detachment and Ñato. Their instructions were to walk as far as possible along this side of the river and to build a raft when it got difficult to proceed any farther. Antonio remained on ambush, together with the entire rear guard. A couple of M-1s were left in a little cave that Ñato and Willi know about. Not hearing any news by 1:30 p.m., we began the march.

It was not possible to ride a mule, and with an attack of asthma beginning I had to leave the animal to León and continue on foot. The rear guard received the order to leave at 3:00 p.m. if there were no counterorders. Approximately at that time, Pablito arrived with word that the ox had reached the area where the animals were to cross, and that the raft was being built one kilometer farther ahead. I waited for the animals to arrive, which did not occur until 6:15, after men had been sent to help them. Then the two mules went across (the ox had done so earlier) and we continued at a tired pace until we reached where the raft was. There I learned that 12 men were still on this side, and that only 10 had gone across. We spent the night divided this way, eating the last ration of half-rotten ox meat.

Altitude = 720 meters. Progress: 2-3 kilometers.

September 15

A little more ground was covered today, five to six kilometers, but we did not reach the La Pesca river. The reason was that the animals had to cross over twice, and one of the mules is stubborn at crossings. We still need to make one more crossing and explore whether the mules can make it through.

The radio carries news of the arrest of Loyola. The photos must be to blame.[6] Our remaining bull died—at the hands of the executioner, naturally.

Altitude = 780 meters.

September 16

The entire day was taken up in constructing the raft and crossing the river. We walked only 500 meters, the distance to the camp, where there is a small spring. The crossing took place without incident on a well-built raft pulled by ropes from both sides of the river.

Later on, when we left them alone, Antonio and Chapaco had another incident and Antonio gave Chapaco six days' punishment for insulting him. I respected that decision, although I am not sure it is justified. At night there was another incident when Eustaquio criticized Ñato for eating an extra meal. It turned out to be a few thick pieces of hide. Another painful situation caused by food. El Médico raised another small problem with me, concerning his illness and the other people's opinion about him, based on some comments made by Julio. None of it seems important.

---

6. Photos of Loyola Guzmán at the guerrilla camp during her stay in late January were found by the army in the guerrillas' caves (mentioned in the August 14 entry). This helped lead to her arrest on September 14.

Altitude = 820 meters.

September 17

Pablito.

A day of dentistry, as I pulled teeth from Arturo and Chapaco. Miguel scouted as far as the river, while Benigno explored the trail. The news is that the mules can make it up, but first they must swim, crossing the river twice. In honor of Pablito, we made a little rice for him. He is 22 today and is the youngest of the guerrillas.

The only news on the radio is the postponement of the trial [of Debray], and a protest over the arrest of Loyola Guzmán.

September 18

The march began at 7:00 a.m., but Miguel arrived shortly with news that three peasants had been spotted behind the next bend. It was not known whether they saw us, and the order was given to apprehend them. Chapaco touched off another dispute, as he does without fail, accusing Arturo of having stolen 15 bullets from his cartridge bag. It is poisonous, and the only good thing is that even though his quarrels are with Cubans, none of the Bolivians pay any attention.

The mules made the whole trip without having to swim. However, while crossing an embankment the black mule got away from us, which was unfortunate because it was dragged about 50 meters. Four peasants were taken prisoner. They were traveling on their donkeys to the Piraypandi, a river located one league upstream from this one. They report that Aladino Gutiérrez and his people are at the banks of the Río Grande, hunting and fishing.

Benigno committed the height of indiscretion by letting himself be seen and then permitting the man, his wife, and another peasant to leave. When I found out, I gave him a full-scale dressing-down and called it an act of treason, which brought Benigno to tears. All the peasants have been advised that tomorrow they will be coming with us to Zitano, the settlement where they live, six to eight leagues from here. Aladino and his wife are somewhat evasive and it was very difficult to get them to sell us food.

The radio is now reporting two suicide attempts by Loyola "from fear of guerrilla reprisals." It also speaks of the arrest of several teachers who, if not directly involved, are at the very least sympathetic to us. It seems that many things were taken from Loyola's house, but it would not be strange if everything stemmed from the photos found in the cave.

At nightfall a small plane and a Mustang aircraft flew over the area in a suspicious manner.

Altitude = 800 meters.

September 19

We did not leave very early because the peasants could not find their animals. Finally, after I let out a healthy outburst, we left with the caravan of prisoners. Because of Moro we walked slowly. When we reached the fork in the river we found out that three more prisoners had been taken. We also learned that the forward detachment had just left, with the intention of reaching a sugar plantation two leagues away. These two leagues were very long ones—as long as the first two turned out to be. Close to nine o'clock at night we reached the plantation, which was only a canefield. The rear guard arrived after 9:00.

I had a discussion with Inti about some weaknesses of his in the matter of food. He was very upset and admitted it was true and said he would make a public self-criticism when the visitors were gone, but he denied some of the accusations. We passed altitudes of 1,404 meters and are now at 1,000. From here to Lusitanos[7] is a three-hour walk, perhaps four, according to the pessimists. Finally, we ate pork, and the sugar eaters were able to fill themselves up on chankaka.

The radio is giving considerable coverage to the case of Loyola. The teachers are out on strike. The students at the sec-

---

7. Los Sitanos.

ondary school where Higueras worked—one of those arrested—are on a hunger strike. And the oil workers are about to go on strike because of the creation of the oil enterprise.

A sign of the times: I have run out of ink.

September 20

I decided the departure would begin at 3:00 p.m., with the goal of reaching the settlement of Los Sitanos at nightfall, since we had been told that three hours was plenty of time. However, due to a variety of problems the start of the trip was delayed until 5:00, and we were overtaken by complete darkness in the hills. Despite lighting a lamp, we did not arrive at Aladino Gutiérrez's house until 11:00 p.m. There were not many grocery items there; some cigarettes and a few trifles were obtained, but no clothing. We took a short nap and at 3:00 a.m. began the march to Alto Seco, which they say is four leagues away. The mayor's telephone was found, but it has not worked in years, and in addition the line is down. The mayor is named Vargas, and has held the position for a short time.

The radio reports no news of any importance. We passed heights of 1,800 meters; Los Sitanos is at 1,400 meters.

We walked about two leagues toward the village.

September 21

We set out at 3:00 a.m. under a bright moon. The route had been mapped out ahead of time and we walked until about 9:00 without encountering inhabitants, crossing altitudes of 2,040 meters, the highest we have yet reached. At that time we came across a couple of herdsmen, who indicated the direction to Alto Seco, two leagues away. We had walked barely two leagues during part of the night and the morning.

Upon reaching the first houses at the bottom of the hill, we purchased some food items and went to prepare a meal at the mayor's house. Later we passed a corn mill run by hydraulic power on the banks of the Piraymiri river (1,400 meters in altitude). The people are very afraid, and try to disappear from us.

We have lost a lot of time owing to our poor mobility. It took us from 12:35 until 5:00 p.m. to travel the two leagues to Alto Seco.

September 22

When we of the center group arrived in Alto Seco, we learned that the mayor had apparently left yesterday to warn that we were nearby. In reprisal, we seized everything in his grocery. Alto Seco is a little village of 50 houses, situated at an altitude of 1,900 meters, and it greeted us with a well-seasoned mixture of fear and curiosity.

The provisioning machine began to function, and we soon had a respectable quantity of food supplies in our camp, which was an abandoned house near the water hole. The small truck that was supposed to arrive from Valle Grande did not come, which would seem to confirm the story about the mayor having gone to warn about us. Nevertheless I had to put up with the crying of his wife, who in the name of God and her children asked for payment, which I refused.

At night Inti gave a talk in the local schoolhouse (first and second grades) to an audience of 15 amazed and silent peasants, explaining the scope of our revolution. The teacher was the only one who spoke, asking whether we were fighting in the towns. He is a mixture of peasant wiliness—with some education—and the naiveté of a child; he asked a number of questions about socialism. A tall youth volunteered to serve as our guide, warning us about the teacher, whom they call a sly fox. We left at 1:30 a.m. en route to Santa Elena, which we reached at 10:00 a.m.

Altitude = 1,300 meters.

Barrientos and Ovando held a press conference, where they went over all the information contained in the documents, and stated that Joaquín's group has been wiped out.

September 23

The place was a beautiful orange grove, which still had a considerable amount of fruit. The day was spent resting and sleeping, but a number of lookouts had to be posted. We arose at 1:00 a.m. and departed at 2:00, heading toward Loma Larga. We reached it at sunrise, passing altitudes of 1,800 meters. The men are loaded down and the march is a slow one. Benigno's cooking gave me indigestion.

September 24

As we reached the settlement called Loma Larga, I was suffering pains in my liver and was vomiting, and the men were exhausted from unproductive hikes. I decided we would spend the night at the junction of the road to Pujio. We killed a pig sold us by the only peasant remaining in town, Sóstenos Vargas. The rest fled when they saw us.

Altitude = 1,400 meters.

September 25

We reached Pujio early in the day, but there we found people who had seen us down below the day before. In other words, our movements are being announced ahead of time by Radio Bemba.[8] Pujio is a little settlement situated up on a hill. The people who fled when they first saw us gradually began to approach us and treated us well.

A carabinero had left there in the morning; he had come from Serrano in the department of Chuquisaca to arrest a debtor. We are at a point where three departments converge.[9] It is becoming dangerous to travel with mules, but I am trying to make it as easy as possible for El Médico, since he is very weak. The peasants claim to know nothing about the army's presence in any part of this region.

We walked in short stretches until reaching Tranca Mayo, where we slept on the side of the road, since Miguel did not take the precautions I had demanded. The mayor of Higueras is in the area and we ordered the sentries to apprehend him.

---

8.   A Cuban expression meaning word of mouth.
9.   Santa Cruz, Chiquisaca, and Cochabamba.

Altitude = 1,800 meters.

Inti and I spoke with Camba, who agreed to accompany us as far as La Higuera, a point close to Pucará. From there he will try to make it to Santa Cruz.

September 26

Defeat. At dawn we reached Picacho, where everyone was outside holding a celebration.[10] It is the highest point we have achieved, 2,280 meters. The peasants treated us very well and we continued without too much fear, despite Ovando's assurance of my capture at any moment.

When we reached La Higuera, everything changed. All the men had disappeared and there were only a few women here and there. Coco went to the telegraph operator's house, where there is a telephone, and brought back a cable dated September 22, in which the subprefect of Valle Grande asks the mayor if there is any news of a guerrilla presence in the region, telling him to cable any information to Valle Grande, and saying that the expenses will be covered. The man had fled, but his wife assured us he had not spoken to anyone today because a celebration was being held in the next town, Jagüey.

At 1:00 p.m., the forward detachment set out on the road to Jagüey, where a decision was to be made about the mules and El Médico. A few minutes later, while I was speaking with the only man in the town, who was very frightened, a coca merchant showed up, saying he had come from V[alle] G[rande] and Pucará and had not seen anything. He too was very nervous, which I attributed to our presence, and I let them both go, despite the lies they had told us.

At approximately 1:30, as I was starting for the top of the hill, shots were heard coming from the ridge above, indicating that our people had fallen into an ambush. I organized the defense inside the little village, awaiting the survivors. I set as the escape route the road leading to the Río Grande. In a few

---

10. For the Feast of Spring.

moments, Benigno arrived, wounded, followed by Aniceto and by Pablito, whose foot was in bad shape. Miguel, Coco, and Julio had been killed and Camba had disappeared, leaving his knapsack behind.

The rear guard advanced rapidly along the road and I followed, still leading the two mules. Those in back of us were under fire at close range and fell behind, and Inti lost contact. After setting up a small ambush and waiting a half hour for Inti, during which time we came under more fire from atop the hill, we decided to leave him. However, he soon caught up to us. Then we noticed that León had disappeared. Inti reported having seen his knapsack along the little gorge that was the only way out. We spotted a man walking hurriedly along a canyon and concluded it was him. Trying to throw the soldiers off our scent, we set the mules loose and sent them heading down the canyon below, while we followed along a little gorge with bitter water in it. We went to sleep at 12:00, since it was impossible to advance.

September 27

At 4:00 a.m. we resumed the march, trying to find a place where we could ascend. This was accomplished at 7:00 a.m., but it was on the side opposite where we intended. In front of us was a barren hill that seemed harmless. We climbed up a little bit, finding a spot protected from aircraft, in a sparsely wooded area. There we discovered that the hill had a road, although no one had been across it all day. Late in the afternoon a peasant and a soldier climbed halfway up the hill and played around a bit, without seeing us. Aniceto had just finished scouting and saw that there was a large group of soldiers in a house nearby. This would have been the easiest road for us to take, and now it was blocked off.

In the morning we saw a column of men going up a nearby hill, with their weapons shining in the sun. Later, at noon, isolated shots were heard, along with a few machine-gun bursts. Later still, we heard shouts of "There he is!" "Come out of there!" and "Are you going to come out or not?" followed by shots. We do not know the fate of the man, whom we presume to be Camba. We left at dusk, trying to climb down to the water along the other side. We stopped at a thicket that was denser than the previous one. To find water it was necessary to go down into the canyon, since there is a cliff preventing us from getting it here.

The radio is reporting that our clash was with the Galindo company, with three dead, whose bodies are to be transported to V[alle] G[rande] for identification. It appears that Camba and León have not been taken prisoner.[11] Our losses this time are very great indeed. The one we will feel most is Coco, but Miguel and Julio were magnificent fighters, and the human value of the three is incalculable. León seemed to have promise.

Altitude = 1,400 meters.

September 28

A nerve-wracking day, which at one point seemed like it would be our last. Early in the morning water was brought up, and right afterward Inti and Willi went to scout another possible descent into the canyon. However, they returned immediately since there is a road spanning across the entire hill in front of us, with a peasant on horseback traveling along it.

At ten o'clock, 46 soldiers passed right in front of us, carrying knapsacks, and it seemed to take centuries for them to pass by. At noon, another group appeared, this time with 77 men. And to top it all off, a shot was heard just then, which made the soldiers take positions. The officer ordered them to go down into the ravine, which appeared to be the one we were in. Finally, however, there was a radio communication and the officer seemed satisfied and resumed the march.

Our refuge has no defense against an attack from above, and if we are detected, the possibilities of escape are remote.

---

11. Both were captured that day.

Later on a soldier passed by, pulling a tired dog behind him, trying to get it to walk. Later still, a peasant went by, guiding another soldier behind him. Later on, the peasant made the return trip, and nothing happened this time. However, the anxiety at the moment when the shot was fired was great indeed.

All the soldiers passing by had knapsacks on, giving the impression they are withdrawing. There were no fires seen at the little house during the night, and the shots they usually fire to greet the evening were not heard. Tomorrow we will spend all day scouting around the village. A light rain got us wet, but did not appear to be enough to erase our tracks.

The radio reported that Coco has been identified and gave a confused piece of news about Julio. They confuse Miguel with Antonio, giving the latter's responsibilities in Manila. Early on there was a news report about my death, but it was later denied.

September 29

Another tense day. The scouting party, Inti and Aniceto, left early to watch the house all day. From early on there was traffic along the road. At mid-morning soldiers without knapsacks passed by in both directions, in addition to others coming from below who were leading donkeys with nothing on their backs, later returning with the animals loaded up.

At 6:15 p.m. Inti returned with word that the 16 soldiers who had descended the hill had gone into the fields and could not be seen any more. This appears to be where the donkeys are being loaded up. Faced with this piece of news, it would have been a difficult decision to take this road. Although it is the easiest and most logical route for us, it would be easy for the soldiers to set an ambush for us, and in any case there are dogs at the house that could give us away. Tomorrow two scouting parties will be sent out. One will go to the same spot while the other will try to walk up the ridge as far as possible to see if there is a way out in that direction, probably by following the road used by the soldiers.

There was no news on the radio.

September 30

Another day of tension. In the morning Radio Balmaseda of Chile announced that high sources within the army have stated that they have Che Guevara cornered in a jungle canyon. The local stations are silent. It appears there may have been a betrayal and that they are certain of our presence in the area.

Shortly afterward, soldiers began moving back and forth. At noon, 40 of them passed by in separate columns, with weapons ready. They stopped at the little house, where they made camp and posted nervous sentries. Aniceto and Pacho brought back this information. Inti and Willy returned with news that the Río Grande was about two kilometers straight ahead, that three houses are located on the upper part of the canyon, and that there are places for us to camp without being seen on either side.

After finding water, the 22 of us began a fatiguing nighttime march. It was slowed up by Chino, who walks very poorly in the dark.[12] Benigno is doing very well, but El Médico has not fully recovered.

SUMMARY OF THE MONTH

This should have been a month of recuperation, and was about to be, but the ambush in which Miguel, Coco, and Julio were killed ruined everything. Since then we have remained in a dangerous position. Moreover, there was the loss of León; losing Camba was a net gain.

We had several small skirmishes: the one where we killed a

---

12. Chino had poor eyesight, and his glasses were broken and missing a lens.

horse; where we killed one soldier and wounded another; where Urbano exchanged fire with a patrol; and the fateful ambush at La Higuera. We have already let the mules go and I think it will be a long time before we again have animals of this type, unless my asthma acts up once more.

On a separate question, some of the news about the death of the other group appears to be true, and it must now be considered eliminated. It is still possible that a small group is wandering about, avoiding contact with the army, since the news about the death of seven of them together could be false, or at least exaggerated.

The characteristics of the month are the same as those of the previous one, except that the army is now showing more effectiveness in action. In addition, the mass of peasants are not helping us at all and are being turned into informers.

The most important task is escaping from here and finding more favorable areas. Then to reestablish contacts, despite the disruption of the entire apparatus in La Paz, where they have also dealt us hard blows. The morale of the rest of the men remains very good. My only doubts are about Willy; unless I talk with him he may take advantage of some clash to try to escape on his own.

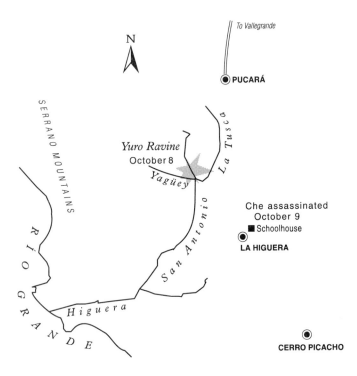

N

To Vallegrande

⊙ PUCARÁ

SERRANO MOUNTAINS

La Tusca

Yuro Ravine
October 8

Yagüey

San Antonio

Che assassinated
October 9
■ Schoolhouse
⊙
LA HIGUERA

RÍO

GRANDE

Higuera

⊙
CERRO PICACHO

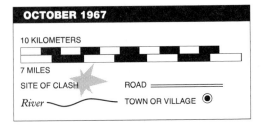

OCTOBER 1967

10 KILOMETERS

7 MILES

SITE OF CLASH   ROAD ════════

River ～～～～   TOWN OR VILLAGE ⊙

OCTOBER 1967

October 1

Altitude = 1,600 meters.

This first day of the month passed without incident. At dawn we reached a sparsely wooded area where we made camp, posting lookouts at the various points of approach. The 40 soldiers moved away from us along a canyon that we had considered following. They fired a few shots, the last of which were heard at 2:00 p.m. There appears to be no one in the little houses, although Urbano saw five soldiers walk down, not following any road.

I decided to remain here another day, since the spot is good and has a guaranteed escape route, in that it overlooks almost all the enemy's troop movements. Pacho, assisted by Ñato, Darío, and Eustaquio, went to look for water and returned at 9:00 p.m. Chapaco cooked fritters, and we had a little charqui, assuaging our hunger.

There was no news.

October 2

Antonio.[1]

The day passed without any sign of soldiers. However, a few small goats passed by our position, led by sheepdogs who barked. We decided to try to leave by passing beside one of the farm plots closest to the canyon. We started the descent at 6:00 p.m., allowing plenty of time for us to arrive and cook before making the crossing. However, Ñato got lost but insisted on continuing ahead. When we decided to make our way back, we got lost and spent the night at the top, without being able to cook and very thirsty.

The radio gave us the explanation for the soldiers' action on September 30. According to a report broadcast by Radio Cruz del Sur, the army reported an encounter at the Abra del Quiñol with a small group of ours, without casualties on either side, although they report finding traces of blood from our withdrawal. According to this dispatch, the group was composed of six individuals.

October 3

A long and unnecessarily intense day. As we were getting ready to return to our base camp, Urbano arrived to report that while we were walking he had heard some peasants passing by saying, "Those are the ones who were talking last night." The report is probably inaccurate, but I decided to treat it as if it were perfectly true. So without mitigating our thirst we climbed back up to a ridge that overlooked the path used by the soldiers.

The rest of the day remained absolutely calm. At nightfall we all climbed down the hill and made coffee, which tasted divine, despite the bitter water and the greasy pot in which it was made. Later we made corn meal, which we ate there, and rice with tapir meat to take with us. At 3:00 a.m. we began the march, after first scouting it out, and circled around the farmland very easily, winding up at the canefield we had chosen.

---

1. A reference to the birthday of the guerrilla Antonio.

There is no water there, and there were signs that the area has been scouted by soldiers.

The radio reported news of two prisoners: Antonio Domínguez Flores (León) and Orlando Jiménez Bazán (Camba). The latter admits having fought against the army; the former says he turned himself in, trusting in the president's word. Both are giving abundant information about Fernando, his illness, and everything else, not to mention what they told them that is not being publicized. Thus ends the story of two heroic guerrillas.

Altitude = 1,360 meters.

An interview with Debray was heard; he was very courageous when faced with a student provocateur.

October 4

After resting in the ravine, we followed it downhill for half an hour, and then came to another one adjoining it, which we climbed. We rested until 3:00 p.m. to escape the sun. At that time we resumed walking for a little over half an hour, when we met up with the scouting party. They had gone to the end of the little canyons without finding water. At 6:00 p.m. we left the ravine and continued along a cattle trail until 7:30, when nothing at all could be seen. We stopped until 3:00 a.m.

The radio reported that the Fourth Division's general command has moved its forward post from Lagunillas to Padilla, in order to better oversee the Serrano region, where it is believed the guerrillas may try to flee. The discussion is that if I am captured by forces of the Fourth Division, I will be tried in Camiri; and if it is by the Eighth, the trial will be in Santa Cruz.

Altitude = 1,650 meters.

October 5

After resuming the march, we walked with difficulty until 5:15 a.m. At that time we abandoned the cattle trail and entered a small, sparsely wooded area, but one where the vegetation was high enough to provide us some cover from indiscreet glances. Benigno and Pacho made several scouting expeditions to find water, thoroughly combing the area by the nearby house without finding any; it is probably in a little well, off to the side. After the scouting was finished, six soldiers were seen arriving at the house, apparently just passing by. We left at nightfall, with the men exhausted from lack of water, and with Eustaquio making a spectacle and crying about needing a mouthful of water. At dawn, after a very bad hike, with many stops and starts, we reached a small wooded area where the barking of dogs could be heard. A high, barren ridge can be seen nearby.

We treated Benigno, whose wound was discharging a little pus, and I gave El Médico an injection. As a result of the treatment, Benigno complained of pain during the night.

The radio reported that our two Cambas were transferred to Camiri to serve as witnesses at the trial of Debray.

Altitude = 2,000 meters.

October 6

Scouting patrols revealed the presence of a house very close by. However, they also found that in a ravine farther away there was water. We headed there and spent all day cooking under a big rock ledge that served as a roof. Nevertheless, I was uneasy all day long, since we had passed by well-populated areas in broad daylight and are now in a hollow. Preparing the meal took longer than expected, so we decided to leave at dawn for a tributary near this little creek, and from there we will make a more detailed scouting trip to determine our future route.

Radio Cruz del Sur reported an interview with the Cambas. Of the two, Orlando was a little less vile. Chilean radio carried a censored news item to the effect that there are 1,800 men in the area searching for us.

Altitude = 1,750 meters.

October 7

Today marks eleven months since our guerrilla inauguration. The day went by without complications, bucolically, until 12:30 p.m., when an old woman, tending her goats, entered the canyon where we were camped and had to be taken prisoner. The woman gave us no reliable information about the soldiers, simply repeating that she knew nothing, and that it had been quite a while since she had last gone there. All she gave us was information about the roads. From what the old woman told us, we gather that we are now about one league from Higueras, one from Jagüey, and about two leagues from Pucará. At 5:30 p.m. Inti, Aniceto, and Pablito went to the old woman's house. One of her daughters is bedridden and another is a half dwarf. They gave her 50 pesos and asked her to keep quiet, but held out little hope she would do so, despite her promises.

The 17 of us set out under a waning moon. The march was very tiring, and we left many traces in the canyon where we had been. There were no houses nearby, just a few potato patches irrigated by ditches leading from the stream. At 2:00 a.m. we stopped to rest, since it was now useless to continue. Chino is becoming a real burden when it is necessary to walk at night.

The army made a strange announcement about the presence of 250 men in Serrano, who are there to cut off the escape of those who are surrounded, 37 in number. They give the area of our refuge as between the Acero and Oro rivers. The item appears to be diversionary.

Altitude = 2,000 meters.

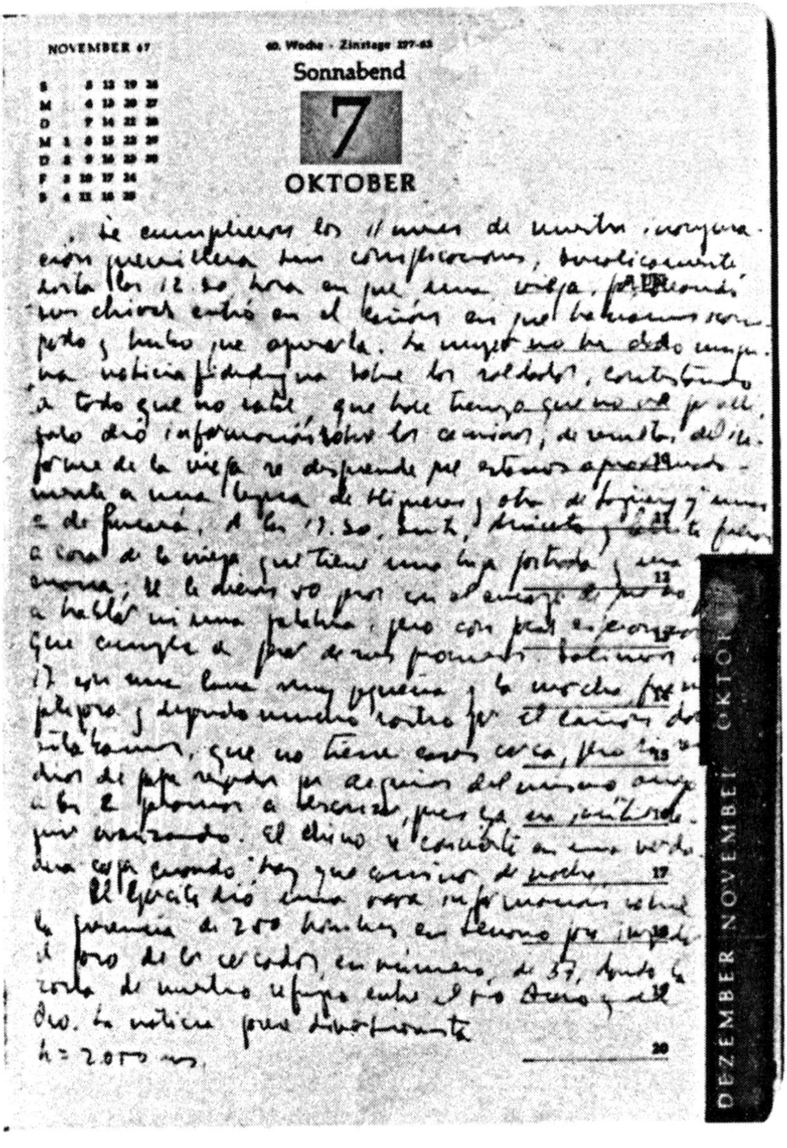

NOVEMBER 67

S   6 13 19 26
M   6 20 27
D   7 14 22 28
M 1 8 15 22 29
D 2 9 16 23 30
F 3 10 17 24
S 4 11 18 25

40. Woche · Zinstage 277-63
Sonnabend
7
OKTOBER

(Handwritten diary entry in Spanish — largely illegible)

Se cumplieron los 11 meses de nuestra incorpora-
ción guerrillera sin complicaciones, simbólicamente
esta tos 12 de hora en que una vieja, por llevando
nos chivos entró en el kedán en que estacamos acam-
pados y hubo que apresarla. La mujer no ha dado ningu-
na noticia fidedigna sobre los soldados, contestando
a todo que no sabe, que hace tiempo que no va por allí.
Solo dió información sobre los caminos, de vuelta, del in-
forme de la vieja se desprende por estamos aproximada-
mente a una legua de Higueras, otra de Jagüey y una
de Pucará. A las 17.30, Inti, y Aniceto y [...] se fueron
a casa de la vieja que tiene una hija postrada y una
enana; se le dieron 50 pesos con el encargo de que no
a hablar ni una palabra, pero con pocas esperanzas
de que cumpla a pesar de sus promesas. Salimos
los 17 con una luna muy pequeña y la marcha fue muy
fatigosa y dejando mucho rastro por el camino del
que íbamos, que no tiene casas cerca, otro 2.00 medios de papa rígido en aquellos del mismo arroyo
a las 2 [...] a se[...]os, pues ya en [...]
iba avanzando. El chivo [...] con[...] en una verda-
dera caja cuando [...] que caminar, de noche.   17

El Ejército dió datos para informarnos sobre
la presencia de 250 hombres en Serrano por impedir
el paso de los cercados, en número de 37, donde la
zona de nuestro refugio entre el río Acero y el
Oro. La noticia parece diversionante
h = 2000 ms.

Documents
and letters
by
Che Guevara

Instructions for Cadres
Assigned to Urban Areas

This document, written by Guevara on January 22, 1967, for members of the guerrillas' urban support network, is mentioned in his diary on page 117. It was given to Loyola Guzmán when she visited the guerrilla camp on January 26.

Building a support network of the type we are aiming at should be guided by a series of norms, summarized below.

Activity will be primarily clandestine in nature. However, it will be necessary at times to establish contact with certain individuals or organizations, which will require some cadres to come up to the surface. This necessitates a very strict compartmentalization, keeping each area of work separate from the other.

Cadres should be strictly governed by the general line of conduct established by our army's general command and transmitted through leadership bodies. At the same time, they will have full freedom in the practical aspect of implementing this line.

To accomplish the difficult tasks assigned, as well as to survive, cadres functioning underground will need to develop highly the qualities of discipline, secrecy, dissimulation, self-control, and coolness under pressure. And they will need to use methods of work that shield them from unforeseen contingencies.

All comrades carrying out tasks of a semipublic character

will operate under the direction of a higher body that is underground. This body will be responsible for passing on instructions and overseeing their work.

To the extent possible, both the leader of the network and those assigned to head up different tasks will have a single function, and contact between different work areas will be made through the head of the network. The following are the minimum posts of responsibility for a network that has already been organized:

The head of the network, under whom are individuals heading up:

1. Supplies
2. Transport
3. Information
4. Finances
5. Urban actions
6. Contacts with sympathizers

As the network develops, someone will need to be in charge of communications, in most cases working directly under the head of the network.

The head of the network will receive instructions from the leadership of the army, and will put these into effect through those in charge of the different work areas. The head of the network should be known only by this small leadership nucleus, to avoid endangering the entire network in the event of his capture. If those in charge of work areas know each other, then their work will also be known to each other, and changes in assignment need not be communicated.

In the event of the arrest of an important member of the network, the head of the network and all those known by the arrested person will take steps to change their residences or methods of contact.

The person in charge of supplies will be responsible for provisioning the army. This task is an organizational one. Starting from the center, secondary support networks will be created, extending all the way to ELN territory. In some cases, this could be organized exclusively through peasants; in other cases, it will include the aid of merchants or other individuals and organizations that offer their help.

The person in charge of transport will be responsible for transferring supplies from storage centers to points where the secondary networks will pick them up, or, in some cases, for bringing them directly to liberated territory.

These comrades should carry out their work under a solid cover. For example, they can organize small commercial enterprises that will shield them from suspicion by the repressive authorities when the scope and aims of the movement become public.

The person in charge of information will centralize all military and political information received through appropriate contacts. (Contact work is conducted partially in the open, gathering information from sympathizers in the army or government, which makes the task particularly dangerous.) All information gathered will be transmitted to our army's chief of information. The person in charge of information for the network will function under dual lines of authority: responsible both to the head of the network and to our intelligence service.

The person in charge of finances should oversee the organization's expenses. It is important for this comrade to have a clear view of the importance of this responsibility. It is true that cadres working under conditions of clandestinity are subject to many dangers and run the risk of an obscure and unheralded death. As a result of living in the city, however, they do not suffer the physical hardships that the guerrilla fighter does. It is therefore possible for them to get used to a certain carelessness in handling supplies and money that pass through their hands. There is also a risk that their revolutionary firmness will grow lax in the face of constant exposure to sources of temptation. The person in charge of finances must keep tabs on every last peso spent, preventing a single centavo from being dispensed without just cause. In addition, this person will be responsible for organizing the collection and administration of money from funds or dues.

The person in charge of finances will function directly under the head of the network, but will also audit the latter's expenses. For all these reasons, the person responsible for finances must be extremely firm politically.

The task of the comrade in charge of urban actions extends to every type of armed action in the cities: elimination of an informer or some notorious torturer or government official; kidnapping of individuals for ransom; sabotage of centers of economic activity in the country, etc. All such actions are to be conducted under the orders of the head of the network. The comrade in charge of urban actions is not to act on his own initiative, except in cases of extreme urgency.

The comrade responsible for sympathizers will have to function in public more than anyone else in the network. This person will be in contact with individuals who are none too firm, who clear their consciences by giving over sums of money or extending support while not fully committing themselves. These are people who can be worked with, although it must never be forgotten that their support will be conditioned by the risks involved. It is necessary, consequently, to try to convert them over time into active militants, urging them to make substantial contributions to the movement, not only in money but also in medical supplies, hideouts, information, etc.

In this type of network some individuals will need to work very closely with each other. For example, the person in charge of transport has an organic connection with the comrade heading up supplies, who will be his or her immediate superior. The person in charge of sympathizers will work with the head of finances. Those responsible for actions and for information will work in direct contact with the head of the network.

The networks will be subject to inspection by cadres, sent directly by our army, who will have no executive function but will simply verify whether instructions and norms are being complied with.

In making contact with the army, the networks should fol-

low the following "route": The high command will give orders
to the head of the network, who in turn will be responsible for
organizing the task in the important cities. Avenues will then
lead from the cities to the towns, and from there to the villages
or peasant houses, which will be the point of contact with our
army, the site of the physical delivery of supplies, money, or
information.

As our army's zone of influence grows, the points of contact
will get closer and closer to the cities, and the area of our
army's direct control will grow proportionately. This is a long
process that will have its ups and downs; and, as in any war
like this, its progress will be measured in years.

The central command of the network will be based in the
capital. From there other cities will be organized. For the time
being, the most important cities for us are Cochabamba, Santa
Cruz, Sucre, and Camiri, forming a rectangle surrounding our
zone of operations. Those heading up work in these four cities
should, to the extent possible, be tested cadres. They will be
put in charge of organizations similar to the one in the capital,
but simplified. Supplies and transport will be headed by a single individual; finances and sympathizers by another one; a
third person will coordinate urban actions; it is possible to dispense with an assignment to information, leaving this to the
head of the network. The coordination of urban actions will increasingly be linked to our army as its territory grows nearer
to the city in question. At a certain point, those involved in urban actions will become semiurban guerrillas, operating directly under the army's general command.

At the same time, it is important not to overlook the development of networks in cities that are today outside our field of
action. In these places we should garner support among the
population and prepare ourselves for future actions. Oruro
and Potosí are the most important cities in this category.

Particular attention must be paid to areas along the borders.
Villazón and Tarija are important for making contacts and receiving supplies from Argentina; Santa Cruz is important for

Brazil; Huaqui [Guaqui] or some other location along the border with Peru; and someplace along the frontier with Chile.

In organizing the supply network, it would be desirable to assign reliable militants who have previously earned a living in activities similar to what we are now asking them to do. For example, the owner of a grocery store could organize supplies or participate in this aspect of the network; the owner of a trucking firm could organize transport, etc.

Where this is not possible, the job of building up the apparatus must be done patiently, not rushing things. By doing so we can avoid setting up a forward position that is not sufficiently protected—leading us to lose it, while at the same time putting other ones at risk.

The following shops or enterprises should be organized: grocery stores (La Paz, Cochabamba, Santa Cruz, Camiri); trucking firms (La Paz–Santa Cruz; Santa Cruz–Camiri; La Paz–Sucre; Sucre–Camiri); shoemaking shops (La Paz, Santa Cruz, Camiri, Cochabamba); clothing shops (the same); machine shops (La Paz, Santa Cruz); and farms (Chapare-Caranavi).

The first two will enable us to store and transport supplies without drawing attention, including military equipment. The shoemaking and clothing shops could carry out the twin tasks of making purchases without drawing attention and doing our own manufacturing. The machine shop would do the same with weapons and ammunition. And the farms would serve as bases of support in the eventual relocation of our forces, and would enable those working on the farms to begin carrying out propaganda among the peasants.

It is necessary to stress once again the political firmness these cadres must possess. These are comrades who receive from the revolutionary movement only what is strictly necessary to their needs; and they give to it all of their time—as well as their liberty or their life, if it comes to that. Only in this way can we effectively forge the network necessary to accomplish our ambitious plans: the total liberation of Bolivia.

Communiqués of the ELN

To the Bolivian People[1]   *Issued*
Revolutionary truth vs. reactionary lies   *March 27, 1967*

The military thugs who have usurped power, murdered workers, and laid the groundwork for surrendering our resources to U.S. imperialism are now mocking the people with a comic farce. As the hour of truth approaches and the people rise up in arms, responding to the armed usurpers with armed struggle, the round of lies continues.

On the morning of March 23, forces of the Fourth Division, based in Camiri and numbering approximately 35 men, under the command of Major Hernán Plata Ríos, entered guerrilla territory along the Ñacahuaso river. The entire group fell into an ambush set by our forces. As a result of the action, 25 weapons of all types fell into our hands, including 3 60-mm. mortars with a supply of shells, and an ample supply of ammunition and equipment. Enemy losses were 7 killed, including a lieutenant, and 14 prisoners, 5 of whom were wounded in the clash. These

---

1. For references to this document in Guevara's diary, Inti Peredo's account, and Rolando's diary, see pages 156, 359, and 420.

were given the best medical treatment at our disposal.

All the prisoners were set free following an explanation of our movement's aims.

The list of enemy casualties is:

Dead: Pedro Romero, Rubén Amenazaga, Juan Alvarado, Cecilio Márquez, Amador Almasán, Santiago Gallardo, and the informer and army guide, named Vargas.

Prisoners: Major Hernán Plata Ríos, Capt. Eugenio Silva, soldiers Edgar Torrico Panoso, Lido Machicado Toledo, Gabriel Durán Escobar, Armando Martínez Sánchez, Felipe Bravo Siles, Juan Ramón Martínez, Leoncio Espinosa Posada, Miguel Rivero, Eleuterio Sánchez, Adalberto Mártinez, Eduardo Rivera, and Guido Terceros. The last five of these were wounded.

In making public the details of the first battle of the war, we hereby establish what our norm will be: the revolutionary truth. Our deeds demonstrated the integrity of our words. We regret the innocent blood shed by the soldiers who fell. Yet peaceful bridges—as the clowns in braided uniform claimed they were constructing—are not built with mortars and machine guns. They are attempting to paint us far and wide as common murderers. There has never been, nor will there ever be, a single peasant with cause to complain of our treatment and of our manner of obtaining supplies—with the exception of those who betray their class and volunteer their services as guides or informants.

Hostilities have begun. In future communiqués we will clearly set forth our revolutionary positions. Today we issue a call to workers, peasants, and intellectuals. We call upon all who believe that the time has now come to respond to violence with violence; to rescue a country being sold piece by piece to the U.S. monopolies; and to raise the standard of living of our people, who with each passing day suffer more and more the scourge of hunger.

The National Liberation Army of Bolivia

Teléfonos: 2901 — 2902.   Plaza Colón Nº 5726, Acera Baja.

AÑO VII   COCHABAMBA, LUNES 1º DE MAYO DE 1967   Nº 1560

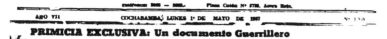

PRIMICIA EXCLUSIVA: Un documento Guerrillero

Primer Comunicado del «Ejército de Liberación Nacional de Bolivia»

Pese a que nos resulta muy difícil, virtualmente imposible, dar a conocer la procedencia del Comunicado No. 1 del "Ejército de Liberación Nacional de Bolivia", denominación que tendrían las guerrillas que operan en el Sudeste de Bolivia, retamos en condiciones de garantizar su autenticidad, ya que dicho documento, que está en nuestro poder desde hace varios días, no fue dado a conocer a la opinión pública porque se tenían algunas dudas sobre su origen. Ahora, una vez confirmada su autenticidad, PRENSA LIBRE llega a conocer en forma primicial y exclusiva, el primer documento emitido por los rebeldes desde el mismo teatro de operaciones:

AL PUEBLO BOLIVIANO
(Comunicado Nº 1)

FRENTE A LA MENTIRA REACCIONARIA, LA VERDAD REVOLUCIONARIA

El grupo de gorilas usurpadores, tras asesinar obreros y preparar el terreno para la entrega total de nuestras riquezas al imperialismo norteamericano, se burló del pueblo en una farsa comicial. Cuando llega la hora de la verdad y el pueblo se alza en armas, respondiendo la usurpación armada con la lucha armada, pretenden seguir su torneo de mentiras.

En la madrugada del 23 de marzo, fuerzas de la 4ta. División, con acantonamiento en Camiri, en número aproximado de 35 hombres, al mando del My. Hernán Plata Ríos, se internaron en territorio guerrillero por el cauce del río Ñancahuazú. El grupo íntegro cayó en una emboscada tendida por nuestras fuerzas. Como resultado de la acción, quedaron en nuestro poder 25 armas de todo tipo, incluyendo tres morteros de 60 mm. con su dotación de obuses, abundante parque y equipo.

Las bajas enemigas fueron: 7 muertos, entre ellos un teniente y 14 prisioneros, cinco de los cuales resultaron heridos en el choque, siendo atendidos por nuestro servicio sanitario con la mayor eficiencia que permiten nuestros medios.

Todos los prisioneros fueron puestos en libertad, previa explicación de los ideales de nuestro movimiento. La lista de bajas enemigas es la siguiente: MUERTOS: Pedro Romero, Rubén Amézaga, Juan Albarado, Cecilia Márquez, Amador Almanza, Santiago Gallardo y el delator y guía del ejército apellidado Vargas. PRISIONEROS: My. Hernán Plata Ríos, Cap. Eugenio Silva, soldados, Edgar Torrico Panoso, Lido Machicado Toledo, Gabriel Durán Escobar, Armando Martínez Sánchez, Felipe Bravo Silva, Juan Ramón Martínez, Leoncio Espinoza Posada, Miguel Rivero, Eleuterio Sánchez, Adalberto Martínez, Eduardo Rivera y Guido Terceros. Los cinco últimamente nombrados resultaron heridos.

Al hacer pública la primera acción de guerra, establecemos lo que será norma en nuestro ejército: la verdad revolucionaria.

Nuestros hechos demostrarán la justeza de nuestras palabras. Lamentamos la sangre inocente derramada por los soldados caídos, pero con morteros y ametralladoras no hacen pacíficos caminos, como afirman los fantoches de uniformes galonados, pretendiendo crearnos la leyenda de vulgares asesinos.

Tampoco hubo ni habrá un solo campesino que pueda quejarse de nuestro trato y de la forma de obtener abastecimiento, salvo los que traicionando su clase se presten a servir de guías o de delatores.

Están abiertas las hostilidades. En comunicados futuros fijaremos nítidamente nuestra posición revolucionaria; hoy hacemos un llamado a obreros, campesinos, intelectuales; a todos los que sientan que ha llegado la hora de responder a la violencia con la violencia y de rescatar a un país vendido en tajadas a los monopolios yanquis y elevar el nivel de vida de nuestro pueblo cada día más hambreado.

EJÉRCITO DE LIBERACIÓN NACIONAL DE BOLIVIA

Communiqué no. 1 of the ELN, published in *La Prensa* of Cochabamba, May 1, 1967.

COMMUNIQUÉ NO. 2

To the Bolivian People[2]
Revolutionary truth vs. reactionary lies   *April 14, 1967*

On the morning of April 10, 1967, an enemy patrol led by Lt.
Luis Saavedra Arombal and composed in its majority of soldiers
of the CITE,[3] fell into an ambush. Killed in the encounter were the
above officer and soldiers Ángel Flores and Zenón Prada
Mendieta; wounded was the guide Ignacio Husarima of the
Boquerón Regiment; taken prisoner were 5 soldiers and a noncommissioned officer. Four soldiers were able to escape, bringing
word of the clash to the company headed by Major Sánchez Castro. The latter went to the aid of his comrades, reinforced by 60
men from a nearby unit. These forces fell into another ambush,
costing the life of Lt. Hugo Ayala, noncommissioned officer Raúl
Camejo, and soldiers José Vijabriel, Marcelo Maldonado, Jaime
Sanabria, and two others not identified by us.

Wounded in the action were soldiers Armando Quiroga, Alberto Carvajal, Fredy Alove, Justo Cervantes, and Bernabé
Mandejara, who were taken prisoner together with the company commander, Major Rubén Sánchez Castro, and 16 other soldiers. In line with the norms of the ELN, the wounded were
treated with the few means at our disposal. The prisoners
were all set free following an explanation of the objectives of
our revolutionary struggle.

The enemy army's losses are summed up as follows: 10
dead, among them 2 lieutenants; and 30 prisoners that included Major Sánchez Castro, 6 of whom were wounded. The
weapons captured include a 60-mm. mortar, automatic weapons, rifles, M-1 carbines, and semiautomatic weapons. Ammunition for all these weapons was also captured.

---

2. For references to this document in Guevara's diary and Rolando's diary, see
   pages 173 and 420.
3. Special Troops Training Center.

On our side we must record with regret the loss of one man. The disparity in casualties is comprehensible if it is recalled that the time and place of all the battles that have taken place have been chosen by us; and that the Bolivian army brass is sending inexperienced soldiers, little more than children, to the slaughter. At the same time, while issuing official statements from La Paz and later pretending to grieve at demagogic funeral ceremonies, they hide who the real culprits are for the bloodshed in Bolivia.

Now they are shedding their mask and beginning to call for U.S. "advisers." This is how the war in Vietnam began, a war that is drowning that heroic people in blood and endangering world peace. We do not know how many "advisers" will be sent against us (we will know how to confront them), but we warn the people about the dangers of this act initiated by the military sellouts.

We call upon the young recruits to follow these instructions: When a battle begins, throw your weapon aside and put your hands on your head, remaining silently where you are at the moment when shooting starts. Never advance at the head of a column marching into combat zones; let the officers who incite you to battle occupy this position of extreme danger. Against those occupying the forward position, we will always shoot to kill. As much as it hurts us to shed the innocent blood of recruits, this is an unavoidable necessity of war.

National Liberation Army of Bolivia

COMMUNIQUÉ NO. 3

To the Bolivian People
Revolutionary truth vs. reactionary lies   *May 1967*

On May 8, in the guerrilla zone of Ñacaguasu, troops from a mixed company under the command of Second Lieutenant

Henry Laredo were ambushed. Those killed in the action include the above-named officer, in addition to Román Arroyo Flores and Luis Peláez, students from the training school for noncommissioned officers.

The following soldiers were taken prisoner: José Camacho Rojas, Bolívar Regiment; Néstor Cuentas, Bolívar Regiment; Waldo Veizaga, noncommissioned officers school; Hugo Soto Lora, noncommissioned officers school; Max Torres León, noncommissioned officers school; Roger Rojas Toledo, Braun Regiment; Javier Mayan Corella, Braun Regiment; Néstor Sánchez Cuéllar, Braun Regiment.

The last two were wounded in a prior action after failing to heed a command to halt. As always, the prisoners were set free after receiving an explanation of the aims and scope of our struggle. Also captured were 7 M-1 carbines and 4 Mausers. Our forces suffered no casualties.

The repressive army has issued frequent statements announcing guerrilla deaths, mixing elements of truth about their own acknowledged losses with fantasy about ours. Growing desperate in their impotence, they resort to lies. Or else they brutalize journalists who, because of their political views, are natural adversaries of the regime, blaming them for all their problems.

Let it be known that the ELN of Bolivia is the only force responsible for the armed struggle, where it stands at the head of its people, and that the struggle will not end until final victory is achieved. At that time we will know how to punish those responsible for crimes committed in the course of the war; this is apart from any reprisals that our army's command feels are appropriate to counter acts of vandalism by the repressive forces.

ELN of Bolivia

COMMUNIQUÉ NO. 4

To the Bolivian People[4]
Revolutionary truth vs. reactionary lies   *June 1967*

In recent dispatches, the army has acknowledged some of its losses suffered in clashes between advance detachments. At the same time, as usual, they attribute to us a large number of dead that are never exhibited. Although we have not received reports from all of our patrols, we can state with assurance that our losses are very small; and in the recent actions acknowledged by the army, we did not suffer any.

Inti Peredo is a member of our army's general command, where he holds the post of political commissar and commanded several of the recent actions. He is in good health and has been untouched by enemy bullets. The falsehood about his death is a tangible example of the absurd lies being spread by the army in their impotency in fighting our forces.

Regarding announcements about the supposed presence of combatants from other Latin American countries, for reasons of military secrecy we will give no figures. In line with our watchword—revolutionary truth—we will simply state that citizens of any country who accept our minimum program, the liberation of Bolivia, are accepted into the revolutionary ranks with equal rights and responsibilities to those of the Bolivian combatants, who naturally constitute the vast majority of our movement. Every man who fights for the freedom of our country arms in hand deserves—and receives—the honorable title of Bolivian, independently of where he may have been born. This is how we interpret genuine revolutionary internationalism.

ELN of Bolivia

---

4. For a reference to this document in Guevara's diary, see page 216.

COMMUNIQUÉ NO. 5

To the Miners of Bolivia[5]   *June 1967*

Comrades:

Proletarian blood has once more been shed in our mines.[6] Over many centuries, the blood of enslaved miners has alternately been sucked dry, and then shed whenever built-up injustice has led to explosions of protest. This repetitive cycle has continued without variation for hundreds of years.

In recent times, the pattern was broken temporarily, and the insurrectionary workers were the decisive factor in the victory of April 9.[7] This event gave rise to hopes that a new day would dawn, and that the workers would finally become masters of their own destiny. But the workings of world imperialism have revealed, for those with eyes to see, that when it comes to social revolution there are no halfway solutions. Either all the power is seized, or the advances won with so much sacrifice and so much blood will be lost.

The armed militias of the mining proletariat were the only serious force at the beginning. Then militias were formed of other sectors of the working class, of declassed elements, and of peasants. The members of these groups were unable to see their fundamental commonality of interests, and, under the demagogy of the antipopular forces, fell into conflict. Finally, the professional army reappeared as a wolf in sheep's clothing. Small and insignificant at the beginning, this army was

---

5. For references to this document in Guevara's diary and Inti Peredo's account, see pages 223 and 378.
6. A reference to the army's massacre at the Siglo XX mines on June 24, leaving 20 dead and scores wounded.
7. April 9, 1952, was the date of an insurrection that toppled the Bolivian military government and installed a new regime led by the Revolutionary Nationalist Movement (MNR). The Bolivian trade unions, led by the miners, played a central role in the uprising.

transformed into the armed tool against the proletariat, as well as the most reliable accomplice of imperialism. For this reason, the imperialists gave their approval to the military coup.

We are now recovering from a defeat caused by a repetition of tactical errors on the part of the working class. We are patiently preparing the country for a deep-going social revolution that will transform the system from top to bottom.

We must not repeat false tactics that are heroic but futile, and would lead the proletariat into a bloodbath and deplete its ranks, depriving us of its most combative elements.

Over long months of struggle, the guerrillas have shaken the country. They have inflicted a large number of casualties on the army and have brought about its demoralization, suffering virtually no losses of its own. Yet this same army, in a confrontation lasting several hours, ended up master of the day, strutting like peacocks over the bodies of workers. The difference between victory and defeat lies in the choice of correct or erroneous tactics.

Comrade miner: pay no further heed to the false apostles of mass struggle, those who interpret this as the people marching forward, in compact formation, against the oppressors' guns. Let us learn from reality! Against machine guns, bare chests, however heroic, are of no avail. Against modern instruments of destruction, barricades, however well constructed, are of no avail. In underdeveloped countries with a large peasant base and a vast territory, mass struggle should revolve around the action of a small, mobile vanguard—the guerrillas—firmly based among the people. This guerrilla force will increasingly acquire strength at the expense of the enemy army, and will act as catalyst for the masses' revolutionary fervor, until a revolutionary situation is created. At that time, state power will be toppled in a single well-aimed and well-timed blow.

Listen well: We are not calling for total inactivity; we simply recommend that forces not be expended in actions that do not guarantee success. The working masses should continuously bring their pressure to bear against the government, since this is a class struggle whose fronts are without limits. Wherever he may be, a worker has the obligation to fight with all his strength against the common enemy.

Comrade miner: the guerrillas of the ELN await you with open arms, and invite you to join the workers of the subsoil already fighting at our side. Here we will rebuild the worker-peasant alliance that was broken by the demagogy of the anti-popular forces. Here we will convert defeat into victory, and transform the lament of proletarian widows into a hymn of victory. We await you.

ELN

Letters

November 20, 1966

Leche:

Things are going well. There are four of us at the refuge, and it appears the others will be able to arrive without difficulty. One of Estanislao's[1] men knows what is up and favors continuing, come what may. The area has very few inhabitants, but is relatively close to population centers. There are indications that the best cadres will leave Estanislao if he does not make up his mind. He is on his way over there. It is necessary to fill his head with a lust for glory, but he should not be given money or commitments, except for what is absolutely necessary. The next steps will be to scout the conditions of the area.

The *ecodofa*[2] has just been sent. It is necessary to avoid having the Uruguayan vaccination certificates require a stamp. They took mine away in São Paulo and I had to get another one made there. The best document is a tourist card. I will try to obtain one for you over there, but it would be better to reproduce them, since it is possible that the number might duplicate another one.

---

1. Mario Monje.
2. A device for manufacturing false documents.

315

TO ERNESTO GUEVARA LYNCH[3]   *January 2, 1967*

Don Ernesto:

Amid the dust kicked up by the heels of Rocinante,[4] with my lance at the ready to do battle with enemy giants, I send you this brief note. Contained in this almost telepathic message is a hug for everyone, along with the ritual wish for a happy new year.

May the young lady, your sister, celebrate her 15th birthday[5] surrounded by the warmth of family. And may she give a tiny thought to this absent and sentimental young beau, whose concrete wish is to see you all soon (in less time than has gone by up to now). I confided this wish to a shooting star that must have been put there by a Magi king whom I met along the road.

Arrivederchi. Si non te veo piu . . . [Goodbye. In case I don't see you again]

D. *Tuijo*[6]

TO IVÁN[7]   *January 26, 1967*

Iván:

It was not possible to decipher anything of what you sent. Arturo is sending you some instructions that might be of use. I asked Manila for new formulas for internal use. I also sent word to them of the break in contact you there have experienced.

---

3. This undated letter to Guevara's father was taken by Tania when she left on January 2, 1967, for Buenos Aires, where it was posted.
4. Don Quixote's horse.
5. Guevara's Aunt Beatriz was celebrating her 80th birthday on January 9.
6. A play on the words *de tu hijo*, meaning "from your son."
7. Iván was a member of the guerrilla support network in La Paz.

Regarding your merchandise, I will send instructions prior to the departure.

Don't worry too much about the business matters; the catastrophe would be if the money were lost. The best thing would be not only for things to go well, but to make a profit. This does not preclude sacrificing money in the interests of security.

René sent a note with C.

Concerning your trip, await confirmation from me.

Regarding your work with the others: you should study the attached document and orient them in accordance with it.[8]

The person in charge (for now it is R.) will hold some meetings with you, but you must be careful and save yourself for the future, when your responsibilities will be of greater scope.

TO FIDEL CASTRO[9]   *July 1967*

This message, if it arrives in time, is for July 26.
Comrade Fidel Castro:

From eastern Bolivia, where we are fighting to duplicate the nation's struggles of the past, we extend our warm and fraternal greetings. We do so inspired by the modern-day example of the Cuban revolution, standard-bearer of the oppressed peoples of the world. Our greetings will be joined with those of millions of others who consider this date as the opening of the final stage of the liberation of the Americas.

We relay to you, your comrades, and your entire people our

8. Probably his "Instructions for Cadres Assigned to Urban Areas."
9. This message, in Guevara's handwriting and found in his notebook after his death, was signed, "Inti, Political Commissar, from the General Command of the ELN B."

unreserved devotion to the common cause, as well as our congratulations on completing another year of intransigent struggle against U.S. imperialism.

To be added: We suffered another failure in our effort to establish contact. We lost Tuma and Papi and a Bolivian from Guevara's group. There is no news on the death of the latter. We remain without communication from Joaquín. Pombo and Pacho were slightly wounded, but are unable to walk. The peasantry is in the stage of fear, and the legend of the guerrilla grows like wildfire. We will attempt to reunite with Joaquín to undertake new adventures. Do not fail to create another front.

Accounts
by
other
combatants

My Campaign with Che
by Inti Peredo

Inti Peredo was one of five guerrilla combatants (the others were Pombo, Benigno, Urbano, and Darío) able to escape the Bolivian military encirclement. He relates how this occurred in the final chapter of this document. Subsequently Peredo sought to reorganize the ELN and relaunch armed struggle against the dictatorship.

In August 1968 he traveled to Cuba, where he spent several months. While there, he was urged by the Italian publisher Giangiacomo Feltrinelli to write an account of his personal experiences.

Peredo returned secretly to Bolivia in October 1968. During the first three months of 1969, living clandestinely in La Paz, he wrote these memoirs, drawing on the collective reconstruction of events by all the veterans. On September 9, 1969, however, before his book could be published, the house he was staying in was raided by 150 police, who had been tipped off by an informer. After resisting for an hour, Peredo was wounded by a grenade, captured, and murdered.

A copy of the manuscript was smuggled out of the country by ELN supporters for safekeeping. In September 1970, a year after Peredo's death, it was published in mimeographed form in La Paz and Cochabamba. The work became widely known that same month when the West German magazine 'Der Spiegel' obtained a copy and printed excerpts. 'Mi campaña con el Che' was subsequently published in several Latin American countries in book form. Excerpts appeared in the Cuban journal 'Pensamiento Crítico' in May 1971.

Published here, for the first time in English, are the initial eleven chapters of the book, containing the entire text of Peredo's memoirs of the campaign.

1. CHE IN ÑACAHUAZÚ

Che was seated on a tree trunk. He had a cigar in his mouth, and was relishing the fragrance of the smoke. He was wearing his cap. As our group arrived, his eyes lit up with joy.

Imperialism's most wanted man, the legendary guerrilla, worldwide strategist and theorist, symbol of struggle and hope—this was the man calmly seated right in front of us, in the heart of one of the most oppressed and exploited countries of the continent.

It was the night of November 27, 1966.

His trip to Bolivia had been one of history's most fascinating secrets. Soon his enemies and the entire world would witness his "resurrection." This image came to mind as I recalled that imperialist news dispatches had already written his death certificate, "a victim of Castro's firing squad."

I was struck by a number of different reactions: confusion because of the respect I had for him (and always will); deep emotion; pride in shaking his hand; and a satisfaction, difficult to describe, in the certain knowledge that from then on I would become one of the soldiers in the army to be led by the most famous of all guerrilla commanders.

Che—or Ramón, as he was introduced to the troop—greeted us warmly. Extending his hand, he said to me, "You must be Inti." I felt more at home. Some comrades, knowing I would be arriving in that group, had told him of my background. On my part, I too knew that Che was in the mountains, waiting for us. Even so, I was unable to control my feelings.

We sat down on some tree trunks. Within a short time, Pombo gave me an M-2 carbine (my first weapon) and my combatant's gear. It was all incredibly simple. Nevertheless, that night was the beginning of my life as a revolutionary.

Conversation came easily, with lively discussion on general topics. I spoke little, still under the impact of that first meeting. Moments later, the group made a toast to the success of the guerrilla struggle, confident in the final victory.

When it got late, Tuma, a man who over time would become one of the most beloved among us, helped me set up my hammock. We had no time to sleep.

Shortly before two o'clock in the morning, with some of us still awake, we were initiated into the "gondola," a term that would become popular around the world as the war went on. The gondola consisted simply in going from our camp to the zinc house to bring back food, weapons, and munitions. It was a difficult task, but Tuma, with his cheerful personality that energized our column, christened it the "gondola." This was an ironic comparison with the ramshackle buses that made their way through the streets of Bolivia's cities, and which carried that name.

The night was very dark.

At the zinc house, Che gave us his first practical lesson of how a modest and capable leader should act: he chose the heaviest sack and put it on his back to begin the return trip. In the course of the journey, he tripped and fell, due to the poor visibility. He picked up his load once again and continued on to the camp. We followed his example.

The guerrilla army was beginning to take shape.

2. BOLIVIA: COUNTRY IN THE VANGUARD

My last day in La Paz was November, 25, 1966. Close to midnight, I left in a jeep with Joaquín, Braulio, and Ricardo. In another vehicle, farther ahead, were Urbano, Miguel, Maymura,[1] and Coco. Twelve hours later we were in Cochabamba. There I bid farewell to my wife, who was living at my father-

---

1. Freddy Maymura (Ernesto).

in-law's house. The conversation was relaxed, free of melodrama. She already knew of my definitive departure into the mountains. Before leaving, I kissed my children.

My decision to join the armed struggle was a product of a series of considerations that had long been maturing. Together with Coco, I had been a member of the Communist Party of Bolivia since 1951, and knew very well that party's strategy, tactics, and internal workings. In addition, because I had worked closely with the party leaders, I was perfectly aware of their mentality.

However, it must also be pointed out that as long as there were no real perspectives for armed struggle in Bolivia, we participated in and fully agreed with the decisions of that leadership. This is an experience that we believe can be of use to members of other Communist parties in Latin America who confuse "unconditional loyalty" with allegiance to principles. For us, principles are the only thing of lasting value.

The policy of the majority of Latin American Communist parties is to go right up "to the edge of armed struggle." In this dangerous game they have become masters. As soon as they reach the edge, they stop short and return to their original position of conciliation, submerging themselves in parliamentarism. As soon as they have gone right up "to the edge of war," they sell their principles, forget their dead, and come up with theoretical justifications for their reformist or traitorous conduct.

The Communist Party of Bolivia was not, and is not, an exception. Committed over many months to preparing for and participating in the guerrilla struggle in our country, it had selected a group of comrades for this work. But the leadership, acting in a two-faced manner that we grasped without difficulty, was always indecisive, always waiting.

We lost confidence in these leaders, and I personally did not believe that the CP as a party would join in the war or offer its wholehearted collaboration, or that it would loyally exert every effort on the struggle's behalf.

Nevertheless, the group assigned to the preparatory work—

Ñato, Loro, Rodolfo, Coco, etc.—had a clear view of what our single and unwavering strategic course had to be. Our resolve to struggle to the end remained firm.

This is natural and has occurred in other countries as well. Many members who are placed right "at the edge of war," rather than retreating together with their conciliatory leaders, take the decisive step and put themselves in the vanguard. Then a new, dynamic, aggressive, and courageous force arises: the guerrilla unit.

Taking a look back at our history, we knew we were on the verge of an opportunity that could mark a new stage in Bolivia's destiny.

For us, the separation of Upper Peru from the Spanish empire was an emancipation struggle that was interrupted.[2] The social foundations were not altered. Political and economic power was transferred to the local aristocracy of Spanish descent and to the wealthy Spaniards living in the country. The people, the principal actor in this struggle of the 19th century, did not enjoy even the crumbs of power. However, over the course of almost a century and a half of struggle, they have fought to break their chains.

The historic opportunity to obtain genuine and definitive independence was now at hand. It was embodied in the development of the guerrilla struggle, whose seeds were germinating in the jungles of Bolivia.

This form of struggle has deep roots in the tradition of the people. For 15 years—from 1810 to 1825—guerrillas such as Padilla, Moto Méndez, the priest Muñecas, Warnes, Juana Azurduy, and others fought heroically against the Spanish colonists, unfurling the continental banner of emancipation of Bolívar and Sucre.

We of course understood and are fully aware that conditions are different. The patriots of the 19th century confronted an

---

2. In 1825 the former Spanish colony of Upper Peru declared itself the independent republic of Bolivia.

imperialism in decline, one that was being pressed by other rising imperialist powers with ambitions of world domination. At the present time, on the other hand, we confront a dominant U.S. imperialism, the strongest military-industrial power in the world, which rules cruelly and unscrupulously, in a brutal, rapacious, and genocidal fashion.

In addition, the motives of the struggle are different. Now we are fighting as the vanguard of the people to conquer power, in order to build socialism and help form the new man, eliminating imperialism and its lackeys.

It is also necessary to caution that a strong sense of chauvinism has grown up among the people of Latin America, stimulated primarily by imperialism. This deformed nationalism has been employed as an instrument to divide the peoples and involve them in fratricidal wars. The traditional parties of the left, far from combating this tendency, have encouraged it and even defended it as an elementary principle, thereby abetting the tactic imposed by the enemy. And Bolivia, at this stage of the guerrilla struggle, was no exception.

This idea passed through our minds as we became convinced with more and more certainty that the Bolivian Communist Party would not join in the guerrilla struggle.

In any case, we had decided to fight to the end, regardless of the attitude taken by the CP. When we learned that Che would be leading the struggle, we were absolutely certain that the revolutionary process would be genuine, without sellouts or backsliding. For that reason, when I saw Ramón on that November night, the emotion I felt was tremendous.

The following day he called Coco, Loro, and me over to discuss the character of the struggle. This was my first political discussion with him, and like all the ones we had during the war, it was interesting and profound.

The first concept that came through clearly and categorically was the continental nature of the struggle. With his usual frankness, Che explained that the struggle would have the following characteristics: it would be long, harsh, and cruel.

Therefore, no one should set their minds on a "short-term" perspective. He then went on to explain why he had chosen Bolivia as the theater for the war.

The choice, he stated, was not an arbitrary one. Bolivia is located in the heart of the southern cone of our continent, bordering five countries, each with a political and economic situation becoming increasingly critical. Bolivia's geographic position thus makes it a strategic region for *extending* the revolutionary struggle to neighboring countries.

It must be kept in mind, he went on, that Bolivia cannot win its liberation alone, or at least it would be very difficult to do so. Even after the army and the state power are defeated, the triumph of the revolution is not assured. The servile governments, led by imperialism—or imperialism directly, with the collaboration of the servile governments—will try to destroy us. Nevertheless, if in the course of the struggle we are faced with the opportunity of taking power, we will not hesitate in assuming that historic responsibility. Clearly this would entail a great quota of sacrifice on the part of the Bolivian revolutionaries.

Later, Che explained to us what he meant by "quota of sacrifice" on the part of the Bolivian revolutionaries. He told us he had written a document for the Tricontinental meeting of the peoples that would be held in Havana in July 1967. In that document, he stressed, the following ideas are spelled out:

"We will be able to triumph over this army only to the extent that we succeed in undermining its morale. And this is done by inflicting defeats on it and causing it repeated sufferings.

"But this brief outline for victories entails immense sacrifices by the peoples—sacrifices that must be demanded starting right now, in the light of day, and that will perhaps be less painful than those they would have to endure if we constantly avoided battle in an effort to get others to pull the chestnuts out of the fire for us.

"Clearly, the last country to free itself will very probably do so without an armed struggle, and its people will be spared the suffering of a long war as cruel as imperialist wars are. But it may be impossible to avoid this struggle or its effects in a conflict of worldwide character, and the suffering may be as much or greater. We cannot predict the future, but we must never give way to the cowardly temptation to be the standard-bearers of a people who yearn for freedom but renounce the struggle that goes with it, and who wait as if expecting it to come as the crumbs of victory."[3]

For Che the "quota of sacrifice" signified the Bolivian people's role as standard-bearers of the guerrilla struggle, and never the postponement of the seizure of power.

In other words, we were becoming a vanguard people that would obtain its liberation in battle, and not as a "crumb of victory."

3. TOWARD A NEW VIETNAM

Che was also correct in spelling out for us the relationship between the struggle of the heroic people of Vietnam against U.S. imperialism and the guerrilla war in our continent. The war in Vietnam, he stated, is one part—although the most important—of the worldwide struggle against imperialism. The war in Vietnam is our own war. Imperialism has converted that heroic country into a laboratory experiment, so that the techniques of military destruction developed there can later be used against the peoples of our continent.

In Vietnam one can see clearly how imperialism not only violates a country's borders, but erases them entirely, claiming its "right" to chase after the patriots of the armed forces of the peoples of Indochina through Cambodia or Laos, bombing vil-

---

3. From "Message to the Tricontinental," in *Che Guevara and the Cuban Revolution*, pp. 356-57.

lages in these countries, and extending its brutal genocide with impunity.

The same thing will happen in Latin America, Che explained. Borders are artificial concepts imposed by imperialism to keep the peoples divided. Any people that recognizes these borders is condemned to isolation, and their liberation will be slow and painful.

The concept of borders must be broken through action. As our guerrilla movement develops, governments in neighboring countries will first send arms, advisers, and supplies, and will try to surround us. Later they will coordinate their actions, uniting in battle against the guerrillas. As they become incapable of defeating us, the U.S. Marines will intervene, and imperialism will unleash all its deadly power. Then our struggle will become identical with the one being waged by the Vietnamese people. The revolutionaries will understand, even if they do not yet feel this imperative, that it is necessary to unite to confront the oppressors in a coordinated manner, as a single force.

Many of the things foreseen by Che came to pass. The rest of them will also undoubtedly be confirmed in practice, since imperialism at that time had carefully studied the writings of our commander, and understood very well the strategic direction of his thinking. Che was also conscious of this question, as we will see later on.

Unfortunately, the "progressive" forces, or those calling themselves "vanguard," were extremely nearsighted or cowardly. They recoiled from, distorted, or failed to understand the meaning of the struggle.

During the course of the war, the United States sent to Bolivia a large quantity of modern arms, with immense lethal power that had already been tested out in Vietnam. They also sent "advisers" with considerable counterinsurgency experience. The job of the latter was to turn the soldiers into sadistic automatons, into inhuman beings without scruples. This was proven later on.

On the other hand, in a crude move, the CIA installed its command headquarters in the Quemado Palace, thereby demonstrating to Barrientos what he really is: a simple decoration. Later they ordered the governments of neighboring countries to close their borders to the revolutionaries and prevent any type of collaboration among them.

The fingerprints of imperialism were visible after each battle, as we captured SIG rifles (a variant of the Belgian FAL), U.S. grenades with NATO inscriptions, or canned food sent as a "fraternal" contribution by the armies of Argentina, Brazil, Paraguay, or Peru, transported unhindered through the territories of these countries.

4. THE DESERTION OF THE COMMUNIST PARTY

Che was a man who spoke with a single voice, and he had an extraordinary sense of loyalty. If one examines his diary, in the entry for November 27, 1966, he addresses two questions that at first glance appear to be of little importance. With the passing of time, however, they acquire great significance.

It says: "Ricardo brought some uncomfortable news: Chino is in Bolivia and wants to send 20 men and to see me. This causes some difficulties since we would be internationalizing the struggle before having worked things out with Estanislao." Later he notes, "In a preliminary discussion, Inti expressed the view that Estanislao will not take up arms. However, he seems determined to cut his ties."

These brief notations by Che, written solely for his personal use, had more of a history than I knew or could appreciate at the time. Later on he was to tell me many of the details. In addition, I was a witness to many events.

Ramón had originally held out hope that the Communist

Party would faithfully carry out its commitment.

"The Latin American Communist parties," he told us on the day following our arrival, "have an institutional structure inadequate for the conditions of today's struggle. As constituted, they are incapable of taking power and defeating imperialism. In addition, many of their leaders, such as Jesús Farías, Victorio Codovilla, etc., have become fossils and are archaic."

After making this analysis, he repeated his faith that in some part of Latin America, one or another of these parties would be able to adopt a revolutionary line. Che thought that the Communist Party of Bolivia might be able to play such a role.

"I am of this opinion," he stated, "because the party is new, its leaders are young, and especially because of the immense moral weight of the commitments it has made, over a considerable period of time, toward the continental revolution."

This statement reflects Che's moral purity, his unblemished loyalty, and his firmness in fulfilling commitments.

But the party and its leaders, especially Monje—whose underground name was Estanislao—did not possess this purity of moral values. Accustomed to making pacts with corrupt parties, with treacherous and opportunist leaders, and with crooked politicians who sell their principles, they had acquired the same traits. That is why I told Ramón that I was certain the party would not take up arms—much less Monje, whom I already considered a coward.

This judgment was not an arbitrary one. Monje had received military training together with other comrades who later died with Che. At that time, on his own initiative, he proposed a "blood pact" among them, to defend the armed struggle until death. This attitude had impressed many of the comrades. But that image would soon be erased.

Monje knew about the preparations of the guerrilla struggle. In July 1966, nine months before the first battle, he was already in direct contact with Ricardo and Pombo in La Paz. At that time he had made a commitment to select 20 men from the

Communist Party of Bolivia to join the armed struggle. One month later, when the comrades asked him about these 20 potential guerrillas, he answered, "What 20 men?"

Several days later, Monje threatened to withdraw the four Bolivian comrades who for several months had been working with the Cuban comrades in preparing the guerrilla base.[4] This was not merely the behavior of a vacillating individual, but of a political extortionist who sought to extract the greatest possible advantage from the conflicts he himself had created.

On September 28, 1966, at a meeting with Ricardo and Pombo in La Paz, he suggested that tasks be assigned to various units of the party to guarantee "better organization" of the struggle.

At that time he was disloyal even to his own organization, because he suggested "not informing the party secretariat, since they talk too much." He even reported that at the congress of the Communist Party of Uruguay, Kolle had known about the existing plans concerning Bolivia, and Arismendi demanded that all the CP general secretaries be informed of the matter. According to Monje, the general secretary of the Uruguayan CP had threatened to personally reveal the information if the Bolivians decided not to do so.

At the beginning of October, Monje had another meeting with the comrades, where he announced that the Central Committee of the Communist Party of Bolivia "had taken a positive step in unanimously accepting the line of armed struggle as the correct road to power." He added, scornfully, "Many of them support the armed struggle only verbally, because they are physically incapable of participating in it."

Several days later, however, he again created problems, going so far as to demand money to pay the salaries of the party functionaries, which the comrades acceded to.

These were the conditions under which we went up into the mountains.

---

4. Coco, Loro, Rodolfo, and Ñato.

My lack of confidence in the leadership of the Communist Party of Bolivia had been deepening as a result of a series of discussions I had with Monje. Without wavering he would jump from one extreme to the other. And he justified his political doubts by referring to his love for his family.

Loving one's family is natural for a guerrilla; because the struggle, although undoubtedly harsh, is motivated by a profound sense of love. For that reason I once told him:

"I think I love my family as much as you do, or more so. But my world does not consist of my family alone; it consists of all the people. I do not want my children to live in a cannibalistic society where the strongest devour the weakest, and where the weakest are always the children of the people. We must make this society better, but we will not make it better with an escapist or cowardly attitude. It is necessary to fight."

That is why, in my first discussion with Che, I frankly expressed my lack of confidence in the party's actions and in Monje's conduct. I even proposed to him that given the position I still held within the party's La Paz regional committee, I could recruit the best people to join our guerrilla nucleus.[5]

Che responded by saying that this attitude was incorrect, since relations with the party had to be based on mutual loyalty. At the same time, he firmly emphasized, "I am willing at any time to impart all my guerrilla experience to the Communist Party of Bolivia, and even to give them political command of the war."

For this reason, the references in the diary to Chino and Estanislao resemble statements written in code, although they appear as two separate questions. Nonetheless, they are clearly related: Che did not want to incorporate combatants from other countries without first clarifying the situation with Estanislao, despite the fact that the latter's conduct had not been honest. In any case, Monje had known previously what the

---

5. Inti Peredo was first secretary of the Communist Party's La Paz regional committee.

scope of the war was to be and had stated his agreement. But Che wanted to go over it with him in person.

That brings us to New Year's Eve. On December 31, there arrived at the zinc house Monje, Coco, Tania, and Ricardo, the latter having come to stay on permanently with us.

As we traveled with Che over to the first camp, Monje was very nervous. During the journey from the city to the farm, Coco had told him that Ramón was willing to give the party political command of the war, but he would not give it military command, a decision that he, Coco, considered correct. Later he pressed Monje to make the decision to join our nucleus.

Monje shook hands with us very coldly. While Che was greeting the other comrades, he asked me, "And how are things here?"

I replied, "They are going very well, as you will see. Moreover, you have arrived at the right time, because the war will soon begin. You should decide to fight with us."

Monje answered, "We shall see, we shall see."

Che and Monje went off by themselves to talk for several hours.

Later we returned to the base camp. When he arrived, Monje saw our people, greeted them, and began to talk to everyone. He later inspected the camp and then made the following comment: "This is a real camp. Clearly there is effective leadership here that knows what it wants, and that has experience."

Later on, he lauded the defenses that Che had planned, and the division of our column into forward detachment, center group, and rear guard. He made another comment that I remember well: "All this demonstrates effective combat preparation."

Shortly afterward, Monje asked me if he could speak with the Bolivian comrades. I immediately consulted with Che to ask whether this would be possible. Che answered affirmatively.

Then there began a meeting that was dramatic, tense at times, persuasive at other moments, harsh at certain points.

Monje related to us in general terms his discussion with Ramón, and later centered the problem around three fundamental questions, which are the ones noted in the diary:

"1. I will resign from the party leadership, because I believe that the party as such will not join the struggle, although I will try to obtain at least its neutrality. I will also try to get the organization to provide a few cadres for the struggle.

"2. I demanded from Che that the political-military leadership of the struggle must rest exclusively with me, at least as long as it takes place in Bolivia. When it becomes continental in character, we can hold a meeting of all the guerrilla groups, and at that time I will hand over command to Che, in front of everyone.

"3. I proposed to Che that I handle relations with other Latin American Communist parties, and try to convince them to support the liberation movements."

He went on to explain these questions in more detail, stating firmly, "We have not reached any agreement."

Monje's words did not surprise us, but their impact was painful, above all for the comrades who still had hopes in him and in the party.

Questions were raised, asking for more background information. Monje developed his point of view in the following manner:

"This guerrilla movement must be led by the party. Therefore, as first secretary I must have total command of both military and political matters. I cannot remain in a secondary position because wherever I am, I represent the party. Having the military command is a question of principle for us, just as much as it is for Che, who does not want to give it to me. Our disagreement is therefore total, even though on other questions we are either in agreement or he has agreed to our requests."

He added, pontifically: "When the people learn that this guerrilla movement is led by a foreigner, they will turn their backs and refuse to support it. I am sure it will fail because it is led by a foreigner, not a Bolivian. You will die very heroically, but you have no prospects of victory."

Monje's words made us indignant, above all his terming Che a *foreigner*, stupidly refusing to recognize him as a revolutionary of the continent. But his shamelessness reached the limit when he proposed that we desert.

"You are free to abandon the struggle, and have been given guarantees of your ability to do so. Leave now with me. We made only one commitment: to provide four comrades to work with Che wherever he goes. The rest of you should leave. Whoever wants to stay can do so. The party will take no punitive measures against you. But as first secretary, I advise you to leave with me."

The mere fact of asking us to abandon Che in the mountains was an act of treason. Perhaps he thought some of us might accept his miserable proposition.

Each one of us replied firmly that we would not leave. We asked him to stay, saying it was false pride for a revolutionary to refuse to serve under the orders of someone else—above all when that "someone else" was none other than Che, the most complete and beloved revolutionary, alongside whom thousands of Latin Americans would want to fight.

Some comrades, Ñato among them, begged him to stay. Ñato loved the party very much, but even more did he love the revolution. With great emotion, he said, "Stay, Mario. Your presence with us will raise the prestige of the Communist Party of Bolivia and all the Latin American Communist parties, which have lost all authority because of their inaction and their conciliation with the enemy. Preserve the prestige of the name Communist and stay with us."

Carlos spoke three or four times in the discussion, insisting, "Mario, don't go. You must not adopt such a vacillating and opportunist position. It is incredible that the party is behaving in such a way. We are sure that we will triumph.

"We have never thought about defeat. We are sure of victory. Without the party it will be more difficult, but with us is Che. In him we have confidence, and he will lead us to victory. Our revolution will triumph because the people will understand sooner or later that our leader is not a 'foreigner,' as you say, but a revolutionary, the best of them all. Your task, and that of the party, is precisely to make it clear among the people that Che is a revolutionary of the continent, and not a foreigner."

Other comrades told Monje that proletarian internationalism should not be confined to such a narrow framework. Che's presence among us, we stressed, was a true demonstration of proletarian internationalism.

Later on he assured us he would resign from the party leadership, because there was no longer anything he could do within the organization.

"It is obvious to me," he stated, "that the only road is that of armed struggle. But not this one. Rather, it should take the form of a general uprising. Since it is not possible to carry this out within the party, my post is of no further value. I will remain as a poor devil. It is therefore better that I go."

We asked him, "What are you going to do? Will you go back to your profession as a teacher, or to some other activity?"

He answered: "Possibly you will have me at your side as just another combatant. I have no other way out than the revolution."

Later on, talking with other Bolivian comrades, he stated that he did not want to become a traitor to the party (although he had already become a traitor to the revolution).

As a finishing touch, he ended the discussion on the following note: "I'm not about to become another Van Troi."

By this he meant that Van Troi—the Vietnamese hero murdered by U.S. troops, a young person who stands as an example for all the world's revolutionaries—had for him become a "useless martyr."[6]

---

6. Nguyen Van Troi was a 19-year-old Vietnamese youth executed in 1964 following an attempt on the life of U.S. defense secretary Robert McNamara. His last words facing the firing squad were "Down with the Yankees!"

This statement was sufficient to instill in us a profound contempt for Monje. But time would show that his conduct, and that of the party, would sink even deeper into the mud.

The meeting was painful in and of itself, not so much because of its emotional impact among the Bolivian comrades, as for what it showed about Monje's attitude and thinking; it revealed him to be a coward, a traitor, and a chauvinist.

That night we made a toast.

I was not present, because at that hour, when the advent of 1967 was being announced in the cities with firecrackers and the ringing of bells, it was my turn for guard duty. The comrades told me that Monje raised his cup and stated that here in Ñacahuazú, a new struggle for freedom was being launched, and he wished our guerrilla effort success.

Che responded that a new struggle for freedom was indeed beginning, and that this call to independence was similar to the one made by Pedro Domingo Murillo.[7] "Perhaps many of us will not live to see the final victory," Ramón said. "But to triumph one must fire the opening shot. And the moment for that has arrived." He added:

"This is a group that is resolved to fight, not as suicidal soldiers but as men who know they will obtain victory. But even supposing that definitive victory is not achieved, we are sure that this call to rebellion will reach the people."

The following morning Monje abruptly left. Che invited him to remain until the afternoon, when the jeep would be returning to the city.

"What are you going to do by yourself at the first camp?" Che asked him. "I prefer to be alone there," responded Monje.

It was obvious that he was nervous and did not dare to remain with us because he felt uncomfortable.

During the afternoon Che met with everyone and explained to us Monje's stance, his demands, and the manner in which he had forced the break. Addressing himself to the Bolivian

7. A reference to the onset of Bolivia's war of independence in 1809.

combatants, he announced:

"You in particular will have difficult days ahead, with moments of moral anguish and emotional conflicts. It may be that at some point in the struggle you will recall this episode, the lack of support by the party, and you will think that perhaps the CP is right.

"Give this a lot of thought. There is still time. Later it will be impossible. If anyone has problems, we will try to solve them through collective discussion or through the commissars."

At that time he told us he would be making contact with all the forces that wanted to join the revolution.

I gave Ramón a detailed report of our discussion with Monje and the objections he had made. "Those are the same ones he told me," he answered.

He later filled me in on other details of his discussion with Monje that are not contained in his diary. I remember clearly the dialogue, as related to me by Ramón:

Monje: "As long as the guerrilla struggle takes place in Bolivia, I insist on having absolute leadership. If the struggle were in Argentina, I would be ready to go with you, even if only to carry your knapsack. But while we are here in Bolivia, I must have absolute command."

Che: "That is a narrow and absurd view of proletarian internationalism. The type of struggle we are calling for goes beyond the national framework. Even if we were operating within your narrow schema, do you believe it is a Marxist position to demand leadership as a right based on nationality? You are mistaken. That is not proletarian internationalism.

"I will give you the following example: If Fidel were to go to Argentina to initiate a war, I would place myself under his command owing to the historic position he holds, and because, as you are well aware, I consider him my teacher. Because of my affection and respect for Fidel, I would gladly accept his command. Or do you believe this would be a question of nationality?

"The same relationship exists between you and me. The historic circumstances have placed me in a certain position. I have military experience that you lack. You have never participated in a military struggle.

"Now I ask you: Would you hold the same view if, instead of me being in Ñancahuazú, it was Malinovsky?"[8]

Monje: "Even if it were Lenin, my position would be the same."

Che replied, ironically, "If Malinovsky were here, you would be speaking differently."

At another point in the discussion, Ramón told him firmly, "I am here now, and the only way I will leave is dead. This is our territory."

At the end of every argument, Monje would return to the vicious circle about absolute command and Ramón's status as a "foreigner." He would get caught up in his own contradictions and insecurities, which appear clearly in the dialogue. Later on, the discussion continued in the following manner:

Che: "The question is real leadership. Imagine that you are the guerrilla leader. What will happen when it is learned that Che Guevara and Mario Monje are here? No one will believe that Mario Monje is leading the guerrilla struggle and that Che Guevara is under his command. Regardless of whether or not this were the case, everybody knows that I am more qualified than you to lead this column. False modesty leads us nowhere. You can appear publicly as the leader, sign all the statements on our behalf, but the real and effective leadership will be in my hands."

Monje: "Leadership has to be real, and from the beginning it must be in my hands. Owing to my lack of experience I will ask your advice and your suggestions until I have acquired the leadership capacity and can take charge of the guerrilla strug-

---

8. Gen. Rodion Malinovsky was Soviet defense minister and commander of its land forces.

gle. You can be my most important adviser."

Che: "Here I am adviser to no one. I do not believe in shirking responsibilities, and being an adviser would be exactly that: shirking responsibilities. I will never consider myself an adviser."

Monje: "But it is ridiculous for me to be leader only in appearance. You know that the CIA could infiltrate this guerrilla army, and the CIA agent will immediately realize that I am not the real leader. This news will be spread abroad and everybody will think I am a 'puppet.'"

Che: "If that is what is involved, I am ready to bow down before you in front of the troops every morning and ask for your instructions. That should satisfy the CIA agent."

Despite the aggressive attitude of Monje at times, Che always maintained great composure. When Monje stated that he would resign from the party, Che answered that this would be a personal decision, although Che felt it was an error, because it would serve to shield those who should be historically condemned for their unwillingness to struggle.

He also acquiesced to Monje's proposal that he solicit support for the guerrilla struggle from other Latin American Communist parties, although he warned that this was a useless effort, destined to fail. He told him: "Asking these parties to collaborate in the armed struggle is like demanding they renounce their reason for existence. Asking Codovilla to support Douglas Bravo would be like asking him to condone an uprising within his own party."

Another point of conflict discussed at that time was contact with Moisés Guevara's group. Monje was fiercely opposed to this, but the arguments he put forward were based solely on party interests, and lacked consistency. He called Moisés Guevara "pro-Chinese." That was enough to stigmatize him.

Che told Monje: "Why do you hold such a sectarian position? Our guerrilla struggle should open its doors to everyone who wants to participate. Our objective is the revolutionary seizure of power. If there are honest people who agree with us, we should not reject them. It is absurd for us to be afraid that when the people seize power, they will be led by this or that group at a given moment. It is from within the armed struggle that new leaders will emerge. And it is not fair to hold prejudices in this regard, because leadership will always be assumed by the most resolute.

"Living together on a daily basis; fighting side by side; permanently risking one's life—this is what cements a brotherhood of blood; this is what makes men better and turns them into more honest and pure human beings. Just as there are good and bad people within what you call the 'pro-Chinese' group, there are also good and bad people within the CP."

Time would prove Che right and would vindicate Moisés Guevara. On the other hand, it would brand Monje and the other sellout leaders as traitors and cowards.

Moisés Guevara was an honest man. A militant leader of the miners highly esteemed by the ranks, he loved the revolution. He joined the pro-Chinese Communist Party convinced that Zamora and the other leaders sincerely intended to join the armed struggle, with a large contingent of workers. He soon realized that Zamora was just as opportunistic and false as the other self-proclaimed "vanguard" elements. Nevertheless, within the party he fought to carry out the promises it had made to the people: to initiate the armed struggle. At a conference of the pro-Chinese CP held in Huanuni—the very region where Moisés had the largest base of support—he was expelled, accused of "collusion with the Monje gang" in order to join the guerrilla struggle.

Although the incorporation of Guevara and the other comrades from this group took place while we were carrying out the exploratory march with Che, it is necessary to examine this question in the present chapter.

The people who worked with us in the city had contacted Moisés in mid-1966. He had made a commitment to bring 20 men into the mountains. After Monje's departure from Ñacahuazú, Ramón decided to speak with Guevara directly, and to demand that his incorporation be unconditional, including disbanding his group. There was a bit of fear that at some point friction would develop over the Sino-Soviet dispute between these comrades and those of us already there.

Moisés arrived at our camp and spoke with Che. With extraordinary modesty and sincerity, he stated, "I have not come here to impose conditions; I come only to request enlistment as just another soldier. For me it is an honor to fight alongside Che, the revolutionary I most admire."

Moisés conducted himself magnificently. There were never any problems with him, and the fear that political disagreements would arise dissipated immediately. What Che had foreseen, happened: the struggle made men into brothers, it developed feelings of solidarity, and it strengthened our ideas. Moisés died several months later, fighting heroically with Joaquín's group.

Zamora's fate was different. The man who presented himself as ultrarevolutionary condemned those who joined the guerrilla struggle.

Che too had formed an opinion about Zamora. Che had held a discussion with him in Havana, while Che was still minister of industry. Zamora, a member of the CP, told Che that he would be returning to La Paz with the aim of splitting the party and forming another one, because the Communist Party of Bolivia was incapable of making the revolution.

Ramón pointed out to him, "Splitting the party to form another one is pointless and useless. It does not contribute in any way to developing the armed struggle. Often such groups are the most sectarian of all, or the most obstinate enemies of the guerrilla struggle, or any other type of struggle that does not accord exactly with the ideas of Mao. I am in agreement with a group that, in order to join the armed struggle, separates from a party that has adopted a vacillating and opportunist position. But splitting for its own sake is nothing but corrupt politicking."

Zamora was offered valuable assistance in undertaking the armed struggle. He was even offered the assistance in the initial efforts of an important collaborator, a man who would later play a great role in preparing the guerrilla nucleus: Ricardo. Che thought that the most propitious objective conditions for initiating the struggle for liberation in the southern cone of South America were in Bolivia. That is where he intended to go in mid-1965, after finishing his tour of Asia and Africa.

However, despite having experienced people assisting him, Zamora was more concerned with splitting the Communist Party of Bolivia and provoking personal quarrels than in devoting himself honestly to preparing such an important and delicate task. He wasted this historic opportunity, postponed the launching of the guerrilla nucleus, and nullified all the work. Later he had the audacity to condemn the members of his own faction who, attempting to turn his statements into reality, joined us in the guerrilla struggle.

The shameless desertion of the Communist Party caused us serious problems. In the city we were left with virtually no organization. The work of Coco, Loyola, Rodolfo, and Tania was insufficient to meet our needs, which were growing larger and larger.

We were on the eve of a war, and for this it was necessary to put together a clandestine network that would function in La Paz, branching out to other cities and towns all the way to the center of our military operations. These were the tasks assigned to the Communist Party of Bolivia. We still had a large quantity of provisions and weapons to be transferred to the mountains, in addition to men who would be joining our column. Coco and Rodolfo conducted a vast amount of work.

Later on a series of events occurred that appear to be "tactical errors." In truth these were not. If such a situation came about, it was the result of Monje's treachery. Because to aggravate his cowardice, he sabotaged the work of the comrades who refused to obey his orders and who loyally joined the guerrilla struggle.

One example:

The farm where the zinc house was located needed a good

"legal facade." Che advocated bringing in an agronomist so that the farm would yield produce, since having such an extensive plot of land with only five hectares of corn under cultivation was already arousing suspicion. On every trip made by comrades from the city, Ramón insisted on an agronomist.

The farm was not meant to be part of our zone of operations. But the comrades were unable to obtain the agronomist—a problem the party was to have solved—because they were devoting their efforts to the most urgent necessities of the war. Che stated, "If the farm's cover is blown, let it not be our fault. The army may discover it, but we must not give it up for no reason."

For the reasons explained above, it was never possible to give the property a legal facade.

On the other hand, when Coco returned to the city after dropping off Monje, he informed us of the first acts by the party against the guerrilla effort. The famous Estanislao, the man who during military training had made a "blood pact" swearing never to abandon the armed struggle, alerted the Central Committee that there was a group in Ñacahuazú initiating guerrilla struggle, composed of many foreigners and a small group of Bolivians.

Some members of the Central Committee decided to actively support our struggle. Then Monje, employing all his talents in corrupt politicking, appealed to the sectarian bent of the CP's leaders and accused us of being "pro-Chinese," factionalists, and enemies of the party allied with the "Zamora gang." Zamora, for his part, condemned the guerrillas as "factionalists," revisionists, and enemies of the party allied with the "Monje gang."

Here we had irreconcilable enemies, united by their hatred of the armed struggle for the liberation of Bolivia!

But their treachery went even further. Monje and the Communist Party of Bolivia went on a campaign throughout the country to turn the rank and file against the "factional group." Through deception they were able to prevent honest members from joining the work in the city. They also intercepted men returning to the country after having received military training, and convinced them not to join the guerrillas. The behavior of those trained to fight but who did not do so under pressure from the party should not be called ideological weakness; it was cowardice.

5. THE MOUNTAINS: A SCHOOL FOR THE NEW MAN

The problems created by the party's desertion, at the time we needed them most, did not prevent our guerrilla group from raising its moral level and carrying out preparatory work of an educational character.

Che felt that when men go up into the mountains, habits of the city are thrown overboard. This is caused not just by the harshness of the struggle and the lack of contact with certain cultural forms or with "civilization." Ragged clothing; lack of personal hygiene; skimpy and sometimes primitive food; frequent lack of domestic utensils—all these force the guerrilla to adopt certain attitudes of a semisavage nature.

Che energetically fought this behavior. He directed our work in such a way as to stimulate a constructive and creative spirit within the guerrilla fighter. This involved concern for one's clothing, knapsack, books, and everything else that constituted our "material belongings." For this reason it was a labor of love for him to direct the "public works" at the second camp, located about eight kilometers from the zinc house. In rapid fashion we built benches, an oven for baking bread—which Apolinar was in charge of—and other types of "conveniences." He regularly ordered us to conduct what he termed the "old guard." This involved cleaning the camp from top to bottom.

Some journalists and critics of our war have said that this camp was meant to be the stable base of operations. That evaluation is false. Ramón never intended to stay there permanently. All the work carried out there—with the exception of the strategic caves—was of the character described above: to involve the men in continual activity and to not let them lose acquired habits.

There also arose at the camp what could be called our first "cadre school." Every day from 4:00 to 6:00 p.m., the most educated comrades, headed by Che, gave classes in grammar and arithmetic (on three levels), the history and geography of Bolivia, topics of general education, and classes in the Quechua language. At night, for those who wanted to attend on a voluntary basis (the classes in the afternoon were obligatory), Che taught French. Another topic that he gave primary importance to was the study of political economy.

He frequently pointed out to us that the guerrillas' role was to be the "vanguard of the vanguard." "But to do justice to this term," he stated, "it is necessary for you to become leading cadres."

"The guerrilla is not simply a gunfighter," Ramón emphasized. "He is someone who may potentially govern a country, a man who at any moment could become a leader of his people. He must therefore be prepared when that moment arrives."

He was always looking for an opportunity to discuss the example of Fidel and the Cuban revolution, especially when referring to the urgent need to consolidate and develop the revolution after victory.

"When we triumphed and took power in Cuba," he told us, "we came face to face with a problem more difficult than the war: we had no people trained to assume responsibilities. At first, bureaucratic posts were practically given out to anyone on hand at the moment. The rapid break with imperialism revealed to us the dramatic reality: we lacked experts to lead the economy, industry, and agriculture. It was especially painful to realize that we had no trained intermediate-level people to orient and lead the masses who, through the revolution, had acquired an extraordinary awareness and were eager to learn.

"We lacked cadres, that is, men with a sufficient political development to be able to interpret the directives issued by the central authority, make them a reality, and convey them without distortions to this aggregate of men and women who have faith in us. At the same time, the cadre must possess sufficient sensibility to perceive the most intimate aspirations of this mass of humanity, while at the same time introducing them to the central authority."

For Che a cadre had to possess, among other things, the following qualities: "Great physical and moral courage; political development enabling one to defend revolutionary principles with one's life; capacity for analysis to make decisions rapidly and effectively; a sense of creativity, discipline, and loyalty."

Through the guerrilla struggle Che wanted us to develop ourselves not only as cadres, but as *new men*. He constantly repeated that we had to be the best, that we were the nucleus responsible for teaching the new combatants who would be joining us.

But the job of training the "man of the future" and acquiring once and for all the class consciousness needed to make us catalysts for the aspirations and concerns of the masses, was something that had to be acquired in the course of the war.

Che believed that man is a very malleable being. This truth had been discovered by capitalist society, which is why we had been educated to respect that system. During the frequent discussions we had with him during marches or scouting missions, Che urged us to eliminate the flaws of the old society in decline, and to "become conscious." Consciousness for him was fundamental. His definition of it was brief and on the mark:

"Communism cannot be seen merely as the result of class contradictions in a highly developed society, gradually resolving themselves during a transition stage on the road to the summit. Man is a conscious actor in history. Without this *con-*

sciousness, which encompasses his social being, communism cannot be built."

Acquiring consciousness signifies breaking the chains that tie man to the society in decline. It is equivalent to his full realization as a human being.

Another characteristic he instilled was love toward one's fellow man. In my opinion, one of the works that best reflects Che as a man, as a revolutionary politician, as the most generous brother of the oppressed peoples, is "Socialism and Man in Cuba." In it he states:

"At the risk of seeming ridiculous, let me say that the true revolutionary is guided by great feelings of love. It is impossible to think of a genuine revolutionary lacking this quality. Perhaps it is one of the great dramas of the leader that he must combine a passionate spirit with a cold intelligence and make painful decisions without flinching. Our vanguard revolutionaries must make an ideal of this love of the people, of the most sacred causes, and make it one and indivisible. They cannot descend, with small doses of daily affection, to the level where ordinary men put their love into practice."[9]

Che was always generous. We witnessed how he treated enemy soldiers without malice, how he tended their wounds even when it meant taking medicine away from our own people, how he treated them fairly and with dignity. Later on, turned into animals by imperialism, they responded to this treatment by cowardly murdering him.

The lessons taught by Che live on. We believe they are being carried forward by the men of the ELN, the army he founded.

---

9. *Socialism and Man in Cuba* (New York: Pathfinder, 1989), p. 15.

6. THE BIRTH OF THE ELN

On the eve of the march that began February 1, planned to last approximately twenty days, it was already possible to speak of a structured guerrilla nucleus, divided into forward detachment, center group, and rear guard. In mid-December, Che had made the first leadership assignments, naming Joaquín second in command militarily and head of the rear guard; Marcos, head of the forward detachment; Alejandro, head of operations; Pombo, in charge of services; Ñato, provisions and armaments; and Rolando and me as political commissars. I was also put in charge of finances. Moro was designated as head of medical services.

Thus, as we began our long exploratory journey, the column was already structured, ready to meet its first test of fire. The objectives Che laid out for this military maneuver were the following:

1. To give the guerrilla nucleus intensive training, enabling it to acquire experience; harden itself; learn to survive under the most difficult conditions; get to know hunger, thirst, lack of sleep, exhausting daytime and nighttime marches; while at the same time learning in the field the most important concepts of tactics.

2. To examine the possibilities for organizing groups of supporters among the peasants, making contact with them to explain the objectives of our struggle. Ramón was fully aware that the attitude of the peasantry at first is distrust. During the second stage they maintain a position of neutrality. And in the third stage, after the guerrilla struggle has developed, they openly take the side of the liberation forces. We therefore had to go through the experience of the first stage, trying to form bases of support in the countryside, even if these were weak. We are certain that had we passed beyond this period, the peasants would have come over to our side, as will undoubtedly occur in the future.

3. Finally, to familiarize ourselves in detail with the terrain in which we were to operate.

From the moment Che went up into the mountains with two other comrades, our forces were always ready for battle. At no time was it ever considered that we would let them capture us peacefully, without offering resistance. For that reason, four comrades were assigned to the defense of the main camp, despite the fact that this was not our "base of operations." These were Arturo, Ñato, Camba, and Antonio. Coco remained at the zinc house, awaiting Moisés Guevara and his men. Foreseeing the possibility of a surprise, an emergency plan was put in place. This included an alarm system to warn us of any attack, instructions for a retreat, and a sketch of the journey we would be making. Finally, Che recommended that each man carry a reserve supply of money at all times.

From the beginning, the exploratory march was extremely arduous, foretelling what would come later. After the first few days many comrades were left practically barefoot, and their clothing was slowly being torn apart. The region was virtually uninhabited, although the official maps listed several houses.

On February 10 we established our first contact with a peasant. It turned out to be Honorato Rojas, a man who Ramón immediately described as "potentially dangerous." Later on Honorato Rojas would become an informer and was the army's principal collaborator in the ambush that cost the life of Joaquín and the rear guard. I was introduced to Rojas as a "hunter," and Che helped out as my "assistant." Moro, our doctor, treated the peasant's children, who had worms in various parts of their bodies. One of them even suffered from severe bruises caused by a kick from a mare. After asking him for information about nearby houses, the location of other peasants, the possibilities for buying food, etc., we said good-bye. He promised to collaborate with us.

Che's idea was to reach the Masicurí river to enable us to see soldiers. This was important for psychological reasons, although we were not to engage in combat with them at that time.

Close to the end of the month, two painful incidents occurred. The first involved an internal conflict, while the second involved the loss of one of our men prior to the start of combat.

Two comrades, Marcos and Pacho, had a major incident. It was provoked not just by personality conflicts, but also because of the conditions we were marching under, with several men sick, no food, hellish conditions for days on end. The problem was brought to my attention, since in my capacity as political commissar together with Rolando, it was my job to help find a solution. A month later Che would learn of other actions Marcos had carried out, and threatened him with dishonorable expulsion from the guerrillas. Marcos replied that he would rather be shot.

Unfortunately, Che's diary is only a compilation of points for his personal use, where he noted above all mistakes that had to be corrected. He therefore did not mention some things that show the political firmness and courage of the comrades. After these incidents by Marcos, for which he was replaced as head of the forward detachment, his conduct was one of absolute discipline and he strived to be the best one among us. He even distinguished himself by carrying the heaviest knapsack, under increasingly difficult conditions; and on top of his Garand rifle, he carried a .30 caliber machine gun. Marcos and Pacho died heroically in combat, establishing themselves as exemplary and beloved men.

Another painful incident was the death of Benjamín. He was a young Bolivian who was physically very weak but who had a strong character, a very high political level, and an unbreakable resolve to defend our ideas with his life. Che was very fond of Benjamín, and during the months he was with us, Che always encouraged him to keep going. Marching along the Río Grande, Benjamín became exhausted and was having difficulty with his knapsack. As we were walking along a cliff, he made a sudden movement and fell into the river, which was very swollen, with a powerful current. He did not have the strength to give more than a few armstrokes. We ran to save him, and Rolando even jumped into the water and dived under to try to rescue him. However, we were unable to find him.

These problems had an impact on us. That was when Che's genius was displayed once again, giving us lessons in solidarity, discipline, and morale.

During the most difficult moments, he told us:

"The main weapons of a revolutionary army are its moral strength and its discipline. Moral strength has two sides to it: ethical conduct and heroism. Our guerrillas must possess both of these. For example if a town falls into our hands, you cannot loot it, nor can you mistreat its inhabitants or show disrespect to women. That is ethical conduct. Heroism is the determination that each one of you must have to triumph, to fight to the death in defense of the revolution. That is the strength that will enable us to carry out the most extraordinary feats.

"To these two characteristics one must add discipline. This is not discipline in the traditional sense of the word, as can be seen in repressive armies. Discipline for us is not bowing down before a superior officer. Such an attitude is external, formal, and automatic. For us discipline is conscious, driven by ideas. Soldiers in repressive armies are cold and mechanical units, empty inside. That is the difference between them and us. And this difference is rooted in the fact that they have no consciousness of the struggle. We, on the other hand, do have it."

He also encouraged the development of solidarity among us. On one occasion he told us:

"It is our duty to retrieve the bodies of dead guerrillas and give them burial. But if doing so means losing another life, then no one should run that risk. Our commitment toward our wounded must be greater. We must risk our lives to rescue them. The effort to save them must be real. Solidarity among combatants is a clear-cut demonstration of humanism."

These discussions were held at every halt in the march, or whenever we gathered together around a fire to eat one of our protein-poor meals.

During the exploratory journey Che became ill. Nevertheless, he motivated us by his example. We knew he did not feel well, but he continued on without stopping for an instant, with an iron will. He even got angry when we tried to look after him or help him out, or if the cook tried to show him preference in food, or if he saw that the hours for guard duty were being changed to give him an easier shift.

A sensitive man, Che too was shaken by the death of Benjamín. For that reason he spoke to us again about the need to respond to these events stoically, as a hazard of war.

"You must not be demoralized," he stressed. "There will be occasions when it will seem like one has reached the limit of one's strength. That is when you must appeal firmly to your will-power and take another step. And after that, another one, and then another one, never stopping."

Another incident I witnessed shows another side of Che's rich personality. Unfortunately it is also not reflected in his diary. On February 5 the forward detachment found two animals: a mare and a colt. Since there were no houses for many kilometers around, we knew that these animals had no owner. Obviously some herdsman had passed through with his herd, and the animals strayed away, remaining in the woods. The hunger we experienced over the subsequent period was so great that many of us made comments that on the return trip the animals should be killed for food. These comments later became a mental attitude, a type of obsession that unsettled us.

Che had said that these animals would be brought to the farm for use in agricultural tasks, since he was looking ahead to the future. Three days before reaching camp, when we were swollen by lack of protein and fats, hungry and tired, the question of the animals was raised again. At one point Che threatened two comrades with not eating if they brought up the subject any more, above all because we were close to our destination. He wanted us to strengthen our characters to the point where we could overcome all obstacles, especially this one, which could arise again in the future.

Some comrades went out to hunt, but only killed a few small birds. Under these circumstances, Che's attitude changed and he ordered us to kill the colt so that our men could restore their energies. What is the significance of this? Simply that Che was a man of sound judgment, who knew how to calmly analyze all circumstances and resolve problems fairly. He was not an obstinate man who defended a decision for its own sake. He knew how to change a decision in line with shifting circumstances.

The loss of another man, Carlos, saddened us once again. He was a combatant belonging to the rear guard. In his diary Che stated, "Up until that point, Carlos was considered to be the best among the Bolivians in the rear guard, owing to his seriousness, discipline and enthusiasm."

His death was similar to Benjamín's. Crossing the Río Grande at the mouth of the Ñacahuazú, the raft was swept up in a powerful current. A whirlpool tossed him violently into the water, together with Braulio, and both of them disappeared in the river's turbulent waters. Braulio saved himself, but Carlos was dragged away, apparently unconscious. Joaquín, who had left earlier together with the rest of the rear guard, did not see him pass.

Che learned of this new loss after Miguel and Tuma, who had gone ahead to bring food to the rear guard led by Joaquín, returned from their mission. We had lost another man prior to combat. This lamentable experience was also utilized to draw lessons and motivate comrades to continue on without wavering. In one of his frequent talks during this period, Che emphasized:

"Nature must be conquered, and man will always triumph over it. But it must not be challenged blindly. Courage should help motivate us, as long as it does not become carelessness. In this particular case the river was rising very fast and the current was violent. Perhaps one could have waited for better conditions. In any case, this situation must be taken into account in the future."

On March 19 we had the first indication that something important was about to happen. A small plane was seen flying over the area in an insistent mission of reconnaissance. Just before reaching the camp, Che met up with Negro (the Peruvian doctor who had come to stay with us) and Benigno, who had gone ahead to bring us food. They came with abundant information. Waiting for us at the main camp were Debray, Chino, Tania, Bustos, and Guevara, along with the new combatants. The army had attacked our farm after two men had deserted. These two had been taken prisoner in Camiri and had given valuable information.

It is necessary to speak of the deserters, with the aim of transmitting our experience to other Latin American revolutionaries. People often join a guerrilla force with little political education, motivated by epic exploits, heroic episodes, or simply by political-military intuition. This leads to a false idealization of the struggle and of the life of a guerrilla. Such a phenomenon is felt especially strongly among university students. The erroneous impression exists that the guerrilla sits comfortably at his camp, sleeping in a hammock, eating a little bit; then a battle is planned, there is an encounter with the army, the dead and wounded are retrieved, and one returns to camp to rest up.

Because of this impression, when they arrive and come face to face with the reality, they receive a shock. This is not what they expected. The extremely difficult life, the constant back-and-forth with supplies, building things, carrying knapsacks so heavy they sometimes make one's legs buckle under, the hunger that often stabs one's stomach like a sharp knife, the long marches over difficult terrain, and the constant possibility of falling into an ambush by soldiers—all these have an impact on the minds of the politically weak. That is why it is necessary to have a very selective criteria in recruiting men for the guerrilla unit, always keeping in mind that it is the "vanguard of the vanguard."

This happened with some of the men. The reality frightened them and they deserted. A deserter is always a potential informer. When these two reached Camiri, the army detained them, assuming they had come from the farm believed to be a cocaine-processing plant. The rest is known in detail: the deserters talked, saying there was a group of insurgents, although they were not able to give more information since we were on an exploratory march and they had not seen us. They nevertheless gave certain indications that Che might be in Ñacahuazú, since they had heard a few careless remarks. They also knew that there were men of other nationalities.

On March 20 Ramón had a discussion with Chino, who had come to join our guerrilla group with three other Peruvian comrades. Che later told me the most important aspects of this discussion, and went into more detail about some tactical questions relating to the continental nature of the struggle, and the conduct to be followed at that moment.

Chino proposed to receive practical *training* with us, and participate in a few battles, with the aim of later taking up arms in Peru. In his diary, Ramón explains this concisely:

"I had a preliminary discussion with Chino. He is asking for $5,000 a month for ten months; when he was in Havana they told him to discuss it with me. . . . I told him that I was in agreement in principle, provided they took up arms within six months. He intends to do so in the Ayacucho region, with 15 men under his command. We also agreed that he would send us 5 men now and 15 more after a period of time, and that they would be sent back with their weapons after receiving training in combat."

Che too did not want a rapid internationalization of the struggle beyond Bolivia's borders, and he did not want his presence there known, for purely tactical reasons. In a number of discussions he told me that if imperialism remained unaware of his presence and of the guerrilla force's composition during the initial stage, it would only send arms and "advisers" to assist the army. However, if they knew from the start the perspectives of the struggle, they would intervene directly with all their might, as they had done in Vietnam, to nip the guerrillas in the bud.

"This will happen sooner or later," Che said, "but the longer it can be delayed, the better. That will permit us to harden ourselves, acquire experience, steel our forces, and turn them into a more efficient nucleus. We know that in the end we will confront the imperialist army directly, but for now it is necessary to take certain tactical precautions. Regardless of the tactical questions, though, if it becomes necessary to confront the imperialist army at this time, we will do so without flinching."

Up to the eve of our first guerrilla battle—the ambush at Ñacahuazú—our column had no name. It existed as an army that was tiny, but one that was ready to give battle at any moment. It is true that certain weaknesses could still be observed, but these were the product of our still-incipient training. Nonetheless, we had already been through a trial by fire during the 47-day march that hardened our men, and we began to get an idea of the characteristics of the struggle, in all its immensity, and that it would acquire epic dimensions.

The programmatic foundations of our nucleus had been studied sufficiently during our exploratory march, so that we all knew what we were fighting for, and what our future perspectives were.

Nevertheless, with his characteristic pedagogical approach, Che decided to read us a manifesto. It was characterized by a total lack of punctuation. And whenever a reference was made to our guerrilla unit, a blank space was left, so that we would "christen" it. His explanation was the following:

"I have written this manifesto with two objectives in mind. The first involves general education and culture. (You must supply the punctuation and fix the errors.) The second objective is political in character. You must read it carefully, add additional information, eliminate what you see fit, and define what we are and why we are here. Finally, you must find a name for our army."

During the exploratory march we continued our usual studies, with some irregularity. However, it was not possible to examine the document thoroughly.

On our return, we were faced with the fact that events had accelerated rapidly: the visitors arrived; the army entered the farm; and later there was the first ambush, a complete success for us. It was then that it became necessary to issue our first manifesto, written completely by Che. Because of its historic value, we reproduce it here in its entirety.[10]

In accordance with the tactical considerations formulated from the beginning by Che, the document was addressed "to the Bolivian people." It denounced the fact that the country was being "sold piece by piece to the U.S. monopolies" and gave a strictly truthful account of the events. It was dated March 23, 1967, and was signed "National Liberation Army of Bolivia." Later other communiqués were simply abbreviated "ELN."

The guerrilla events that moved public opinion during the eight subsequent months popularized the initials ELN, its current designation.

Missing from the documents is our slogan of "Victory or death!" also created by Che. That is not a mere phrase. It has a very important motivation that was explained by Ramón in this way:

"The people have a single alternative: victory. Our enemies too have a single alternative: death. We can be defeated, or our struggle can suffer setbacks, but regardless of these transitory difficulties, the people will win. That is an indisputable truth. The alternatives of victory or death—both of them—are for us, the guerrillas. We can reach the final victory, or we can fall along the way. But if we die, the struggle will continue forward without letup."

---

10. Published on pages 305-6. For an account by Che, see page 156.

7. THE FIRST BATTLES

Che's initial plan to rest up for several days in order to recover our strength and train the new comrades was abruptly
altered. On March 17 approximately 60 soldiers took the road
leading to Algarañaz's house and captured Salustio, one of the
recruits who was starting out with us as a messenger. During
their attack on the zinc house, Lorito killed one of the soldiers.
On learning this news, Marcos ordered a retreat, believing we
should not be defending fixed positions. In his diary, Che describes the problem in the following way:

"Rolando had been sent to organize the withdrawal of
everything. A mood of defeat was in the air. Shortly afterward,
there arrived a Bolivian doctor who has recently joined us,
with a message for Rolando, telling him that Marcos and Antonio were by the pond, and that he should go meet them
there. I ordered the same messenger to go back and tell them
that wars are won with bullets, and that they should immediately return to the camp and wait for me there. Everything
gives the impression of total chaos; no one knows what to do."

Che later explained his decision to me: "It is correct that
guerrillas do not defend fixed positions. But it was necessary
to take into account a whole series of factors that had been ac-
cumulating up to that point."

In the first place, he said, we were not "defending a fixed
position," since the camp was not of that character. Moreover,
in conducting the work in preparation for military action,
many signs of our presence had been left, owing to the lack of
cadres to carry out a series of preliminary tasks. This forced us
to "blow the cover" of certain comrades. The zinc house itself
had become a focus of suspicion, and Algarañaz had even sent
a hunter to keep a constant eye on us. To retreat at that moment without giving battle, after the guerrilla unit had been
detected through the information provided by the deserters,
would simply have meant the beginning of a vigorous pursuit

of us by the army, with troops who were fresh and whose morale was high.

On the contrary, to fight meant steeling ourselves to meet future battles with determination. One must realize that in any case it would have been necessary to fight sometime during the following days, owing to the factors mentioned above. Another alternative, although it seems extreme, would have been to disappear as guerrillas, create new conditions in the city, make new contacts, recruit new forces, and begin all over again. That would have been absurd.

Furthermore, because of the privations suffered during the exploratory march, our morale coming back was not very high, nor was our combat readiness very good. Now a tactical opportunity had been presented to us, with very favorable prospects.

That was why Che considered it a serious error to retreat at that moment, and ordered Rolando to set up an ambush downriver. He immediately ordered the defense of the entrance to the camp and sent a group of comrades to explore downriver.

March 22 was a day of tense preparations. At 7:00 a.m. on March 23, as Rolando was reviewing the position of the guerrillas on ambush, they noticed splashing in the river. Rapidly everyone took positions and awaited the troops, who were advancing slowly. Silence was maintained until a large group penetrated the area. Rolando, as the person in charge of our first action, opened fire, taking them by surprise. Many soldiers assumed combat positions; those doing so in front were quickly struck by bullets. The rest fled. The firing lasted approximately six minutes, according to the report Rolando gave Che, until the enemy forces surrendered.

The participants in this battle were Rolando, Benigno, Coco, Guevara, Pablito, Ernesto, Apolinar, and Walter. Seven soldiers were killed, 6 were wounded, and 11 were taken prisoners. Another 8 soldiers escaped. As can be appreciated, the enemy forces were four times greater than our own. We suffered no losses. In addition, we captured 3 60-mm. mortars, 8 boxes of grenades, 1 .30-caliber machine gun with 500 rounds, 2 BZ machine guns, 2 Uzi submachine guns, 16 Mausers with 2,000 rounds, 2 radio sets, and other items.

Coco reached us at 8:00 a.m. to report the results of the battle. Immediately Che ordered Marcos to leave along the first path of operations, with the objective of cutting off the army's retreat from behind, if it advanced along the river canyon trying to reach the camp. Braulio was sent, with the rear guard, along the second path of operations, to prevent them from leaving the canyon, which was a death trap in the fullest sense of the term. The center group would attack from the positions already held. Che ordered me to interrogate the prisoners, presenting myself as the person in command. I carried out this role throughout the entire course of the war.

Major Plata, commander of the forces taken prisoner, wept for a long time, while the soldiers asked us to shoot him because of the mistreatment and abuse he had committed. On Che's orders I told him that all the prisoners would be set free, and that we were giving them until noon on March 27 to gather their dead. Very frightened, he told us that he would retire from the army. He gave us a number of important pieces of information about the operations they were conducting. For example, he told us that this attack was planned to coincide with a bombing raid that was to begin at noon. They were to signal their position to avoid suffering casualties. The ambush made them lose radio contact and prevented the air attack. In fact, the bombing occurred the following day.

Captain Silva, another prisoner, also spoke in detail, informing us that he had rejoined the army at the request of the Communist Party of Bolivia and that he had a brother studying in Cuba. He later gave the names of two other officers who were possible collaborators.

We took all the prisoners' clothing, with the exception of the two officers, who kept their uniforms, and we gave them our civilian clothes stored in one of the caves. We also treated their wounded and explained to the soldiers the aims of our struggle. They replied that they did not know why they had been sent to fight us, that they agreed with what we were saying, and repeated the request that we shoot Major Plata. This officer had been a despot within the unit, but now, in front of the troops, he was behaving like a coward. We explained to them that we did not kill unarmed enemies and that we treated them like human beings, with dignity and respect.

The days following the ambush were full of euphoria, pressure, and happiness. A new historic stage had begun with a combat force that was small, but with a high morale. In addition, the resounding and astonishing triumph revealing the presence of a guerrilla force was the center of the news we heard on the radio. The pressure we felt was a product of the two visitors: Régis Debray and Ciro Bustos (Pelao). Tania's identity had been discovered and she was forced to remain with us while awaiting an appropriate time to leave with absolute security. Chino, who had also come as a visitor, decided to stay on as a combatant. But Debray and Bustos had to leave in the shortest possible time. At a meeting held on March 27, Che presented the immediate tasks:

(a) To get the visitors out through a secure route, close to the city.

(b) To hide all the weapons and supplies that had fallen into our hands after the first ambush, in addition to some of our own things. For this reason it was necessary to open a new strategic cave, a task that would be headed by Moisés Guevara.

(c) To send ten men to gather corn at the farm. This task had to be conducted with great care to avoid having the army take them by surprise.

The following day, when our men went to the farm to gather corn, they discovered that the tactical cave had been discovered by the army. Suddenly seven officials from the Red Cross arrived, along with a number of unarmed soldiers and two doctors. Later on, a truck appeared full of soldiers. However, our comrades ordered them to withdraw, which the army complied with obediently.

These events occurred 24 hours after the elapse of the time period we had given them to gather their dead. It thus revealed the demoralization in their ranks and their respect for us.

Meanwhile, Débray raised that for him it was a moral duty to join our guerrilla nucleus. The famous author of *Revolution in the Revolution*, known among us as Danton, wanted to demonstrate that he was not simply a theoretician but was also a man of action.

Che explained to us that under the circumstances, the French philosopher would be more valuable outside than inside. Danton would be able to lead a great movement of solidarity with our guerrilla force, to obtain declarations by intellectuals, raise funds, take charge of propaganda, etc. Because of its succinct and personal nature, Che's diary does not reflect his full opinion about Debray, a man he thought highly of and whose intellectual stature he appreciated. Che told him that at the present time he should leave, and that there would be plenty of time later for him to gain his guerrilla experience.

With the aim of getting the visitors out and changing our zone of operations, in conformity with the plans Ramón had made previously, we set out for Gutiérrez. We did so because, according to our information, the road to Muyupampa was closed off by the army. However, when we reached Pirirenda we learned that there were troops in Gutiérrez as well. We therefore decided to return to the Ñacahuazú, but not before the departure of one of the villagers who, we assumed, would be informing the army of our presence.

At the Iripití we joined up with the rear guard, which was under Rolando's command, and with the personnel who were ill, among them Joaquín. There we camped and sent out scouting patrols so we could head out once again to Gutiérrez, which we believed was the indicated spot for evacuating the visitors.

Iripití was the scene of our second battle and the gravesite of our first comrade killed, Rubio—Jesús Suárez Gayol. He was a magnificent human being and an excellent comrade, simple and courageous. He had been vice minister of the sugar industry and left everything behind—family, honors—to join our struggle.

At 10:00 a.m. on April 10, our rear guard, waiting in ambush, spotted an army patrol with a number of men. They let them advance up to a suitable distance. Twenty minutes later the battle began, with a toll of 3 soldiers dead, 1 wounded, and 7 captured. We also captured 6 Garand rifles, an M-1 carbine, and 4 Mauser rifles. On our side we lost Rubio.

Four soldiers escaped. For this reason Che ordered us to move up the ambush, anticipating that the army would send reinforcements to investigate what had happened.

It again fell on me to interrogate the prisoners. They told us they were part of a company located upriver, at the Ñacahuazú. They had come down through the canyon, gathered their dead, and captured the camp.

Just as we had expected, a company of approximately 120 men, under the command of Major Sánchez, fell into our ambush. At 5:10 p.m. the battle began, with another victory for us. Enemy losses included 7 dead, 6 wounded, and 13 prisoners, including the commander of the column. In addition, we captured 1 Browning, 1 mortar, 15 Garands, 4 M-3s, 2 M-1s, and 5 Mausers.

Inexplicably, this column walked right into our ambush, without taking any security measures. When we opened fire, they tried to look for protection. Since they did not find any cover, they dispersed and the remainder of the troops fled into the woods. We gave pursuit, firing sporadically at them. Through this effort Coco took Major Sánchez prisoner. Rolando, who was nearby, threatened him into giving the order for his troops to surrender. Sánchez ordered his men to surrender.

Major Sánchez thought we were going to shoot him, and during my interrogation he asked me to please allow one of the soldiers to relay a message to his wife. As I had done previously with the coward Major Plata, I told Major Sánchez that our norm was to respect a defeated enemy, to guarantee their lives, treat their wounded, and permit them to gather their dead along with their personal effects. I then asked him why he had entered our ambush so confidently. He answered:

"We came to look for our dead and to investigate what had occurred. Since we have been taught that guerrillas attack and then withdraw, we did not imagine that you would be here waiting for us."

Major Sánchez's response is a lesson for guerrilla forces. We should not limit ourselves to schemas; we should always strive to disconcert the enemy.

The following morning we set the prisoners free and permitted them to take their dead and wounded from the two battles. We also granted them a 24-hour truce.

The interrogation of the prisoners led us to the conclusion that the troops that had closed off the Ñacahuazú upstream were the same ones who had been moved to the zinc house. This meant that the road to Muyupampa was clear. Since our presence in the Iripití region had been discovered, Ramón changed our itinerary, and instead of heading toward Gutiérrez, we began a march to Muyupampa, with the sole aim of getting Debray and Bustos out safely.

The death of Rubio saddened everyone. I had noticed that he was occupying a bad position, visible from the river, so I suggested he move. When they went to find him after the morning's ambush was over, he had a bullet in his head and died a few moments later. This was his first and only battle. Che gave a moving speech in his memory, stressing that the first blood to be shed was Cuban. For that reason, it was more necessary than ever to unite together wholeheartedly, and eliminate any tendency toward chauvinism.

On April 17 we remained in waiting for the army to advance, after a peasant had escaped. There was no combat. That same day Pelao spoke with Pombo and raised with him that he was very concerned about his children, that he had not left them monetary resources to get by, and that he had other responsibilities to fulfill in Buenos Aires. He also requested that his departure not occur in an area where the guerrillas had been operating, so as not to attract the army's attention. Pombo answered that there was no reason for him to get excited, and that he should wait calmly for the right moment. The first symptoms of desperation in him were already noticeable.

It is necessary to mention a series of dates, since these were to have important consequences later on. That very day Che ordered Joaquín to remain behind with four men considered "rejects," and he added to the group Moisés Guevara, Alejandro, and Tania, who were ill. Moisés had been suffering from an acute gall bladder attack, and Tania and Alejandro had swelling and fever fluctuating between 38 [100.4° F] and 39 [102° F] degrees. Joaquín was to wait in the region, moving about, but without clashing head on with the army.

As can be appreciated, two things were foreseen: our rapid return (three to five days) after evacuating the visitors; and the possibility to bring the center squad commanded by Che back to full strength with the return of the four comrades—the three ailing ones plus the doctor, Negro, who had remained with them. However, this was to be the last contact we had with the rear guard, due to a series of factors we will relate subsequently. It should be noted that always, at every opportunity, we tried to locate these comrades. We even thought that Joaquín would be at the Rosita, a region we had explored in February and March, which was one of the operational areas Che had mentioned to the head of the rear guard. We knew that Joaquín's group did not have combat strength, with 4 "rejects," 3 ailing comrades receiving care, and only 10 others who had to carry the entire load of the operations. For this reason our desire to link up with them was a permanent and pressing goal.

April 18 was spent on the march and scouting. We also detained a few peasants so they would sell us food and give us information.

The following day there was another unusual development. An Anglo-Chilean journalist, George Andrew Roth, came to our camp, guided by a few young boys from the area where Joaquín had remained behind to operate. The journalist seemed suspicious to us. In his passport the occupation of student was crossed out and changed to that of journalist, although he claimed to be a professional photographer working freelance for several foreign publications. He also had documents listing him as an instructor for the Peace Corps, with a Puerto Rico visa. Moreover, his notebook contained a list of questions that, according to him, were to be used to confirm the rumors being spread by the army that Che was with us under the name of Ramón, in addition to the presence of Tania and Debray. This information had been provided to the army by the informers.

I was again called on to interrogate the prisoner. He said that he had been with the army at our camp and that a diary by Braulio had even been found, in which it said that Ramón was Che. Roth and the little boys guiding him later stated that the army was in Lagunillas and knew of our presence.

I handed Roth an interview with me as "head" of the guerrillas. The document had been drafted by Che and contained a short account of the actions that had occurred in the previous days and the objectives of our struggle.

Che remained with Pombo, Tuma, and Urbano close to Muyupampa. When we reached the outskirts of the town, we dropped off Pelao, Debray, and Roth. Régis asked me earnestly to tell Che that he was leaving then only so as not to abandon Bustos, who was in a very desperate state and was very afraid. At that stage Pelao was already showing what would happen later. We were therefore not very surprised that he became a useful collaborator of the army, identifying the bodies of our dead comrades, and making drawings of our faces, in addition to supplying a series of factual descriptions about us.

Our objective and the request of the visitors had been carried out. That night we did not want to take Muyupampa because of information we had received that the army was waiting for us in the town.

April 20 was a day of agitation, "parliamentarism," and bombing. During our return trip to reunite with Joaquín, we tried to obtain food supplies, which had now become a serious objective.

We reached the house of Nemesio Caraballo, a man who had offered us coffee the night before and had been friendly toward us. Now he was not there. He had departed and left behind only a few workers, who were very frightened. We purchased some items of food and prepared lunch. Sometime after noon, a van appeared bearing a white flag. In it were a priest, a doctor, and the subprefect from Muyupampa. The priest was German. As a gesture of good will they brought us some candy and cigarettes. The delegation offered us "peace on a national level," and begged us not to attack Muyupampa because the army was dug in there. "We do not want bloodshed," they repeated.

I answered them that we did not want any "national peace" unless they handed power over to us, which was the aim of our struggle as vanguard of the people. I asked them how the peasants in the area lived, the manner in which they were exploited, and I asked the doctor for facts on infant mortality. As in all of Bolivia, the general picture was a sorry one. I told them, "Do you find this situation to be just? We are fighting so that the poor do not become poorer while the rich become richer. We are fighting for the people's progress, so that no longer will there be so much hunger and poverty."

The priest, in particular, answered by criticizing us for the participation of foreigners. I replied that the poor, that revolutionaries of all countries, had the right to unite together to fight a common enemy that was united long before we were, an enemy that was cruel and powerful. I said that this situation gave the struggle an international character. For this reason our army opened its doors to patriots from anywhere in the world who wanted to participate with us in the great endeavor to liberate Bolivia. (*On Che's specific instructions, I was not to categorically deny the presence of comrades of other nationalities, nor to confirm it, since he knew that this conversation would be published and disseminated internationally.*)

Finally, I offered them peace for Muyupampa, on the condition that they bring us a truckload of food supplies and medicines that we needed by 6:00 p.m. Through these same individuals we learned that Danton, Roth, and Bustos had been arrested.

The delegation withdrew, but in place of medicine and food, what arrived were planes to bomb us. Three AT-6 aircraft dropped their lethal loads close to the little house where we were located, and a piece of shrapnel wounded Ricardo slightly in the leg.

That night we set out en route to Ticucha. From that moment on our goal was to locate Joaquín, and at the same time to stock up on as much food as possible. On April 22 we had a brief clash with the army. In the morning we had surprised the driver of a small truck belonging to the Bolivian State Petroleum Reserves (YPFB), who was examining our tracks in the company of a peasant who had informed them of our presence. We took them prisoner. We then set up an ambush to detain other vehicles and deal a blow to the army if they approached our positions. We were only able to obtain a few items, plus some bananas from a truck that fell into our hands later. At 8:00 p.m., as we were preparing to leave, a brief exchange of fire was heard. It was Ricardo, who had surprised a group of soldiers and a guide who were coming over a ridge and were about to fall upon us. We were not able to tell whether the enemy suffered any casualties. That was the occasion in which Loro Vásquez was lost.

Our men were waiting in ambush, and Rolando had issued the order to abandon positions at 6:30 p.m. When this time was up, they waited for Loro for a considerable period, but he did not appear. Days later the radio announced he had been wounded and captured. Later his "escape" from the Camiri hospital was announced. Some journalists have spread the idea that Che sent him on a mission by himself. That is absolutely false.

We never learned what happened to him. Ramón himself explains in his diary that the balance sheet was "negative," among other factors because of "the loss of a man (temporary I hope)." Through information we have pieced together over time, however, we know that Loro died valiantly. Wounded, he was bestially tortured by President Barrientos's thugs. Since they were unable to extract even a single confession that would reveal information about us, they threw him out of a helicopter, still alive, over the jungle. Lorito was a courageous, audacious, and loyal man. He was one of the four who worked unstintingly in the early preparation of the guerrilla war.

The day after this small skirmish, Ramón sent Benigno and Aniceto on a four-day mission to find Joaquín. In the meantime, we remained in the area, awaiting the results of the mission.

On April 25 we suffered another deeply felt loss: Rolando. While on guard duty, Pombo and Eustaquio discovered an army column approaching with approximately 30 soldiers. Later Eustaquio returned, saying the number of soldiers was 60, not 30. Che rapidly ordered the taking of positions, but we were forced to fight in a location not suitable for an ambush. Rolando, a man of great courage, placed himself in the most difficult position at the end of a curve, and he had to directly face a machine gunner, who fired several bursts at him. A bullet split open his thighbone and the entire nerve and vascular bundle. Despite efforts to save him, he rapidly lost blood. Rolando, a political commissar, a man barely 24 years old, had a brilliant future. Of all the comrades there, he was the most developed politically and militarily.

That was the ambush Che directed personally, and he recounts it in the following way:

"Soon the army's advance unit appeared. To our surprise, it

included three German shepherds and their guide. The animals were restless, but I did not think they would give us away. However, they continued advancing and I shot at the first dog, but missed. When I went after the guide, my M-2 jammed. Miguel shot the other dog, according to what I could see, although it could not be confirmed. No one else entered the ambush. Intermittent firing began along the army's flank. When it stopped I sent Urbano to order the withdrawal, but he came back with news that Rolando was wounded. They brought his lifeless body back a short time later, and he died as they began to give him plasma."

The withdrawal was slow and we were preoccupied with gathering all the things and burying Rolando. In the afternoon Benigno and Aniceto arrived, having lost their knapsacks after a brief exchange of fire with the army. This created a new situation. Soldiers had now come between us and Joaquín, and our natural outlets were blocked off. It was therefore necessary to head up into the mountains, clearing trails. We would have to distance ourselves somewhat from Joaquín in order to reach his position from the other side.

At that moment, the balance sheet for us was completely favorable. We had the deaths of Rubio and Rolando to lament, as well as Loro's disappearance. Morale was very high and combat readiness was excellent. Determined efforts were being made to reunite with Joaquín, which was our main operational aim.

In May there were three battles as we circled the area conducting work of persuasion among the peasants and searching vigorously for Joaquín. All the clashes were resounding victories for us, despite radio reports and official dispatches that invented stories of "many guerrilla casualties."

The first battle was on May 8. Che had ordered an ambush set up at our camp at the Ñacahuazú, which we had retaken. It was under the command of Pacho. At 10:30 a.m. we wounded two soldiers who were advancing carelessly. After treating their wounds, we kept them as prisoners. At noon we captured another two who were coming down the Ñacahuazú, unarmed. The four were out-and-out liars. They tried to give us false information, claiming they had gone hunting and their company had disappeared, and they had gone looking for them. Everything was false; the company was located farther upriver.

The ambush continued in place until 7:00 p.m. Then, as it was getting dark, the army appeared, taking many security precautions. They reached the entrance into the canyon and pulled back, apparently to see whether or not any shots would be fired. On one of these occasions they entered the canyon and fell into the trap. The battle was brief. In the action Second Lieutenant Laredo was killed, together with 2 soldiers. We took 6 additional prisoners, but the rest of the company fled. The tally was 3 dead, 10 prisoners (2 of them wounded), 7 M-1s, 4 Mausers, personal gear, ammunition, and a little food.

Second Lieutenant Laredo had a campaign diary and a letter from his wife, which provoked great surprise among us. In the diary, under the date marked May 1, he refers to the workers as "shiftless and lazy" and uses other insulting adjectives. Regarding his troops he speaks of their lack of combat morale, mentioning soldiers who wept when informed of the presence of guerrillas nearby. The letter from his wife referred to her concern for Laredo, but later on added the following request, more or less: "Our friend asks you to bring her the scalp of a guerrilla, and I ask you the same, to put up in our living room."

This episode brings to mind the sad and sinister days of Nazism, as well as the profound gap between the conduct or spirit of the army with respect to the guerrillas, contrasted to the dignified treatment we gave to our prisoners.

The letter and the diary caused an uproar and provoked disgust among us.

Che's respect for human beings, independently of how they behaved, was underscored once again when he decided to wait for an appropriate opportunity to return Lieutenant Laredo's diary to his mother, since the enemy officer had made this an express wish in the event he died in combat or was captured by us. Laredo's diary remained in Che's knapsack until the ambush at the Yuro ravine on October 8.

The second battle of the month was on May 30. We had reached the railroad tracks leading to Santa Cruz, looking for the Michuri. In doing so our thoughts were constantly on Joaquín, who apparently had moved north. Along a road used by the oil company Che set up an ambush, while a scouting patrol was sent out in a jeep requisitioned from the state oil enterprise. At three o'clock in the afternoon the clash occurred. Once again we dealt them a blow: 3 soldiers killed and 1 wounded.

The following day we closed out the month of May with another triumph, although less than what we hoped. Two army trucks advancing along the road were attacked by us. One fled, but we destroyed the other. We could have caused greater casualties among their ranks, but Ñato, in his rush, fired a real shell instead of a blank from his grenade launcher, causing a big explosion that frightened off the soldiers. Fortunately, Ñato was unhurt, although the barrel of his gun was destroyed.

8. THE SEARCH FOR JOAQUÍN

The three months of military operations registered a notable advance for us. We had inflicted over 50 casualties on the enemy, including dead, wounded, and prisoners, among whom were three high-ranking officers. We had seized a large quantity of arms, ammunition, clothing, and some food. However, the most noteworthy result was the demoralization and lack of combativity among the soldiers, in contrast to the aggressiveness and daring of our guerrillas. On the negative side, there was the loss of Rubio and Rolando, the disappearance of Loro, and the lack of contact with our rear guard and with the city.

Under these circumstances we began our eighth month in the mountains of Bolivia, and the fourth month of sustained combat. Despite the difficulties—hunger, illness, lack of contact with the city, and being unable to find Joaquín—our morale was high. The guerrillas were an aggressive force, conscious of their power, inflicting blows on the army powerful enough to prevent them from reorganizing themselves, modifying their tactics, or responding to us swiftly.

During the short course of the war, Che gave us lessons in human solidarity that frequently extended even to the enemy. One of these events occurred on June 3. We were still close to the oil company road, where we had previously clashed with the army. For several days we had been searching for water and food and had devoured a great-tasting pig. That morning, after walking along the edge of a creek, Che ordered an ambush along this road, waiting for army trucks to pass by. Pombo was to give the signal with a yellow handkerchief when a vehicle entered our line of fire. After five and a half hours of waiting, a military truck passed by and Pombo made the anxiously awaited signal. Inexplicably to us, Che—who was to have opened fire on the vehicle, after which we were to have joined in— did not pull the trigger of his M-2.

Later, so that everyone could hear, he told us, "It would have been a crime to shoot those little soldiers."

The incident is related in his diary almost as if it were lacking in importance. It says: "At 2:30 a truck drove by with pigs in it, and we let it pass. We did the same with a small truck carrying empty bottles that drove by at 4:20. At 5:00 p.m. an army truck came by—the same one as yesterday—with two very young soldiers lying down in back wrapped in blankets. I did not have the heart to shoot them and did not think fast enough to apprehend them, and we let them pass."

What a difference from the officers and soldiers of the Bolivian army who murdered Che and the comrades captured with him at the Yuro ravine! Perhaps the same soldiers whom Che considered it a crime to kill were the ones who months later were photographed smiling over his body.

The majority of the analyses made about the course of our guerrilla war are superficial and very often frivolous. They have not sufficiently studied its development, or they have simply taken isolated facts in order to combat the theory of the guerrilla nucleus.

Despite the limitations caused by our constant search for Joaquín, which prevented us from moving to areas more suitable for our operations, we were able to confirm that day-to-day contact with the peasants would, as one would expect, work in our favor. This was proved in Moroco, a small village on the edge of the river. We arrived there on June 19, and several events occurred that must be examined in detail, since they give an indication of the impact of the prolonged presence of a guerrilla force on the population.

As was natural, the initial response was cold, a mixture of curiosity and distrust. That same day three individuals arrived in the village armed with revolvers and Mausers, saying they were merchants selling pigs. We did not hold any meetings as was customary in these cases, to inform the population of our principles and ask for their incorporation or solidarity. We simply devoted ourselves to talking to them, asking about roads and trails, information about neighbors, etc. This informal conduct enabled us to obtain valuable friends. In addition, we gained our first recruit: Paulino, a peasant youth whose family lived there and who knew the entire area. Despite his youth (he was about 22), he suffered from tuberculosis, a product of poor diet and the miserable life of that region.

The following day, a spectacular event occurred. Paulino informed us that the three "merchants" were not that at all, but were spies sent by the army to conduct intelligence work. Paulino's valuable piece of information, which he had received from his girlfriend, also from the village, enabled us to take them prisoner. This collaboration was extremely important and demonstrated to us the rich potential from prolonged contact with the peasants. Paulino subsequently continued on with us, and was sent to Cochabamba carrying several messages. These did not reach their destination because the youth was arrested by the army.

At this same place Che worked as a dentist, earning the affectionate nickname "Fernando the Toothpuller."

We resumed our search for Joaquín along the Río Grande and later along the mouth of the Rosita, in order to reach Samaipata. This was a spot where Joaquín might be, since Che had told him it was a probable zone of operations.

On June 10 a squad of ours composed of Coco, Ñato, Pacho, and Aniceto had an unforeseen clash with the army. The event unfolded in the following way: The four comrades were conducting a mission to reach a peasant's house to gather food and information, when they unexpectedly ran into the soldiers, who were advancing along the opposite bank of the river. There was an immediate heavy exchange of fire, with a large expenditure of ammunition on our side. Ñato and Aniceto withdrew, followed later by Coco and Pacho. We had no news of enemy losses until two days later, when reports on the radio announced that one soldier had been killed and another wounded.

We suffered no losses, although the army released official dispatches announcing my death and that of two other comrades not identified. This was simply a psychological maneuver to undermine in part the impact of our blows, which were having a disastrous effect on public opinion for them. As a result, at the same time as we were reaching the Río Grande and later the Rosita in search of our rear guard, whom we had lost contact with for almost three months, the army was diverting part of its resources to repression against the miners.

Although Bolivian radio was not reporting it owing to censorship, an Argentine station reported the San Juan massacre at the Siglo XX mines, with a toll of 87 victims. In this manner the servile government of the military thug Barrientos was attempting to stifle the clamor of the workers for their demands, as well as the clear signs of working-class support for our struggle. This act clearly demonstrated the weakness of the regime. We were becoming aware of the potential power of a small vanguard group in destroying the foundations of a corrupt society—and in infinitely less time than all the efforts spent by the corrupt politicians in conciliating, making pacts, and granting unimportant reforms that eventually frustrate the people.

On that occasion Che issued a call to the miners (Communiqué no. 5), urging them to unite with the guerrilla struggle and explaining the correct tactics the people should adopt in the struggle. This manifesto became known only after Che's death.[11]

Two days later, on June 26, we clashed with the army once again. We were camped at Piray, on the banks of the Durán river. Che had ordered an ambush to be set while another group of comrades went looking for food in the tiny village of Florida. Around 4:30 p.m., he sent Pombo, Arturo, Antonio, Ñato, and Tuma to relieve Miguel and the forward detachment. As soon as they arrived, a heavy exchange of gunfire broke out. Left lying in the sand were four soldiers, although not all of them were dead. The army troops were deployed on the other side of the river bed, which was totally dry, and were well situated.

Che took his battle position alongside Benigno, and ordered the comrades sent as relief—who had now become reinforcements—to position themselves on the flank where Miguel was. We heard some branches breaking, revealing that the army was moving to new positions. The sound of a truck indicated the arrival of enemy reinforcements. Immediately we were met by a round of fire that took us by surprise in an area without good defenses. Pombo was wounded in the leg with a .30-caliber machine-gun bullet. Che subsequently gave the order to withdraw.

---

11. See pages 312-14.

As these instructions were being carried out, it was learned that Tuma had been wounded in the stomach. He was rapidly moved to one of the houses in Piray several kilometers from the ambush site. Moro gave him an anesthetic and began to operate on him. But Tuma, or Tumaini, as we affectionately called him, did not make it through the operation. His liver was destroyed and he had suffered intestinal perforations.

That day was an intensely painful one for us. We lost one of our best comrades, the most cheerful among us, an exemplary and beloved combatant. As Che wrote, "With his death I have lost an inseparable comrade and companion over all the recent years. His loyalty was unwavering, and I feel his absence almost as if he were my own son. After he fell he asked that I be given his watch, and since they did not do so while he was being treated, he took it off and gave it to Arturo. Behind this gesture was the desire that it be given to the son whom he did not know, as I had done with the watches of many comrades who had died in the past. I shall carry it throughout the entire war."

Pombo, who was wounded, felt the death of Tuma as if he had lost his closest relative. They had practically grown up together during Cuba's war of liberation; they had participated together in the Congo. And now, death pulled them apart in Piray.

That same afternoon two new spies were taken prisoner, one of them an officer in the carabineros. After being advised of the norms of war and threatened with severe punishment if they were caught in the act again, they were set free, but in their underwear. Their clothes were taken away due to a misinterpretation of an order by Che that they be stripped of anything of value. When Che learned of this, he became indignant. He assembled the comrades who had done it and told them that human beings must be treated with dignity, that they must not be subjected to humiliations or gratuitous mistreatment. At his side was the body of Tuma.

July was a month of combat, as the crisis of the Barrientos

government sharpened. At the same time, we received the first
news of Joaquín, through various radio reports of battles between guerrilla forces and the army far from our location. For
this reason we decided to head toward Samaipata. This spot,
as we had anticipated, was one of the zones of operations previously agreed to with Joaquín. Our immediate plan was to
take the town, including the police station, and purchase food
supplies and medicines, particularly those needed for Che's
asthma.

First we passed through Peña Colorada, a heavily populated region that received us with little enthusiasm, and later we
regrouped at Alto de Palermo. To get to Samaipata we decided
to capture a suitable vehicle. We stopped several, but one of
them attempted to flee, forcing us to shoot its tires. Subsequently Pacho, Coco, Ricardo, Julio, Aniceto, and Chino set
out in a truck to carry out the mission.

Our squad first reached a small soda fountain, where they
had a few soft drinks. Two carabineros who came in to see what
was going on were taken prisoner and disarmed. Later a lieutenant named Vacaflor came in, and he too was taken prisoner.
While Chino, Julio, and Aniceto stayed to guard the two carabineros and carried out the task of looking for medicines, the
rest of the squad went with the lieutenant to the garrison, with
the aim of capturing it. The officer gave the password and the
door was opened without difficulty. Immediately Ricardo,
Pacho, and Coco entered, capturing a few soldiers while others
put up resistance. One of them even fired at Pacho, but Ricardo
alertly shoved him aside and saved him. This was the only soldier who put up a fight during the entire operation, and it was
necessary to fire at him. He died instantly.

The tally was 9 soldiers captured, 1 killed, 1 BZ-30 machine
gun seized, and 5 Mausers. The action was carried out in the
presence of the entire population and a number of travelers
who were there. It therefore had an enormous repercussion.
The prisoners were left on the road one kilometer from the
town. In addition, food was purchased and medicines were

obtained, although nothing for asthma.

Among the material we requisitioned was a map with our entire route traced out, and a possible way out was seen toward the highway. After this lightning operation, we withdrew. During the following days we walked in the direction of Florida. In the course of the march we heard radio reports of two guerrilla actions: one in El Dorado, between Samaipata and the Río Grande, and the other in Iquirá. Casualties on our side were announced in both of these. We immediately realized that the group doing the fighting was Joaquín's.

Simultaneously the radio stations announced a crisis affecting the government's political base of support, with the withdrawal of the PRA from the so-called Revolutionary Front, which propped up the military thug Barrientos. At the same time, we heard some pitiful declarations by Barrientos, begging to be allowed to finish his presidential term. That was when Che, in a conversation with a group of us, said that it was a pity we did not have 100 more guerrillas to accelerate the regime's disintegration.

At the close of the month we heard news of two other military actions by Joaquín, while at the same time we clashed with the army twice.

On July 27 we were preparing to look for a path that would avoid Moroco, where, according to information provided us by peasants, there were a large number of soldiers. Then Willy announced that a group of soldiers were entering an ambush we had set. At the site were Chapaco, Willy, León, Arturo, Ricardo, Chino, Eustaquio, Aniceto, and me. The soldiers were walking slowly, taking virtually no precautions. They made some signals and later fired three mortar rounds. When no response was forthcoming, they continued advancing. There were only eight of them, because the rest were lagging behind. When they got close we opened fire, killing four of them. The rest fled into the woods. We immediately organized our withdrawal without gathering up their weapons or equipment, since this would have meant an unnecessary risk of men, and we continued on.

Two days later we had another skirmish, but under different conditions. We were on the banks of the Rosita, one hour's walk from the mouth of the Suspiro. It was approximately 4:30 a.m. Che had not slept all night due to asthma. Miguel was awake to organize the changing of guards, and Moro was heating coffee. At that moment the latter spotted a light from a lantern at the river bank. Moro asked: "Who goes there?"

From the embankment they answered, "Trinidad Detachment."

Che heard the whole dialogue, since he was in the improvised kitchen. Immediately our comrades opened fire. Moro's M-2 jammed, but Miguel protected him with his Garand. Che then ordered the formation of a line of defense. The soldiers were hidden in a small gully. Benigno threw a grenade that landed in the water. The sound of the explosion frightened them, and they ran away in terror. This enabled us to shoot at them with ease. Miguel, an audacious man, went right up to one of the wounded soldiers, took his M-1 and his cartridge belt and interrogated him, obtaining valuable information. He learned that the group consisted of 21 men en route to Abapó, and that in Moroco, the place we were avoiding, there were 50 soldiers stationed.

During this ambush we committed various errors. Loading up our horses went very slowly. In addition there was an excess of confidence in our capabilities, as well as an underestimation of the enemy's power.

One comrade fell behind trying on a new pair of boots. Another dropped a load of beans. A horse became frightened and ran off with a mortar, some rifles, clothing, etc. This was the situation when daybreak came. The soldiers recovered from their surprise, received reinforcements from Moroco, regrouped, and gave us pursuit.

We crossed a plot of land where we ran into the sister of one of the peasants who had helped us. The woman was friendly and very calm despite the shooting, telling us that all the peas-

ants of Moroco had been taken prisoner and brought to La
Paz. She sold us a can of milk and offered us some chickens.
She acted with amazing tranquility, despite the soldiers who
were already near, and were shooting at us with sustained fire.

Crossing through one of the fords, Che's horse slipped and
fell. However, Coco, Julio, and Miguel set up a line of fire to
prevent the army from concentrating their fire on him. Later
on Julio tripped, and the soldiers shouted gleefully, "We got
one! We got one!"

Our group crossed the ford on the run, but later on one part
of the forward detachment, including Ricardo, was unable to
do so. While crossing the ford, Ricardo was wounded, and
Pacho and Raúl flew to his rescue. Raúl was shot dead with a
bullet in the mouth, and Pacho wounded by a shot
through the buttocks that brushed lightly against his testicles.
Pacho propped himself up behind the now lifeless body of
Raúl and was able to silence a machine gun. Arturo and other
comrades rescued Ricardo and placed him in a hammock. Unfortunately, however, the plasma was lost in Willy's knapsack.
Despite every effort by our doctor, Ricardo died during the
night.

Two new losses!

Raúl was a very quiet comrade who never asked questions.
He was disciplined, but in general did not stand out from the
rest. The day of the battle he surprised everyone with his daring and heroic conduct. His magnificent and necessary solidarity with a wounded comrade led to his death. Our respect
for him grew.

Ricardo, or Papi, as we all affectionately called him, was the
man who bore the brunt of the preparatory work of the guerrilla nucleus. He was beloved by the Bolivian comrades and
respected by the Cubans and Peruvians fighting there. We
could not abandon him at such a painful moment. For this reason, and because the guerrilla struggle sows deep fraternal
sentiments among men, incredible efforts were made by Raúl,
Pacho, and other comrades to drag him away and save him.

August was a bad month for us. We returned to the banks of the Río Grande with the hope of finding Joaquín. With increasing frequency the local radio stations were reporting skirmishes between soldiers and guerrillas who were not us. During this period we experienced great hunger and a thirst that tortured us to such an extent that some comrades, attempting to mitigate it, drank their own urine, provoking a series of intestinal disorders. To make matters worse, Moro, our doctor, was ill from lumbago, an affliction so painful it practically left him immobilized. We therefore had to show him the greatest care.

On another matter, Camba began to display the first symptoms of cowardice. He raised with me his desire to abandon the struggle, saying his "physical condition would not permit him to continue." He added that he saw few prospects for the guerrilla struggle. The pretext of his physical inability was false, since Camba had shown himself to be a man of great strength. He was simply scared and wanted to desert. The question of the negative prospects for the struggle was another shameful pretext. I told Che about this situation and he spoke with Camba, informing him that he would not be able to leave until our small column reached the end of the route already announced. Camba accepted this.

On August 26 we had our only skirmish with the army of the month. We had planned an ambush at the Río Grande. The soldiers, who already showed themselves to be more prepared, divided into two groups and took a series of precautions they had previously scorned. For example, in a squad of seven men, five were left downriver and two were sent to cross in front of us. Antonio, who was at the front of the ambush, fired prematurely and missed. The two fled in search of reinforcements and the other five ran away at full speed along the sand. Coco and I proposed to Che that he let us follow them up to the embankment and try to take them prisoner. However, they dug in and repulsed us.

These were harsh and tense days, and a drop in morale was

seen. Under these conditions strong will-power was needed, along with firm and respected political leadership. Without these qualities, the disintegration of our column was possible. That was when Che's spirit flourished once again in all its grandeur, along with his qualities as a rounded leader with undisputed authority, decisive in giving orders, clear in his conceptions, rapid in making decisions, emphatic in eliminating any signs of disintegration, and determined to defend his ideals to the very end.

Then, as never before, he issued his historic, precise, and unequivocal call for us to stand up as revolutionaries:

"We have reached a moment," he said on August 8, "when great decisions are called for. This type of struggle provides us the opportunity to become revolutionaries, the highest level of the human species. At the same time, it enables us to emerge fully as men. Those who are unable to achieve either of these two states should say so and abandon the struggle."

The men who continued the struggle at his side not only increased their love and admiration for this exceptional leader, but also committed themselves, whatever the circumstances, to victory or death on behalf of the ideals that were inspiring men and women the world over.

Although we were then unaware of it and only realized it days later, the entire remainder of Joaquín's group was killed in the ambush at the Vado del Yeso on August 31, miserably informed on by the peasant Honorato Rojas. The army waited patiently for Rojas to take Joaquín's group into the trap, and as they forded the river, the soldiers shot them in the back.

Among the lives snuffed out was that of Tania, the woman guided by revolutionary ideals and by her admiration for Che. She had worked patiently in Bolivia for two years, laying the groundwork for our final effort. Later, she picked up a rifle to fight for the freedom of our people. Tania, with her legend consisting of myth and reality known throughout the world, has gone down in history as a heroine of Latin America.

By itself, the rear guard lacked combat capability, owing to the manner in which it was formed. We operated with it for only one month, and were separated from it for four months. The death of Joaquín and the rear guard was a stroke of luck for the army. One or two days prior to the ambush, our column, with Che at the head, reached one of the places where Joaquín had camped. The tracks were still fresh.

The facts we have since gathered enable us to know that Joaquín and his squad suffered indescribable hardships, hunger, and anguish. They searched for us as much as we did for them. However, they never got discouraged, their morale remained high, and they all were resolved to die for our ideals rather than give themselves up, faithful to Che's slogan of "Victory or death!"

We were only 22 men. Of these, El Médico was in poor condition; Camba was a deserter who was terrorized and accompanied us only by force of circumstance; and León was also ready to flee, although he never said anything to us about it. Nevertheless, our small army had earned the enemy's respect, maintained its aggressiveness, and was ready to fight to the end.

Once again, Che energetically reinitiated his educational work with our group, in particular, to correct some weaknesses he had noted. His talks, challenges, or "salvos," as he called them, had the character, on occasion, of a father's advice to his children, and at other times were energetic and harsh, depending on the circumstance. He also knew how to be tender, especially when remembering his family, or comrades who had been part of his military life, such as Tuma or Rolando.

One day, thinking about his children, he told us with a deep sense of affection and nostalgia of his last conversation with his daughter Celita. Just before leaving Cuba for good, he went to his house to see his children for the last time and to say goodbye to them. Naturally, he went disguised as Ramón, the middle-aged man with a businessman's appearance who traveled around much of the world eluding the eye of the CIA. His disguise was so good that the sentries at the house did not recognize him, nor did his daughter. Che took her in his arms, and then sat her on his lap and caressed her hand. The little girl said to Aleida, his wife, who witnessed the scene:

"Mommy, this old man loves me."

Che did not find it painful to relate this incident, although his voice revealed great tenderness. We understood what it meant to him to hear this statement by his beloved daughter, to whom he could not even say goodbye, as any other father would do in a similar situation.

He showed the same tenderness toward his guerrilla comrades, who reciprocated with a total and unlimited affection and admiration for him. It was precisely during these days that Che punished himself with kitchen duty because he had let his rifle get wet while wading through a river. Crossing the Río Grande again, he lost his shoes. Immediately Ñato, a man who resolved all the little problems that came up, crafted a pair of leather sandals for him, entirely closed up. These homemade shoes were the ones that awakened curiosity and comment the day of his death at the Yuro ravine, and later at Vallegrande. In this way Ñato prevented Che from going barefoot. Any one of us would have given him our own shoes, but I'm sure that Che would have vehemently rejected such a gesture.

At the same time, Che reciprocated this affection with a series of acts that we fully appreciated. For example, on September 17, during the days when we had very little food and our situation was not good, he ordered us to prepare rice, a luxury dish, to celebrate the 22nd birthday of Pablito, a comrade of great courage and the youngest of the guerrillas. He had also celebrated Benigno's birthday on September 6.

9. THE AMBUSH AT LA HIGUERA

September was a month of battles, of the loss of valuable men, of long marches and privations, of promising contacts with the peasants, and of ups and downs in our morale. It was also the month when the definitive loss of Joaquín and his group began to sink in.

Our first skirmish occurred on September 2. It could have had very favorable results for us had it not been for an incident that took place. I will relate it with the sole aim of transmitting experiences that might be of value in the future.

Chino was on guard duty with Pombo, when he saw a soldier on horseback. Instead of firing, he shouted, "A soldier!" Naturally the soldier was alerted, and immediately fired in the direction where the shout had come from. As Chino fumbled with his weapon, Pombo was quicker and got off several shots, killing the horse. The soldier fled.

The next day a squad of ours composed of Benigno, Pablito, Coco, Julio, León, and myself clashed with some 40 soldiers in Masicurí, at the house of a large landowner.

The encounter took us by surprise. We were talking with the person in charge of the house and his wife when the soldiers appeared. As soon as they saw us they retreated and formed a semicircle, and immediately opened fire on us. We answered with sustained gunfire, and saw at least one of them fall. However, we were not able to collect any food, and withdrew.

On September 6—Benigno's birthday—there was another skirmish. An army patrol almost took us by surprise due to carelessness by the forward detachment. However, after a brief exchange of fire, nothing happened and we left peacefully.

The following days were ones of constant marches, where we observed with concern that the illness of Moro, our doctor, was steadily worsening and he was suffering from intense pain. Che treated him devotedly and went to great lengths to help alleviate even slightly the effects of his illness. On the other hand, he himself was troubled by new attacks of asthma, and lacked medicine to control it.

On September 22 we reached Alto Seco, a little village of about 50 very modest houses, with horrendous sanitary conditions. Nevertheless, the village was of some importance. In the center was a little plaza, a church, and a school. There was also a dirt road over which motorized vehicles could travel. We immediately learned that the mayor had hurried off to Vallegrande to inform the army of our presence.

The reaction of the population was interesting. The inhabitants did not withdraw from the area. Slowly they began to approach us, with great distrust. Their fear—and it was fear—was not of the guerrillas, but of the possibility that there might be fighting in the town, or of reprisals the army might take against its inhabitants.

It should be noted that for the first time we held a meeting, at the school, attended by peasants who watched in amazement and silence, listening attentively. I was the first to speak. I explained our objectives and went over their harsh conditions of life, the significance of our struggle, and the people's stake in it, since the possibility of a positive change in their lives depended on our triumph.

For the first time, Che also addressed the village inhabitants, although no one recognized him. Che described the state of neglect in which the village had been left and went over the exploitation suffered by the peasants of the area, giving various examples. Among them, he noted that Alto Seco had only one unsanitary well that supplied water to the residents. "Remember this," he told them. "Our presence through here will remind the authorities that you exist. Then they will offer to build a polyclinic for you, or to make some other improvements. But that offer will be a result solely and exclusively of our presence in the area. And if they do carry out some project, you will feel, indirectly, the beneficial effect of our guerrilla struggle."

This was the only meeting we held during the entire war.

Our propaganda in the countryside was conducted through our successful battles. The continual contact between guerrillas and peasants does the rest.

During the following days we passed through Santa Elena and Loma Larga, reaching Pujío on September 25. Again the initial response was curiosity and distrust, but it later turned friendly. The people began to approach us, and we gradually won their trust.

Two facts characterized our situation:

1. Moro continued to be ill and was very weak.

2. Camba was a quivering wreck. At this time Che and I spoke with him to tell him that that very night he was to shave and change clothes so that he could later make his way out without being spotted by the army. Camba said this was not necessary, and that he would continue on with the column until we changed course. That way he could reach Santa Cruz with relative ease.

That night we slept on the side of the road.

The walk from Pujío to Picacho during the early morning of September 26 went off without incident. The population treated us very well. Two little old peasant women even invited Julio and Coco to sleep in their house, and gave them some eggs. For obvious security reasons, both comrades did not accept such a welcome and generous offer. These acts of solidarity undoubtedly had a comforting effect. They also demonstrated that peasants are not so impervious to contact with guerrillas. Through regular, sustained work they can be won over and mobilized as an important auxiliary in combat-related tasks, leading up to obtaining their total integration into the guerrilla ranks.

We reached Picacho very early. The population was holding a celebration, and treated us very well. They offered us *chicha*[12] and some snacks, and when we left they showered us with hugs. Chapaco said a few words as he gave a toast.

---

12. A homemade alcoholic beverage made from fermented corn.

We decided to continue the march. Our next spot was La Higuera. As could be expected, our presence was known by everyone. Coco confiscated a telegram that was at the telegraph operator's house, in which the subprefect of Vallegrande informed the town's mayor of the presence of guerrillas in the area.

A few minutes later came the opening of our most negative battle of the war.

During the preceding days, Moro's illness had been getting worse. On September 26 his health continued to be poor, and this was one of Che's most serious concerns. Perhaps it was his most pressing concern, since the radio reports about Joaquín, although still fragmentary, led us to the supposition that the group was definitively finished. This meant the end of our circling operation to find them; now the column would relocate to another zone of operations.

That day, at 1:00 p.m., the forward detachment set out to reach Jagüey. A half hour later, as the center group and rear guard were preparing to follow them, heavy shooting was heard at the entrance to La Higuera.

Che immediately organized the defense of the town, awaiting the forward detachment. No one doubted at that moment that our people had fallen into an ambush. We therefore waited nervously and tensely for the first reports.

The first one to return was Benigno, with a bullet through his shoulder, the same one that had killed Coco. Later Aniceto and Pablito arrived, the latter with a dislocated foot. Julio and Miguel had also been killed in the ambush.

The battle was quick and unequal. With great fire power and a sizable number of men, the army had attacked our combatants by surprise in an area with no natural defenses, totally lacking in vegetation. The soldiers were able to dominate the area, looking down from a long ridge, with high-caliber weapons.

Miguel was killed almost instantly while Coco was badly wounded. The rest of the comrades fought heroically trying to rescue him, in a noble demonstration of solidarity. As Benigno grabbed Coco's blood-soaked body, a machine-gun volley finished him off, with one of the bullets wounding Benigno. Another burst of fire killed Julio.

Coco and I were more than brothers, if that can be said. We were inseparable comrades in many adventures. Together we were members of the Communist Party. Together we felt the weight of police repression on many occasions and shared imprisonment. Together we worked in Tipuani. Together we roamed Mamoré, learning agriculture and spending long days hunting alligators. Together we joined the guerrilla struggle. In this new adventure I will not see him at my side, but I feel his presence, urging me on more and more.

One day, talking in the woods about the death of Ricardo, which had a powerful impact on his brother Arturo, Coco said to me:

"I would not wish to see you dead; I don't know how I'd handle it. Fortunately, I think that if anyone dies first, it will be me."

Coco was a very generous man, capable of becoming emotional and crying like a man for someone he held dear, as he did the day Ricardo died.

I did not see him die. Nor did I shed tears. It is not in my character to cry. But that does not mean that my pain, my feelings, or my affection for a man so beloved to me was any less intense.

Coco, Julio, and Miguel, comrades of heroic episodes, reached the highest level of the human species, and emerged fully as human beings. Just as Joaquín, Tania, Rolando, Marcos, Tuma, Rubio, Aniceto, and other dear comrades had done so earlier.

That is why Che, who was not given to lavish eulogies, said of them:

"Our losses this time are very great indeed. The one we will feel most is Coco, but Miguel and Julio were magnificent fighters, and the human value of the three is incalculable."

10. THE YURO RAVINE

The ambush at La Higuera marked a new stage for us, difficult and agonizing. We had lost three men and had virtually no forward detachment. El Médico continued doing poorly, and the column was reduced to only 17 guerrillas who were malnourished due to prolonged protein deficiency. With the question of Joaquín's fate now settled, Che's next steps were directed toward looking for another zone of operations with more favorable terrain. Our immediate need was to make contact with the city to solve logistical problems and receive human reinforcements, since our forces were being spent without being able to replace the men who had fallen.

However, it was first necessary to break out of two encirclements. One of these was practically in our very face, while we learned of the army's other circle from journalists' reports that filtered out and were broadcast on Argentine and Chilean radio. It was no mystery to anyone that our presence had been clearly detected, and this was also announced on international broadcasts. Local stations, however, which were silenced by the regime, gave only very general information.

Between September 27 and October 1 we remained in constant hiding, although some comrades carried out scouting missions to look for a way out along one of the ridges that would enable us to elude the enemy forces. Our rations were considerably reduced and consisted only of three-quarters of a small can of sardines and a canteen of water for the entire day. To make matters worse, the water was bitter. But that was all there was, and we went out looking for it at night, or when it was still dark during the early morning hours. Two comrades carried all the canteens. They climbed down into the ravines taking every precaution, erasing their tracks.

Up until September 30, large numbers of fully equipped soldiers passed in front of us without detecting our presence. On October 1 we began to move a little more rapidly. After days of privation, we ate fritters cooked by Chapaco, and Che ordered that each of us get a small piece of fried charqui. So that the fire would not be detected by the soldiers, we covered it with blankets.

The radio stations began to provide more information. One report of note was that Camba and León, who had deserted on September 26, had turned informer. Another report was that the army's general command had moved its forward post. Our marches were made with extreme caution, although at times we passed by fairly populated areas in broad daylight.

This was the situation as we came to October 8.

The previous evening marked eleven months since Che had gone into the mountains of Bolivia. Up to that point the balance sheet was not particularly unfavorable for us. The army had dealt us only one serious blow, at La Higuera, which on the other hand was accidental. Everything else had been positive on balance. Despite our small numbers, we had captured almost a hundred soldiers, including high-ranking officers; we had put a large number of enemy troops out of commission; and we had captured various weapons and a lot of ammunition.

We now faced a new tactical phase, where it was absolutely necessary to break out of the encirclement in order to reach a new zone of operations. There we would have been able to engage the enemy under conditions set by us, while at the same time making contact with the city, an important question in this period, in order to reinforce our column.

Anyone who reads Che's diary will realize that at no time can one detect desperation or lack of faith, despite the many anguished moments we had passed through. (It should be kept in mind that the diary contains only notations for Che's personal use, primarily reflecting negative aspects, with the aim of analyzing these and later correcting them.) That is why, in reviewing eleven months of operations, Che summed up his thoughts by saying that the time had passed "without complications, bucolically."

The early morning of October 8 was cold. Those of us with

wool ponchos put them on. Our hike was slow because Chino walked badly at night, and because Moro's illness was getting worse. At 2:00 a.m. we stopped to rest, resuming our hike at 4:00. We were 17 silent figures, camouflaged in darkness, walking through a narrow canyon called the Yuro ravine.

At dawn a beautiful sun broke out over the horizon, enabling us to carefully scan the terrain. We were looking for a hillcrest we could take to the San Lorenzo river. Extreme security measures were taken, particularly because the gorge and the hill were semibarren, with very low bushes, making it almost impossible to hide.

Che then decided to send out three pairs of scouts: one along the hill to the right, made up of Benigno and Pacho; another along the hill to the left, made up of Urbano and another comrade; and the last one to the area in front of us, assigned to Aniceto and Darío. Benigno and Pacho soon returned with news that left no doubt as to the situation: soldiers were closing off the pass. The problem was to know whether they had detected us or not.

What were the alternatives left to us?

We could not turn back, since the path we had taken, very unprotected, would make us easy targets for the soldiers. Nor could we go forward, since this would mean walking straight into the position occupied by the soldiers. Che made the only decision possible at that moment. He gave the order to hide in a small lateral canyon, and organized the taking of positions. It was approximately 8:30 a.m. The 17 of us were positioned at the center and at both sides of the canyon, waiting.

The great dilemma faced by Che, and all of us, was to know whether the army had discovered our presence, or whether this was simply a tactical maneuver within the broader encirclement they had been putting in place for several days.

Che made a rapid analysis. If the soldiers attacked between 10:00 a.m. and 1:00 p.m., we would be at a profound disadvantage, and our prospects would be minimal, since it would be very difficult to resist for a prolonged period of time. If they attacked between 1:00 and 3:00 p.m., our prospects for neutralizing them were better. If the battle occurred from 3:00 p.m. on, the advantage would be ours, since night would soon be falling, and night is comrade and ally to the guerrilla.

At approximately 11:00 a.m., I went to replace Benigno at his position, but he did not climb down and instead remained there spread out on the ground, since the wound in his shoulder had become infected and was very painful. Benigno, Darío, and I would remain there from then on. On the other side of the ravine were Pombo and Urbano, and in the center was Che with the rest of the combatants.

At approximately 1:30 p.m., Che sent Ñato and Aniceto to relieve Pombo and Urbano. To cross over to their position, we had to cross a clearing that the enemy's position overlooked. The first to try it was Aniceto, but he was killed by a bullet.

The battle had begun. Our exit was closed off. The soldiers shouted, "We got one! We got one!"

From the same narrow gorge, in a position occupied by soldiers, one could hear the regular rattle of machine guns, which appeared to cover the path we had come through the night before.

The group I was in was positioned directly facing one section of the army, at an equal height, which enabled us to observe their movements without being seen. We therefore fired only when fired upon, to not give ourselves away. The army, for its part, believed that all our firing was coming from down below, i.e., from Che's position.

The most difficult situation was that of Pombo and Urbano. Hidden behind a rock, they were under constant fire. They were unable to leave, because if they crossed the clearing they could be wiped out with ease, as happened to Aniceto. Attempting to force them out from that natural fortification, the enemy threw a grenade. The explosion raised a cloud of dust that Pombo and Urbano seized upon. With impressive speed they ran across the clearing as the soldiers fired in their general direction and shouted aggressively. Both of them ended up right where Ñato was waiting for them.

The three of them tried to retreat along a path indicated previously by Che in order to reach a meeting place agreed upon earlier. Nevertheless, they were able to see us, and understood our signal to stay where they were.

The battle continued without interruption. We fired only when fired upon to not give ourselves away and to save ammunition. From our position we put a number of soldiers out of action.

When it got dark we climbed down to meet up with Pombo, Urbano, and Ñato and to look for our knapsacks. We were now in our element. We asked Pombo, "Where's Fernando?"

"We thought he was with you," they responded.

We put on our knapsacks and headed quickly to the contact point. Along the way we found food supplies thrown on the ground, including flour. This troubled us deeply, because Che never permitted anyone to throw food on the ground. When it was necessary to do so, it would be carefully hidden. Farther ahead I found Che's plate, completely trampled. I recognized it immediately, because it was a wide bowl made of aluminum with unique characteristics. I picked it up and stored it in my knapsack.

We found no one at the meeting place, although we recognized footprints from Che's sandals, which left a different mark than the others, making it easy to identify. But these tracks disappeared farther ahead.

We assumed that Che and the others had headed toward the San Lorenzo river, as foreseen, with the aim of hiding out in the woods, far from the army's reach, until arriving at the new zone of operations.

That night the six of us walked along: Pombo, Benigno, Ñato, Darío, Urbano, and myself. Our load was lighter, since at the bottom of the ravine we had thrown out a number of items that seemed unnecessary. Lightening our burden meant we could walk faster.

My knapsack was open and the radio had been taken out.

Undoubtedly the person who took it out was Che before retreating. This was natural. A cool-headed man, always looking
ahead, Che never organized an unplanned, desperate retreat.
On the contrary, at moments of great decision, his stature as a
leader, both militarily and politically, grew gigantically. It was
therefore obvious that he took out the radio to listen to news,
since obtaining information is a very important element in the
woods.

We marched silently. None of us could hide our immense
concern for the fate of Che and the other comrades.

After losing the tracks of our people, we came once again to
La Higuera, a place that brought back painful memories that
had still not been erased. We sat down almost in front of the
schoolhouse there. The dogs barked persistently, but we did
not know whether they were barking at us or were responding
to the songs and shouts of the soldiers who were in a state of
drunken euphoria that night.

Never did we imagine that so close to us was our beloved
commander, wounded but still alive!

Over the course of time, I have thought that perhaps had we
known it, we would have attempted a desperate action to save
him, even though we would surely have died in the process.

But on that tense and agonizing night, we knew absolutely
nothing of what had happened. In low voices we asked each
other if other comrades had perhaps been killed in the battle,
in addition to Aniceto.[13]

We continued walking, circling around La Higuera without
moving very far away. At dawn, with the first ray of daylight,
we hid ourselves in not very dense brush. We had decided to
walk only at night, since daytime required rigorous vigilance.

October 9 was calm and peaceful. Twice we saw a helicopter
pass overhead. This was precisely the one carrying the still-

---

13. Also killed in the battle were Antonio and Arturo. Pacho was captured,
gravely wounded; he received no medical attention and died during the
night. Captured and murdered were Chino, Willy, and Che.

warm body of Che, cowardly murdered on the orders of the CIA and of the military thugs Barrientos and Ovando. However, we knew nothing of this.

Our only communication with the outside world was a small radio that had belonged to Coco, but was now carried by Benigno. That afternoon Benigno heard a confused report. A local station announced that the army had captured a seriously wounded guerrilla who seemingly was Che. We immediately discounted this as a possibility, since if it were true they would be making a big fuss out of it. We thought the wounded person might be Pacho, and that the confusion resulted from a certain resemblance between the two.

That night we walked through hellish ravines and over steep and jagged cliffs that even goats would not have chosen. But Urbano and Benigno, with their extraordinary sense of direction and unbreakable resolve, guided us slowly out of the encirclement.

We moved slowly. On October 10 we found ourselves at a spot still close to La Higuera, and we joked that the water we were drinking was the same as the soldiers were drinking down below. We again waited for nightfall to reach Abra del Picacho, through which we hoped to break out of the encirclement.

At approximately one o'clock in the afternoon, Urbano heard a news report that left us frozen: the radio was announcing the death of Che and described his physical appearance and clothing. There was no possibility of a mistake, because in describing his clothing they listed the sandals made by Ñato, a wool poncho that had belonged to Tuma and that Che wore at night, and other details we knew perfectly.

A profound pain came over us, leaving us mute. Che—our leader, comrade, and friend; the heroic guerrilla; the man of exceptional ideas—was dead. The horrendous and lacerating news produced deep anguish.

We remained there unable to utter a sound, with fists clenched, as if afraid of breaking into tears at the first word. I looked at Pombo; tears were streaming down his face.

Four hours later the silence was broken. Pombo and I spoke briefly. The night of the ambush at the Yuro ravine, the six of us had agreed that he would assume command of our group until we met up with Che and the rest of our comrades. It was necessary at that very special moment, to make a decision that would honor the memory of our beloved leader. We exchanged some ideas, and later the two of us spoke to our comrades.

It is difficult to recall exactly, in minute detail, a moment filled with so many emotions, with such deep feeling, with such intense pain, and with such a desire to cry out to revolutionaries that all was not lost, that Che's death was not a burial of his ideas, that the war was not over.

How can one describe each of our faces? How can one faithfully reproduce all the words, the gestures, the reactions made amid that awesome solitude, under the constant threat of the military cannibals seeking to assassinate us, offering rewards for our capture "dead or alive"?

All I remember is that with a very great sincerity and an immense desire to survive, we swore to continue the struggle, to fight until death or until reaching the city, where we would begin again the task of rebuilding Che's army, in order to return to the mountains and continue fighting as guerrillas.

With firm voices, but laden with emotion, we made our pledge that afternoon—the same pledge that hundreds of men in all parts of the world have now taken—to turn Che's dream into reality.

Thus, on the afternoon of October 10, Ñato, Pombo, Darío, Benigno, Urbano, and I stated out loud, in the jungles of Bolivia:

"Che: Your ideas have not died. We who fought at your side pledge to continue the struggle until death or the final victory. Your banners, which are ours, will never be lowered. Victory or death!"

11. BREAKING THE ENCIRCLEMENT

How did we survive the encirclements placed around us after the battle at the Yuro ravine, against forces vastly superior in both numbers and weapons?

Some may think it was solely the result of the elemental factor called the "survival instinct" or the desire to continue living. I sincerely believe this was not the only reason.

It is true we wanted to continue living, but that was not all. In essence, we maintained our aggressiveness and were ready to engage in combat at any moment, as we had always been.

Was it impossible, then, to break out of the tight enemy encirclement and return to the city in search of contacts to continue the struggle?

On the afternoon of October 10, after pledging never to desert the revolutionary process, we made plans to break out of the encirclement and decided to look for the other survivors. Through radio reports we learned that the army knew that only ten guerrillas remained alive. Our group was composed of the six already mentioned. The other group, whose direction we did not know but assumed to be the same as ours, was composed of Chapaco, Moro, Eustaquio, and Pablito. The deserters Camba and León collaborated with the army in identifying us and giving the exact number of those remaining.

We had already realized how the enemy's encirclement was organized, and we knew how the soldiers were proceeding. We therefore decided to break through at the most abrupt point. Unfortunately, on October 11 Moro, Pablito, Eustaquio, and Chapaco were killed at the mouth of the Mizque river.[14] These comrades would surely have made the same decision we did to never give themselves up, and they died in combat

---

14. Moro was killed in the fighting. The three others were wounded (Chapaco gravely) and captured; they were subsequently murdered. The fighting took place in the early morning of October 12.

with dignity. They chose a route in the opposite direction from ours (to the south), obviously attempting to reach the city, as we were. The only ones remaining now were us.

We were in poor physical condition. We had eaten little and had exerted great efforts during the previous days. In addition, the great tension we had been under also left its mark on us.

We lightened our load once again. Ñato, who carried all the medical supplies, buried them, since these would be of no use to us in the future. The metal box that had been used previously for sterilization was turned into a cooking pot. The flour soup we prepared after so many days of privation served only to "fool our insides," but did not restore our strength.

In the early morning hours of October 12, we began walking in the direction of one part of the circle. At 3:00 a.m. we crossed the road to La Higuera at the Abra del Picacho, just as we had done earlier with Che. It was completely silent all around. When it got light we were at the other side of the pass. We came upon a hut and decided to go ask its inhabitants for the exact location, reorient ourselves, try to stock up on food supplies, and continue on. We looked for the peasants but found no one. Remaining in the hut was too dangerous, so we decided it would be better to hide ourselves in the bushes surrounding the house.

Two totally opposite events marked the day. A boy about twelve years old, very alert, identified our exact location for us. He pointed out the direction of the river, offered us a pot to cook in, and began to milk a cow for us. Unfortunately, a peasant passing by saw us and ran off toward the pass to denounce us to the soldiers, large numbers of whom were concentrated there as part of the strategic encirclement around our dwindling column. Owing to our physical weakness, we were unable to catch up with him. And because he was a peasant, we did not want to shoot him.

In this emergency situation, we were compelled to leave immediately, without cooking and without waiting for the milk. We circled around a steeply sloped creek that emptied into the San Lorenzo river. Then Urbano, who was walking at the front, saw soldiers who were already in position. Possessing all the technical resources, they had passed ahead of us and were there waiting for us.

Urbano, who had rapid reflexes, opened fire immediately. The soldiers returned the fire.

This was the last time we carried knapsacks. Forced by circumstance to escape the enemy at great speed, we took only the ration of sugar and our respective wool ponchos. The rest we threw away.

We climbed a hill beside us that was very steep and dangerous, as one could fall to the other side of the creek. Since the ravines were the only place in the area with trees, we were forced to get out any way possible to seek a better position. We dragged ourselves to a type of wooded "island," with an area of approximately 50 square meters. The situation was relatively worse than before, because the small grove was surrounded by open plains where the soldiers could easily kill us. We hid and kept silent, hoping they would not spot us, waiting for nightfall, when we could leave.

Some peasants began to circle around the area, and the army began to surround it. At approximately 4:30 p.m. on October 12, a tight circle of soldiers was moving in on the "island." This was their best opportunity to eliminate us, but the final word had not been spoken.

The six of us resolved to group ourselves in the highest part of the small wood, and to respond to enemy fire only when we were sure of hitting the mark. The soldiers opened fire, insulting us and calling on us to surrender. We kept our silence, aware of their movements.

These were extremely difficult moments. We thought our last moment had arrived, and prepared ourselves to die with dignity. At one point I proposed that we bury the remaining money and watches, to avoid having these fall into the hands of the soldiers. Pombo, however, with much assurance, stated that we would be able to break out of the circle at night. We all kept our respective belongings.

Our silence disconcerted the army. Some soldiers, showing their fear, shouted, "There's no one here. Let's go." Others insulted us.

A new operation was soon begun. Groups of soldiers began to "comb" the little island, an easy task given its small size. When they were close, we opened fire. Three soldiers and a guide fell dead.

The troops retreated, but immediately began to fire bursts of machine gun fire and grenades, since our position was now located. They also changed their insolent tone. Now they no longer insulted us, but shouted, "Guerrillas, surrender. Why continue fighting when your leader is dead?"

As Pombo had foreseen, the firing stopped when night fell. But to our misfortune, there appeared a beautiful moon, showering its light on every corner. To try to leave under such circumstances was too risky.

We remained vigilant. A terrible chill had fallen and went right through one's clothing down to the bone. We shivered as we watched the sky, waiting for the moon to be obscured.

At 3:00 a.m., clouds came down over the entire area. This was the moment we had been waiting for with impatience. We crawled slowly. To our surprise, the soldiers had pulled back a bit. Apparently the four losses they suffered during the afternoon drove them to take precautions. Soon we were close to enemy positions. The soldiers were posted five meters apart from each other. The weather and the wait had affected them as well.

We continued advancing until suddenly one of the soldiers, instead of firing, shouted, "Halt! Who goes there?"

That was our salvation. We threw ourselves at one of the trenches, killed a few of the soldiers, and crouched together there. An intense exchange of fire broke out on all sides, lasting approximately 15 minutes or longer. When it ended, we began to leave. The army's encirclement had been broken.

Our escape from the mountains has been utilized by writers and journalists to concoct fantastic tales. Some day—because now is not the time, since we would be hurting the peasants who helped us—we will relate the details of this action, which in truth did have its incredible and fascinating aspects. We will only say that had it not been for this solidarity, our survival would have been extremely difficult.

Beginning in the early morning of October 13, we walked only at night, trying to avoid contact with the population, except when this was absolutely necessary for acquiring food or obtaining information. We were somewhat wary, since some peasants—not all and not the majority—motivated by the 10 million peso reward for our "heads," as the radios announced, would run off to denounce us to the soldiers. But there were many peasants who helped us leave this vulnerable area, guiding us to Vallegrande, providing us with food, giving us valuable information, and remaining silent despite the beatings, threats, and even robbery they suffered at the hands of the army.

For a month we walked toward the Cochabamba-to-Santa Cruz highway. On November 13 we made our first serious attempt to head toward the city. Ñato and Urbano reached Mataral to buy sandals and clothes, to change our threadbare "suits" and modify our sinister appearance. At the store in town, they obtained information that the soldiers were aware of our presence and were preparing for combat against us. They immediately returned to warn us. In the afternoon we noticed several patrols persistently looking for us. We remained in hiding all day. That night we started walking again, crossed the highway, and tried to leave the area. However, on November 14 the army discovered us, and once again we engaged in unequal combat. At the top of a hill, when we were close to escaping the enemy forces, Ñato was struck by a bullet. We formed a line of defense and dragged him toward our position, but he was already dead.

Ñato was a man dear to all, firm in his convictions, courageous, ready to find solutions to the small domestic problems that sometimes accumulate and lead to so many unpleasant consequences. He died in our last battle, after having faced greater dangers than this one in which he lost his life. Such are the fortunes of war. As a simple tribute to this prototype of a man of the people, one can only say: He was a complete guerrilla and a man loyal to the ideas of liberation.

From Mataral we marched parallel to the highway, hoping that our people in the city, who had received hard blows, would realize our maneuver and come to help get us out of the mountains. However, fierce repression had destroyed the weak organization we still had left, and the remaining cadres found themselves in a difficult situation, making it very hard for them to operate. Our movements were easily detected by the army, since we inevitably left signs of our passage. Therefore, until December we had many other skirmishes with the soldiers, inflicting new casualties on them.

We have deliberately never told how we emerged from the mountains, because this would endanger the lives of a number of peasants and their families who risked everything for us, along with honest revolutionaries from the city.[15] They understood the meaning of our struggle and risked what little they had to create the conditions for us to be able to initiate the stage of rebuilding the ELN. Some day in the not-too-distant future, we will be able to acknowledge them. It is necessary to state, however, that this type of generous solidarity gives the categorical lie to those who hold that the rural population is immune to revolutionary ideas and that "nothing can be done." Fortunately, we can proudly say the opposite. Moreover, we are certain that in the next stage of the guerrilla struggle, the peasants will sooner or later come over massively to our side, since our army represents their aspirations of social, economic, and political progress.

As a brief epilogue, we can state the following: Urbano and I were the first to reach the city. There we made contact with

---

15. An account of this escape, written by Peredo's father-in-law, at the time a prominent member of the Communist Party, is contained in Jesús Lara, *Guerrillero Inti* (Mexico City: Editorial Diógenes, 1972).

other comrades and organized the arrival of Pombo, Benigno, and Darío.

The rest of the story is known, although it has not yet ended. The second part will soon be written, with new guerrilla actions in the jungles of Bolivia.

Talks by Che Guevara to the Guerrilla Unit
From diaries of other combatants

The diaries of Pombo (Harry Villegas) and Rolando (Eliseo Reyes),
excerpted below, were captured by the Bolivian military and sub-
sequently published in Latin America, together with those of Pacho
(Alberto Fernández) and Braulio (Israel Reyes).

Pombo was one of the three Cuban surviving veterans. Rolando,
second-in-command of the guerrilla unit and a former member of the
Central Committee of the Communist Party of Cuba, was killed at El
Mesón April 25, 1967. Pacho was wounded and captured October 8,
1967, at the Yuro ravine and died that night. Braulio was killed near
the Vado del Yeso on August 31, 1967.

The third item in this section is taken from an account by Benigno
(Dariel Alarcón), one of the other Cuban survivors.

FROM POMBO'S DIARY

November 7, 1966
After searching for the entrance to the road leading to the
farm, we stopped in a remote area. There, while we ate, Mongo[1] introduced himself to Bigotes, informing him of his deci-

---

1. Che.

sion to come and fight in Bolivia because it has the best conditions on the continent for guerrilla warfare. He realizes that both the [scope of the] plans and his presence would postpone the possibility of a rapid victory. However, we cannot afford the luxury of dreaming about a revolution in Bolivia alone, without a revolution in a country on the coast at the very least, if not in all of Latin America. If that does not happen this revolution will be crushed.

November 15, 1966

Mongo spoke to us of the points he will lay out to Estanislao: He has no political power in Bolivia. Nevertheless, he feels his experience is sufficient to direct military operations and control the finances. He knows where money can be obtained. We can ask China and the Soviet Union for aid, explaining to the Chinese that this would not involve any political commitment on China's part. We could send [Moisés] Guevara with a letter from us to Chou En-lai, and we can send Mario together with a comrade to the Soviet Union, so that at the very least they can inform us what they will contribute.

Mario must understand that the struggle in Bolivia will be a long one, because the enemy will concentrate all his forces against it. Bolivia's sacrifice will help create conditions in neighboring countries. We have to create another Vietnam in America, centered in Bolivia.

December 4, 1966

We held a meeting with Ramón, where he spoke to us about discipline and the obligation we had, in view of our guerrilla experience, to serve as examples for the Bolivians. Later he stated:

"Some of the [Bolivian] comrades have taken courses in the use of weapons and are better trained than many of us, who have spent our time in political activities and have not kept up with these things.

"It is our privilege to be proven soldiers. We have experienced all the tests of guerrilla life, which are extraordinarily difficult, and have overcome them. We are the authors of a victorious revolution. Our moral obligation is therefore much greater, for we must be true communists, full of an immense spirit of sacrifice.

"Taking every security measure is not sufficient. There are examples in Latin America of guerrilla movements that were wiped out. We too [in Cuba] received blows that scattered us, surprises such as Alegría de Pío and Alto de Espinoza.[2] We had no experience and lacked the most basic knowledge; nevertheless, we survived those surprises. The spirit of Fidel and his ability to organize men saved us from defeat. This was an advantage that our comrades in Peru and Argentina lacked. In Venezuela the outcome is still in the balance. It is not a question of victory or defeat; after the initial blow they did not have to pass through a formative stage.

"One problem facing the guerrillas: leisure time must be spent fighting leisure time. We must not slip into being neglectful, doing only what is absolutely necessary. Yesterday, for example, I conducted a little test: a lantern had fallen on the ground, and I waited to see who would pick it up. No one did. If you were at home you would have done so. In my battle against idleness, I seek to overcome an attitude of indifference toward things that do not belong to us personally, because that can destroy the internal cohesion essential for unity in the guerrilla ranks.

"The Manilans [Cubans] will hold positions of leadership temporarily in order to begin training the Bolivians—the future cadres who will lead the battle in this country as part of the continent-wide struggle. The [*illegible*] must be formed by the liberation armies from neighboring countries.

---

2. Two battles from the early stages of the Cuban revolutionary war in December 1956 and February 1957 respectively, in which the Rebel forces were taken by surprise.

December 12, 1966

During a meeting Ramón discussed organizational plans that were decided several days ago at a meeting which we—Marcos, Rolando, Pombo, Miguel, Pacho—did not attend, even though the main point under discussion was the responsibilities of the political instructors. The duties assigned are the following:

Second in command: Joaquín. Head of operations: Alejandro. Political commissars (the only responsibility assigned to two comrades): Rolando and Inti. Information, collection of data on the organization of the troops, etc.: Antonio. Head of supplies: Ñato. Head of all services: Pombo (food, medicine, transport, and so forth).

Ramón discussed the responsibility of each position and the absolute duty of all the men to obey the orders of each leader in his respective field. He also stated that the political instructors are subordinate to the military commander. The political leader is on top of the troops' political situation and acts as a catalyst. He is responsible for the men's morale and their problems, and must keep the military leader informed at all times. "We do not ask that he always be overly strict; on the contrary, each man should seek him out for orientation or help at difficult moments."

"Those of us from Manila have already been through these things, and we must analyze our experiences so that we do not repeat our mistakes here. . . .

"In a few days, Comrade Estanislao will be visiting us, and I hope we will be able to come to agreement on the future organization of the revolutionary struggle. I also hope that we receive the total support of the vanguard organization of the working class and of the Bolivian [Communist] party.

"It is not necessary for us to choose a name for our movement at the present time, but we will have to select one in the future. The Bolivians, who are still few in number, must bear the greatest burden in future marches, since we of Manila cannot remain in the forefront. The Bolivians will therefore have to sacrifice much, and will need to have a great capacity for work.

"The principal thing we are discussing here—assigning areas of responsibility—does not require further elaboration, because this has been done on previous occasions. In addition, the specific duties of each post are straightforward; those assigned are familiar with them. All these assignments are temporary because ultimately the leadership cadres for this struggle will emerge from among the Bolivians: their officials, future economic administrators, and so on.

December 20, 1966

We held a meeting at which Ramón explained what this struggle represents. He stressed repeatedly that it will not be a rapid one, for we need ten years or more to conclude the insurrectional stage. Power must be seized in Bolivia, but unless some neighboring countries do the same, we will inevitably be annihilated, because [*illegible*], and a blockade like the one against Cuba would be sufficient.

February 18, 1967

We have a meeting with Ramón where he announces that owing to the army's presence in Masicuri, and the fact that it is not advantageous for us to attack it, we will head toward the Rosita river. To get there we have to cross the entire Masicuri mountain region, and after reaching the mouth of the Rosita we will return to the Ñacahuazú by way of the Río Grande.

February 26, 1967

"Everyone is aware of the purpose of this meeting," Ramón began. "For us it has been a great surprise to witness that comrades already tested are the first to become a problem. The march we are on is aimed at enabling the Bolivian comrades to adapt to the trials and difficulties of guerrilla life, which in our view is the hardest part of the struggle. We want them to get used to hunger, thirst, constant hikes, loneliness out in the woods, etc. What we have discovered is that it is not the Bolivians who are having problems, but comrades who could be classified as veterans, owing to the many times they have been through these situations. This should provide us a lesson for the future: men who once gave their heart and soul for a cause have become used to life in an office; they have become bureaucrats, accustomed to giving orders, having everything solved in the office, having everything come to them already worked out.

"Such is the case with Comrades Marcos and Pacho, who are unable to adapt to this life. I would not like to think that the reason for their constant problems with the other comrades is that they do not have the courage to say they want to leave.

"Comrade Marcos has commanded large units, and this case is typical of him. Pacho is a comrade who has been in combat, but needs to go through the school of guerrilla training because he is not a complete revolutionary, and is an incomplete guerrilla combatant. If we have any further problems on Pacho's account, he will be punished and sent back to Manila, because he lied about what happened."

April 15, 1967

Ramón spoke to us about our future activities: wiping out the enemy through ambushes along roads and trails; the need to win the support of the peasants in order to organize our rural base.

He pointed out the great truth that theft is incompatible with socialism, and it is also incompatible with the principles followed by this guerrilla unit. Therefore, anyone caught committing this crime will be punished, including the death penalty.

Inti

Pombo

Rolando

Ñato

Four of the members of the guerrillas' general staff. Inti Peredo and Rolando were assigned by Guevara as political commissars, with responsibility for day-to-day political leadership of the unit. Pombo was head of services; Ñato, head of supplies and armaments.

FROM ROLANDO'S DIARY

January 6, 1967

We held the first meeting of all the people. Ramón indicated
a number of cases of carelessness and violation of discipline.
He pointed to a lack of interest in the classes on the part of
some comrades. He reviewed the experiences in Manila and
the C[ongo], referring to comrades having a spirit of self-
sacrifice but lacking instruction, and how in Manila this led to
placing unqualified people in certain positions, etc. He spoke
of the perspective of combat in the future and the time it
would take for us to reach our objective. In doing so, he
warned against false illusions, etc.

He stated that methods and procedures need to be introduced to help steel our guerrilla unit, so that new members,
upon their arrival, feel the positive influence of the group. He
later pointed to the need to establish a political leadership body.
After analyzing the present difficulties, he concluded by stating
that for the moment we could function without such a body.

Ramón later explained the reasons he had selected Joaquín
as second in command rather than Marcos, saying a few
things about each one. He ended by assigning various tasks
and reporting on his upcoming meeting with [Moisés]
Guevara, and referring to the consequences it would entail.

February 26, 1967

At 8:00 a.m. we stopped and held a meeting of all the people
in which Ramón reviewed the results of the journey up to
now. He pointed to its usefulness, stressing the fact that we
were beginning to experience the harsh and difficult moments
of guerrilla life. He emphasized that what we have gone
through so far is infinitesimal compared to what lies ahead. As
he had done earlier, he explained that the people from Manila
had an advantage over the Bolivians in that they have been
through this type of combat.

He stated that in the recent period our defects had become

clear, that seven years of revolution had left their mark on certain comrades. He spoke of how having chauffeurs, secretaries, and others working under them had made them accustomed to giving orders and having things done for them, and how a relatively easy life had led them to forget to a certain extent the rigors and sacrifices of the life we are again living through. Ramón continued by saying that among the Manilans are comrades who have been in combat, but have never experienced the difficult moments we are going through.

He concluded this part of his talk by saying that the people from Manila were all known to him personally, and this was precisely the reason we had come. However, he had to admit to being unaware of the personal traits of Marcos, as well as Pacho's demonstration that he is far from being a true guerrilla. The merits of the Manilans had merely given them the right to participate in this glorious and extremely important struggle.

"What I had in Manila were not friends, but comrades," he said. "Whenever I defended someone in difficulty, I did so because it was correct, and not out of friendship. Whoever is deserving here can have responsibilities and the opportunity to set an example. The next time Comrade Pacho has a problem of this type he will be dishonorably discharged and sent back to Manila. Comrade Marcos must change his manner of addressing comrades; the insulting manner he employs undermines his authority."

He declared the meeting closed, and ordered the march to continue until 6:00 p.m.

March 25, 1967

At 6:30 p.m. Ramón held a meeting with all the people and reviewed the journey. He commented on the deeply felt loss of Benjamín and Carlos, pointing to the personal qualities of the latter. Although not very strong physically, he possessed a high degree of morale and spirit. He mentioned the comrades who were exemplary during the training march: Miguel, Inti, Pombo, and Rolando. He noted that there are few Bolivians in this list, adding that this is natural given that the Manilans include comrades who have been through this type of experience before. However, he hopes that in the future the number of Bolivians will be greater.

Later he referred to the case of Marcos, reviewing his mistakes and improper behavior, while stating that he is a comrade with many merits. Among his defects, Ramón noted his tendency to have others serve him, his lack of discipline, his despotic attitude toward comrades, his cockiness, and his lack of authority. Ramón accused Marcos of not obeying the order he had given to return along the Ñacahuazú; of having arrived at the farm in broad daylight, disobeying orders; and that in doing so a shot was fired at them by a presumed army collaborator without this being reported. He also accused him of having camped at the house of a peasant who accompanied them for three leagues and later guided the army in its pursuit. Although the army did not catch up to them, it was later confirmed that this man was killed in the ambush of March 23 while acting as the army's guide.

Ramón concluded by announcing that Marcos was being relieved as head of the forward detachment and as third in command of the guerrilla unit, giving him the choice of returning to Manila or remaining as an ordinary combatant. He stated that Marcos had spoiled a large part of his good record. Miguel will replace Marcos as head of the forward detachment. Marcos agreed to remain as a combatant and has been assigned to the rear guard.

Ramón continued by saying that among the people brought by Guevara are comrades who are not guerrilla material, but are rejects, referring to Chingolo, Pepe, and Paco. They do not want to work, do not want weapons, do not want to carry things, pretend to be ill, etc. In addition, there were two deserters from this group. What shall we do with these people? We want to get them out of here as soon as it is possible. In the meantime, they are warned that if they do not work they will not eat. As soon as we hide our belongings, keeping the location secret from them, Ramón said, we will give them a few pesos—this money belongs to the people—and let them make their way back as best they can.

He went on to stress once again the harshness and difficulty of the struggle, as well as how long it will last. The new recruits were then given the opportunity to decide whether or not they wanted to stay. He referred to the case of Eusebio: a thief, liar, and hypocrite, who states he wants to leave because he is tired. We will treat him the same way as the three others brought by Guevara.

He referred to the declaration made in Manila by the [Bolivian Communist] party that it would not demand leadership of the war, but would collaborate with us, stating their intention to send a commission to speak with Ramón. We are willing to discuss with them, Ramón said, and to accept their collaboration. However, it must be in deeds, not words. Let them send us cadres to work in the cities. Let them send us arms and economic assistance, which is a form of aid. But at the same time as they speak of aid, Comrades Aniceto, Pedro, and Loyola have been expelled from the youth organization. Once again their deeds are at variance with their words. We will hold discussions with them again, comrades, and will not hide anything from them. We will keep them informed on all political and [illegible] questions. We must have confidence in this group. But what is important are the comrades who have firmly resolved to fight.

April 15, 1967

At 8:00 p.m. Ramón held a meeting with us, where he told us that we would be heading toward another region. (It is to the south, along the Sucre-to-Monteagudo road.) In this area, he pointed out, are peasants with whom we will be establishing our base. He explained that we would be in contact with many more peasants, and should keep in mind that their initial reaction will be fear. It is possible that at first they will not be very responsive to the guerrillas, he said, and that some might even inform the army of our presence. His advice was to act carefully toward them, seeking to win their confidence. Additional aims of the trip are to obtain food, get Danton and Carlos out, and familiarize ourselves with the area.

Ramón also reported that 20 cans of milk were missing from the cave. He explained that this was not a case of a comrade taking a can and drinking it, which would merit reproach, but is not as bad as this premeditated act. He stated that a man capable of doing such a thing does not deserve to be among us and should be shot; that if milk continues to disappear and the thief is not found, he would halt the purchase of milk for six months.

He concluded by reading communiqués 1 and 2, which we are attempting to deliver to the press.[3]

FROM BENIGNO'S ACCOUNT[4]

September 27, 1967

Che pointed out to everyone how extraordinarily difficult our situation was. He gave the Bolivians the option of leaving the column if they so desired, to save themselves. All of them expressed their determination to remain with us.

To us Cubans he spoke more or less along the following lines: "We represent something more than the Bolivian revolution. In these moments we represent the Cuban revolution. What we symbolize here is the prestige of the Cuban revolution, and we are going to defend that prestige to the last man and to the last bullet. Does anyone have anything to say?" A total silence underlined our absolute determination to continue the struggle.

---

3. See pages 305-9.
4. "La emboscada de La Higuera" (The La Higuera ambush) published in *OCLAE*, November-December 1971.

Accounts by Cuban veterans

On February 15, 1968, the three Cuban guerrillas who had survived—Pombo (Harry Villegas), Urbano (Leonardo Tamayo), and Benigno (Dariel Alarcón)—eluded a massive army search effort and crossed into Chilean territory. A week later they made contact with supporters inside Chile. Bowing to widespread demands to ensure the Cubans' safety, the Chilean government provided a military plane to fly them to Tahiti, escorted by Socialist Party leader and future president Salvador Allende. From there a Cuban plane flew them home, where they arrived March 6.

Below are excerpts from accounts they have provided, published in Cuba.

On the selection of the guerrillas' zone of operations

by Pombo

Papi, Tuma, and I left for Bolivia, with instructions from Che.[1] Our objective at that stage was to organize and prepare the armed struggle in that country. We therefore did

---

1. Pombo and Tuma arrived in Bolivia in July 1966. Ricardo (Papi) had been there since March.

not participate in the training.

The zone in which we later conducted operations was not the one we had originally foreseen. Che's aim was to conduct operations a little farther to the north, and the base at the Ñacahuazú had been chosen as an extreme rear, to be used for organizing the guerrilla unit. Later on, avoiding any confrontation with the army, we were to advance toward the north, on our way to a more centrally located region. Our primary line of communication and movement was to be the Cordillera Occidental of the Andes, a mountain chain through which one could reach the Argentine border.

The region Che intended to operate in had taller vegetation, a higher population density, and better conditions. But as is known, the guerrilla unit was compelled to begin action in the Ñacahuazú region. There were many comrades who were still arriving, or who would soon be coming, including a large group of Bolivians then undergoing training. Due to circumstances everybody knows, this group never arrived.[2]

The initial group assigned to organize the struggle was small. At the beginning we were four, later reduced to three, because one comrade who had joined us said he did not want to continue. We were joined by a Peruvian with the last name Pacheco, and he was with us throughout this entire organizational stage. He did not become part of the guerrillas but continued his organizational work in the urban underground apparatus; he would be killed much later on, during the second stage, after Che was dead and Inti was leading the movement. This Peruvian participated with us in scouting out the different regions of Bolivia.

We purchased arms and conducted reconnaissance in three regions of the country, so that the entire organizational phase could be completed without great difficulties. We purchased clothing, medicine, and the Ñacahuazú farm. We had scouted the terrain from the Ñacahuazú to Chapare; we were also in

---

2. See pages 345-46.

Alto Beni, which was a little closer, near the border of Peru, Brazil, and Bolivia. We went through that entire area over there, and we had also been through the area to the south of the Ñacahuazú.

Of the regions explored, the site that had the best conditions for establishing a base, from the guerrilla point of view, was the zone to the south—keeping in mind that Che wanted this to be a temporary location. Because he had even instructed us to concentrate a large quantity of arms and munitions in the upper Chapare region, to purchase a farm in that region, and to prepare conditions for concentrating the entire group there after we had begun the guerrilla struggle. All this had already been foreseen when Che arrived at the Ñacahuazú. The aim was to stay in this zone for a brief period of preparation and organization.

The first guerrilla battle took place in the Ñacahuazú region, because we had been discovered and had to fight. There was a whole sequence of events regarding how the army came to realize that something abnormal was going on in the area. This began with Algarañaz, the peasant who had a farm next to ours. This man thought that we were setting up a cocaine-processing factory, and he wanted to participate in the supposed business. To pressure us, he denounced us to the police and army, and we thus had to move farther into the woods, to the Ñacahuazú camp. . . .

Upon our return to the Ñacahuazú camp following the reconnaissance expedition to the mouth of the Rosita and Río Grande, the army had become aware of our presence. Waiting for us at the camp were Tania, the Frenchman Debray, and the Argentine Bustos. The first battle occurred in an area we had not foreseen, and Che decided—in order to keep the latter two out of danger—to get them out of the area, escorting them to a secure point. Vilo[3] and his people were to be left in the region, since his troops were almost all sick, and

---

3. Joaquín.

unable to undertake such a march.

On our return, we spent some four and a half months look-ing for them in that dangerous, very barren and thorny re-gion. After we heard reports on the radio of battles in that re-gion, we even headed in the direction where, according to the radio reports, these clashes were taking place. Our goal was to help and reinforce them, to unite with them, using these same radio reports to guide us. They, for their part, were extraordinarily heroic, trying to survive and resist, stay-ing in the region Che had told them to, surrounded, with the army right behind them.

Che could not abandon them even though in the journey we had made to transport the foreigners, after reaching Muyu-pampa all we had to do was cross the highway and enter the zone of operations we had initially selected, where we had contacts, munitions, everything. But Che decided to return, and not only that; but to spend almost five months searching for Vilo's group.

After Che learned of the death of Joaquín and the extermi-nation of his group, the last thing he tried to do was head to-ward the spot that we had been so close to when we dropped off the foreigners. But to go there meant resolving another problem—the sick men who were accompanying him. We be-gan to head there with the sick.

At the time we fell into the ambush of September 26, Che's idea was to launch a surprise attack and enter Vallegrande. We knew that the army had a division stationed there, but we intended to enter the town with the aim of capturing a pharmacy, stocking up on medicine, and resolving the prob-lem of El Médico and the other comrades who because of ill health were unable to walk.

Heading north, Che's goal was to reach Alto Beni and re-main there for a relatively long period of time, avoiding com-bat. There we would make contact with the city, which had been broken, and reorganize our forces to a certain extent. The aim was to obtain 150 new recruits who were undergoing training, 50 Bolivians more than had been promised, and some Peruvians. In other words, we would create a force, because in that region we had a large quantity of arms and munitions. These were the aims when the battle at the Yuro ravine took place. These were our perspectives on October 7.

Prior to the battle at the Yuro ravine, we had tried to capture a small truck that came by every day to deliver bread to a small settlement in the area, and use it to get to Vallegrande. However, it seems that the army understood what we were trying to do and stopped it from coming. That was Che's idea: to get medicine for the sick.

In addition, Che was aware that we were inside a large encirclement extended by two army divisions, and that our location was known—not precisely but in general terms. We had to hop out of there at all costs, somewhere or another, and avoid the encounter at the Yuro ravine, because the conditions were not the best.

Analyzing the situation in which he fell, we can state that had Che, who was in good physical condition, continued the march and left the sick behind, he would have gotten out of the encirclement. But Che could not abandon them; his human qualities, his high concept of human solidarity prevented him from escaping the encirclement at the Yuro ravine. To leave those sick men there was to sign their death sentence.

When I last saw Che he was in good spirits, not discouraged, confident; and the possibility of crossing over to our future zone of operations heartened us all.[4]

The immediate objective [at the time of the La Higuera ambush] was to reach Pucará and, once there, decide what to do with the sick; either leave them in a safe place with some peasant and continue on foot into the woods, with the healthy fighters, or else pull a daring coup: take the risk of getting

---

4. From interview with Harry Villegas (Pombo), in *Verde Olivo*, October 7, 1982.

transportation there in Pucará—which is the road's end in that area—get out into Vallegrande—the town where the command post of the Eighth Division was based—stock up with medicine, food, and equipment, and from there move on to a different area—Chapare or Alto Beni, farther to the north.

What would be the point of doing this? We hoped to begin a one- or two-month recovery period hidden in the woods; to reestablish contact with the city; to recruit new fighters, who, we knew, were ready to join up; to reorganize ourselves; and to carry on the struggle. That was the general idea we had. Besides this, in the new zone we had chosen, the peasants had greater political development.[5]

On the guerrillas' battle for culture

by Pombo

From the time of our arrival in Bolivia, one of the first tasks that Che laid out was aimed at preventing a repetition of what he considered to be a weakness of the Cuban revolution. This was that the members of the Rebel Army, its leading cadres, had not acquired a sufficient educational grounding and political level to be able to hold the type of leadership responsibilities required. He said that the cadres had to have a cultural and intellectual level that would allow them to carry out their tasks without committing barbarities.

He later explained, "That must not happen to us. We have to forge in this army what will become the backbone of our fu-

---

5. From interview with Pombo, Benigno, and Urbano in *Granma*, October 8, 1969. Published in English in *Tricontinental*, July-October 1970.

ture government. Because it is from here, this nucleus, that the cadres will arise who will lead the National Liberation Army of this continent."

For this reason he established compulsory study of a whole series of subjects, including political economy, history (specifically that of Bolivia), higher mathematics, and languages. He felt it was indispensable for us to be able to speak the same language as the inhabitants there, and for that reason we studied Quechua or Aymará, in addition to French for those who wanted it. He drove us to systematic study because he felt it was a necessity.

Moreover, he himself continuously studied the classics. He greatly admired Marx, in particular. In Bolivia the notes from his studies of Marx and mathematics must have filled up 15 or 20 notebooks. Che systematically studied higher mathematics and enjoyed teaching it to everyone. He explained that it was the basis for mastering any science.

With regard to classes, he established a system whereby he taught some subjects and utilized instructors for others. He taught history, French, and mathematics, with Suárez Gayol and San Luis[6] as instructors. Aniceto and Pedro (both Bolivians) taught Quechua.

He also instituted discussions on what we read, rotating books among all the comrades. In this way we read a very interesting novel with historic and social themes, dealing with an uprising of women in Cochabamba during the colonial period.

There also existed among us a great movement with regard to reading. Che was the leader in this, reading *The Young Hegel* and *Capital*. He always carried one or two volumes of *Capital* in his knapsack.

We came to have a good library in Bolivia, composed of 300-400 books. A system was established whereby each comrade carried one or two books in his knapsack, read them, and then passed them on to others.

The objective Che was pursuing was to raise our cultural

---

6. Rubio and Rolando.

level. At the same time, he always made us see clearly that even though war presented difficult circumstances, in which one had to live under constant tension, nevertheless we could not let ourselves take an easy-going and conformist attitude that would have us put off study until later. We had to study right there in the guerrilla camp, he said, with an enthusiasm and determination equal to the way we confronted the vicissitudes and difficulties we faced. And one of the biggest such difficulties to overcome was precisely the one he sought to instill: the habit of study.[7]

On the selection and training of the Cuban combatants

by Benigno

I remember once [during the Cuban revolutionary war] we held a meeting of the two columns, Che's and Camilo's. Che steered the conversation onto the need to continue the struggle not only in Cuba but in other countries. He spoke about the revolution in Argentina and other Latin American countries. And four or five of us told him that whenever he intended to go someplace to fight, that he could count on us. He looked at us and said, "I'll keep you in mind."[8]

Our happiness was immense when we learned that Commander Ernesto Guevara, Che of the Sierra, of the invasion, of the battle of Santa Clara, had chosen us to form the ranks of the internationalist army he was going to command. But at

---

7. From interview with Harry Villegas (Pombo), in *Verde Olivo*, October 10, 1971.
8. From interview with Dariel Alarcón (Benigno), in *La Nueva Gaceta*, April 1981.

first we didn't know who our commander was going to be. It's curious how we found out.

The entire group was already together, headed by Pinares.[9] Then they told us that we would be studying the history of various countries. Because of its tradition of workers' struggles, Bolivia was stressed in particular.

It was then that a wartime comrade came to tell us that we were going to meet a "Galician" who was to be our leader. He warned us that the man had a difficult personality, and asked whether we were prepared to put up with a difficult personality. We said yes. Commander Antonio Sánchez Díaz said, "Of course. No problem."

So with our weapons and everything they took us to a mountain, a hill, and there we saw a house. Shortly thereafter a middle-aged man came out, completely bald, with spectacles, smoking a pipe, wearing a suit, with shoes that sparkled. He walked toward us, and the comrade who had brought us presented him as the "Galician" in question. Pinares, acting as the one in charge, gave the order to stand at attention. Then the "Galician" went about shaking our hands and responding brusquely to certain questions addressed to him about us. Well, something was bothering us. I could see that Pinares was uncomfortable, as if he could hardly stand the difficult personality of this "Galician," who had already been addressed in front of us as Ramón.

Finally, we saw him stop in front of Pinares and ask him whether or not he had been in Pinar del Río as head of operations during the October crisis.[10] Pinares answered yes, but that he had never met the "Galician," that he had never seen him before. Ramón made a joke about certain details during those days but Pinares did not catch on. Suddenly we saw

9. Marcos (Antonio Sánchez Díaz).
10. During the October 1962 crisis over the installation of Soviet missiles in Cuba, Guevara was sent to Pinar del Río province to organize the defense for an anticipated U.S. invasion. Pinares (Marcos) served under him as head of operations.

Suárez Gayol[11] run up and embrace the "Galician," saying, "It's Che, fellows, it's Che!"

Imagine our surprise. We did not recognize him. Che enjoyed the joke he had made at our expense, with his unsurpassable disguise. Later Pinares, with his characteristic sense of humor, swore: "I always recognized him. I always recognized him."

Later, when we were training in camp, Che warned us that in the future we would have to forget our status as officials, as men used to leading, and become soldiers. For the same reason that he explained in his letter of farewell to Fidel,[12] we also resigned our ranks and posts. By then we were already soldiers of the future internationalist army, as we would concretize it later on in the Latin America for which we were going to fight for human dignity and freedom.

And as soldiers we gave ourselves sentry duty and other tasks to fulfill to keep the place in order. It happened that on the third day, without prior warning, Che came and asked when it was his turn for guard duty. We told him he was last before leaving. He responded that here everyone was equal, that he was the same as everyone else, and that he would do guard duty that very night.

A little later he asked when it was his turn to do the cleaning and serving in the kitchen. When he was assured that he would be informed and that his name was on "the list," he asked to see it. Of course, by then those who had made up the aforementioned "list" had written in his name, to avoid being called to order as had happened with the guard duty. His name had been written down but they had not thought to inform him. And what happened? He had to put down the day, and on that day we saw him cleaning and serving in the kitchen.

The question of cultural and political improvement was a constant preoccupation of his. He established the daily study of certain subjects, such as Spanish and languages, which served

---

11. Rubio.
12. See pages 71-73.

to raise the cultural level of the comrades. He also explained to us conscientiously the rationale for our struggle. He told us about the Indians there, exploited and subjugated over centuries, who lived in total misery, without the most elementary human rights; without food to eat and without food for the mind, since where we would be going illiteracy was total. He pointed out the role played in this by imperialism, colonialism, and neocolonialism, the brutal tyrants of the underdeveloped peoples who make up Latin America. He did this constantly.

He wanted each one of us to know clearly what we were facing there and he warned us of the harshness of the struggle: of the hunger, thirst, fatigue, and the danger of losing one's life at any moment—all of which are inseparable companions of the guerrilla soldier, the revolutionary soldier. He pointed out that one day the people among whom we would be fighting would consider us to be part of that people—as had happened to him in Cuba—but that we would have to earn this through our daily effort, by being organized, disciplined, and exemplary combatants at each moment of our lives as revolutionaries. . . .

[When the time came to depart], Che—honest as always in all his acts—asked us if anyone wanted to stay behind, that there was still time to say so, and that he personally would not consider the person a coward, since human beings feel fear and the person who doesn't is not human. He said that he had felt fear not just once but a number of times, and that the shield against it was precisely the political convictions that a revolutionary has, his firmness, the knowledge of the justice of the cause he is defending and for which he could give his life at any moment.

He emphasized that where we were going, each Cuban combatant had to be the first in facing danger and sacrifice; that this was the best way of making us worthy representatives of the feelings and generosity of our people.[13]

---

13. From account by Dariel Alarcón (Benigno) in Mariano Rodríguez Herrera, *Abriendo senderos* (Opening paths) (Havana: Editorial Gente Nueva, 1980).

List of combatants

FROM CUBA
Alejandro
Antonio (Olo)
Arturo
Benigno
Braulio
Joaquín (Vilo)
Marcos (Pinares)
Miguel (Manuel)
Moro (El Médico, Morogoro, Muganga)
Pacho (Pachungo)
Pombo
Ramón (Fernando, Mongo, Che)
Ricardo (Chinchu, Mbili, Papi)
Rolando (San Luis)
Rubio (Félix)
Tania
Tuma (Tumaini)
Urbano

FROM PERU
Chino
Eustaquio
Negro

FROM BOLIVIA
Aniceto
Apolinar (Apolinario, Polo)
Benjamín
Camba*
Carlos
Chapaco (Luis)
Chingolo*
Coco
Daniel*
Darío
Ernesto (El Médico)
Eusebio*
Inti
Julio
León* (Antonio)
Loro (Bigotes, Jorge)
Moisés (Guevara)
Ñato
Orlando*
Pablito (Pablo)
Paco*
Pedro (Pan Divino)
Pepe*
Raúl
Salustio
Serapio (Serafín)
Víctor
Walter
Willy (Willi, Wily, Wyly)

---

* Deserters or expelled

Division of column (as of April 1, 1967)

FORWARD DETACHMENT	**CENTER GROUP**	**REAR GUARD**
Miguel (*head*)	Ramón (*head*)	Joaquín (*head*)
Aniceto	Alejandro	Apolinar
Benigno	Antonio	Braulio
Camba	Arturo	Ernesto
Coco	Chapaco	Marcos
Darío	Chino	Pedro
Julio	Eustaquio	Rubio
Loro	Inti	Víctor
Pablito	León	Walter
Pacho	Moisés	Chingolo (*expelled*)
Raúl	Moro	Eusebio (*expelled*)
	Ñato	Paco (*expelled*)
	Negro	Pepe (*expelled*)
	Pombo	
	Ricardo	
	Rolando	
	Serapio	
	Tania	
	Tuma	
	Urbano	
	Willy	

Prior to April 1, 1967
died: Benjamín, Carlos
captured: Salustio
deserted: Daniel, Orlando

JOAQUÍN'S COLUMN (after April 17, 1967)

Joaquín	Marcos	Tania	Chingolo (*expelled*)
Apolinar	Moisés	Víctor	Eusebio (*expelled*)
Braulio	Pedro	Walter	Paco (*expelled*)
Ernesto	Serapio		Pepe (*expelled*)

Glossary

(Guerrilla fighters are in bold type, listed under the pseudonyms used in the diary. The biographies of the Cuban combatants list the responsibilities each of them held prior to resigning all posts, ranks, and official duties to join the guerrilla column in Bolivia.)

Alejandro
> *Gustavo Machín* (1937-1967) – Active in the movement against Batista at the University of Havana, and a leader of the Revolutionary Directorate. In February 1958 he organized the landing of a Directorate guerrilla column, based in Cuba's Escambray mountains. Fought in the battle of Santa Clara in December 1958 with Guevara's column. Ended the war with the rank of commander. Held a number of government posts after 1959, including vice minister of industry, before returning to active military duty. Joined the guerrilla column in Bolivia December 11, 1966. Assigned as head of operations. Originally part of the center group, he became a member of Joaquín's column. Killed near the Vado del Yeso August 31, 1967.

Algarañaz, Ciro – Owner of property next to Ñacahuazú farm. Arrested by Bolivian troops as guerrilla collaborator; tried and acquitted.

Almeida, Juan (1927-) – A commander in the Rebel Army during Cuba's revolutionary war. Held numerous posts after 1959 including commander of the air force, vice minister of the armed forces, and vice president of the Council of State and

Council of Ministers. A longtime member of the Central Committee and Political Bureau of the Communist Party of Cuba.

Aniceto

Aniceto Reinaga (1940-1967) – Former student from La Paz, and member of the national leadership of the Bolivian Communist Youth. Studied in Cuba. Joined the guerrilla column by early January 1967, assigned to the center group. Expelled from the Executive Committee of the Communist Youth in February 1967. Killed at the Yuro ravine October 8, 1967.

Antonio (Olo)

Orlando Pantoja (1933-1967) – Native of Jiguaní in eastern Cuba. A veteran of the anti-Batista struggle and an early member of the July 26 Movement, jailed for underground activities. Joined the Rebel Army in October 1957, becoming a captain in Guevara's column. After 1959 he headed the Las Villas regiment, served in the Ministry of the Interior, and was head of the border guards. Joined the guerrilla column December 19, 1966. A member of the center group. Killed at the Yuro ravine October 8, 1967.

Apolinar (Apolinario, Polo)

Apolinar Aquino (1935-1967) – Factory worker from Viacha in the department of La Paz; local union leader and member of the Bolivian Communist Party. Originally a worker at the Ñacahuazú farm, he requested to become a combatant and was incorporated into the unit December 19, 1966. Assigned to the rear guard under Joaquín. Killed near the Vado del Yeso August 31, 1967.

Argañaraz. See *Algarañaz, Ciro*

Arismendi, Rodney (1913-1989) – General secretary of the Communist Party of Uruguay 1955-88.

Arturo

René Martínez (1941-1967) – Jailed for underground activities against Cuba's Batista dictatorship; joined the Rebel Army in November 1958. After 1959 he served in the Cuban air force, the Rebel Army's Department of Investigations, and the Ministry of the Interior, achieving the rank of lieutenant in the armed forces.

Joined the guerrilla column in Bolivia December 11, 1966. Assigned as radio operator attached to the center group. Brother of guerrilla combatant Ricardo. Killed at the Yuro ravine October 8, 1967.

Azurduy de Padilla, Juana (1781-1862) – Heroine of Bolivia's independence war against Spain, achieving rank of colonel.

Barrientos, René (1919-1969) – Bolivian air force general and a leader of the November 1964 military coup. President of Bolivia 1966-69; died in a helicopter crash.

Béjar, Héctor (1935-) – Leader of guerrilla struggle in Peru waged by the National Liberation Army (ELN) from 1962 until his arrest in 1966.

Benigno

Dariel Alarcón (1939-) – Former peasant from Cuba's Sierra Maestra. Joined the Rebel Army in July 1957, serving under Camilo Cienfuegos. After the revolution's triumph, he continued working in the armed forces, reaching the rank of lieutenant in the Cuban army. He joined the guerrilla column in Bolivia December 11, 1966. Assigned to the forward detachment. One of the five surviving veterans of the guerrilla struggle, he reached Cuba in March 1968.

Benjamín

Benjamín Coronado (1941-1967) – School teacher from La Paz and member of the Bolivian Communist Youth. Studied in Cuba, returning to join the guerrilla column January 21, 1967. Assigned to the forward detachment. Drowned in the Río Grande February 26, 1967.

Bigotes. See *Loro*

Bolívar, Simón (1783-1830) – Led armed rebellion that helped win independence from Spain for much of Latin America.

Braulio

Israel Reyes (1933-1967) – Born in Cuba's Sierra Maestra, where he worked as a sharecropper and day laborer. Joined the Rebel Army in 1957, serving in Raúl Castro's column. After the revolution's triumph he was assigned to Raúl Castro's escort, and later served as liaison officer of the Oriente Army's general staff. Sent on a special internationalist assignment in April 1966, he was promoted to first lieutenant upon returning to Cuba. Joined the guerrillas in Bolivia November 27, 1966. Assigned to the rear guard, he became second in command of Joaquín's column. Killed near the Vado del Yeso August 31, 1967.

Bravo, Douglas (1933-) – Leader of the guerrilla struggle in Venezuela waged by the Armed Forces for National Liberation (FALN). Expelled from the Venezuelan Communist Party in 1967 for refusing to suspend the armed struggle.

Bustos, Ciro Roberto (Mauricio, Pelao, Carlos) – Painter and journalist from Argentina who helped raise funds for the 1963-64 guerrilla movement in northern Argentina led by Jorge Masetti. Summoned to Bolivia by Guevara to discuss support activities in Argentina, he arrived in early March 1967. Captured by the Bolivian army April 20 in Muyupampa. Tried and sentenced to 30 years imprisonment; pardoned and released in 1970.

Calvimonte – Member of the guerrilla urban support network.

Camba

Orlando Jiménez – Born in Riberalta and a member of the Bolivian Communist Party. Assigned to a guerrilla-owned farm in Caranavi in mid-1966. Incorporated as a combatant at Ñacahuazú December 11, 1966, assigned to the forward detachment. Deserted September 26, 1967, and was captured by the army the following day. Sentenced to 10-year prison term; released in 1970.

Carlos

Lorgio Vaca (1934-1967) – Native of Santa Cruz and member of the Bolivian Communist Party. A national leader of the social security workers union and of the Bolivian Communist Youth. Studied economics in Cuba. Returned to Bolivia to participate in the armed struggle, arriving at the guerrilla camp December 11, 1966. Assigned to the rear guard. Drowned in the Río Grande March 17, 1967.

Carlos. See *Bustos, Ciro Roberto*

Castro, Fidel (1926-) – Leader of the Cuban revolution. Led the 1953 attack on the Moncada garrison; founder and leader of the

July 26 Movement; organized the *Granma* landing November-December 1956 and commanded the Rebel Army during the revolutionary war. Cuban prime minister 1959-76; president of the Council of State and Council of Ministers since 1976; commander in chief of the armed forces; first secretary of the Communist Party of Cuba.

Castro, Raúl (1931-) – A central leader of the Cuban revolutionary struggle and a commander in the Rebel Army. Armed forces minister 1959-present; vice premier 1959-76; vice president of Council of State and Council of Ministers since 1976; second secretary of the Communist Party of Cuba since 1965.

Chapaco (Luis)

Jaime Arana (1938-1967) – Native of Tarija in southern Bolivia. A leader of the Revolutionary Nationalist Movement (MNR) at the University of San Andrés. Went to Cuba in 1963 to study hydraulics, and became a member of the Bolivian Communist Youth. Joined the guerrilla column in March 1967 and was assigned to the center group. Killed at the Mizque river October 12, 1967.

Chinchu. See *Ricardo*

Chingolo

Hugo Choque – Arrived at Ñacahuazú March 1967 as part of Moisés Guevara's group. Expelled from guerrilla ranks March 25; accompanied Joaquín's column. Deserted in July 1967 and was captured by the army, leading them to the guerrilla supply caves.

Chino

Juan Pablo Chang (1930-1967) – Peruvian revolutionary of Chinese ancestry, he joined the Aprista Youth in 1945 and was active in the movement against the military dictatorship. Arrested in 1948, he was jailed for two years, the first of many periods of imprisonment and exile. Joined the Communist Party of Peru in the early 1950s, becoming a member of its Central Committee. Expelled from the CP in the early 1960s, he participated in a guerrilla movement organized by the National Liberation Army (ELN) in 1963; after its defeat he escaped through Bolivia and spent two years living clandestinely in La

Paz. In January 1966 he attended the Tricontinental Conference
in Havana, after which he began organizing a new guerrilla
movement in Peru. He joined the guerrilla column in Bolivia in
March 1967, assigned to the center group. Captured at the Yuro
ravine October 8, 1967, and murdered the following day.

Coco

Roberto Peredo (1938-1967) – Native of Beni and brother of Inti
Peredo. Joined the Bolivian Communist Party in 1951 at age 13
and was active in the student movement. Helped found the
Bolivian Communist Youth after moving to La Paz. There he
organized a printshop at his home for the CP's newspaper.
Imprisoned several times for his political activities. In 1963-64
he assisted guerrilla movements in Peru and in northern
Argentina. One of the original cadres assigned to help begin
guerrilla preparations in Bolivia, he was the legal proprietor of
the Ñacahuazú farm. Assigned to the forward detachment.
Killed at La Higuera September 26, 1967.

Codovilla, Victorio (1894-1970) – General secretary of the Communist
Party of Argentina 1941-63; CP president 1963-70.

Daniel

Pastor Barrera – Native of Oruro, Bolivia. He arrived at the
guerrilla camp February 1967 as part of Moisés Guevara's
group. Deserted March 11 and captured by the army three
days later, becoming an informer.

Danton. See *Debray, Régis*

Darío

David Adriazola (1939-1969) – Mine worker from Oruro. A
former member of the Bolivian Communist Party, he was
recruited to the guerrilla struggle as part of Moisés Guevara's
group. Arrived at the guerrilla camp March 1967 and was
assigned to the forward detachment. One of two Bolivian surviving veterans of the struggle, he lived clandestinely in La
Paz, seeking to resume armed actions. His hideout was located
through an informer, and he was killed December 31, 1969.

Debray, Régis (Danton, Frenchman) (1940-) – Journalist from France;
author of *Revolution in the Revolution?* Summoned by Guevara

to the guerrilla camp to discuss support activities, he arrived in
early March 1967. Captured by the Bolivian army April 20 in
Muyupampa. Tried and sentenced to 30-year prison term;
pardoned and released 1970.

El Médico. See *Ernesto*

El Médico. See *Moro*

Ernesto (El Médico)

> *Freddy Maymura* (1941-1967) – Native of Trinidad in Bolivia,
> of Japanese ancestry. Went to Cuba in 1962 to study medicine.
> Member of the Bolivian Communist Youth. Returned to Bolivia
> to participate in the armed struggle, joining the guerrilla
> column November 27, 1966. Assigned to the rear guard under
> Joaquín. Captured and murdered near the Vado del Yeso
> August 31, 1967.

Estanislao. See *Monje, Mario*

Eusebio

> *Eusebio Tapia* – Born in La Paz, he joined the guerrilla column
> January 21, 1967. Expelled from the guerrilla ranks March 25,
> he accompanied Joaquín's column. Deserted in July 1967, and
> was captured by the army; imprisoned until 1970.

Eustaquio

> *Lucio Edilberto Galván* (1937-1967) – Born in Huancayo, Peru,
> he worked as a bakery worker, pharmacy hand, and radio
> technician. Participated in the 1963 guerrilla movement in that
> country led by the National Liberation Army (ELN). A member
> of Juan Pablo Chang's group, he arrived at the Ñacahuazú
> sometime around December 31, 1966. Assigned to the center
> group in March. Killed at the Mizque river October 12, 1967.

Farías, Jesús – General secretary of the Communist Party of
Venezuela.

Félix. See *Rubio*

Fernando – Ernesto Che Guevara. See biography on pages 9-10.

Frenchman. See *Debray, Régis*

Gelman, Juan (1930-) – Member of the Communist Party of
Argentina.

Guevara. See *Moisés*

Guzmán, Loyola – Leader of the guerrilla urban support network and head of finances for the ELN. Joined the Bolivian Communist Youth in 1956 and subsequently became a member of its national leadership. In February 1967 she was expelled from its Executive Committee for her activities in support of the guerrillas. Arrested September 14, 1967; released 1970.

Honorato. See *Rojas, Honorato*

Hugo. See *Lozano, Hugo*

Inti

    Guido Alvaro Peredo (1937-1969) – Born in Cochabamba, he grew up in Beni. Joined the Bolivian Communist Party in 1951 at age 14; became an alternate member of its Central Committee in 1959 and a full member in 1964. Imprisoned several times for his political activities. Helped give logistical support to the guerrilla movement in northern Argentina in 1963-64. Became secretary of the CP regional committee in La Paz in 1965. Joined the guerrilla unit November 27, 1966. Together with Rolando, assigned as political commissar—a member of the general staff with responsibility for political leadership of the unit; assigned to the center group. One of two Bolivian surviving veterans of the guerrilla struggle. Attempted to reorganize the ELN and re-launch armed struggle. Wrote *Mi campaña con el Che* (My campaign with Che). Tipped off by an informer, the army raided the house where he was staying in La Paz. After determined resistance he was wounded, captured, and executed.

Iván – member of the guerrilla support network in La Paz.

Joaquín (Vilo)

    Juan Vitalio Acuña (1925-1967) – Former peasant from Cuba's Sierra Maestra, he joined the Rebel Army in April 1957. Promoted to lieutenant by Fidel Castro, he headed the rear guard in Guevara's column and became a leading recruiter of peasants to the rebels. Promoted by Castro to commander in November 1958 with his own column. Held a number of posts in the armed forces after 1959. Elected to the Central Committee of the Cuban Communist Party in October 1965. Joined the guerrilla column in Bolivia November 27, 1966. Second in command of the unit, he commanded the rear guard, which operated as a separate column after April 17, 1967. Killed near the Vado del Yeso August 31, 1967.

Jorge. See *Loro*

Jozami, Eduardo – Journalist and lawyer; member of a grouping that split from the Communist Party of Argentina.

Julio

Mario Gutiérrez (1939-1967) – Native of Trinidad in the department of Beni. A national leader of the Bolivian student movement from 1957 to 1960. Later became a leader of the social security workers union in Trinidad. A member of the Bolivian Communist Youth. Studied medicine in Cuba, returning to join the guerrilla column March 10, 1967. Assigned to the forward detachment. Killed at La Higuera September 26, 1967.

Kolle, Jorge – Leader of the Communist Party of Bolivia. Replaced Monje as first secretary in December 1967, holding that post until 1985.

Lagunillero (Mario Chávez) – Guerrilla collaborator and Bolivian Communist Party member assigned to live in Lagunillas, where he maintained contact with Coco Peredo.

Leche. See *Castro, Fidel*

Lechín, Juan (1920-) – Central leader of the Bolivian trade union federation since the 1940s. Organized the Revolutionary Party of the National Left in 1964.

León (Antonio)

Antonio Domínguez – native of Trinidad and member of the Bolivian Communist Party. Assigned as a worker at Ñacahuazú farm, he was later incorporated as a combatant in the center group. Deserted September 26, 1967, and captured by the army the following day, providing information. Released in 1970.

Loro (Bigotes, Jorge)

Jorge Vázquez (1939-1967) – Son of a well-known Bolivian historian and writer. Active in the student movement, he joined the Communist Party of Bolivia and became an alternate member of its Central Committee. Helped provide logistical support to the guerrilla movement in northern Argentina 1963-64. One of the original cadres assigned in 1966 to help prepare the guerrilla movement in Bolivia. Arrived at the Ñacahuazú November 7, 1966, carrying out logistical and other tasks. Incorporated into the forward detachment January 25. On April 22, 1967, he was separated from the column during a clash with the army; subsequently wounded and taken prisoner. Held incommunicado, he was tortured and murdered, his body thrown from a helicopter into the jungle.

Loyola. See *Guzmán, Loyola*

Lozano, Hugo – Radio operator for the guerrilla urban support network.

Luis. See *Chapaco*

Lumumba, Patrice (1925-1961) – Leader of independence struggle in the Congo (today Zaire) and prime minister after independence from Belgium in June 1960. In September 1960 his government was overthrown in a U.S.-backed coup. Lumumba was jailed and murdered by his captors in January 1961.

Maceo, Antonio (1845-1896) – Prominent military leader and strategist in Cuba's three independence wars; killed in battle.

Malinovsky, Rodion (1898-1967) – Soviet minister of defense 1957-67 and commander of its land forces.

Manuel. See *Miguel*

Marcos (Pinares)

Antonio Sánchez (1927-1967) – A native of Pinar del Río province in western Cuba, where he worked as a bricklayer. Went to the Sierra Maestra in early 1957 and after a three-month search encountered the Rebel Army, becoming a captain and head of the rear guard in Camilo Cienfuegos's column. Promoted to commander in January 1959. Subsequently held various posts in the armed forces, including head of operations in Pinar del Río, corp chief in Camagüey, and military commander at the Isle of Pines. Elected to the Central Committee of the Cuban Communist Party in October 1965. He joined the guerrilla column in Bolivia November 20, 1966. Originally the head of the forward detachment, he was replaced and assigned to the rear guard under Joaquín. Killed at Bella Vista June 2, 1967.

Martí, José (1853-1895) – Cuban national hero. Noted poet, writer, speaker, and journalist who founded the Cuban Revolutionary Party in 1892 to fight Spanish rule and oppose U.S. designs on Cuba. Lived in the U.S. 1881-95. Launched Cuba's 1895 independence war and was killed in battle.

Masetti, Jorge Ricardo (Segundo) (1929-1964) – Journalist from Argentina who traveled to Cuba's Sierra Maestra in January 1958 and joined the Rebel movement. Founding director of Prensa Latina, the press service launched by the new revolutionary government. Killed while leading a guerrilla nucleus in the Salta mountains of northern Argentina.

Mauricio. See *Bustos, Ciro Roberto*

Maymura. See *Ernesto*

Mbili. See *Ricardo*

Megía – Member of the guerrilla urban support network.

Mella, Julio Antonio (1903-1929) – Student leader of the university reform movement in Cuba in 1923; a founding leader of the Communist Party of Cuba in 1925. Assassinated in Mexico, probably by agents of Cuba's Machado dictatorship.

Méndez, Eustaquio "Moto" – Peasant fighter in Bolivia's war of independence from Spain.

Merci (Mercy) – Code name of an individual sent from Havana to collaborate with the underground guerrilla support organization in Bolivia.

Miguel (Manuel)

Manuel Hernández (1931-1967) – A native of Jiguaní in eastern Cuba, where he worked as a sugarcane cutter and magnesium miner. A member of the July 26 Movement, he joined the Rebel Army in mid-1957. Served in and helped lead Guevara's column, in which he became a captain. Wounded in the battle of Fomento. Held various posts after 1959 in the army and interior ministry, and attained the rank of first captain in the armed forces. Joined the guerrilla column in Bolivia November 27, 1966, and became head of the forward detachment in March 1967. Killed at La Higuera September 26, 1967.

Mito – Member of the guerrilla urban support network.

Moisés (Guevara)

Moisés Guevara (1939-1967) – Bolivian miner from Huanuni, in the department of Oruro. A leader of the miners union, he was arrested for his union activities in 1963. Joined the Bolivian Communist Party in 1956. Sided with Oscar Zamora in the 1965 split, but was soon expelled from the pro-Maoist party together with his supporters. After months of negotiations and a meeting with Che Guevara in January 1967, twelve members of his group joined the guerrilla column, arriving in February-March. Originally assigned to the center group, he became part of Joaquín's column. Killed near the Vado del Yeso August 31, 1967.

Monje, Mario (Estanislao) – General secretary of the Communist Party of Bolivia until December 1967. Subsequently a leading member of its Central Committee.

Moro (El Médico, Morogoro, Muganga)

Octavio de la Concepción (1935-1967) – Became active in the anti-Batista struggle while studying medicine at the University of Havana. Joined the July 26 Movement in 1957 and became a member of the Rebel Army in September 1958, serving in the Second Front of Oriente as doctor and combatant. After 1959 he worked in a number of medical posts, including head of surgery at the Baracoa hospital, and as a doctor in the countryside. From August to December 1965 he carried out an internationalist mission, and upon returning to Cuba was promoted to first lieutenant. Joined the guerrilla column in Bolivia December 11, 1966, as head of medical services. Killed at the Mizque river October 12, 1967.

Morogoro. See *Moro*

Muganga. See *Moro*

Muñecas, Ildefonso de las (1776-1816) – Argentine priest; killed fighting in the war for independence from Spain.

Murillo, Pedro Domingo (1757-1810) – Bolivian patriot who led an uprising against Spanish rule launched July 16, 1809. Captured by Spanish troops and executed.

Ñato

Julio Luis Méndez (1937-1967) – Native of Beni and member of the Bolivian Communist Party. In 1963 he escorted a group of guerrilla survivors from Peru through the mountains of Bolivia. One of the original cadres assigned to assist guerrilla preparations in Bolivia in 1966. Incorporated as a combatant November 11, 1966, heading up supplies and armaments and assigned to the center group. A survivor of the Yuro ravine battle, he was killed at Mataral November 15, 1967.

Negro

Restituto José Cabrera (1931-1967) – Peruvian who studied and practiced medicine in Argentina. Inspired by the revolution in Cuba, he moved there in the early 1960s. Worked in the cardiology department at the provincial hospital of Santiago de Cuba until November 1965. A member of Juan Pablo Chang's group, he joined the guerrillas in Bolivia in March 1967. A member of the center group, he was later moved to the rear guard led by Joaquín. Escaped from the Vado del Yeso ambush, but was captured and murdered September 4, 1967.

Olo. See *Antonio*

Onganía, Juan Carlos (1914-) – Argentine general; seized power in a 1966 coup; president of Argentina 1966-70.

Orlando

Vicente Rocabado – Native of Oruro, Bolivia. He arrived at the guerrilla camp in February 1967 as part of Moisés Guevara's group. Deserted March 11 and was captured by the army three days later, turning informer.

Ovando, Alfredo (1918-) – A leader of the November 1964 coup in Bolivia; commander in chief of the armed forces. President of Bolivia 1965-66, 1969-70.

Pablito (Pablo)

Francisco Huanca (1945-1967) – Native of Challapa in the department of Oruro. A former member of the Bolivian Communist Youth, he was recruited to the guerrilla struggle as part of Moisés Guevara's group. Arrived at the guerrilla camp in February 1967, and was subsequently assigned to the forward detachment. After the Yuro ravine battle, he led a group of four survivors who were killed at the Mizque river October 12, 1967.

Pacheco. See *Sánchez*

Pacho (Pachungo)

> *Alberto Fernández* (1935-1967) – Veteran member of the July 26 Movement's urban underground in Santiago de Cuba and then Santa Clara, he joined the Rebel Army in November 1958, serving with Guevara's column in Las Villas. From 1961 to 1963 he was a factory administrator in Pinar del Río, and then headed the state mining enterprise. He held the rank of captain in the armed forces. He arrived at the Ñacahuazú November 7, 1966. Assigned to the forward detachment. Wounded and captured at the Yuro ravine on October 8, 1967; died from his wounds.

Pachungo. See *Pacho*

Paco

> *José Castillo* – Arrived at Ñacahuazú early March 1967 as part of Moisés Guevara's group. Expelled from the guerrilla ranks March 25, he accompanied Joaquín's column. Captured following the Vado del Yeso ambush August 31, 1967; released 1970.

Padilla, Manuel Ascencio (1774-1816) – Guerrilla leader in Bolivia's independence war against Spain.

Pan Divino. See *Pedro*

Papi. See *Ricardo*

Pareja, Walter – A leader of the urban support network and member of the Bolivian Communist Party. Arrested October 1967.

Paulino (Paulino Baigorria) – Peasant from Abapó who accompanied the guerrillas for several days in June 1967 and asked to join. Volunteered as messenger; captured by the army and tortured.

Pedro (Pan Divino)

> *Antonio Jiménez* (1941-1967) – University student and native of Tarata in the department of Cochabamba. A member of the national leadership of the Bolivian Communist Youth. After studying in Cuba, he returned to join the guerrilla column December 31, 1966. Expelled from the Executive Committee of the Communist Youth in February 1967. A member of the rear guard under Joaquín. Killed near Monteagudo August 9, 1967.

Pelado. See *Bustos, Ciro Roberto*

Pepe

> *Julio Velasco* – Arrived at Ñacahuazú early March 1967 as part of Moisés Guevara's group. Expelled from the guerrilla ranks March 25 and accompanied Joaquín's column. Deserted May 23; captured by the army the following day and murdered.

Peredo, Coco. See *Coco*

Peredo, Inti. See *Inti*

Pinares. See *Marcos*

Polo. See *Apolinar*

Pombo

> *Harry Villegas* (1940-) – Former peasant from Cuba's Sierra Maestra. Joined the Rebel Army in 1957, serving in Guevara's column as part of his personal escort, which he headed after the revolution's triumph. After working in the Ministry of Industry, he returned to active military duty as a battalion commander and then head of personnel for the Western Army. Prior to volunteering for internationalist missions with Guevara, he was a captain in the Cuban armed forces. Served in the Congo with Guevara in 1965. Arrived in Bolivia July 1966 to assist in preparations for the guerrilla movement. Accompanied Guevara to the Ñacahuazú November 7, 1966. A member of the center group, he was assigned as head of services and was a member of the general staff. A survivor of the Yuro ravine, he led the group of guerrilla fighters who escaped following Guevara's death. Reached Cuba with Benigno and Urbano in March 1968. Later served three tours of duty in Angola. Currently a brigadier general in the Cuban army.

Ramírez, Humberto – A leader of the Communist Party of Bolivia. Became CP general secretary in 1987.

Ramón

> *Ernesto Che Guevara.* See biography on pages 9-10.

Raúl

> *Raúl Quispaya* (1939-1967) – Tailor from Oruro, Bolivia, of Aymara Indian ancestry. A former member of the Bolivian Communist Youth, he was recruited to the guerrilla struggle as

a part of Moisés Guevara's group. Arrived at the guerrilla
camp in February 1967; subsequently assigned to the forward
detachment. Killed at the Rosita river July 30, 1967.

Remberto (Remberto Villa) – Proprietor of the Ñacahuazú property
who sold it to Coco Peredo. Subsequently arrested by the army
as a guerrilla collaborator.

Renán – Member of the guerrilla urban support network.

Reyes, Simón – Leader of the Communist Party of Bolivia and the
mine workers union; CP general secretary 1985-87.

Rhea, Humberto – Member of the guerrilla urban support network;
in charge of supplying medical equipment.

Ricardo (Chinchu, Mbili, Papi)

José María Martínez (1936-1967) – Native of Guaro, in Cuba's Oriente Province, where he worked as a tractor driver. A member of
the July 26 Movement, he joined the Rebel Army in April 1958,
serving in the Second Front of Oriente. Embarked on his first
internationalist mission in October 1962, assisting the revolutionary movement in Guatemala. Went to Bolivia in March 1963 to
help organize logistical support for the guerrilla movement in
northern Argentina headed by Jorge Massetti. Served in the
Congo in 1965 with Guevara. He achieved the rank of captain in
the Cuban armed forces. Arrived in La Paz March 1966 to help
organize guerrilla preparations. Incorporated as a combatant on
December 31, 1966, assigned to the center group. Killed at the
Rosita river July 30, 1967.

Rodolfo. See *Saldaña, Rodolfo*

Rojas, Honorato – Bolivian peasant visited by the guerrillas in February 1967. Led Joaquín's column into the ambush near the Vado
del Yeso on August 31, for which he received an award from
the government. Executed by an ELN commando unit in 1969.

Rolando (San Luis)

Eliseo Reyes (1940-1967) – Native of San Luis in Cuba's Oriente
Province. Active in the underground struggle against Batista,
he joined the Rebel Army in 1957, serving in Guevara's
column. Following the triumph of the revolution he headed the
military police at the La Cabaña garrison, held military

responsibilities in Las Villas, and became head of the G-2, the undercover division of Cuba's police. Sent to Pinar del Río in 1962 to help lead operations against counterrevolutionary bands. Elected to the Central Committee of the Cuban Communist Party in October 1965. Prior to volunteering for the internationalist mission with Guevara, he was a captain in the armed forces. He joined the guerrilla unit in Bolivia November 20, 1966. A member of the general staff, he was assigned together with Inti as political commissar of the unit, with responsibility for political leadership of the troops; assigned to the center group. Killed at El Mesón April 25, 1967.

Roth, George Andrew – Anglo-Chilean journalist believed to have been a CIA agent. Met up with guerrillas April 19, 1967. Arrested in Muyupampa with Debray and Bustos April 20; released July 8. Shortly after, he disappeared from public view without a trace.

Rubio (Félix)

Jesús Suárez Gayol (1936-1967) – member of July 26 Movement from Camagüey, Cuba. Forced into exile, he participated in an armed expedition that landed in Pinar del Río in April 1958. After carrying out armed actions in that province, he went to Las Villas and joined Guevara's Rebel Army column, becoming a lieutenant. After 1959 he held a number of posts in the Rebel Army and government, including vice minister of the sugar industry. Joined the guerrilla column in Bolivia December 19, 1966, where he was assigned to the rear guard. Killed at the Iripiti river April 10, 1967.

Russell, Bertrand (1872-1970) – Philosopher and mathematician from Britain. An opponent of the U.S. war in Vietnam, he organized an international tribunal that found Washington guilty of war crimes.

Saldaña, Rodolfo – Member of the Bolivian Communist Party who helped provide logistical support to the guerrilla movement in northern Argentina in 1963-64. One of the original cadres assigned in 1966 to help organize guerrilla preparations in Bolivia, functioning as a leader of the urban support network.

Salustio

Salustio Choque – Born in La Paz, he arrived at the guerrilla camp in February 1967 as part of Moisés Guevara's group. Captured March 17, 1967.

San Luis. See *Rolando*

Sánchez (Julio Dagnino Pacheco) – Peruvian revolutionary and a leading member of the guerrilla urban support network in La Paz.

Sartre, Jean-Paul (1905-1980) – Writer and philosopher from France. Opponent of the U.S. war in Vietnam.

Serafín. See *Serapio*

Serapio (Serafín)

Serapio Aquino (1951-1967) – Native of Viacha in the department of La Paz. Assigned by the Bolivian Communist Party as a worker at the Ñacahuazú farm. Subsequently incorporated as a combatant and assigned to the rear guard under Joaquín. Killed at the Iquira river July 9, 1967.

Siles Salinas, Luis Adolfo (1925-) – Vice president of Bolivia 1966-69; president 1969.

Stamponi, Luis Faustino (1935-1976) – Member of the Socialist Party of Argentina. Lived in Bolivia after 1969 and founded the Revolutionary Workers Party of Bolivia. Kidnapped and murdered in 1976.

Sucre, Antonio José de (1795-1830) – Leader of Latin American revolt against Spanish rule and liberator of Ecuador. Ousted Spanish troops from Bolivia.

Tania

Haydée Tamara Bunke (1937-1967) – Born in Argentina of German parents who had fled the Nazi rise to power. In 1952 her family moved to East Germany, where she later joined the German Communist Party. Moved to Cuba in 1961, working in the Ministry of Education and as a translator. In March 1963 she volunteered for internationalist duty and was trained in clandestine work. In 1964 she was assigned by Guevara to move to Bolivia. Working under the name of Laura Gutiérrez, she began advance preparations for the guerrilla movement. In

March 1967, while visiting the Ñacahuazú camp, her cover was
blown, leading to her incorporation as a combatant. A member
of Joaquín's column, she was killed near the Vado del Yeso
August 31, 1967.

Tuma (Tumaini)

Carlos Coello (1940-1967) – Former agricultural worker from
eastern Cuba. Joined the July 26 Movement in Manzanillo and
became a member of the Rebel Army in November 1957,
serving in Guevara's column. Assigned to Guevara's personal
escort from 1959 on, accompanying him to the Congo in 1965.
A lieutenant in the armed forces. He went to Bolivia in July
1966 to help with advance preparations for the guerrilla
movement. Arrived at the Ñacahuazú November 7, 1966.
Killed at Florida June 26, 1967.

Tumaini. See *Tuma*

Urbano

Leonardo Tamayo (1941-) – Former peasant from Cuba's Sierra
Maestra. Joined the Rebel Army in mid-1957, serving in
Guevara's column. In 1959 he became a member of Guevara's
personal escort, which he later headed up. Subsequently
worked as Guevara's adjutant and accompanied him on
internationalist missions. A first lieutenant in the armed forces.
Joined the guerrilla column in Bolivia November 27, 1966.
Assigned to the center group. One of five surviving veterans of
the guerrilla struggle, he reached Cuba in March 1968. Later
served on internationalist missions in Angola and Nicaragua.
Currently a colonel in Cuba's Ministry of the Interior.

Vallegrandino (Tomás Rosales) – Farmhand on the Algarañaz plot
near the Ñacahuazú farm. Arrested by the Bolivian army as a
suspected guerrilla collaborator; tortured and killed.

Víctor

Casildo Condori (1941-1967) – Baker and truck driver from Coro
Coro in the department of La Paz; of Aymara Indian ancestry.
A former member of the Bolivian Communist Party, he joined
the guerillas as a member of Moisés Guevara's group, arriving
at the Ñacahuazú in February 1967. Subsequently assigned to

the rear guard led by Joaquín. Killed near Bella Vista June 2,
1967.

Vilo. See *Joaquín*

Walter

Walter Arancibia (1941-1967) – Native of Macha in the
department of Potosí. A national leader of the Bolivian
Communist Youth. Studied in Cuba. Returned to join the
guerrilla unit in January 21, 1967. Assigned to the rear guard
led by Joaquín. Killed near the Vado del Yeso August 31, 1967.

Warnes, Ignacio (1770-1816) – General in Argentina's war of independence from Spain.

Willy (Willi, Wily, Wyly)

Simón Cuba (1932-1967) – Bolivian miner and longtime leader
of the miners union in Huanuni, in the department of Oruro.
Close collaborator of Moisés Guevara. A member of the
Communist Party of Bolivia, he subsequently became a leader
of Moisés Guevara's group, arriving at the guerrilla camp in
February 1967. Subsequently assigned to the center group.
Captured October 8, 1967, at the Yuro ravine while trying to
rescue Che Guevara; murdered the following day.

Zamora, Oscar (1934-) – Led a split from the Communist Party of
Bolivia in 1965, becoming general secretary of Communist
Party Marxist-Leninist, with Maoist political orientation.
Refused to support the guerrilla movement of 1966-67. Ran
for vice president of Bolivia in 1993 as running mate of former
military dictator Hugo Banzer.

Index

455

Basic works of...

To Speak the Truth

WHY WASHINGTON'S 'COLD WAR' AGAINST CUBA DOESN'T END

Fidel Castro, Che Guevara

In historic speeches before the United Nations and its bodies, Guevara and Castro address the workers of the world, explaining why the U.S. government is determined to destroy the example set by the socialist revolution in Cuba and why its effort will fail. Introduction by Mary-Alice Waters. 232 pp. $16.95

Che Guevara and the Cuban Revolution

WRITINGS AND SPEECHES OF ERNESTO CHE GUEVARA

The most complete collection in English. Guevara writes about the revolutionary war that brought the workers and farmers to victory; Cuba's efforts to overcome economic backwardness while transforming the economic foundations and social relations inherited from capitalism; and Cuba's commitment to freedom struggles around the world. $21.95

Che Guevara Speaks

SELECTED SPEECHES AND WRITINGS

"A faithful reflection of Che as he was, or, better, as he developed"—from the preface by Joseph Hansen. Includes works by Che not available elsewhere in English. $12.95

ERNESTO CHE GUEVARA

Socialism and Man in Cuba

Guevara's best-known presentation of the political tasks and challenges in leading the transition from capitalism to socialism. Includes Fidel Castro's speech on the 20th anniversary of Guevara's death. [Also available in Spanish, French, Swedish, and Farsi.] Booklet. $3.50

Che Guevara: Economics and Politics in the Transition to Socialism

Carlos Tablada

Quoting extensively from Guevara's writings and speeches, explains why building socialism is the task of free men and women transforming themselves and society at the same time. Also available in Spanish and French. $17.95

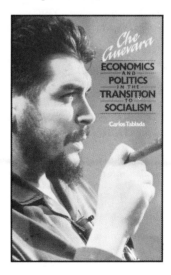

Escritos y discursos

WRITINGS AND SPEECHES

The most extensive selection in print. 9-vol. set. In Spanish. $75.00

FIDEL CASTRO

Speeches & interviews...

In Defense of Socialism
FOUR SPEECHES ON THE 30TH
ANNIVERSARY OF THE CUBAN
REVOLUTION

Not only is economic and social
progress possible without the dog-
eat-dog competition of capitalism,
Castro argues, but socialism remains
the only way forward for humanity.
Also discusses Cuba's role in the
struggle against the apartheid regime
in southern Africa. $13.95

Selected Speeches of Fidel Castro
Includes 1961 speech, *"I Shall Be a Marxist-Leninist to the End of My
Life,"* explaining why only a socialist revolution could bring about the
profound changes Cuban working people had overthrown the Batista
dictatorship to achieve. 8½ x 11 format. $14.00

The Second Declaration of Havana
In 1962, as the example of Cuba's socialist
revolution spread throughout the Americas,
the workers and farmers of Cuba issued their
call for revolutionary struggle from Tierra del
Fuego to the Río Bravo. Booklet. $3.00

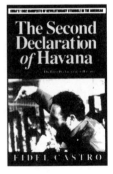

How Far We Slaves Have Come!
SOUTH AFRICA AND CUBA IN TODAY'S WORLD
Nelson Mandela and Fidel Castro

Speaking together in Cuba in 1991, Mandela and Castro discuss the
unique relationship and example of the struggles of the South African
and Cuban peoples. $8.95

Also by Fidel Castro

Cuba Will Never Adopt Capitalist Methods (1988), $2.50
War and Crisis in the Americas (1984-85), $17.95
Nothing Can Stop the Course of History (1985), $17.95
Cuba's Internationalist Foreign Policy (1975-80), $19.95
Building Socialism in Cuba (1960-1982), $19.95
History Will Absolve Me (1953) (Together with *Fidel Castro's Political Strategy* by Marta Harnecker), $12.95

Also from Pathfinder

The Leninist Strategy of Party Building

THE DEBATE ON GUERRILLA WARFARE IN LATIN AMERICA

Joseph Hansen
In the 1960s and '70s, revolutionists in the Americas and throughout the world debated how to apply the lessons of the Cuban revolution to struggles elsewhere. A record of that debate. $26.95

Che Guevara and the Fight for Socialism Today

CUBA CONFRONTS THE WORLD CRISIS OF THE '90s

Mary-Alice Waters
Socialism can be built only by free men and women working together to lay the foundations for a new society and transforming themselves in the process. That practical commitment was championed by Ernesto Che Guevara in the early years of the Cuban revolution. It remains central for Cuban working people today. Booklet. $3.50

Also from Pathfinder

The Changing Face of U.S. Politics
WORKING-CLASS POLITICS AND
THE TRADE UNIONS
Jack Barnes
   A handbook for workers coming
into the factories, mines, and mills, as
they react to the uncertain life,
ceaseless turmoil, and brutality that
will accompany the arrival of the
twenty-first century. It shows how
millions of workers, as political
resistance grows, will revolutionize
themselves, their unions, and all of
society. $19.95

Dynamics of the Cuban Revolution
Joseph Hansen
   To understand the first socialist revolution in the Americas, Hansen
says, "it is not necessary to begin from zero. The problems presented
to Marxist theory by the uniqueness of the events were solved at the
time." This compilation, written with polemical clarity as the
revolution advanced, presents the conclusions that guide fighters
worldwide. $19.95

The Struggle for a Proletarian Party
James P. Cannon
   In a political struggle in the late 1930s with a petty-bourgeois
current in the Socialist Workers Party, Cannon and other SWP leaders
defended the political and organizational principles
of Marxism. The debate unfolded as Washington
prepared to drag U.S. working people into the
slaughter of World War II. A companion to *In
Defense of Marxism* by Leon Trotsky. $19.95

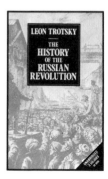

The History of the Russian Revolution
Leon Trotsky
   The social, economic, and political dynamics of
the first victorious socialist revolution, as told by
one of its principal leaders. Unique in modern
literature. Unabridged edition, 3 vols. in one.
1,358 pp. $35.95

The Communist Manifesto

Karl Marx and Frederick Engels

Founding document of the modern working-class movement published in 1848. Explains how capitalism arose as a specific stage in the economic development of class society and how it will be superseded through revolutionary action on a world scale by the working class. Booklet. $2.50

Imperialism: The Highest Stage of Capitalism

V.I. Lenin

"I trust that this pamphlet will help the reader to understand the fundamental economic question, that of the economic essence of imperialism," Lenin wrote in 1917. "For unless this is studied, it will be impossible to understand and appraise modern war and modern politics." Booklet. $3.95

Cosmetics, Fashions, and the Exploitation of Women

Joseph Hansen, Evelyn Reed, and Mary-Alice Waters

How big business uses women's second-class status to generate profits for a few and perpetuate the oppression of the female sex and the exploitation of working people. $12.95

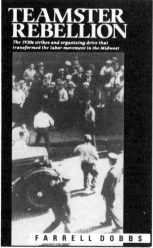

Teamster Rebellion

Farrell Dobbs

The 1934 strikes that built a fighting union movement in Minneapolis, recounted by a leader of that battle. The first in a four-volume series on the Teamster-led strikes and organizing drives in the Midwest that helped pave the way for the CIO and point a road forward toward independent labor political action. $15.95

Malcolm X Talks to Young People

"I for one will join in with anyone, I don't care what color you are, as long as you want to change this miserable condition that exists on this earth"—Malcolm X, Britain, December 1964. Also includes Malcolm's 1965 interview with the *Young Socialist* magazine. $10.95

Nelson Mandela Speaks

FORGING A DEMOCRATIC, NONRACIAL SOUTH AFRICA

Charts a course of struggle to open a deep-going transformation of political, economic, and social conditions in the former land of apartheid. $18.95

Revolutionary Continuity

MARXIST LEADERSHIP IN THE UNITED STATES

Farrell Dobbs

How successive generations of fighters took part in the struggles of the U.S. labor movement, seeking to build a leadership that could advance the class interests of workers and small farmers and link up with fellow toilers around the world. 2 volumes, $16.95 each

Peru's 'Shining Path'

Martín Koppel

How can Shining Path's growth, and its mounting internal political crisis, be explained? Why are its perspectives so destructive to the working class in Peru and worldwide? What is the alternative for workers and peasants fighting to defend their interests against the landlords and factory owners? Booklet. $3.50

The Revolution Betrayed

WHAT IS THE SOVIET UNION AND WHERE IS IT GOING?

Leon Trotsky

Classic study of the degeneration of the Soviet workers state under the brutal domination of the privileged social caste whose spokesman was Stalin. Illuminates the roots of the Russian crisis of the 1990s. $19.95

Capital

Karl Marx

Marx explains that the capitalist system is a specific stage in the development of class society; how large-scale modern industry draws men, women, and children into the factories and into the army of wage-laborers who compete for jobs. And he shows how this exploitative social system produces the insoluble contradictions that breed class struggle and make possible the revolutionary transformation of society into one ruled for the first time in history by the majority: the producers. Volume 1, $13.95

America's Revolutionary Heritage

MARXIST ESSAYS

Edited by George Novack

Explanatory essays on Native Americans, the first American revolution, the Civil War, the rise of industrial capitalism, and the first wave of the fight for women's rights. $21.95

The Jewish Question

A MARXIST INTERPRETATION

Abram Leon

Traces the historical rationalizations of anti-Semitism to the position of Jews as a "people-class" of merchants and moneylenders in the centuries preceding the domination of industrial capitalism. Leon explains how in times of social crisis renewed Jew-hatred is incited by the capitalists to mobilize reactionary forces against the labor movement and disorient the middle classes and layers of working people about the true source of their impoverishment. $17.95

Sandinistas Speak

Tomás Borge, Carlos Fonseca, Daniel Ortega, and others

The best selection in English of historic documents of the FSLN and speeches and interviews from the opening years of the 1979 Sandinista revolution. $13.95

AVAILABLE FROM PATHFINDER. WRITE FOR A FREE CATALOG. SEE ADDRESSES AT FRONT OF BOOK.

New International

A MAGAZINE OF MARXIST POLITICS AND THEORY

No. 10

Imperialism's March toward Fascism and War *by Jack Barnes*

What the 1987 Stock Market Crash Foretold

Defending Cuba, Defending Cuba's Socialist Revolution *by Mary-Alice Waters.*

No. 9

The Triumph of the Nicaraguan Revolution

Washington's Contra War and the Challenge of Forging Proletarian Leadership

The Political Degeneration of the FSLN and the Demise of the Workers and Farmers Government. $14.00

No. 8

The Politics of Economics: Che Guevara and Marxist Continuity *by Steve Clark and Jack Barnes*

Che's Contribution to the Cuban Economy *by Carlos Rafael Rodríguez*

The Creativity of Che's Economic Thought *by Carlos Tablada*. $10.00

No. 7

Opening Guns of World War III:
Washington's Assault on Iraq
by Jack Barnes

Communist Policy in Wartime
as well as in Peacetime
by Mary-Alice Waters

Lessons from the Iran-Iraq War
by Samad Sharif. $12.00

No. 6

The Second Assassination of Maurice
Bishop *by Steve Clark*

Washington's 50-Year Domestic
Contra War *by Larry Seigle*

Land, Labor, and the Canadian
Socialist Revolution *by Michel Dugré*

Renewal or Death: Cuba's
Rectification Process
two speeches by Fidel Castro. $10.00

No. 5

The Coming Revolution
in South Africa
by Jack Barnes

The Future Belongs to
the Majority
by Oliver Tambo

Why Cuban Volunteers
Are in Angola *two
speeches by Fidel Castro*.
$9.00

No. 4

The Fight for a Workers and
Farmers Government in the
United States *by Jack Barnes*

The Crisis Facing Working
Farmers *by Doug Jenness*

Land Reform and Farm
Cooperatives in Cuba *two
speeches by Fidel Castro*. $9.00

New International

New International
A MAGAZINE OF MARXIST POLITICS AND THEORY

1848 TO TODAY
Communism and the fight for a popular revolutionary government
by Mary-Alice Waters

'A nose for power': Preparing the Nicaraguan revolution
by Tomás Borge

National liberation and socialism in the Americas
by Manuel Piñeiro

3

No. 3

Communism and the Fight for a Popular Revolutionary Government: 1848 to Today
by Mary-Alice Waters

'A Nose for Power': Preparing the Nicaraguan Revolution
by Tomás Borge

National Liberation and Socialism in the Americas
by Manuel Piñeiro. $8.00

New International
A MAGAZINE OF MARXIST POLITICS AND THEORY

THE WORKING CLASS FIGHT FOR PEACE
by Brian Grogan

ARISTOCRACY OF LABOR _by Steve Clark_
ARSENAL OF MARXISM
SOCIAL ROOTS OF OPPORTUNISM
by Gregory Zinoviev

2

No. 2

The Aristocracy of Labor: Development of the Marxist Position _by Steve Clark_

The Working-Class Fight for Peace _by Brian Grogan_

The Social Roots of Opportunism _by Gregory Zinoviev_. $8.00

No. 1

Their Trotsky and Ours: Communist Continuity Today
by Jack Barnes

Lenin and the Colonial Question _by Carlos Rafael Rodríguez_

The 1916 Easter Rebellion in Ireland: Two Views
by V.I. Lenin and Leon Trotsky. $8.00

Many of the articles that have appeared in **New International** are also available in Spanish in **Nueva Internacional**, in French in **Nouvelle Internationale**, and in Swedish in **Ny International**.

DISTRIBUTED BY PATHFINDER